POST-TRAUMATIC STRESS
DISORDERS

The Wiley Series in

CLINICAL PSYCHOLOGY

J. Mark G. Williams
(Series Editor)

*School of Psychology, University
of Wales, Bangor, UK*

Further titles in preparation: *A list of earlier
titles in the series follows the index*

POST-TRAUMATIC STRESS DISORDERS

Concepts and Therapy

Edited by
William Yule

*University of London, Institute of Psychiatry
and Bethlem and Maudsley NHS Trust, London, UK*

JOHN WILEY & SONS

Chichester · New York · Weinheim · Brisbane · Singapore · Toronto

Copyright © 1999 by John Wiley & Sons Ltd,
Baffins Lane, Chichester,
West Sussex PO19 1UD, England

National 01243 779777
International (+44) 1243 779777
e-mail (for orders and customer service enquiries):
cs-books@wiley.co.uk
Visit our Home Page on http://www.wiley.co.uk
or http://www.wiley.com

Other Wiley Editorial Offices

John Wiley & Sons, Inc., 605 Third Avenue,
New York, NY 10158-0012, USA

WILEY-VCH Verlag Gmbh, Pappelallee 3,
D-69469 Weinheim, Germany

Jacaranda Wiley Ltd, 33 Park Road, Milton,
Queensland 4064, Australia

John Wiley & Sons (Asia) Pte Ltd, 2 Clementi Loop #02-01,
Jin Xing Distripark, Singapore 129809

John Wiley & Sons (Canada) Ltd, 22 Worcester Road,
Rexdale, Ontario M9W IL1, Canada

Library of Congress Cataloging-in-Publication Data
Post-traumatic stress disorders: concepts and therapy / edited by
  William Yule.
      p.   cm.—(Wiley series in clinical psychology)
    Includes bibliographical references and index.
    ISBN 0-471-96058-6 (alk. paper).—ISBN 0-471-97080-8 (pbk. alk. paper)
    1. Post-traumatic stress disorder. 2. Psychic trauma. 3 Adjustment (Psychology) I.
  Yule, William. II. Series.
  RC552.P67P673   1998   98-24146
                                                                              CIP

British Library Cataloguing in Publication Data
A catalogue record for this book is available from the British Library

ISBN 0-471-96058-6 (cased)
ISBN 0-471-97080-8 (paper)

Typeset in 10/12 pt Palatino by Best-set Typesetter Ltd., Hong Kong
Printed and bound in Great Britain by Biddles Ltd, Guildford and King's Lynn
This book is printed on acid-free paper responsibly manufactured from sustainable forestry, in which at least two trees are planted for each one used for paper production.

To Bridget, Claire and Alastair
who have supported me throughout

CONTENTS

ABOUT THE EDITOR

William Yule Professor of Applied Child Psychology, University of London, Institute of Psychiatry. Formerly Head of Clinical Psychology Services, The Bethlem Royal and Maudsley Hospitals.

William Yule trained as a clinical psychologist at the Institute of Psychiatry and Maudsley Hospital in London. He has published over 300 articles and 9 books on a wide range of topics in child psychology including reading retardation, epidemiology, autism, parent training, the effects of lead on children's development, the effects of the Chernobyl radiation on children, behavioural phenotypes and the effects of war on children.

For the past ten years, he has been heavily involved in the study and treatment of PTSD in both adults and children. He has studied the effects of the capsize of the cross-channel car ferry the *Herald of Free Enterprise*, and the sinking of the cruise ship, *Jupiter*, in Athens harbour. He has shown that PTSD is both a commoner and more chronic reaction in children and adolescents than had hitherto been suspected.

Since the summer of 1993, he has been an adviser to UNICEF on its psychosocial programme for war-affected children in former Yugoslavia and is Technical Director of a major programme to develop services for war-affected children in Mostar in Bosnia.

He has been active among British and European PTSD researchers and has presented at many international meetings. He was a member of the Board of the International Society for Traumatic Stress Studies, and is on the editorial boards of both the *Journal of Traumatic Stress* and the new electronic journal, *Traumatology*. He has currently developed links with researchers in the countries of the former Soviet Union and would want to explore how best to foster good practice there.

He was elected Chair of Association for Child Psychology and Psychiatry in June 1996 and elected to the Green Cross Foundation Academy of Traumatology in January 1998.

LIST OF CONTRIBUTORS

Rachel Canterbury
Department of Psychology, Institute of Psychiatry, De Crespigny Park, London SE5 8AF

Tim Dalgleish
MRC Cognition and Brain Sciences Unit, 15 Chaucer Road, Cambridge CB2 2EF

Padmal de Silva
Department of Psychology, Institute of Psychiatry, De Crespigny Park, London SE5 8AF

Laura Goldstein
Department of Psychology, Institute of Psychiatry, De Crespigny Park, London SE5 8AF

Hassan Hagh-Shenas
Department of Psychiatry, Hafez Hospital, Abiverdi Avenue, Shiraz, Iran 71046

Stephen Joseph
Department of Psychology, University of Essex, Wivenhoe Park, Colchester CO4 3SQ

Karina Lovell
University of Manchester, Manchester

Melanie Marks
Private Practice, 10 Upper Wimpole Street, London WIM FTD

Sean Perrin
Department of Psychology, Institute of Psychiatry, De Crespigny Park, London SE5 8AF

David Richards
R&D Directorate, Leeds Community Mental Health Services NHS Trust, 24 Hyde Terrace Leeds LS2 9LN

Patrick Smith
*Department of Psychology, Institute of Psychiatry, De Crespigny Park, London
SE5 8AF*

Sian Thrasher
*Private Practice, Holmlea, High Street, Hook Norton, Banbury, Oxon. OX15
5NQ*

Ruth Williams
*Department of Psychology, Institute of Psychiatry, De Crespigny Park, London
SE5 8AF*

William Yule
*Department of Psychology, Institute of Psychiatry, De Crespigny Park, London
SE5 8AF*

FOREWORD

Post-traumatic stress disorders are the simplest and also the most complex of the anxiety disorders: simplest because the initiating cause of the disorder, the stress which it is post, is generally all too evident, but they are also complex because of the puzzling unpredictability of the symptoms, their seemingly functionless effects, and the mixture of psychological processes (memory, imagery, startle, fear, etc.) that are involved. The astonishing tricks of memory are particularly intriguing. It is a nasty and distressing disorder but replete with scientific challenges.

Why do the majority of people who are exposed to the common stresses fail to develop PTSD? A grasp of these natural processes of absorption or recovery will, I believe, provide the key to understanding PTSD—the physiology, as it were, on which to base an analysis of the pathology. From this point of view, PTSD is best regarded as a failure or delay in the natural processes of protection and recovery. PTSD arises when the natural, spontaneous path of emotional processing is impaired.

Regarding PTSD as an isolated psychological phenomenon, an intrinsically pathological and independent psychological phenomenon, begs the question—and may also lead to the formulation of explanations that remain remote from the corpus of the behavioural sciences. In keeping with Professor Yule's views, the approach adopted by all of the contributors to the present volume is a splendid vindication of the value of regarding PTSD as an unfortunate disturbance of normal psychological processes. The authors approach PTSD with the tools and knowledge of information processing, attributional styles, personality traits, cultural psychology and psychobiology. The result is an extremely informative and stimulating book that covers the territory.

How much progress has been accomplished in the past decade? The best and quickest answer is to read this volume; but, in brief, the phenomenology is well described, and the nature and occurrence of PTSD in children are now fully recognized thanks to the work of Yule, Joseph, Williams and their colleagues. Interest and understanding in PTSD have been expanded well beyond the earlier preoccupation with combat trauma, the value of particular types of social support is well established, the importance of intrusive thinking and of intense/unpredictable memories is very clear, and useful progress has been made in helping people overcome their distress.

Many important questions remain to be tackled, but the view expressed by the Editor, and the contributors, is worth reiterating. The problems of PTSD are best approached as disruptions of normal processes of absorption and recovery from stress. The growing infusion of cognitive concepts into current explanations of such absorption and recovery, and indeed into explanations of PTSD itself, is a progressive and extremely promising move, and the book provides an instructive and helpful guide to these new trends. We can expect the emergence of a cognitive-emotional processing account of PTSD during the coming decade.

Professor S. Rachman
Vancouver, October 1997

SERIES PREFACE

The Wiley Series in Clinical Psychology aims to provide a comprehensive set of texts covering the application of psychological science to the problems of mental health and disability. Of all the aspects of psychopathology that have received increased attention over the last two decades, post-traumatic stress disorder must be ranked one of the most prominent. Professor Bill Yule of the University of London's Institute of Psychiatry has been responsible for much of the most exciting new research in this field. Focusing especially, in his own work, on PTSD reactions in children and adolescents, he has been an influential figure in the whole emerging field. In this book he draws together colleagues who review the research on both adults and young people, examining how social support, personality, biological and cultural factors affect the presentation of this disorder. Different theoretical paradigms are reviewed, and a variety of treatment approaches examined (including the controversial Eye Movement Desensitisation and Reprocessing Therapy). This text is comprehensive, written by clinicians of international standing who have both rich clinical experience and an extensive academic knowledge. It will be an invaluable guide for both students and practitioners across the whole range of mental health disciplines.

J. Mark G. Williams
Series Editor

PREFACE

Shortly after the cross-channel ferry, the *Herald of Free Enterprise*, capsized as it left Zeebrugge harbour with considerable loss of life, I was contacted by lawyers acting for survivors and asked whether my colleagues and I would be able to assess and help some of the survivors. That telephone call was to change my life and the activities of the Department of Psychology considerably. More than 25 years of clinical experience of children and their families left me ill-prepared to meet the enormous distress of the surviving adults and children whom we worked with over the following few years.

As a group, we realised there was a great deal to be done and a great deal to be learned. We had little experience of *Post-Traumatic Stress Disorder* until then but a great deal of experience working with anxiety disorders, depression and bereavement. It soon became obvious that we had an unique opportunity to contribute to professional understanding of the effects of a major transport disaster on the lives of survivors and their families. We worked closely with lawyers and determined that, without violating the need to consider each individual's unique experience and reactions, we would, as far as possible, adopt a semi-structured standard assessment of all the survivors. The database so developed proved invaluable in allowing us to follow up selected samples of survivors and learn more about the natural course of their difficulties and those factors that moderated their distress.

When, a year later, the cruise ship *Jupiter* was sunk outside Athens harbour, we followed a similar approach and so were in a position to say a great deal about the effects of that disaster on the teenagers on board. Indeed, we were able to follow them over the next seven years and so establish that the stress reactions developed by the majority of them were not short lived. In a significant minority of cases, that single catastrophe had an indelible effect on their lives.

As colleagues discussed our experiences and shared ideas, so a distinctive way of viewing stress reactions emerged. This book represents the fruits of 10 years of working with survivors of accidents and disasters. It contains a coherent approach to the psychology underpinning these reactions. It places the disorders within a broad social psychological perspective. It applies many of the latest insights from experimental cognitive psychology to the experiences of the survivors. We have learned a great deal from all of this and we trust that readers will also.

None of this would have been possible without the cooperation and generosity of the survivors and their families. Despite at times being severely distressed, they put up with our questioning and questionnaires, secure in the belief that together we were trying to improve our understanding of traumatic stress reactions so that future survivors would benefit. Our readers can decide for themselves the extent to which we have achieved that goal.

William Yule
London, 22 May 1998

Chapter 1

POST-TRAUMATIC STRESS DISORDERS IN ADULTS

William Yule*, Ruth Williams*
and Stephen Joseph[†]

All human beings are complex organisms who constantly strive to adapt to the demands placed on them by their physical and social environments. We constantly strive to make sense of what happens to us, and we build up internal models of the world as we experience it. When threatened, we react with distress and fear. This response serves a survival function for each individual and for our species. We learn from encounters with danger—and hopefully we learn to deal with them or not to place ourselves in similar dangerous situations. Thus, once danger has passed, we may ponder over the characteristics of whatever threatened us. We may think about it or see or hear it in our imagination—all ways of helping us to recognise signs of danger in the future. Having done so, we can better avoid such dangers or prepare ourselves to face them.

From the beginning of recorded history, people have reacted in fairly characteristic fashion after particularly threatening experiences. Shakespeare described reactions to acute stress in many of his plays. Samuel Pepys recorded his own reactions of terror to the great fire of London in 1666 (Daly, 1983). The advent of mass transport in Victorian times also brought with it the experience of mass transport disasters. Psychological reactions that seemed out of scale with the actual accident were explained as the effects of direct damage to the spine and central nervous system, and so the concept of "railway spine" was born (Erichsen, 1866; Trimble, 1981).

But it was the reactions of serving soldiers in times of war that led to the greatest advances in our understanding of the effects of life-threatening

*Institute of Psychiatry, London, and [†]University of Essex, Colchester

Post-Traumatic Stress Disorders: Concepts and Therapy. Edited by William Yule.
© 1999 John Wiley & Sons Ltd.

traumatic stressors on psychological adjustment. Officers and enlisted men, faced with the high casualty rates in trench warfare during World War I, often broke down on the battlefield. Shell shock (Mott, 1919; Southward, 1919) was the term favoured for reactions to stress that had previously been labelled nervous shock (Page, 1885), traumatic neurosis (Oppenheim, 1892), anxiety neurosis (Freud, 1894, 1919) or fright neurosis (Kraepelin, 1886). Pat Barker's fictionalised account of shell shock, and how it was treated either humanely or brutally, graphically describes the way that trench warfare at times affected serving soldiers (Barker, 1991).

Each description built on previous ones and reflected the understanding of the day. At first, shell shock was conceived solely in physical terms—a shock that caused damage to the physical nervous system. Then it was realised that some people developed very similar symptoms without having experienced a shell explode near them. Such soldiers were often accused of cowardice and some were even executed when they refused to fight on.

By World War II, mental health professionals were more involved in the care of serving soldiers and concepts such as post-trauma syndrome (Kardiner, 1941) and war neurosis (Grinker & Spiegel, 1943) held sway. Kardiner (1941) recognised that the syndrome incorporated feelings of irritability and outbursts of aggression, exaggerated startle response, and fixations on the traumatic event.

Slowly at first, and then with a great rush, other mental health professionals began to recognise similar constellations of symptoms among civilians exposed to acute stressors that often fell short of those confronting fighting soldiers (see Joseph, Williams & Yule, 1997 for a listing).

The Vietnam War and its horrendous aftermath brought to the attention of American mental health professionals the devastating effects that the war experiences had on many enlisted men. In many ways, one of the legacies of that futile conflict has been the recognition of the syndrome of Post-Traumatic Stress Disorder (Figley, 1978). Work undertaken in Veterans' Administration hospitals and clinics forced people to recognise not only the short-term effects of being exposed to horrors in war, but also the long-term effects on personality and adjustment. In part, as with previous reformulations, the latest way of conceptualising the disorder is a product of its social times and it is as well today to remember that the current diagnostic category of PTSD has its origins in post-Vietnam War North America. Some of the reported phenomena and part of the supposedly natural course of recovery may well have been influenced by the reactions of American society to men returning from a war they had lost so spectacularly. Had the affected soldiers returned to heroes' welcomes and massive social support from their communities, the tale may well have been different. Had they had access to socialised medical care, rather than rely on a system where symptoms led to compensation, again one might speculate that things may have been different.

As it was, the American Psychiatric Association was much influenced by Horowitz's (1975, 1976, 1979) work on the phenomenology of trauma-related reactions. Horowitz worked within a framework utilising concepts from psychodynamic and information-processing theories and he saw the traumatised individual as being initially assailed by intrusive and emotionally disturbing memories. The affected individuals then try to use avoidant strategies to ward off the distressing thoughts, images and feelings. They "work through" the reactions in alternating phases of intrusion and avoidance. Avoidance or "denial" could be seen as a perfectly normal defence against overwhelming emotions. Thus, in the third edition of its *Diagnostic and Statistical Manual of Mental Disorders* (APA, 1980), the APA recognised a syndrome of PTSD which acknowledged that, following particularly traumatic events, some people developed symptoms of intrusive re-experiencing of the trauma, avoidant behaviours, and a set of symptoms of increased physiological arousal.

Case Example

Mrs. Stirling had taken a day trip to Belgium on a cross-channel ferry with her husband and two sons. After a pleasant day together, they rushed to catch the ferry back. They were settling in the restaurant to take a meal, two members of the family seated at either side of the small table, when the ship suddenly rolled over and failed to right itself. She and one of her sons found themselves thrown into the water that was rushing in through broken portholes. Her older son had been grabbed by his father and they managed to remain holding on to the table. Even so, they had to clamber up from one table to the other as the water rose quickly in the dark.

At first, she thought they were all going to die. She hoped that at least they would all die together.

Mrs. Stirling became separated from her husband. When rescue vessels arrived, she eventually saw a rope lowered near her, but was too numb from the cold to be able to climb up without assistance. She saw dead bodies floating in the water around the bottom of the rope. Somehow she pulled herself up, got on to a tug and was taken to dry land. Then she spent a few anxious hours touring the wards and hospitals until she found that all her family were alive and well, apart from cuts and bruises.

The flight back to England was terrifying. Once at home, she just wanted all of them to be close together. The children's constant questioning about what happened was very upsetting to her. She found it very difficult to sleep and the sleeping tablets given her by her GP just made her feel drowsy all the day. She began to have vivid dreams about the accident and to have intrusive images about it at any time during the day.

A few months later when she was assessed psychologically, she was weepy and complained of constant tiredness. She had lost interest in housework, from having been a meticulous home-maker, and her former hobbies were not pursued. She worried about any form of travel, and also worried about the safety of all members of her family. She was constantly on the look out for dangers and the slightest noise made her jump. She felt guilty about taking the children on the ferry crossing in the first place. She was ruminating constantly about death—something she had rarely considered before.

Overall, she felt that literally her world had been turned upside down. From being a happy, contented lady who took pride in her family and enjoyed a full social life, she had become tired, listless and worried, feeling that she had undergone a total personality change. She constantly asked, "Why me?"

Comments

Mrs. Stirling's reactions to the accident that threatened not only her own life but also those of her loved ones are, in many ways, typical of a post-traumatic stress reaction. In other ways, they are unique to her. Initially, during the incident, she could not believe it was really happening. Lots of thoughts about herself, her life, her family passed through her mind. She feared she was going to die. And yet, she managed to look after her son as best she could. She summoned up strength to clamber up a slippery hawser to be rescued. She was in a highly anxious state until she was reunited with her family.

Once home, she wanted them all to be together and safe. As the reality of what had happened to them dawned on her, and as she thought of what else might have happened, she began to relive the whole experience in vivid recollections, both during the day and at night in dreams. She soon lost interest in hobbies and friends. She did not want to talk about the experience yet felt a pressure to do so, even if that upset her. She began to avoid using any form of public transport. She could only trust her husband to drive her, and even then with difficulty. Such difficulty in entrusting one's life to another driver is not uncommon after a transport accident.

Survivors may be able to drive themselves, sometimes quite recklessly as if tempting fate, but still be unable to be driven or flown.

Her sleep was disrupted; her concentration shattered. She became hypervigilant and reacted quickly to any sudden noise. Any reminder of the accident on television or the newspapers brought her out in sweats and she became very upset.

In addition to these symptoms which form part of the cardinal triad recognised as PTSD—the re-experiencing, the numbing and avoidance, and the hyperarousal—she also showed guilt at having survived and, most clearly, her model of her world—her assumptive world as Janoff-Bulman (1989) puts it—had been shattered. She could not trust her judgement. She felt totally lost and bewildered.

After the APA first officially recognised the syndrome of PTSD in 1983, the attention of mental health professionals was focused on the disorder. A great many studies were undertaken and this led to the criteria whereby the disorder was defined being revised both in DSM-III-R (APA, 1987) and again in DSM-IV (APA, 1994). Internationally, the official classification of diseases sanctioned by the World Health Organisation—WHO's International Classification of Diseases or ICD—had recognised two reactions to acute stress: an "Acute Reaction to Stress", which was very transient, lasting only a few hours or days; and an "Adjustment Reaction", which lasted slightly longer. In the tenth revision of ICD in 1993, WHO defined PTSD along similar lines to DSM, although placing slightly different emphasis on some of the symptoms. Thus, by the early 1990s, PTSD had been defined and recognised internationally, and this led to a massive increase in the amount of research into its nature and treatment.

COMPARISON BETWEEN DSM-IV AND ICD-10

The two official definitions are given below.

The ICD-10 criteria for PTSD are very similar to those of DSM-IV, involving the identification of a threatening event which is thought necessary in the onset of the disorder. However, as with all other diagnoses, the approach to reaching a diagnosis is very different between the two systems. ICD requires the clinician to match an overall pattern of symptoms to the example given, whereas DSM provides somewhat more mechanistic guidelines and rules to follow. ICD prefers that only one diagnosis is given to a patient, whereas DSM encourages the making of multiple diagnoses and so increases the amount of "co-morbidity".

ICD-10 describes various stress disorders and notes the relative roles of the traumatic event and psychosocial factors. The biggest single difference lies in the emphasis placed on "emotional numbing"—ICD sees that as a frequent accompaniment to PTSD but not as being necessary for the diagnosis. Both systems agree that it is the re-experiencing symptoms that are the hallmark sign of PTSD and mark it out from most other psychopathology.

Table 1.1 DSM-IV Criteria for PTSD

A. The person has been exposed to a traumatic event in which both the follow-ing were present:
   (1) The person experienced, witnessed, or was confronted with an event or events that involved actual or threatened death or serious injury, or a threat to the physical integrity of self or others.
   (2) The person's response involved fear, helplessness, or horror. *Note:* In children, this may be expressed instead by disorganised or agitated behaviour.

B. The traumatic event is persistently re-experienced in one (or more) of the following ways:
   (1) Recurrent and intrusive distressing recollections of the event, including images, thoughts, or perceptions. *Note:* In young children, repetitive play may occur in which themes or aspects of the trauma are expressed.
   (2) Recurrent distressing dreams of the event. *Note:* In children, there may be frightening dreams without recognisable content.
   (3) Acting or feeling as if the traumatic event were recurring (includes a sense of reliving the experience, illusions, hallucinations, and dissocia-tive flashback episodes, including those that occur on awakening or when intoxicated). *Note:* In young children, trauma-specific re-enactment may occur.
   (4) Intense psychological distress at exposure to internal or external cues that symbolise or resemble an aspect of the traumatic event.
   (5) Physiological reactivity on exposure to internal or external cues that symbolise or resemble an aspect of the traumatic event.

C. Persistent avoidance of stimuli associated with the trauma and numbing of general responsiveness (not present before the trauma), as indicated by three (or more) of the following:
   (1) Efforts to avoid thoughts, feelings, or conversations associated with the trauma.
   (2) Efforts to avoid activities, places, or people that arouse recollections of the trauma.
   (3) Inability to recall an important aspect of the trauma.
   (4) Markedly diminished interest or participation in significant activities.
   (5) Feeling of detachment or estrangement from others.
   (6) Restricted range of affect (e.g., unable to have loving feelings).
   (7) Sense of foreshortened future (e.g., does not expect to have a career, marriage, children, or a normal life span).

Table 1.1 (*continued*)

D. Persistent symptoms of increased arousal (not present before the trauma) as indicated by two (or more) of the following:
   (1) Difficulty falling or staying asleep.
   (2) Irritability or outbursts of anger.
   (3) Difficulty concentrating.
   (4) Hypervigilance.
   (5) Exaggerated startle response.

E. Duration of the disturbance (symptoms in criteria B, C, and D) is more than one month.

F. The disturbance causes clinically significant distress or impairment in social, occupational, or other important areas of functioning.

Specify if:
   Acute: if duration of symptoms is less that three months.
   Chronic: if duration of symptoms is three months or more.

Specify if:
   With delayed onset: if onset of symptoms is at least six months after the stressor.

Reprinted with permission from the *Diagnostic and Statistical Manual of Mental Disorders*, Fourth Edition. Copyright 1994 American Psychiatric Association.

Table 1.2 ICD-10 Criteria for Post-traumatic Stress Disorder

This disorder should not generally be diagnosed unless there is evidence that it arose within six months of a traumatic event of exceptional severity. A 'probable' diagnosis might still be possible if the delay between the event and the onset was longer than six months, provided that the clinical manifestations are typical and no alternative identification of the disorder (e.g., as an anxiety or obsessive–compulsive disorder or depressive episode) is plausible. In addition to evidence of trauma, there must be a repetitive, intrusive recollection or re-enactment of the event in memories, daytime imagery, or dreams. Conspicuous emotional detachment, numbing of feeling, and avoidance of stimuli that might arouse recollection of the trauma are often present but are not essential for the diagnosis. The autonomic disturbances, mood disorder, and behavioural abnormalities all contribute to the diagnosis but are not of prime importance.

The late chronic sequelae of devastating stress, i.e., those manifest decades after the stressful experience, should be classified under F62.0.

Includes: traumatic neurosis.

Reproduced, by permission of WHO, from: The ICD-10 Classification of Mental and Behavioural Disorders: Clinical descriptions and diagnostic guidelines. Geneva, World Health Organization, 1992.

Overlap with Other Disorders

Since first being defined in 1980, the criteria for making a diagnosis of PTSD have been revised twice by APA in DSM-III-R (APA, 1987) and DSM-IV (APA, 1994). In part, this has been in response to the mass of new empirical findings, but also in part it reflects the reality of arriving at consensus in committee of different theoretical persuasion. Thus, "survival guilt" figured as an important symptom in DSM-III but is dropped thereafter. It is not that new studies failed to find it—on the contrary, many survivors express guilt at having survived, guilt that others died, guilt that they did not do enough to help others, and even guilt at what they themselves had to do in order to survive. The clinician may still find it useful to enquire about survival guilt and take note of the patient's reactions when formulating the client's problems and planning therapy. The point here is that there are many associated reactions that do not go towards making the formal diagnosis but which may be present and may be important. Indeed, in an ideal world, studies of survivors of traumatic events would enquire systematically about the broadest range of reactions possible rather than concentrate only on the 17 approved signs. That way, we would get a far better understanding of the range of symptoms that can occur after a life-threatening experience. In other words, while the recognition of PTSD was enormously helpful, too slavish a following of the definition may inadvertently constrain better understanding.

As noted above, in addition to PTSD, survivors may undergo enduring personality changes (Horowitz, 1986a, 1986b), as well as high levels of anxiety and depression. Where there have been deaths in the particular incident, survivors may also develop both normal and pathological grief reactions. The extent of the overlap between diagnosed conditions will depend almost entirely on the rules being followed by the particular investigator. DSM encourages multiple diagnoses and so almost invented the phenomenon of "co-morbidity", whereas ICD specifies that where possible only one main diagnosis should be made. Thus, if we look at studies where continuous measures of other symptoms, signs, syndromes and diagnoses are all made, we may get a better picture of the associated symptoms of PTSD.

McFarlane and Papay's (1992) community study of over 450 firefighters who experienced an Australian bush fire found that 77% of the 70 (18%) who were diagnosed as having PTSD also had at least one other psychiatric diagnosis. Other studies report high levels of depression among survivors of traumatic events (North, Smith & Spitznagel, 1994; Loughrey, Bell, Kee, Roddy & Curran, 1988).

Substance abuse is commonly reported among combat veterans who have survived traumatic events (Solomon, Mikulincer & Kotler, 1987b; Keane, Caddell, Martin, Zimmering & Fairbank, 1983; Roth, 1986). In one study, it was clearly established that in 75% of cases the the abuse of alcohol had predated the war experience and the same was true for 23% of the drug abuse (Kulka et al., 1990). Such increase in substance abuse is also found in survivors of civilian trauma (Abrahams, Price, Whitlock & Williams, 1976; Logue, Hansen & Struening, 1979; Gleser, Green & Winget, 1981; Goenjian, 1993). Our own follow-up studies of adult survivors of the *Herald of Free Enterprise* capsize (Joseph, Yule, Williams & Hodgkinson, 1993a) reported large increases in their use of alcohol, cigarettes, sleeping tablets, antidepressants and tranquillisers some 30 months after the event. All these, of course, add significantly to the health risks facing the survivors.

Physical health is affected in a number of different ways in addition to the effects of increased substance abuse. In general, there is a decline in overall subjective health ratings (Logue et al., 1979; Melick, 1978; Price, 1978), an increased use in medical services (Abrahams et al., 1976; Bennet, 1970; Price, 1978) as well as reports of increased incidence of tiredness, headaches, chest pains, gastrointestinal disorders, cardiovascular disorders and impairment in the immune system. Of course, it could be argued that many of these physical signs are also signs of depression and certainly there has been insufficient attention paid to somatisation in relation to PTSD. However, the reports of fatigue and increased minor illnesses and infections are all too much a reality to many survivors.

Social relationships can be affected, usually adversely. McFarlane's (1987) report of the effects of the bush fire disaster on family functioning found increased levels of intrafamilial irritability, increased fighting, and decreased enjoyment in shared activities. Goenjian (1993) also noted the increase in marital discord, intrafamilial and interpersonal violence in survivors of the large-scale Armenian earthquake. All this is more than just unfortunate for, as will be seen later, good social support from family and friends can be a major factor in coping with the reactions to the traumatic stressor.

Cognitive impairment has been reported by many investigators. Difficulties in concentrating were found in 44% of the survivors of the Hyatt Regency Hotel skywalk collapse and 27% were found to have memory difficulties (Wilkinson, 1983). These symptoms tend to be assessed clinically but more recently techniques developed in experimental cognitive psychology have been applied to the study of survivors. Thus, McNally, Lasko, Macklin and Pitman (1995) have established autobiographical memory disturbance in patients with PTSD. Biases in attention and memory difficulties are further explored in later chapters of this volume (Chapter 9, Thrasher and Dalgleish; Chapter 7, Hagh-Shenas, Goldstein and Yule).

WHAT IS A TRAUMATIC EVENT?

The very label chosen implies that it is the nature of the event that is traumatic. This at times leads to a lack of clarity with clinicians following rather outdated ways of formulating psychological distress, where the word "trauma" is often used to describe the *reactions* to the event.

What sort of events are regarded as traumatic? Initially, the creators of DSM-III saw it as being an event outside the range of usual human experience—events such as " . . . a recognizable stressor that would evoke significant symptoms of distress in almost anyone" or, as in DSM-III-R:

> . . . an event that is outside the range of usual human experience and that would be markedly distressing to almost anyone, e.g., serious threat to one's life or physical integrity; serious threat or harm to one's children, spouse, or other close relatives and friends; sudden destruction of one's home or community; or seeing another person who has recently been, or of being, seriously injured or killed as the result of an accident or physical violence.

DSM-IV further clarified the nature of Criterion A saying that both the following have to be present:

(1) The person experienced, witnessed or was confronted with an event or events that involved actual or threatened death or serious injury, or a threat to the physical integrity of self or others.
(2) The person's response involved fear, helplessness or horror. *Note:* In children, this may be expressed instead by disorganised or agitated behavior.

Some events clearly fulfil Criterion A: earthquakes, hurricanes, sinking of ships, explosions and so on. But what about the death of a spouse through cancer? The person may develop all the other symptoms, but is death from cancer "outside the range of usual human experience"? It is clearly a tragedy to the individual involved and his or her suffering is nonetheless real and severe.

Slowly, it is being accepted that whereas the objective description of events that satisfy Criterion A is helpful in many instances, it is insufficient. One needs to take cognisance also of the way in which the individual interprets those events. Criterion A also has a subjective element, and so the same event may not be traumatic for nearly everyone. As can be seen, DSM-IV goes a long way towards taking both the objective and subjective aspects into account.

The definition also recognises that children may develop PTSD in response to a traumatic experience, and this is followed up in Chapter 2. Moreover, it firmly recognises that PTSD is one of a number of *anxiety* disorders, distinguished from most others by having a clear aetiological event.

A paradox in all these discussions is that, on the one hand, the definitions recognise that if the stress is sufficient, almost anyone may develop PTSD. It is, therefore, seen as a normal response to an abnormal event. On the other hand, it is given a psychiatric label and this upsets many people who develop it. How can it be normal and yet be seen as a serious psychiatric disorder at the same time? Clinicians have to be prepared to discuss these issues with their patients.

PREVALENCE

The point prevalence (i.e. at a particular point in time) of PTSD will clearly depend on what traumatic events have occurred and how many people were exposed to them. At first sight, this makes the concept of "prevalence" seem unusual in relation to this condition. And yet, one can speak of the prevalence of influenza, which is a reaction to a virus that strikes and spreads irregularly, so why not consider prevalence in relation to a myriad of traumas and disasters that strike randomly? Indeed, why not consider how many people may be exposed to potentially traumatic events?

Research on life events gives some clues. Kilpatrick (1992) estimated that 13% of adult women had been sexually assaulted—a very traumatic experience. Other potentially traumatic events affect anything from 40 to 70% of the population (Breslau, Davis, Andreski & Peterson, 1991; Norris, 1992). As will be seen below, the prevalence of PTSD is much lower than this and so straightaway it can be seen that not all people exposed to a traumatic event go on to develop a major stress reaction. Individual differences are important.

The proportion of those exposed who go on to develop PTSD varies in part according to the nature and severity of the traumatic event. By and large, there is good agreement in finding an exposure–effect relationship. People who are more severely exposed are more likely to develop a disorder. In mass transport disasters, such as the sinking of the cruise ship, Jupiter, well over 50% of the survivors went on to develop PTSD and others developed other psychopathology (Boyle, Bolton, Nurrish, O'Ryan, Udwin & Yule, 1995). Some 15 to 50% of people exposed to high levels of combat went on to develop PTSD (Foy, 1992).

When people are interviewed and asked whether they currently have symptoms or have ever had them, it is possible to get estimates of current and lifetime rates of PTSD. These will obviously differ if one studies a highly exposed group or a sample drawn from the general population. The US Epidemiological Catchment Area study (Kessler, Sonnega, Bromet, Hughes & Neison, 1995) estimated a population point prevalence rate of 1%. Other studies of more exposed samples give ranges from 5 to 15% for current levels and 4 to 12% for lifetime diagnosis.

This all indicates that PTSD is a very common disorder—as common as schizophrenia and almost as common as depression. It makes one wonder how it was overlooked for so long!

INDIVIDUAL DIFFERENCES, EMOTIONAL PROCESSING AND RISK AND PROTECTIVE FACTORS

The finding that, in certain extreme circumstances, most people may develop PTSD but that even then there are many exceptions, indicates that, as in most things, there are wide individual differences between people. Some people are more vulnerable than others; some are more resilient. In part, these differences will be genetically and biologically determined; in part, they arise because of different histories of experience with stress. In classic experimental studies, the reader is well aware of problems generalising the findings from one study to a different sample. What is less well understood is the problem facing the clinician of *particularising* findings from any or many studies and applying these to understanding the problems presented by an individual client. There is no greater turn-off for a traumatised patient than for the therapist to say, with all the summoned up empathy, genuineness and warmth at his or her disposal, "There, there; I understand what you are going through." Patients rightly concentrate on the unique experience they are trying to cope with and feel that only someone who has undergone identical experiences can even begin to understand. The therapist should rather say something like, "I can never fully understand what it is like for you, but all my experience with survivors of other terrible events suggests there may be some similarities. We need to find out which things you have in common and which you do not. Then, we can begin to plan what to do about it."

Having said that, there are things that can guide the therapist towards factors in the survivor as well as factors in the traumatic event that make for easier or more difficult recovery. These were well reviewed by Rachman (1980) in a seminal paper on "Emotional processing" published around the time that PTSD was first so labelled. Rachman argued that when individuals are threatened, they may react with strong emotions. These are natural, largely in-built mechanisms. In the normal course of events, the individuals may suffer a few bad nights or think a great deal about what happened to them, but the usual thing is for the anxiety and distress to wane as they realise that the threat no longer remains. However, when the initial threat has been very great and the initial reactions have been overwhelming, then, the survivors have many more problems. Frequently, they will not place themselves in situations that may be threatening and so are not exposed to the feared stimuli in a setting where no further harm occurs—in other words, normal habituation of anxiety does not occur. This, then, interferes with the normal processing of emotional reactions to stressful situations.

Rachman (1980) went on to analyse factors in the person, factors in the situation and factors in treatment that either help or hinder emotional processing. His argument was that the symptoms of what came to be called PTSD are the signs that emotional processing is incomplete. Disturbed sleep, tiredness, and high arousal as opposed to relaxation are state factors that militate against satisfactory emotional processing. Personality factors such as neuroticism, introversion and being inner-oriented likewise predict greater difficulty (see Chapter 5, Williams, for a fuller discussion).

More precise predictions can be made about stimulus factors in the stressful situation that seem to lead to difficulties in emotional processing derived from the experimental behaviour therapy literature. These include the event being sudden; being intense—there is increasing evidence for an exposure–effect relationship between the objective measure of the severity of the traumatic event and the subsequent distress; being dangerous—especially when many people are killed or injured; involving "prepared" fears, in Seligman's (1971) sense of the term; and the somewhat more subjective judgement that the event was uncontrollable and unpredictable. This list provides one way of emergency planners characterising different types of disaster events and estimating which are likely to give rise to greater levels of psychopathological reactions. Indeed, subsequent research has broadly found that traumatic events can be roughly scored on these dimensions and that high scores are related to higher degrees of problems among the survivors (Yule, 1993).

Once established, various factors can then either promote or impede emotional processing. High on the list of impeding factors is avoidance. Also in that sector is treatment that involves excessively brief presentations or poorly presented material. As will be seen later, good cognitive behavioural therapy involving both imaginal and in vivo exposure also requires considerable attention to detail on the part of the therapist (Richards and Lovell, Chapter 12 in this volume). Inexperienced therapists can too readily get a patient aroused and distressed and then cut the session short, thereby only sensitising the patient to the feared material and distressing him or her further. Thus, as early as 1980, Rachman was advocating therapy that involved long, vivid presentations with repeated practice. The patient had to be helped to be emotionally involved in the sessions and relaxation was seen as a useful adjunct, although it was recognised that relaxation at times serves to increase the vividness of the images conjured up. This finding can be put to good use in therapy, but can lead to premature avoidance if the patient and therapist do not expect it.

This formulation of reactions to severe, acute stressors has been very influential, both in developing better forms of treatment and in devising experimental ways of assessing more precisely how emotions are processed cognitively—see Thrasher and Dalgleish (Chapter 9) and Dalgleish (Chapter 10) for detailed accounts.

NATURAL COURSE OF THE DISORDER

While the short-term effects of traumatic events are fairly well described, less is known about the long-term effects, for the simple reason that the condition has not long been systematically diagnosed. Raphael (1986) summarised what was known around the time the diagnosis was gaining credibility. She concluded that, in the first year after a disaster, some 40% of survivors would show significant psychopathology. Over the following five years this dropped to 20–30%, indicating a chronic course for a significant minority of sufferers.

Since then, evidence is indeed accumulating that for some survivors of some events, the effects can be very long lasting. Holen (1991) studied the survivors of the Alexander Keilan oil rig collapse in the North Sea. Some were still severely affected eight years later. One of the earliest systematic studies of a man-made disaster was that of the collapse of the dam at Buffalo Creek. Fourteen years later, Green et al. (1990) found that 17% of the adult survivors still met the criteria for PTSD.

Seventeen years after being sexually assaulted, 17% of women were found still to have PTSD (Kilpatrick, Saunders, Veronen, Best & Von, 1987).

People are still found to suffer from PTSD, 40 to 50 years after World War II and the Holocaust of the Nazi Concentration Camps.

Studies of Vietnam veterans reported that many former soldiers had a delayed onset of PTSD, sometimes delayed by many years. This feature was incorporated into the definition of the disorder. However, it is rarely reported in studies of the medium-term aftermath of civilian disasters. To the contrary, the evidence seems to be that there is remarkable stability and predictability of early symptoms. People who respond most strongly initially go on to have more severe forms of the disorder and it lasts for longer.

In some studies, survivors report only being intermittently troubled by their symptoms (Zeiss & Dickman, 1989) and PTSD can have a varied course (Blank, 1993). McFarlane (1988) assessed over 300 firefighters called to deal with a bush fire in Australia in which some of their colleagues were killed. Using the self-completed screening scale, the General Health Questionnaire (Goldberg & Hillier, 1979), the proportions found to meet criteria for having a psychiatric disorder at 4, 11 and 29 months after the fire were:

(1) 50% never reached criteria for caseness
(2) 9% formed an acute group who reached caseness at 4 months but not thereafter
(3) 10% developed a persistent and chronic set of disorders
(4) 6% were distressed at 4 and 11 months but had resolved by 29 months
(5) 5% were well at 11 months but reached "caseness" at 4 and 29 months and so were considered to be a recurrent group
(6) 3% reached caseness at 11 and 29 months
(7) 5% were affected at only 11 months
(8) 11% were a delayed onset group reaching caseness only at 29 months.

Thus, McFarlane's study suggests that 19% had delayed onsets, but against this is the fact that the men only completed a screening scale, which is a broad indicator of common psychiatric disorders, such as anxiety and depression, rather than a specific measure of PTSD. The study suggests that the course of reactions is not always linear and can be delayed, but does not directly address the issue of the course of PTSD.

McFarlane and Papay (1992) did interview a sub-sample of the firefighters using a standard interview schedule, the Diagnostic Interview Schedule (Robins & Helzer, 1985), some 42 months after the fire. Eighteen per cent were found to have PTSD, with the next most common diagnosis being depression (10%). Of those who did have PTSD, the vast majority (77%) also had another major psychiatric disorder.

ASSESSMENT

There can be no substitute at present for a clinical interview directly with the survivor in order to obtain information both for the purposes of making a diagnosis and for planning treatment. It may be that in the near future some of this information can be obtained by sophisticated, interactive computer programs, but at present most services rely on well-trained mental health professionals.

But it is not just any old clinical interview, however sympathetically undertaken. The interview must systematically gather information about the traumatic event and the survivor's perceptions of it and its effects. It is vital to know about the survivor's pre-trauma history and levels of adjustment, and preferably to have some of this corroborated by a significant other. And the reactions to stress and current symptomatology must be carefully appraised.

There are now a number of semi-structured interviews that assess the symptoms of PTSD (Watson, 1990). Some of these are extensions of more general interviews such as the Diagnostic Interview Schedule (DIS: Robins & Helzer, 1985) and the Structured Clinical Interview (SCID: Spitzer, Williams & Gibbon, 1987). Of those that aim solely to measure and diagnose PTSD, the Clinician-Administered Post-Traumatic Stress Disorder Scale (CAPS: Blake et al., 1990) probably has the most useful supporting data.

As suggested earlier, one of the weaknesses of some of these structured interview schedules is that they may follow DSM too slavishly. Thus, merely asking for presence or absence of 17 DSM symptoms is rather mechanistic and may miss idiosyncratic reactions or wider psychopathology. At the very least, one must enquire about wider anxiety and phobias, depression and bereavement reactions.

Elsewhere, we have argued that there is a strong case for regarding PTSD to occur along a continuity of normal to abnormal stress reactions, rather than view it as a dichotomous variable which is either diagnosed or not (Joseph, Williams & Yule, 1997). Many people may not make the full, strict criteria for a diagnosis of PTSD but they may be equally as impaired in functioning and require the same level of care as those who do. Increasingly, clinical researchers see the need to classify such reactions as partial PTSD or sub-threshold PTSD (Blank, 1993; Carlier & Gersons, 1995).

Further, in assessing long-term outcome and change in response to treatment, it is necessary to have more finely calibrated instruments that provide continuous scales of measurement. For this purpose, there has been a great deal of interest in devising appropriate self-report instruments. Again, some of these merely restate the 17 DSM symptoms as questions, but even this has proved useful in clinical and research practice (Solomon, Weisenberg, Schwarzwald & Mikulincer, 1987; Solomon, Benbenishty, Neria, Abramowitz, Ginzburg & Ohry, 1993). Specialist scales were developed for use with Vietnam veterans. The Mississippi Scale (Keane, Caddell & Taylor, 1988) assessed features of depression, substance abuse and suicidal tendencies as well as the PTSD symptoms.

Some authors have looked at existing batteries and used techniques such as discriminant functions analysis to create sets of items that differentiate those with PTSD from those without. In the USA, the MMPI has been particularly targeted for such exercises, despite the fact that the items in the MMPI were developed long before PTSD was recognised. This seems an odd way of developing clinically useful measures.

A measure that was specifically developed to tap the main features of PTSD—namely, intrusion and avoidance—is the 15 item Impact of Event Scale (Horowitz, Wilner & Alvarez, 1979). Independent studies have confirmed that this scale possesses a factor structure that does indeed tap these two main constructs, although some minor factors may also be present (Joseph, Williams, Yule & Walker, 1992; Joseph, Yule, Williams & Hodgkinson, 1993a; Schwarzwald, Solomon, Weisenberg & Mikulincer, 1987; Zilberg, Weiss & Horowitz, 1982). The scale correlates well with a diagnosis of PTSD, has been translated and used successfully in other languages than English, and is sensitive to change brought about in treatment. However, it does not measure features of increased physiological arousal, and results from principal components analysis suggests that a few items are unnecessarily complicated and require rewording.

When making a full assessment, it can also be very useful to have the survivor complete measures of depression and anxiety as well as the fear survey schedule.

TREATMENT

When a traumatic event occurs, the individual directly affected is likely to be in shock for a matter of hours or a few days. Whether the traumatic event has hit at only one individual or at many hundreds of thousands, as in some of the recent earthquakes and civil wars, the first need of the survivor is to get to a place of safety, then to be reunited with his or her loved ones. In these first few hours, there is a limited role for mental health professionals other than to flag up to the survivors that they are there to help.

It has rapidly become the orthodox approach to service delivery for the authorities then to set up help lines and "counselling". Indeed, this has become so much part of the western scene in the past decade that firms sometimes fear that they lay themselves open to charges of negligence if they do not make trauma counselling available to their employees. And yet, controversy surrounds the provision of crisis intervention (see Canterbury and Yule, Chapter 11 this volume, for a fuller treatment).

It is clear that some response must be made by mental health services. Acting on the assumption that prevention is better than cure, proactive services have been set up. Rather than wait for things to go wrong, a member of the service reaches out to the survivor. So far, so good. The controversy comes in what is actually offered.

Following the capsize of the *Herald of Free Enterprise*, the Herald Assistance Unit was established by Kent Social Services. It sent out a leaflet which originated after the Australian Bushfires and was called Coping with a Personal Crisis. This went to all known survivors and the vast majority found it helpful, but a significant minority were upset even to receive it—again, individual differences affect responses to interventions. Most would agree that even where a few people get upset, the issuing of such a leaflet will be, on balance, a good thing to do.

Mitchell (1983) developed a particular protocol to help emergency service personnel deal with their emotional reactions to unpleasant work events. Working with the fire service, he devised "Critical Incident Stress Debriefing" which was a way of helping the firefighters deal with stress responses before they went home after their shift. It was developed as a collegiate, group support system and is widely practised. The problem comes when it has been extended and applied to the primary victims, many of whom will still be in shock in the first few days. Many services provide similar debriefing for primary victims, but few have evaluated it. Until recently, many thought it was obviously "a good thing".

Currently, some doubts have been raised as to its value and it is even suggested that debriefing may make things worse for some people (Raphael, Meldrum & McFarlane, 1995). As noted much earlier, inexperienced therapists can inadvertently cause problems for their clients if they raise their levels of distress and do not allow the fear or anxiety to habituate. Thus, it must be accepted that inappropriate debriefing which, by its very nature must make clients recall the traumatic event, has the propensity for making people worse. It is a weak argument to point out that many thousands of clients have been given this intervention and most appreciate it, as such vague endorsement is no substitute for hard evidence from random control trials which is sadly lacking at present.

It is also worth noting in passing that this controversy takes place in the context of the rapidly developing profession of trauma counsellors fighting for the turf of traditional mental health professionals, and the scientific debate may not be entirely uninfluenced by this battle.

Little has been written on treating survivors in groups and much more on treatment individually. Direct Exposure Therapies within a cognitive behavioural framework appear to offer the promise of greatest benefit. Most treatment packages include a selection of anxiety management techniques such as relaxation training, breathing retraining, stress inoculation therapy, guided self-dialogue and cognitive restructuring. But the core of successful treatment remains confronting the feared situation. This has been achieved by systematic desensitisation, flooding, prolonged exposure, implosive therapy—all either in imagination or in real life (see Chapter 12, this volume, for more detail).

There are many single case descriptions of treatment outcome and some of these are undertaken within rigorous single case experimental methodologies that permit drawing the conclusion that the treatment was responsible for the change observed. Such studies are useful in establishing that a treatment package can be effective, but cannot tell whether it is more effective than other approaches. For such studies one needs group comparison studies, preferably with random assignment of subjects. Very few such studies have been conducted.

Keane, Fairbanks, Cadell and Zimmering (1989) reported one random control treatment study and demonstrated convincingly that anxiety management was not enough on its own to help people with PTSD. Foa, Rothbaum, Riggs and Murdock (1991) compared exposure treatment with stress inoculation therapy with supportive therapy and a waiting list control. In the short term, stress inoculation therapy seemed better than prolonged exposure, but the reverse was found at long-term follow-up. The results of the Richards, Lovell and Marks (1994) study are discussed in Chapter 12 of this volume. Chemtob, Novaco, Hamada, Gross and Smith (1997), working with Vietnam veterans, found that anger management was a superior intervention than a control condition in veterans with PTSD.

New to the scene is Eye Movement Desensitisation and Reprocessing Therapy (Shapiro, 1995) (see also Smith and Yule, Chapter 13 in this volume). This intervention was originally promulgated as a specific treatment for PTSD but has since been applied, somewhat indiscriminately, by enthusiasts to many other conditions. Partly because the method is so bizarre and has no obvious theoretical rationale, it has sparked a great deal of interest—coupled with the fact that very strong claims were made for its efficacy. At present, it appears that some people do improve rapidly when asked to recall the traumatic event in images while systematically moving their eyes rapidly. Whether the eye movement is necessary is a debatable point. Whether it merely acts as a distracter allowing individuals to expose themselves to the feared situation and so allow habituation to occur is still unclear. Whatever the eventual verdict, it is a rapid treatment method that deserves further empirical validation.

REFERENCES

Abrahams, M.J., Price, J., Whitlock, F.A. & Williams, G. (1976). The Brisbane floods, January 1974: Their impact on health. *Medical Journal of Australia*, **2**, 936–939.

APA (1980). *Diagnostic and Statistical Manual of Mental Disorders* (3rd Edition). Washington, DC: American Psychiatric Association.

APA (1987). *Diagnostic and Statistical Manual of Mental Disorders* (3rd Edition, Revised). Washington, DC: American Psychiatric Association.

APA (1994). *Diagnostic and Statistical Manual of Mental Disorders* (4th Edition). Washington, DC: American Psychiatric Association.

Barker, P. (1991). *Regeneration*. London: Viking.

Bennet, G. (1970). Bristol floods 1968: Controlled survey of effects on health of local community disaster. *British Medical Journal*, **3**, 454–458.

Blake, D.D., Weathers, F.W., Nagy, L.M., et al. (1990). A clinician rating scale for assessing current and lifetime PTSD: The CAPS-I. *Behavior Therapy*, **13**, 187–188.

Blank, A.S. (1993). The longitudinal course of posttraumatic stress disorder. In J.R.T. Davidson & E.B. Foa (Eds.), *Posttraumatic Stress Disorder: DSM-IV and Beyond*. Washington, DC: American Psychiatric Press.

Boyle, S., Bolton, D., Nurrish, J., O'Ryan, D., Udwin, O. & Yule, W. (1995). The Jupiter sinking follow-up: Predicting psychopathology in adolescence following trauma. Poster presented at Eleventh Annual Meeting of the International Society for Traumatic Stress Studies, Boston, 2–6 November 1995.

Breslau, N., Davis, G.C., Andreski, P. & Peterson, E. (1991). Traumatic events and posttraumatic stress disorder in an urban population of young adults. *Archives of General Psychiatry*, **48**, 216–222.

Carlier, I.V.E. & Gersons, B.P.R. (1995). Partial posttraumatic stress disorder (PTSD): The issue of psychological scars and the occurrence of PTSD symptoms. *The Journal of Nervous and Mental Disease*, **183**, 107–109.

Chemtob, C.M., Novaco, R.W., Hamada, R.S., Gross, D.M. & Smith, G. (1997). Anger regulation deficits in combat-related posttraumatic stress disorder. *Journal of Traumatic Stress*, **10**, 17–36.

Daly, R.J. (1983). Samuel Pepys and post traumatic disorder. *British Journal of Psychiatry*, **143**, 64–68.

Erichsen, J.E. (1866). *On Railway and Other Injuries of the Nervous System*. London: Walton & Maberly.

Figley, C.R. (1978). Psychosocial adjustment among Vietnam veterans. In C.R. Figley (Ed.), *Stress Disorders among Vietnam Veterans*. New York: Brunner/Mazel.

Foa, E.B., Rothbaum B.O., Riggs D.S. & Murdock T.B. (1991). Treatment of posttraumatic stress disorder in rape victims: A comparison between cognitive-behavioural procedures and counselling. *Journal of Consulting and Clinical Psychology*, **59**, 715–723.

Foy, D.W. (Ed.) (1992). *Treating Post-Traumatic Stress Disorder: Cognitive Behavioral Strategies*. New York: Guilford Press.

Freud, S. (1894). On the grounds for detaching a particular syndrome from neurasthenia under the description "anxiety neurosis". *The Standard Edition of the Complete Psychological Works of Sigmund Freud*, vol. 3. London: Hogarth Press.

Freud, S. (1919). *Introduction to the Psychology of the War Neurosis* (Standard edn., vol. 18). London: Hogarth Press.

Gleser, G.C., Green, B.L. & Winget, C.N. (1981). *Prolonged Psychosocial Effects of Disaster*. New York: Academic Press.

Goenjian, A. (1993). A mental health relief programme in Armenia after the 1988 Earthquake: Implementation and clinical observations. *British Journal of Psychiatry*, **163**, 230–239.

Goldberg, D.P. & Hillier, V.F. (1979). A scaled version of the General Health Questionnaire. *Psychological Medicine*, **9**, 139–145.

Green, B.L., Grace, M.C., Liny, J.D., Gleser, G.C., Leonard, A.C. & Crummier, T.L. (1990). Buffalo Creek survivors in the second decade: Comparison with unexposed and nonlitigant groups. *Journal of Applied Social Psychology*, **20**, 1033–1050.

Grinker, R.R. & Spiegel, J.P. (1943). *War Neurosis in North Africa, the Tunisian Campaign, January to May 1943*. New York: Josiah Macy Foundation.

Holen, A. (1991). A longitudinal study of the occurrence and persistence of post-traumatic health problems in disaster survivors. *Stress Medicine*, **7**, 11–17.

Horowitz, M. (1975). Intrusive and repetitive thoughts after stress. *Archives of General Psychiatry*, **32**, 1457–1463.

Horowitz, M. (1976). *Stress Response Syndromes*. New York: Jason Aronson.

Horowitz, M. (1979). Psychological response to serious life events. In V. Hamilton & D.M. Warburton (Eds.), *Human Stress and Cognition: An Information Processing Approach*. Chichester: Wiley.

Horowitz, M.J. (1986a). *Stress Response Syndromes*, Northvale, NJ: Jason Aronson.

Horowitz, M.J. (1986b). Stress-response syndromes: A review of posttraumatic and adjustment disorders. *Hospital and Community Psychiatry*, **37**, 241–249.

Horowitz, M., Wilner & Alvarez, W. (1979). Impact of Event Scale: A measure of subjective stress. *Psychosomatic Medicine*, **41**, 209–218.

Janoff-Bulman, R. (1989). Assumptive worlds and the stress of traumatic events: Applications of the schema construct. *Social Cognition*, **7**, 113–136.

Joseph, S., Williams, R. & Yule, W. (1997). *Understanding Post-Traumatic Stress: A Psychosocial Perspective on PTSD and Treatment*. Chichester: Wiley.

Joseph, S., Williams, R., Yule, W. & Walker, A. (1992). Factor analysis of the Impact of Events Scale in survivors of two disasters at sea. *Personality and Individual Differences*, **13**, 693–697.

Joseph, S., Yule, W., Williams, R. & Hodgkinson, P. (1993a). Increased substance use in survivors of the Herald of Free Enterprise disaster. *British Journal of Medical Psychology*, **66**, 185–191.

Joseph, S., Yule, W., Williams, R. & Hodgkinson, P. (1993b). The Herald of Free Enterprise disaster: Measuring post-traumatic symptoms thirty months on. *British Journal of Clinical Psychology*, **32**, 327–332.

Kardiner, A. (1941). *The Traumatic Neurosis of War*. Psychosomatic Medicine Monograph II–III. New York: Paul B. Hoeber.

Keane, T.M., Caddell, J.M., Martin, B., Zimmering, R.T. & Fairbank, J.A. (1983). Substance abuse among Vietnam veterans with posttraumatic stress disorders. *Bulletin of Psychologists and Addictive Behaviour*, **2**, 117–122.

Keane, T.M., Caddell, J.M. & Taylor, K.L. (1988). Mississippi scale for combat-related posttraumatic stress disorder: Three studies in reliability and validity. *Journal of Consulting and Clinical Psychology*, **56**, 85–90.

Keane, T.M., Fairbank, J.A., Cadell J.M. & Zimmering, R.T. (1989). Implosive (flooding) therapy reduces symptoms of PTSD in Vietnam combat veterans. *Behavior Therapy*, **20**, 149–153.

Kessler, R.C., Sonnega, A., Bromet, E., Hughes, M. & Nelson, C.B. (1995). Posttraumatic stress disorder in the national comorbidity survey. *Archives of General Psychiatry*, **52**, 1048–1060.

Kilpatrick, D.G., Edmunds, C.N. & Seymour, A.K. (1992). *Rape in America: A Report to the Nation*. Arlington, VA: National Victims Center.

Kilpatrick, D.G., Saunders, B.E., Veronen, L.J., Best, C.L. & Von, J.M. (1987). Criminal victimization: Lifetime prevalence reporting to police, and psychological impact. *Crime and Delinquency*, **33**, 479–489.

Kraepelin, E. (1886). *Psychiatrie*, Vol. 5. Auflage. Leipzig: Barth.

Kulka, R.A., Schlenger, W.E., Fairbank, J.A., Hough, R.L., Jordon, B.K., Marmar, C.R. & Weiss, D.S. (1990). *Trauma and the Vietnam war generation: Report of findings from the National Vietnam Veterans Readjustment Study*. New York: Brunner/Mazel.

Loughrey, G.C., Bell, P., Kee, M., Roddy, R.J. & Curran, P.S. (1988). Post-traumatic stress disorder and civil violence in Northern Ireland. *British Journal of Psychiatry*, **153**, 554–560.

Logue, J.N., Hansen, H. & Struening, E. (1979). Emotional and physical distress following Hurricane Agnes in Wyoming Valley of Pennsylvania. *Public Health Reports*, **4**, 495–502.

McFarlane, A.C. (1987). Family functioning and overprotection following a natural disaster: The longitudinal effects of post-traumatic morbidity. *Australian and New Zealand Journal of Psychiatry*, **21**, 210–218.

McFarlane, A.C. (1988). The longitudinal course of posttraumatic morbidity: The range of outcomes and their predictors. *Journal of Nervous and Mental Disease*, **176**, 22–29.

McFarlane, A.C. & Papay, P. (1992). Multiple diagnoses in posttraumatic stress disorder in the victims of a natural disaster. *Journal of Nervous and Mental Disease*, **180**, 498–504.

McNally, R.J., Lasko, N.B., Macklin, M.L. & Pitman, R.K. (1995). Autobiographical memory disturbance in combat-related posttraumatic stress disorder. *Behaviour Research and Therapy*, **33**, 619–630.

Melick, M.E. (1978). Life change and illness: Illness behavior of males in the recovery period of a natural disaster. *Journal of Health and Social Behavior*, **19**, 335–342.

Mitchell, J.T. (1983). When disaster strikes. . . . The critical incident stress debriefing process. *Journal of Emergency Medical Services*, **8**, 36–39.

Mott, F.W. (1919). *War Neuroses and Shell Shock*. London: Oxford University Press.

Norris, F.H. (1992). Epidemiology of trauma: Frequency and impact of different potentially traumatic events on different demographic groups. *Journal of Consulting and Clinical Psychology*, **60**, 409–418.

North, C.S., Smith, E.M. & Spitznagel, E.L. (1994). Posttraumatic stress disorder in survivors of a mass shooting. *American Journal of Psychiatry*, **151**, 82–88.

Oppenheim, H. (1892). *Die traumatischen Neurosen*. Berlin: August Hirschwald.

Page, H. (1885). *Injuries of the Spine and Spinal Cord without Apparent Mechanical Lesion*. London: Churchill.

Price, J. (1978). Some age-related effects of the 1974 Brisbane floods. *Australian and New Zealand Journal of Psychiatry*, **12**, 55–58.

Rachman, S. (1980). Emotional processing. *Behaviour Research and Therapy*, **18**, 51–60.

Raphael, B. (1986). *When Disaster Strikes*. London: Hutchinson.

Raphael, B., Meldrum, L. & McFarlane, A.C. (1995). Does debriefing after psychological trauma work? Time for randomized control trials. *British Medical Journal*, **310**, 1479–1480.

Richards, D.A., Lovell, K. & Marks, I.M. (1994) Post-traumatic stress disorder: Evaluation of a behavioural treatment. *Journal of Traumatic Stress*, **7**(4), 669–680.

Robins, L.N. & Helzer, J.E. (1985). *Diagnostic Interview Schedule (DIS) Version III-A*. St. Louis, MO: Washington University.

Roth, L.M. (1986). Substance use and mental health among Vietnam veterans. In G. Boulanger & C. Kadushin (Eds.), *The Vietnam Veteran Redefined*, pp. 61–78. Hillsdale, NJ: Lawrence Erlbaum.

Seligman, M.E.P (1971). Phobias and preparedness. *Behavior Therapy*, **2**, 307–320.

Schwarzwald, J., Solomon, Z., Weisenberg, M. & Mikulincer, M. (1987). Validation of the impact of event scale for psychological sequelae of combat. *Journal of Consulting and Clinical Psychology*, **55**, 251–256.

Shapiro, F. (1995). *Eye Movement Desensitization and Reprocessing: Basic Principles, Protocols and Procedures*. New York: Guilford Press.

Solomon, Z., Benbenishty, R., Neria, Y., Abramowitz, M., Ginzburg, K. & Ohry, A. (1993). Assessment of PTSD: Validation of the Revised PTSD Inventory. *Israel Journal of Psychiatry and Related Sciences*, **30**, 110–115.

Solomon, Z., Mikulincer, M. & Kotler, M. (1987). A two year follow-up of somatic complaints among Israeli combat stress reaction casualties. *Journal of Psychosomatic Research*, **31**, 463–469.

Solomon, Z., Weisenberg, M., Schwarzwald, J. & Mikulincer, M. (1987). Post-traumatic stress disorder among frontline soldiers with combat stress reaction: the 1982 Israeli experience. *American Journal of Psychiatry*, **144**, 448–454.

Southward, E.E. (1919). *Shell Shock and Neuropsychiatric Problems*. Boston: Leonard.

Spitzer, R.L., Williams, J.B.W. & Gibbon, M. (1987). *Structured Clinical Interview for DSM-III-R, Version NP-V*. New York: New York State Psychiatric Institute, Biometrics Research Department.

Trimble, M.R. (1981). *Post-traumatic Neurosis: From Railway Spine to the Whiplash*. New York: Wiley.

Watson, C.G. (1990). Psychometric posttraumatic stress disorder measurement techniques: A review. *Psychological Assessment*, **2**, 460–469.

Wilkinson, C.B. (1983). Aftermath of a disaster: The collapse of the Hyatt Regency Hotel Skywalk. *American Journal of Psychiatry*, **140**, 1134–1139.

Yule, W. (1993). Risk and protective factors in childhood post traumatic stress disorder. In S.M.J. van Hekken, N.W. Slot & J.W. Veerman (Eds.), *Pedologie tussen wetenschap en praktijk*, pp. 204–210. Utrecht: De Tijdstroom.

Zeiss, R. & Dickman, H. (1989). PTSD 40 years later: Incidence and person-situation correlates in former POW's. *Journal of Clinical Psychology*, **45**, 80–87.

Zilberg, N.J., Weiss, D.S. & Horowitz, M.J. (1982). Impact of Event Scale: A cross-validation study and some empirical evidence supporting a conceptual model of stress response syndromes. *Journal of Consulting and Clinical Psychology*, **50**, 407–414.

Chapter 2

POST-TRAUMATIC STRESS REACTIONS IN CHILDREN AND ADOLESCENTS

William Yule, Sean Perrin* and Patrick Smith**

It has always been obvious that children may get upset when confronted by some frightening experience. Until 15 years ago, it was widely accepted that children only responded to frightening events with transient distress, although it was recognised that, in some circumstances, they might develop circumscribed phobic reactions that could last a long time and seriously disrupt their lives. Garmezy and Rutter (1985) reviewed the existing evidence and concluded that, following a variety of stressors,

> . . . behavioural disturbances appear to be less intense than might have been anticipated; a majority of children show a moderate amount of fear and anxiety but this subsides; regressive behaviour marked by clinging to parents and heightened dependency on adults appears and then moderately mild sleep disturbance persists for several months; a later less severe stressor such as a storm may lead to a temporary increase in emotional distress, although this is variable; enuresis occurs in some cases, while hypersensitivity to loud noises may be evident in others. (Garmezy & Rutter, 1985, p. 126)

They concluded that, in the majority of children, any disturbances following a traumatic event are short lived. Because children were reported as not showing amnesia for such events, nor as showing "psychic numbing" or intrusive flashbacks, they argued that there was no need for a specific diagnostic category for stress reactions in children to parallel the category of PTSD in adults.

Garmezy and Rutter rightly stressed that not all children who experience a potentially traumatic event react with disabling stress reactions. By

*Institute of Psychiatry, London

Post-Traumatic Stress Disorders: Concepts and Therapy. Edited by William Yule.
© 1999 John Wiley & Sons Ltd.

focusing attention on *resilience* rather than pathology, they have emphasised that we can learn a lot from the study of children who do not react badly to stress. However, like the rest of us, they were misled because the evidence was incomplete. Put simply, the bulk of the then existing evidence came from data provided by parents and teachers. Few investigators had done what is now so obvious—*they had not asked the children themselves*!

It has long been appreciated that parents and teachers under-report anxiety symptoms in children. The same has now been demonstrated with respect of symptoms of post-traumatic stress. Some studies, such as that of the Three Mile Island nuclear accident (Handford et al., 1986), not only established that parents under-report the extent and severity of their children's reactions, but also that the most widely used observer rating scales are insensitive to the reactions of children and adolescents following traumatic incidents (Galante & Foa, 1986; McFarlane, Policansky & Irwin, 1987). In part, this under-reporting is likely to be due to children not talking to their parents about their symptoms so as to protect the adults, and in part because adults often may wish to deny how children have been affected by horrendous incidents.

Thus, it is really only in the past 15 years or so that traumatic stress reactions in children have been studied in a scientific, clinical manner. The term *"traumatic stress reactions"* is used as opposed to PTSD to emphasise that, while broadly similar to adult reactions, the narrow confines of either DSM (APA, 1980, 1987, 1994) or ICD (WHO, 1987, 1988, 1991), as described in Chapter 1, may not do justice to the range of reactions shown by children and, in particular, ignores the different manifestations in very young children. The chapter will describe these reactions in children and then summarise what is known about prevalence, aetiology and natural history before considering more technical issues of assessment and treatment.

MANIFESTATIONS OF STRESS REACTIONS IN CHILDREN AND ADOLESCENTS

Immediately following a very frightening experience, children are likely to be very distressed, tearful, frightened and in shock. They need protection and safety. They need to be reunited with their familes wherever possible.

Starting almost immediately, most children are troubled by *repetitive, intrusive thoughts* about the accident. Such thoughts can occur at any time, but particularly when the children are otherwise quiet, as when they are trying to drop off to sleep. At other times, the thoughts and vivid recollections are triggered off by reminders in their environment. Vivid, dissociative *flashbacks* are uncommon. In a flashback, the child reports that he or she is re-experiencing the event, as if it were happening all over again. It is almost a dissociated experience. *Sleep disturbances* are very common, particularly in the first few weeks. *Fears* of the dark and bad dreams, *nightmares*, and waking through the night are widespread (and often manifest outside the developmental age range in which they normally occur).

Separation difficulties are frequent, even among teenagers. For the first few days, children may not want to let their parents out of their sight, even reverting to sleeping in the parental bed. Many children become much more *irritable and angry* than previously, both with parents and peers.

Although child survivors experience a *pressure to talk* about their experiences, paradoxically they also find it very *difficult to talk with their parents and peers*. Often they do not want to upset the adults, and so parents may not be aware of the full extent of their children's suffering. Peers may hold back from asking what happened in case they upset the child further; the survivor often feels this as a rejection.

Children report a number of *cognitive changes*. Many experience *difficulties in concentration*, especially in school work. Others report *memory problems*, both in mastering new material and in remembering old skills such as reading music. They become very *alert to danger* in their environment, being adversely affected by reports of other disasters.

Survivors have learned that life is very fragile. This can lead to a loss of faith in the future or a *sense of foreshortened future*. Their priorities change. Some feel they should live each day to the full and not plan far ahead. Others realise they have been over-concerned with materialistic or petty matters and resolve to rethink their values. Their "assumptive world" has been challenged (Janoff-Bulman, 1985).

Not surprisingly, many develop *fears* associated with specific aspects of their experiences. They avoid situations they associate with the disaster. Many experience *survivor guilt*—about surviving when others died; about thinking they should have done more to help others; about what they themselves did to survive.

Adolescent survivors report significantly high rates of *depression*, some becoming clinically depressed, having suicidal thoughts and taking overdoses in the year after a disaster. A significant number become very *anxious* after accidents, although the appearance of *panic attacks* is sometimes considerably delayed. When children have been *bereaved*, they may need bereavement counselling.

In summary, children and adolescents surviving a life-threatening disaster show a wide range of symptoms which tend to cluster around signs of re-experiencing the traumatic event, trying to avoid dealing with the emotions that this gives rise to, and a range of signs of increased physiological arousal. There may be considerable co-morbidity with depression, generalised anxiety or pathological grief reactions.

EFFECTS ON YOUNGER CHILDREN

Many writers agree that it is very difficult to elicit evidence of emotional numbing in children (Frederick, 1985). Some children do show loss of interest in activities and hobbies that previously gave them pleasure. Pre-school children show much more regressive behaviour as well as more antisocial, aggressive and destructive behaviour. There are many anecdotal accounts of pre-school children showing repetitive drawing and play involving themes about the trauma they experienced.

Although parents and teachers initially report that young children do not easily talk about the trauma, recent experience has been that many young children easily give very graphic accounts of their experiences and were also able to report how distressing the re-experiencing in thoughts and images was (Sullivan, Saylor & Foster, 1991; Misch, Phillips, Evans & Berelowitz, 1993). All clinicians and researchers need to have a good understanding of children's development to be able to assist them express their inner distress.

Scheeringa, Zeanah, Drell and Larrieu (1995) examined the phenomenology reported in published cases of trauma in infants and young children and evolved an alternative set of criteria for diagnosing PTSD in very young children. Re-experiencing is seen as being manifested in post-traumatic play; re-enactment of the trauma; recurrent recollection of the traumatic event; nightmares; flashbacks or distress at exposure to reminders of the event. Only one positive item is needed. Numbing is present if one of the following is manifested: constriction of play; socially more withdrawn; restricted range of affect; or loss of previously acquired developmental skill. Increased arousal is noted if one of the following is present: night terrors; difficulty getting off to sleep; night waking; decreased concentration; hypervigilance; or exaggerated startle response. A new subset of new fears and aggression was suggested and is said to be present if one of the following is recorded: new aggression; new separation anxiety; fear of toileting alone; fear of the dark or any other unrelated new fear. To date, these altered criteria have not been tested against the traditional ones. Almqvist and Brandell-Forsberg (1997) provide evidence on how a standard set of play material can be used to obtain objective data on traumatic stress reactions from pre-school children. Thus, one can anticipate a refining of criteria and methods of assessment of PTSD in pre-school children in the next few years.

Risk and Protective Factors

Age

This has been thought to be a factor in the development of PTSD. Indeed, DSM cited children as being at a high risk of psychopathology following a trauma. This seems to owe more to a particular theoretical view of child development than to any hard evidence. Age was not found to be related to Stress Reaction Index scores within the Armenian earthquake group (Pynoos et al., 1993). Indeed, it can be argued that developmental age in the sense of cognitive understanding could act in different ways— younger children may not fully appreciate the dangers they faced and so may be protected from strong emotional reactions (Keppel-Benson & Ollendick, 1993). This would imply that brighter children would be at an increased risk, and this does not appear to be the case by teenage years.

Gender

It is generally found that girls score higher than boys on self-report measures of anxiety, depression and stress reactions following a trauma (Gibbs, 1989; Yule, 1992a, 1992b; Lonigan, Shannon, Finch, Daugherty & Saylor, 1991; Pynoos et al., 1993). There only a few unexplained exceptions to this pattern of findings and, as always, it is far from clear whether these are culturally or biologically determined differences.

Ability and Attainment

In general, higher ability is seen as a protective factor against developing psychopathology. The developmental concern around appraisal of the threat noted earlier complicates the issue, insofar as, in very young children, those who are brighter may appreciate the implications of danger to a greater extent. Early studies of *Jupiter* survivors indicated that high risk was associated with prior *low* pre-accident attainment (Yule & Udwin, 1991). There are now many individual case examples of children's educational careers being thrown off-course by the after-effects of traumas happening at crucial times, and there is also evidence that, in general, academic attainment falls temporarily after a major trauma (Tsui, Dagwell & Yule, 1993).

Family Factors

It has already been noted that children often try to protect their parents from learning about their reactions to a trauma for fear of upsetting the parents. Where parents have difficulty processing their own emotional reactions, they are less successful in helping their children (McFarlane, 1987). Families who had difficulty sharing immediate reactions had more problems later. While some authors argue that all of children's reactions to trauma are mediated by parental reactions, in our clinical and research experience this is far from the case. The evidence for there being direct effects on the children is overwhelming. Equally, the reactions of parents must be important in moderating the effects, but quite in which ways is far from established.

Recently, a preliminary analysis of consecutive cases assessed in a specialist children's traumatic stress clinic found that where mother and children were involved in the same road traffic accident, those children were likely to be less badly affected than cases where the children were not accompanied by their mother at the time of the accident (Perrin, Smith & Yule, 1996). However, a similar study of RTA survivors at a different, general outpatient clinic reached opposite conclusions (Ellis, Stores & Mayou, 1998). While these differences may be related to referral biases and/or differences in methodology, the point to note is that the interaction between the family and the child's reaction, even in RTAs, is not well understood at present.

Prevalence

Epidemiological investigations of adults in the general population estimate a lifetime prevalence of PTSD between 1 and 9.2% (see Fairbank, Schlenger, Saigh & Davidson, 1995 for a review of epidemiological investigations of PTSD). The prevalence of PTSD among children in the community is unknown. There have been no epidemiological investigations of the disorder to date. However, there have been several studies of PTSD in children exposed to war, natural disaster, violent crime and sexual abuse ("at-risk" groups).

Prevalence rates from studies of at-risk children vary widely (from 0 to 100%). This extreme variability is consistent with findings from studies of at-risk adults (Fairbank et al., 1995), and is reflected in the estimates given for at-risk groups in DSM-IV (3–58%) (APA, 1994). Therefore, the following studies must be interpreted with caution. Specific diagnostic criteria for PTSD were not widely available until 1980. The term "psychic trauma", which included extreme fear reactions, grief, agitation and depression, was more often found in the literature. Also, few, if any, reliable screening instruments for childhood PTSD had been developed which severely undermined reliable estimation of the prevalence of PTSD (Galante & Foa, 1986; Yule & Williams, 1990).

In one of the earliest studies of at-risk children, Terr (1979) noted that the incidence of psychic trauma was 100% among 26 children involved in the Chowchilla bus-kidnapping. This rate was independent of the child's background and developmental history (Terr, 1979).

Two additional studies provide estimates for PTSD among children exposed to civilian acts of violence. Pynoos et al. (1987) examined the occurrence of PTSD in 159 children one month after an attack by a sniper on their school playground. Seventy-seven per cent of the children under direct threat (i.e. those on the playground) had moderate or severe PTSD as measured the PTSD Reaction Index. Moderate or severe PTSD were also high (67%) among children not exposed to the sniper but at the school on the same day (Pynoos et al., 1987).

More recently, Schwarz and Kowalski (1991) assessed 64 pre-adolescent school children six months after a shooting spree by a woman in their school. Prevalence rates were presented separately for the three diagnostic categorisations of PTSD under DSM-III, DSM-III-R and DSM-IV and the PTSD Reaction Index. Using "conservative" symptom thresholds (i.e. symptoms occurring "much" or "most of the time"), the prevalence of PTSD under DSM-III was 16%. By contrast, the prevalence of PTSD under DSM-III-R was only 8%, and 9% under DSM-IV (Schwarz & Kowalski, 1991). Using "liberal" symptom threshold levels (i.e. symptoms occurring at least "a little of the time"), prevalence rates ranged from 91% under DSM-III to 50% for DSM-III-R, and 26% for DSM-IV. This study underlines the difficulty with comparing PTSD prevalence rates across studies using which use different versions of the DSM. Arguably, it also points out the risk of not identifying true cases of PTSD when using the subsequent revisions of the criteria under DSM-III-R and DSM-IV.

Five months after the sinking of the cruise ship, *Jupiter*, with over 400 British school children on board, Yule, Udwin and Murdoch (1990) studied self-reported fears, anxiety and depression in a party of 24 adolescent girls from one school. Yule (1992a) reports the data on 334 of the survivors, confirming the high scores on the Impact of Events Scale as well as increased fears. Around half of the survivors were found to meet the criteria for a diagnosis of PTSD in the first year following the sinking. While there was a slow improvement in symptoms over the following six to seven years, almost one in five of those who developed PTSD still met the criteria five years after the sinking. Many others had anxiety or depression and so it was demonstrated that PTSD is not a transient disorder and is associated with long-term morbidity in a sizeable minority of cases (Boyle, Bolton, Narrish, O'Ryan, Udwin & Yule, 1995).

Several investigations have examined the prevalence of PTSD among children exposed to war. Most have used self-completed questionnaires rather than individual diagnostic interviews. In general, early studies conducted in association with UNICEF in former Yugoslavia found not only high levels of traumatic stress symptoms, anxiety and depression while the fighting was still in progress, but also that the greater the level of exposure of children to war traumas, the higher their subjective distress (Stuvland et al., 1994). These findings have been confirmed and extended in a study of more than 3,500 children in the Bosnian city of Mostar, conducted a few months after the Dayton agreement brought an uneasy peace to the region (Smith, Yule, Perrin & Schwartz, 1996).

McFarlane, Policansky and Irwin (1987) found a high frequency of PTSD symptom clusters (94%) obtained from parent and teacher versions of the Rutter Scales in 808 children two months after large-scale brushfires in Australia. Similarly, Milgram, Toubiana, Klingman, Raviv and Goldstein (1988) observed a 40% prevalence rate for PTSD in children one month after a bus accident. Bradburn (1991) reported prevalence rates of 27% for moderate PTSD and 36% for mild PTSD in 22 children aged 10–12 years, some six to eight months after the San Francisco earthquake. Of 179 children aged 2–15 years who were examined two years after the Buffalo Creek disaster, 37% received probable PTSD diagnoses based on retrospective examination of records (Green et al., 1991).

A series of large-scale investigations of PTSD in children were conducted following Hurricane Hugo which struck South Carolina in 1989. Based on self-report data, Lonigan et al. (1991) reported PTSD prevalence rates of 5.06% in a no-exposure group, 10.35% in a mild group, 15.54% in a moderate group, and 28.95% in a high-exposure group of hurricane survivors. The overall prevalence rate for PTSD in the sample was 5% ($n = 5687$) nearly three months after the hurricane (Shannon et al., 1994). Similarly, Garrison, Weinrich, Hardin, Weinrich and Wang (1993) reported current prevalence rates ranging from 1.5 to 6.2% one year after the hurricane in 11- to 17-year-olds.

From the above studies it can be seen that reliable estimation of the prevalence of PTSD in children and adolescents is extremely difficult, particularly from data collected prior to the operationalising of PTSD in DSM. Moreover, there is considerable variability in prevalence estimates depending upon the age of the child, time since the trauma, assessment methods used, and version of DSM under which caseness was established.

Single versus Repeated or Chronic Stressors

Both DSM and ICD in different, and changing, ways discuss the nature of the event that gives rise to the stress reaction. Each concentrates on single, acute stressors such as an unexpected disaster or a violent attack, each of which occurs in the context of ongoing normality. Gradually, the nature of the stressor is being discussed more and more as one in which the "victim" felt that his or her life was under threat or in which such a threat was perceived in relation to a loved one. This is a difference from the earlier formulations in which the stressor was seen as one that would cause significant distress to almost anyone.

Thus, it is increasingly recognised that the stressor cannot be fully defined in objective terms. There is a very important element of subjective evaluation which goes some way towards explaining individual differences in reactions to extreme stressors. Rachman (1980) had examined the objective and subjective factors which he saw as being related to continuing difficulties in processing the emotions that arose from life-threatening experiences.

Objective Factors

Rachman's (1980) list included the suddenness with which a disaster strikes, the severity in the sense of the numbers killed or maimed, and the extent to which the incident involved "prepared fears". This way of considering the stimulus properties of a disaster opens the way for emergency services to develop a profile of potential scenarios indicating those that are most likely to give rise to high proportions of people with severe psychopathology. As researchers are increasingly using standard assessments in their studies, it is becoming clearer that there are differences which tend to follow Rachman's model. Thus, the level of reported distress was greater following the capsize of the *Herald of Free Enterprise* in which many people were killed compared with that following the sinking of the cruise ship, *Jupiter*, in which only one pupil, one teacher and two rescuers were killed. In both cases, the level of distress reported in teenagers was greater in these shipping disasters than that recorded after a school bus crash in which no one was killed (Stallard & Law, 1993). Children who survived the Lockerbie air disaster (Parry Jones, 1992) and those who survived Hurricane Hugo (Lonigan et al., 1991) presented with intermediate levels of distress on standard measures.

Within particular disasters there is evidence of a dose–response, or more specifically an exposure–response, relationship. Pynoos et al. (1987) reported the effects of a sniper attack on children in a Californian school. There was a clear relationship between the distance from the sniper (and hence the objective, personal danger) and later psychopathology, with some individual differences such as a boy who had left early to play football, leaving his sister in the line of fire. Although he was in a safe area when the firing started, he experienced considerable post-traumatic stress.

In a systematic follow-up study, Nader, Pynoos, Fairbanks and Frederick (1990) reported that 74% of the most severely exposed children in the playground still reported moderate to severe levels of PTSD, whereas only 19% of the unexposed children reported any PTSD. It is of note that in this study the lower the objective level of threat, the more did other subjective factors enter the equation to produce stress reactions. Pynoos et al. (1993) studied three large groups of children following the Armenian earthquake—one from a town at the epicentre where buildings were totally destroyed; one from a town on the periphery; and one from a city outside the affected area. Again, a very clear exposure–effect relationship was demonstrated.

A further consensus is appearing in the published literature to the effect that greater psychopathology follows the witnessing of death and mutilation, as well as the feeling that the child's own life was under threat.

Subjective Factors

In PTSD work in general, there has been an increasing interest in cognitive appraisal, coping strategies and attributional processes (Joseph, Brewin, Yule & Williams, 1991, 1993). Yule, Udwin and Murdoch (1990) presented some evidence that there was a subjective exposure–effect relationship insofar as children who had experienced a school trip disaster were much more badly affected than children in the same school who had wanted to go on the cruise but had not obtained places; there was even less distress among children who had never wanted to go. In another study of a larger group of adolescents who survived that same ship disaster, Joseph et al.

(1993) reported on the attributions of 16 adolescent survivors of the *Jupiter* sinking and found that more internal and controllable attributions were related to intrusive thoughts and feelings of depression one year after the accident.

Single versus Multiple Traumas

Naturally, as work on PTSD in children and adolescents began to appear, people tried to extend the paradigm to help understand other experiences that affect children's development. Wolfe, Gentile and Wolfe (1989) were among the first to try to formulate the effects of child sexual abuse within a PTSD framework, and this certainly helped to focus attention on aspects of the whole experience that were perhaps more amenable to intervention. Thus, by drawing attention to many of the avoidance behaviours, it was possible to think of desensitisation and exposure treatments that might help alleviate some of the distress.

However, there are important differences between child sexual abuse and a one-off civilian disaster. In the first place, the latter happens in the context of ongoing normality. The threat comes out of the blue and the event is public. Thus the therapist or researcher can quickly gain a reasonably clear picture of what each survivor must have encountered during the event and can guide the survivor in remembering what happened. By contrast, sexual abuse takes place in conditions of secrecy and shame, often with threats of violence should the child ever tell anyone else about it. Important details surrounding the violations are therefore private and not readily accessible to the investigator. Moreover, the abuse often occurs on many occasions over many years, and so it is very difficult to focus on one particular incident when investigating cause–effect relationships in research or trying to help the victim relive the experiences in therapy.

Two other sorts of chronic stressors that affect children have been discussed in recent years, and each brings yet more variables into play. Worldwide concern was focused on the psychological effects on children following the Chernobyl nuclear disaster in 1986. The World Health Organisation has coordinated a number of studies of the health effects on children in Ukraine, Byelarus and Russia, and a number of local studies have also tried to assess the effects on psychological adjustment. The problem here is that while the acute stage of the disaster can be pinpointed, there has been continuing concern about the delayed effects of radiation to the extent that, nine years later, people in the affected areas still restrict children from playing outdoors and avoid eating mushrooms and other foods that are thought to be contaminated. Thus, there is a continuing, chronic level of stress and the symptoms displayed by the population affected appear to be expressed much more somatically than is found in classic PTSD.

The other chronic stressor being investigated is that which occurs in war situations. UNICEF has been at the forefront of stimulating research into the effects of war on children, particularly the dreadful war in former Yugoslavia. Stuvland et al. (1994) used a version of the War Trauma Questionnaire and showed that children in Sarajevo had experienced very high levels of stressful events such as sniping and shooting. Over 50% of their large sample had seen dead people, and in half the cases they had actually witnessed the killings. The level of exposure to war-related stress correlated highly with symptoms of PTSD reported on the Impact of Events Scale and with levels of depression reported on the Birleson scale. But again, it is difficult to disentangle the effects of the many other things that happen during a bloody war—the ethnic cleansing, the break-up of families, the forced move from home and school, the loss of parents and so on. Children take on adult roles prematurely and then find it difficult to adjust to more normal, more age-appropriate demands when they return to school after hostilities cease.

DESNOS

The debate about the different effects of single versus repeated stressors continues and the need to agree on a classification of stressors is clearly identified. Terr (1991) argued the need to distinguish what she termed Type I and Type II stressors—with greater dissociative symptoms being associated with the Type II, repeated stressors. Others, working with adults, have argued the need to recognise a category called DESNOS—disorders of extreme stress not otherwise specified (Herman, 1992). As noted above, it is highly likely that different types of stressor will be associated with different psychological reactions, both in terms of severity and content. A better understanding of these links will lead to better assessment and intervention.

DEVELOPMENTAL ISSUES

Earlier, the different ways in which stress reactions manifest in children of different ages was briefly outlined. Here, we will examine the different ways in which traumatic events *may* have differential effects depending on the developmental level of the child at the time.

Although it was claimed in early versions of DSM that young children were at greater risk of developing PTSD following a trauma, this seems to have been based on particular theoretical models of development rather than on empirical findings. Pynoos (1994) has articulated the most detailed developmental model of potential effects of trauma on children's development.

Pynoos (1994) draws on a model by Steinberg & Ritzman (1990) to consider the complex interactions that may develop following traumatic stress and its sequelae. Indeed, this is the major point that is empasised—it is not simply that a stressor has an effect in a simple linear fashion, but rather that the stressor interacts with the child at a particular point in development and sets in train a number of complicated reactions. Elsewehere (Yule, Bolton & Udwin, 1992) we have indicated that it is important to consider both the objective nature of the stressor and the subjective way in which any threat is interpreted. In turn, that subjective threat is determined by the developmental stage the child has reached, the circumstances surrounding and following the incident, and the subsequent supports offered the child.

This model goes beyond solely considering the child's level of cognitive development, important as that is. It considers the proximal traumatic reminders and the proximal secondary stresses as well as the distal reminders and the effects on development much further down the line. Within a framework of developmental psychopathology, resilience and vulnerability are considered. Early reactions in young children may interfere with the mastery of imporant developmental goals. The child's physiological and biochemical systems may be compromised with a resulting lack of resilience and an increased tendency to break down under later stress. Pynoos's model suggests many opportunities for much better focused research studies.

To date, there are few empirical studies to test the predictions from this model. While the emerging longitudinal studies of PTSD do indeed show that many children are knocked off their normal developmental trajectory, the studies are conceived within different frameworks and so the findings are difficult to map onto Pynoos's model.

Keppel-Benson and Ollendick (1993) argued that very young children may be protected from strong emotional reactions because of their limited cognitive capacity. In particular, children's awareness of the possible serious consequences of any event will be related both to their understanding of causality and their understanding of the concept of death. Many adults for far too long took comfort in the rather crude stage theorising of Piaget, and assumed that children had no complete understanding that death was both universal and irreversible until they reached the age of 13 years or so. Now we know that children as young as 4 years of age can have partial, and sometimes complete, understanding of death and so when they are involved in fatal incidents they can become aware all too soon of their own mortality. Thus, some young children will not appreciate that their lives were under threat and so they may not develop a full blown traumatic stress reaction; other children of the same chronological age may be cognitively more mature and will appreciate that their own lives were at risk and so may develop PTSD. As always, clinicians and researchers must remember the wide individual differences there are in children's development and reactions. (See case examples below.)

As Schwarz and Perry (1994) argue, infants and very young children are more sensitive to emotional states and behaviour of parental care-givers than to assessments of danger. As such, a trauma to either the child or primary care-giver may result in global dysfunction, apathy and failure to thrive, excessive crying, eating and sleeping, psychophysiological lability, and overstimulation (Schwarz & Perry, 1994). Consistent with Schwarz and Perry's hypothesis, Green et al. (1991), in reviewing data from the Buffalo Creek Disaster, noted that the pre-school child's perception of the dangerousness of the trauma (i.e. life threat) was not correlated with PTSD symptoms, while life threat was positively associated with PTSD symptoms in school-aged children and adolescents.

Pynoos (1994) points out that while very young children may be partly protected by their lack of understanding of danger, they do respond to the reactions of their parents. This places adults in a very difficult position as they often assume that the best way to protect a child is to pretend that everything is safe and unthreatening. Thus, they may do their best to disguise their own emotional reactions. In turn, this may confuse the child who is feeling alarmed and, in the long term, it may undermine the trust the child has in that adult. As so often occurs in real life, complicated situations do not yield to nice simple solutions.

Case Examples

Mark, aged 5, was playing in the kitchen while his parents were preparing the evening meal when three masked robbers burst in on them. The robbers tried to place handcuffs on his mother as they ripped her jewellery from her hands. As his father tried to go to his wife's aid, he was felled by a blow and kicked in the face such that his nose was broken and blood poured everywhere. Mark began to cry and scream and this upset the robbers who fled when the front door bell rang.

Mark had always been a quiet boy, but at home he had been confident. Immediately afterwards, he became very scared to be out of sight of his parents. He wanted to sleep in their bed and would not go upstairs on his own. From being a child who abhorred violence, he began playing violent games of cops and robbers with his play people. This change in him upset his parents who realised that his sense of security had been compromised. His parents tried to tell him that the robbers had been caught, but a letter from the police apologising for not apprehending the gang undermined that strategy.

During a clinical interview, Mark was able to describe in detail what had happened and what he had feared. He was most worried that the robbers were going to take his parents away and he would be left without a mummy or daddy. He had not been able to share this separation anxiety with his parents even though they were both very gentle, open and supportive. He agreed to share the worries after the interview and this seemed to help him and his parents recreate a secure and protective relationship.

His parents had not been able to say that they, too, were scared to be in the large house on their own. Even his father felt uneasy going out in the garden at night. They decided to move house rather than tolerate these feelings of dread. On balance, the therapist agreed that this was appropriate and not avoiding the issues.

Mark showed a fairly typical set of reactions to the traumatic events—re-experiencing the events in thoughts and acting them out in play, albeit in uncharacteristic aggressive play. He showed separation anxiety. Being a bright 5-year-old, he understood rather more of what had happened than his parents would have hoped for and he was also responding to their helplessness when they were overpowered.

By contrast, Julie was not quite 3 years old when she was nearly electrocuted. She was climbing some stairs in their apartment house, holding on to the metal railing when she also tried to push the front door closed. The door was lined with metal and the automated entrance system had been badly wired so she received an electric shock. A neighbour spotted her standing still, realised what had happened and herself was thrown backwards as she pushed Julie off the door, breaking the circuit.

Fortunately, Julie survived without even a burn. For a long time, she showed fear when passing the door but that did not generalise to other doors. She also developed a fear of railings and bannisters and will not hold on when climbing stairs. Apart from these avoidance behaviours, she showed no other signs of PTSD when evaluated at age 5. In this instance, while her parents were all too aware of what might have happened to her, Julie remained blissfully unaware of how near to death she had been. In interview, she had very good recall of what had happened and described the "tingly" sensation on her arms. No one had explained anything about the effects of electricity to her and so she was not able to differentiate between touching wooden bannisters and touching metal ones. Such concepts are still complex for most 5-year-olds, but her parents were advised to educate her at a level that she would understand as, it was felt that, in the interests of safety, she should be helped to used bannisters when appropriate.

In this case, it seems clear that Julie's lack of understanding had protected her from the worst consequences of the trauma, but that, even so, she developed some specific avoidance behaviours along with more general distress.

ASSESSING PTSD IN CHILDREN

The clinical assessment of traumatic stress reactions in children will normally depend on good interviews with parents as well as interviews with the children. The interview with the parents should cover the family history, the child's developmental history prior to the traumatic event as well as the parents' perceptions of how the child has changed subsequently. In as far as they can give it, a detailed description of what actually happened is essential. This also needs to be checked with the child, who should be asked not only about the objective aspects of the event, but also how it impinged upon him or her—what he or she saw, heard, smelled, felt and so on. In addition, asking about the child's thoughts and feelings at various points can be very illuminating.

There has been a rush to develop semi-structured interviews to elicit and quantify PTSD in children. It is laudable that at last children are being asked to give their own accounts of internal distress direct to professionals, but a number of the attempts at developing suitable interviews are misguided as they only rephrase DSM criteria into question format. Since some of the criteria are irrelevant to children, then the exercise seems doomed. Far better to consider the suggestions of Pynoos and Eth (1986) on conducting a good clinical interview. These include asking the child to draw something, preferably connected with the incident, and then talking the therapist through it.

While childhood PTSD can be very similar to the manifestation of PTSD in adults, it differs sufficiently to warrant separate assessment tools that are more relevant to their developmental level. There are now many measures suitable for establishing post-traumatic reactions in children (Finch & Daugherty, 1993). The Children's Post-Traumatic Stress Reaction Index

(Frederick & Pynoos, 1988) has been widely used in a number of major studies (Nader et al., 1991; Pynoos et al., 1987, 1993; Pynoos & Nader, 1988) and has been shown to have good internal consistency and to relate well to clinical judgement of the severity of PTSD (Yule, Bolton & Udwin, 1992). Saigh's (1989) Children's Post-traumatic Stress Disorder Inventory also has good psychometric properties.

The Impact of Events Scale (Horowitz, Wilner & Alvarez, 1979) has been found useful with children aged 8 and over (Yule & Williams, 1990; Yule & Udwin, 1991), especially when used in conjunction with measures of anxiety and depression (Yule & Udwin, 1991; Stallard & Law, 1993). However, factor analyses of the IES indicate that some items are misunderstood by children and should be replaced (Yule, ten Bruggencatte & Joseph, 1994). A shortened version of eight items to assess intrusion and avoidance has been developed by Dyregrov and Yule (1995) and, together with additional items to assess physiological arousal, has now been used in studies of children in Bosnia and Rwanda with promising results.

It is important also to obtain estimates of the levels of children's anxiety and depression when assessing their stress reactions. The Revised Children's Manifest Anxiety Scale (Reynolds & Richmond, 1978) and the Spence Child Anxiety Scale for Children (Spence, 1997) are among the commonest anxiety scales; the Birleson Depression Scale (Birleson, 1981) and the Child Depression Inventory (Kovacs, 1983) are used to assess depression. To assess the extent of fears developed subsequent to a trauma, the Fear Survey Schedule for Children (Ollendick, 1983) has been found helpful. Work is currently underway on the value of the nine-item Grief index (Nader et al., 1993). The point being made is that it is necessary to examine a wide range of potential psychopathology following a major trauma (Yule & Udwin, 1991).

There is a dearth of standardised approaches to assess stress reactions in children under the age of 8, although at least those in the age range 3 to 8 can give adequate verbal responses. There is a need to develop additional measures for younger children, as has been started by Almqvist and Brandell-Forsberg (1997).

Assessment could also involve psychophysiological assessments of alterations to heart rate as well as biochemical assays, but these promising techniques are not yet in widespread clinical use.

TREATMENT OF PTSD

While there have been a number of single case reports of treatment of children suffering from PTSD, as yet there are no accounts of randomised controlled studies. For the most part, treatment approaches are predominantly cognitive-behavioural and appear to consist of adaptations of approaches used with adults (Yule, 1991).

Critical Incident Stress Debriefing

Techniques of this type have been adapted for use with groups of children following a variety of traumas (Dyregrov, 1991). Such a structured crisis intervention approach was used with some children following the *Jupiter* sinking, with good effects on lowering the levels of intrusion and of fears (Yule & Udwin, 1991). Stallard and Law (1993) used two debriefing sessions to reduce distress in girls who survived a school bus crash.

Currently, the role of crisis intervention with adults is being called into question with some evidence being cited to the effect that early intervention may cause more rather than less PTSD (see Canterbury, this volume). Following the arguments of Rachman (1980) and of Saigh (1986), there is a clear danger that inappropriate exposure sessions that are too short and leave the child in an aroused state may sensitise them rather than help the anxiety habituate. Moreover, the wide range of individual differences to experience have already been emphasised. Even as apparently simple an intervention as giving out a leaflet to survivors has been found to be helpful to the majority, but distressing to a significant minority (Yule, Hodgkinson, Joseph & Williams, 1990). Thus, one must entertain the notion that any crisis intervention might have untoward effects in at least some children. Thus, the onus is on therapists to monitor which children are helped and which are not by any of the crisis intervention techniques.

Group Treatments

These are obviously to be preferred as a first line of intervention when large numbers are involved. Gillis (1993) suggests that groups of six to eight are optimum, and advises that separate groups should be run for boys and for girls. However, different types of incident surely require different responses from professionals (Galante & Foa, 1986; Yule & Williams, 1990) and it is too soon to pontificate on what should be a standard approach.

As with debriefing, the aims of such therapeutic groups will be to share experiences and feelings, to boost children's sense of mastery and control, and to share ways of solving common problems. Pynoos and Nader (1993) point out that it is not sufficient for groups to provide a forum for the expression of feelings: this may only renew feelings of anxiety unless a constructive, therapeutic approach is taken.

While the group treatment approaches reported above are well described and appear promising, there are no controlled studies providing evidence for the efficacy of such groups. There is a consensus that group interventions will be effective for some, but not all, children. However, one function of therapeutic groups is to screen for high-risk children who may need individual therapy. More generally, children whose problems persist despite group help should be treated individually.

Individual Treatment

Individual treatment centres mainly on cognitive behavioural therapies that aim both to help the survivors make sense of what happened and to master their feelings of anxiety and helplessness. Drug treatments, as in the rest of child psychopathology, have little place. Asking children to draw their experiences can be useful in helping them recall both the event and the emotions associated with it (Blom, 1986; Newman, 1976; Galante & Foa; 1986; Pynoos & Eth, 1986) but merely drawing the trauma is not a sufficient therapy. A recent study from former Yugoslavia, where great emphasis was placed on getting children to express their emotions through drawing, found that six months after having had very structured sessions on drawing and other expressive techniques, there was no measurable change in children's adjustment on a whole range of self-report measures of stress reactions (Bunjevac & Kuterovac, 1994).

Saigh (1986) was one of the first to provide clinical evidence that, as Rachman (1980) had predicted, there were dangers in using standard systematic desensitisation approaches as the length of exposure sessions may be too short to permit adequate habituation of anxiety. It should also be remembered that where children are frightened by the vividness of their memories, then relaxation may only serve to intensify the vividness. The theoretical aspects of exposure therapy in treating PTSD in children are discussed elsewhere (Saigh, Yule & Inamdar, 1996) and other suggestions of techniques to promote emotional processing are described in Rachman (1980), Yule (1991), Richards and Lovell (1990) and Saigh (1992).

Given the nature of traumatic events, children are not infrequently bereaved as a consequence. Pynoos and Nader (1988) emphasise the need to help children to distinguish their trauma-related responses from those related to grief, and suggest that, where several children are bereaved, small groups can be beneficial in the initial stages. Dyregrov's (1993) account of the distinguishing features of traumatic bereavement implies that the traumatic nature of the death and post-trauma reactions need to be addressed before grieving can begin. Black (1993) uses a wide variety of techniques, including the use of drawings and play, in her work with children who have been bereaved as a consequence of one parent killing another. Importantly, she also describes how family work—including that with new carers—is necessary in cases where a child has lost a parent.

Pynoos's (1994) developmental framework for understanding trauma reactions has a number of implications for therapeutic intervention. The model suggests that the interaction over time of many critical factors (including the complexity of the traumatic experience and the interactions of traumatic reminders, secondary stress, post-traumatic distress and development) play a role in the progression from traumatic exposure to psychopathology. Each of these factors can be seen as a potential focus for intervention. Similarly, James (1989) describes the use of early intervention with subsequent "pulsed intervention" over time, using multifaceted treatment approaches.

There is considerable interest and scepticism in Eye Movement Desensitisation and Reprocessing (EMDR) treatment (Shapiro, 1991). To date there are no published accounts of controlled trials with children and adolescents, although claims for its value are being made on the conference circuit! As with all techniques that have no clear rationale, caution has to be exercised. However, if symptomatic relief can really be attained in a few brief sessions, then the approach needs to be evaluated carefully. Since there does seem to be a different quality to the memories of a trauma that appear at the same time to be locked in, vivid and unchangeable by merely talking about them, then any technique that will allow emotional processing to proceed must be examined.

Contingency Planning

When trauma affects a large number of children at once, as in an accident at school, then a public health approach to dealing with the emergency is required (Pynoos, Goenjian & Steinberg, 1995). Schools need to plan ahead not only to deal with large-scale disasters, but also to respond to the needs of children after threatening incidents that affect only a few of them. Thus, there are now a number of texts written especially for schools to help them develop contingency plans to deal with the effects of a disaster (Yule & Gold, 1993; Johnson, 1993; Klingman, 1993).

CURRENT ISSUES AND FUTURE TRENDS

With the recognition that major stressors produce stress reactions in children and adolescents that are not merely transient, the need is to understand more about the effects of single and repeated trauma on the short- and long-term adjustment of children.

The most elaborated model of a developmental approach to understanding the effects of trauma has been articulated by Pynoos and his colleagues (Pynoos, 1994; Pynoos, Steinberg & Wraith, 1995). The point is strongly argued that trauma may disrupt development and so the effects must be looked at within a developmental perspective. There may be immediate and distal effects. Pynoos pays particular attention to the potential retraumatising effects of children being repeatedly exposed to reminders of the original trauma. Such a model highlights the need for different types of study that can help improve our interventions.

The issue of vividness of memory looms large in trying to help traumatised children. There is a need to integrate the clinical interventions with work in the mainstream of experimental cognitive and developmental psychology (Siegel, 1997). Conway (1995) discusses the parameters associated with "flashbulb memories"—namely, that they tend to be associated with experiences that are both very surprising and very emotionally relevant to the individual. Van der Kolk (1994) produced evidence from SPET scanning to show that traumatic memories are indeed encoded non-verbally on the right temporal lobe; a further indication that such memories are less accessible to verbally mediated processing. As yet there are few studies of any psychophysiological, neurochemical or neurophysiological aspects of PTSD in children or adolescents, and the time is approaching when these will be done to shed light on the developmental aspects of the condition.

Experimental studies of the cognitive processing of emotions in children with PTSD, anxiety and depression using a modified Stroop paradigm and other tests of memory processing have recently been reported (Moradi, Taghavi, Doost & Yule, 1995). The preliminary results indicate that children and adolescents aged 9 to 16 respond very similarly to the Stroop as do adults (Thrasher, Dalgleish & Yule, 1994), in that they show more interference when trauma-related words, as opposed to emotionally neutral or positive words, are displayed. Having developed paradigms that appear to work with much younger subjects than have been investigated previously, a whole new line of investigations is possible.

But, above all, the time has come to institute proper treatment studies with children. The pioneering single-case studies of Saigh (1986) were vital in establishing that cognitive behavioural treatments work in individual cases. In the following decade, little progress has been made in extending this work and no randomised controlled studies have been published. There are uncontrolled studies of large-scale interventions by rapidly trained therapeutic aides in times of disaster and war, and these are certainly very promising. But we now need to develop a much more rigorous approach to evaluating alternative treatments, as well as to dissecting treatment packages to identify the necessary elements. The children are out there needing help. Ways of identifying them and assessing changes during treatment are sufficiently well developed as to be of clinical value. What is needed is the resolve to undertake proper evaluations.

REFERENCES

Almqvist, K. & Brandell-Forsberg, M. (1997). Refugee children in Sweden: Post-traumatic stress disorder in Iranian preschool children exposed to organized violence. *Child Abuse and Neglect*, **21**, 351–366.

APA (1980). *Diagnostic and Statistical Manual of Mental Disorders* (3rd Edition). Washington, DC: American Psychiatric Association.

APA (1987). *Diagnostic and Statistical Manual of Mental Disorders* (3rd Edition, Revised). Washington, DC: American Psychiatric Association.

APA (1994). Diagnostic and Statistical Manual of Mental Disorders (4th Edition). Washington, DC: American Psychiatric Association.

Birleson, P. (1981). The validity of depressive disorder in childhood and the development of a self-rating scale: A research report. *Journal of Child Psychology and Psychiatry*, **22**, 73–88.

Black, D. (1993). When father kills mother. In G. Forrest (Ed.), *ACPP Occasional Papers*, Number 8. London: ACPP.

Blom, G.E. (1986). A school disaster—intervention and research aspects. *Journal of the American Academy of child Psychiatry*, **25**, 336–345.

Boyle, S., Bolton, D., Nurrish, J., O'Ryan, D., Udwin, O. & Yule, W. (1995). The Jupiter sinking follow-up: Predicting psychopathology in adolescence following trauma. Poster presented at Eleventh Annual Meeting of the International Society for Traumatic Stress Studies, Boston, 2–6 November 1995.

Bradburn, L.S. (1991). After the earth shook: Children's stress symptoms 6–8 months after a disaster. *Advances in Behavioural Research Therapy*, **13**, 173–179.

Bunjevac, T. & Kuterovac, G. (1994). Report on the results of psychological evaluation of the art therapy program in schools in Hercegovina. Zagreb: UNICEF.

Conway, M. (1995). *Flashbulb Memories*. Hove: Lawrence Erlbaum.

Dyregrov, A. (1991). *Grief in Children: A Handbook for Adults*. London: Jessica Kingsley.

Dyregrov, A. (1993). The interplay of trauma and grief. In G. Forrest (Ed.), *ACPP Occasional Papers*, Number 8. London: ACPP.

Dyregrov, A. & Yule, W. (1995). Screening measures—the development of the UNICEF screening battery. Paper presented at Symposium on "Children and War" at Fourth European Conference on Traumatic Stress, Paris, 7–11 May 1995.

Ellis, A., Stores, G. & Mayou, R. (1998). Psychological consequences of road accidents in children. *European Child and Adolescant Psychiatry*, **7**, 61–68.

Fairbank, J.A., Schlenger, W.E., Saigh, P.A. & Davidson, J.R.T. (1995). An epidemiologic profile or post-traumatic stress disorder: Prevalence, comorbidity, and risk factors. In M.J. Friedman, D.S. Charney & A.Y. Deutch (Eds.),

Neurobiological and Clinical Consequences of Stress: From Normal Adaptation to PTSD. Philadelphia: Lippincott-Raven.

Finch, A.J. & Daugherty. T.K. (1993). Issues in the assessment of posttraumatic stress disorder in children. In C.F. Saylor (Ed.), *Children and disasters*, pp. 45–66. New York: Plenum.

Frederick, C.J. (1985). Children traumatized by catastrophic situations. In S. Eth & R. Pynoos (Eds.), *Post-Traumatic Stress Disorder in Children*, pp. 73–99. Washington: American Psychiatric Press.

Frederick, C.J. & Pynoos, R.S. (1988). *The Child Post-Traumatic Stress Disorder (PTSD) Reaction Index*. Los Angeles: University of California.

Galante, R. & Foa, D. (1986). An epidemiological study of psychic trauma and treatment effectiveness after a natural disaster. *Journal of the American Academy of Child Psychiatry*, **25**, 357–363.

Garmezy, N. & Rutter, M. (1985). Acute reactions to stress. In M. Rutter & L. Hersov (Eds.), *Child and Adolescent Psychiatry: Modern Approaches* (2nd Edition), pp. 152–176. Oxford: Blackwell.

Garrison, C.Z., Weinrich, M.W., Hardin, S.B., Weinrich, S. & Wang, L. (1993). Posttraumatic stress disorder in adolescents after a hurricane. *American Journal of Epidemiology*, **138**, 52–53.

Gibbs, M.S. (1989). Factors in the victim that mediate between disaster and psychopathology: A review. *Journal of Traumatic Stress*, **2**, 489–514.

Gillis, H.M. (1993). Individual and small-group psychotherapy for children involved in trauma and disaster. In C.F. Saylor (Ed.), *Children and Disasters*, pp. 165–186. New York: Plenum.

Green, B.L., Korol, M., Grace, M.C., Vary, M.G., Leonard, A.C., Glesser, G.C. & Smithson-Cohen, S. (1991). Children and disaster: Age, gender, and parental effects on PTSD symptoms. *Journal of the American Academy of Child and Adolescent Psychiatry*, **30**, 945–951.

Handford, H.A., Mayes, S.O., Mattison, R.E., Humphrey, F.J., Bagnato, S., Bixler, E.O. & Kales, J.D. (1986). Child and parent reaction to the TMI nuclear accident. *Journal of the American Academy of Child Psychiatry*, **25**, 346–355.

Herman, J.L. (1992). Complex PTSD: A syndrome in survivors of prolonged and repeated trauma. *Journal of Traumatic Stress*, **5**, 377–391.

Horowitz, M.J., Wilner, N. & Alvarez, W. (1979). Impact of event scale: A measure of subjective stress. *Psychosomatic Medicine*, **41**, 209–218.

James, B. (1989). *Treating Traumatized Children: New Insights and Creative Interventions*. Massachusetts: Lexington Books.

Janoff-Bulman, R. (1985). The aftermath of victimization: Rebuilding shattered assumptions. In C.R. Figley (Ed.), *Trauma and its Wake*. New York: Brunner/Mazel.

Johnson, K. (1993). *School Crisis Management: A Team Training Guide*. Alameda, CA: Hunter House.

Joseph, S.A., Brewin, C.R., Yule, W. & Williams, R. (1991). Causal attributions and psychiatric symptoms in survivors of the Herald of Free Enterprise disaster. *British Journal of Psychiatry*, **159**, 542–546.

Joseph, S., Brewin, C., Yule, W. & Williams, R. (1993). Causal attributions and psychiatric symptoms in adolescent survivors of disaster. *Journal of Child Psychology and Psychiatry*, **34**, 247–253.

Keppel-Benson, J.M. & Ollendick, T.H. (1993). Posttraumatic stress disorders in children and adolescents. In C.F. Saylor (Ed.), *Children and Disasters*, pp. 29–43. New York: Plenum.

Klingman, A. (1993). School-based intervention following a disaster. In C.F. Saylor (Ed.), *Children and Disasters*, pp 187–210. New York: Plenum.

Kovacs, M. (1983). The Children's Depression Inventory: A self-rated depression scale for school-aged youngsters. Unpublished Manuscript: University of Pittsburgh School of Medicine.

Lonigan, C.J., Shannon, M.P., Finch, A.J., Daugherty, T.K. & Saylor, C.M. (1991). Children's reactions to a natural disaster: Symptom severity and degree of exposure. *Advances in Behaviour Research and Therapy*, **13**, 135–154.

McFarlane, A.C. (1987). Family functioning and overprotection following a natural disaster: The longitudinal effects of post-traumatic morbidity. *Australia and New Zealand Journal of Psychiatry*, **21**, 210–218.

McFarlane, A.C., Policansky, S. & Irwin, C.P. (1987). A longitudinal study of the psychological morbidity in children due to a natural disaster. *Psychological Medicine*, **17**, 727–738.

Milgram, N.A., Toubiana, Y., Klingman, A., Raviv, A. & Goldstein, I. (1988). Situational exposure and personal loss in children's acute and chronic reactions to a school bus disaster. *Journal of Traumatic Stress*, **1**, 339–532.

Misch, P., Phillips, M., Evans, P. & Berelowitz, M. (1993). Trauma in pre-school children: A clinical account. In G. Forrest (Ed.), *Trauma and Crisis Management*. ACPP Occasional Paper.

Moradi, A., Taghavi, R., Doost, H.N. & Yule, W. (1995). The performance of children with PTSD on the Stroop colour interference task. Poster presented at Fourth European Conference on Traumatic Stress, Paris, May 1995.

Nader, K., Pynoos, R.S., Fairbanks, L. & Frederick, C. (1990). Childhood PTSD Reactions one year after a sniper attack. *American Journal of Psychiatry*, **147**, 1526–1530.

Nader, K.O., Pynoos, R.S., Fairbanks, L.A., Al-Ajeel, M. & Al-Asfour, A. (1993). A preliminary study of PTSD and grief among children of Kuwait following the Gulf war. *British Journal of Clinical Psychology*, **32**, 407–416.

Newman, C.J. (1976). Children of disaster: Clinical observation at Buffalo Creek. *American Journal of Psychiatry*, **133**, 306–312.

Ollendick, T.H. (1983). Reliability and validity of the Revised Fear Survey Schedule for Children (FSSC-R). *Behavior Therapy*, **21**, 685–692.

Parry Jones, W. (1992). Children of Lockerbie. Paper presented at Guys Hospital meeting.

Perrin, S., Smith, P. & Yule, W. (1996). Post traumatic stress in children as a function of sibling and parental exposure to the trauma. Paper presented at the 12th Annual Convention of the International Society for Traumatic Stress Studies (November), San Francisco, CA.

Pynoos, R.S. (1994). Traumatic stress and developmental psychopathology in children and adolescents. In R.S. Pynoos (Ed.), *Posttraumatic Stress Disorder: A Clinical Review*. Lutherville, MD: Sidran Press.

Pynoos, R.S. & Eth, S. (1986). Witness to violence: The child interview. *Journal of the American Academy of Child Psychiatry*, **25**, 306–319.

Pynoos, R.S., Frederick, C., Nader, K., Arroyo, W., Steinberg, A., Eth, S., Nunez, F. & Fairbanks, L. (1987). Life threat and posttraumatic stress in school-age children. *Archives of General Psychiatry*, **44**, 1057–1063.

Pynoos, R.S., Goenjian, A., Karakashian, M., Tashjian, M., Manjikian, R., Manoukian, G., Steinberg, A.M. & Fairbanks, L.A. (1993). Posttraumatic stress reactions in children after the 1988 Armenian earthquake. *British Journal of Psychiatry*, **163**, 239–247.

Pynoos, R.S., Goenjian, A. & Steinberg, A.M. (1995). Strategies of disaster interventions for children and adolesacents. In S.E. Hobfoll & M. de Vries (Eds.), *Extreme Stress and Communities: Impact and Intervention*. Dordrecht, Netherlands: Kluwer.

Pynoos, R.S. & Nader, K. (1988). Psychological first aid and treatment approach for children exposed to community violence: Research implications. *Journal of Traumatic Stress*, **1**, 243–267.

Pynoos, R.S. & Nader, K. (1993). Issues in the treatment of posttraumatic stress in children and adolescents. In J. Wilson & B. Raphael (Eds.), *International Handbook of Traumatic Stress Syndromes*. New York: Plenum Press.

Pynoos, R.S., Steinberg, A.M. & Wraith, R. (1995). A developmental model of childhood traumatic stress. In D. Cicchetti & D. Cohen (Eds.), *Manual of Developmental Psychopathology*. New York: Wiley.

Rachman, S. (1980). Emotional processing. *Behaviour Research and Therapy*, **18**, 51–60.

Reynolds, C.R. & Richmond, B.O. (1978). What I think and feel: A revised measure of children's manifest anxiety. *Journal of Abnormal Child Psychology*, **6**, 271–280.

Richards, D. & Lovell, K. (1990). Imaginal and in-vivo exposure in the treatment of PTSD. Paper read at Second European Conference on Traumatic Stress, Netherlands, September 1990.

Saigh, P.A. (1986). In vitro flooding in the treatment of a 6-year-old boy's posttraumatic stress disorder. *Behaviour Research and Therapy*, **24**, 685–688.

Saigh, P.A. (1989). The development and validation of the Children's Postraumatic Stress Disorder Inventory. *International Journal of Special Education*, **4**, 75–84.

Saigh, P.A. (1992). The behavioral treatment of child and adolescent posttraumatic stress disorder. *Advances in Behaviour Research and Therapy*, **14**, 247–275.

Saigh, P.A., Yule, W. & Inamdar, S.C. (1996). Imaginal flooding of traumatized children and adolescents. *Journal of School Psychology*, **34**, 163–183.

Scheeringa, M.S., Zeanah, C.H., Drell, M.J. & Larrieu, J.A. (1995). Two approaches to the diagnosis of posttraumatic stress disorder in infancy and early childhood. *Journal of the American Academy of Child and Adolescent Psychiatry*, **34**, 191–200.

Schwarz, E.D. & Kowalski, J.M. (1991). Posttraumatic stress disorder after a school shooting: Effects of symptom threshold selection and diagnosis by DSM-III, DSM-III-R, or proposed DSM-IV. *American Journal of Psychiatry*, **148**, 592–597.

Shannon, M.P., Lonigan, C.J., Finch, A.J., et al. (1994). Children exposed to disaster. I: Epidemiology of posttraumatic symptoms and symptom profiles. *Journal of the American Academy of Child and Adolescent Psychiatry*, **33**, 80–93.

Shapiro, F. (1991). Eye movement desensitization and reprocessing procedure: From EMD to EMD/R—a new treatment model for anxiety and related traumas. *Behavior Therapist*, **14**, 133–135.

Siegel, D.J. (1997). Memory and trauma. In D. Black, M. Newman, J. Harris-Hendricks & G. Mezey (Eds.), *Psychological Trauma: A Developmental Approach*, pp. 44–53. London: Gaskell.

Smith, P., Yule, W., Perrin, S. & Schwartz, D. (1996). Maternal reactions and child distress following the war in Bosnia. Paper presented at the 12th Annual Convention of the International Society for Traumatic Stress Studies, San Francisco, CA, November 1996.

Spence, S.H. (1997). Structure af Anxiety Symptoms among children: A confirmatory factor-analytic study. *Journal of Abnormal Psychology*, **106**, 280–297.

Steinberg, A.M. & Ritzman, R.F. (1990). A living systems approach to understanding the concept of stress. *Behavioral Science*, **35**, 138–146.

Sullivan, M.A., Saylor, C.F. & Foster, K.Y. (1991). Post-hurricane adjustment of preschoolers and their families. *Advances in Behaviour Research and Therapy*, **13**, 163–171.

Stallard, P. & Law, F. (1993). Screening and psychological debriefing of adolescent survivors of life-threatening events. *British Journal of Psychiatry*, **163**, 660–665.

Stuvland, R. et al. (1994). A UNICEF report on war trauma among children in Sarajevo. Zagreb: UNICEF.

Terr, L.C. (1979). The children of Chowchilla. *Psychoanalytic Study of the Child*, **34**, 547–623.

Terr, L.C. (1991). Childhood traumas—An outline and overview. *American Journal of Psychiatry*, **148**, 10–20.

Thrasher, S., Dalgleish, T. & Yule, W. (1994). Information processing in post-traumatic stress disorder. *Behaviour Research and Therapy*, **32**, 247–254.

Tsui, E., Dagwell, K. & Yule, W. (1993). Effect of a disaster on children's academic attainment. Unpublished paper, Institute of Psychiatry.

van der Kolk, B. (1994). Plenary presentation at Trauma, Memory and Dissociation. 10th Annual Meeting of the International Society for Traumatic Stress Studies, Chicago, 5–9 November 1994.

Wolfe, V., Gentile, C. & Wolfe, D.A. (1989). The impact of sexual abuse on children: A PTSD formulation. *Behavior Therapy*, **20**, 215–228.

World Health Organisation (1987/1988/1991). *International Classification of Diseases—10th Edition* (ICD-10). WHO: Geneva.

Yule, W. (1991). Work with children following disasters. In M. Herbert (Ed.), *Clinical Child Psychology: Social Learning, Development and Behaviour*, pp. 349–363. Chichester: Wiley.

Yule, W. (1992a). Post traumatic stress disorder in child survivors of shipping disasters: The sinking of the "Jupiter". *Psychotherapy and Psychosomatics*, **57**, 200–205.

Yule, W. (1992b). Resilience and vulnerability in child survivors of disasters. In B. Tizard & V. Varma (Eds.), *Vulnerability and Resilience: A Festschrift for Ann and Alan Clarke*, pp. 82–98. London: Jessica Kingsley.

Yule, W., Bolton, D. & Udwin, O. (1992). Objective and subjective predictors of PTSD in adolescents. Paper presented at World Conference of International Society for Traumatic Stress Studies, "Trauma and Tragedy", Amsterdam, 21–26 June 1992.

Yule, W. & Gold, A. (1993). *Wise Before the Event: Coping with Crises in Schools*. London: Calouste Gulbenkian Foundation.

Yule, W., Hodgkinson, P., Joseph, S. & Williams, R. (1990). Preliminary follow-up of adult survivors of the Herald of Free Enterprise. Paper presented to Second European Conference on Traumatic Stress, Netherlands, September 1990.

Yule, W., ten Bruggencatte, S. & Joseph, S. (1994). Principal components analysis of the Impact of Events Scale in children who survived a shipping disaster. *Personailty and Individual Differences*, **16**, 685–691.

Yule, W. & Udwin, O. (1991). Screening child survivors for post-traumatic stress disorders: Experiences from the "Jupiter" sinking. *British Journal of Clinical Psychology*, **30**, 131–138.

Yule, W., Udwin, O. & Murdoch, K. (1990). The "Jupiter" sinking: Effects on children's fears, depression and anxiety. *Journal of Child Psychology and Psychiatry*, **31**, 1051–1061.

Yule, W. & Williams, R. (1990). Post traumatic stress reactions in children. *Journal of Traumatic Stress*, **3** (2), 279–295.

Chapter 3

ATTRIBUTIONAL PROCESSES, COPING AND POST-TRAUMATIC STRESS DISORDERS

*Stephen Joseph**

Several theorists have noted that the behavioural disturbances which are observed in animals subjected to uncontrollable and unpredictable aversive events resemble post-traumatic stress disorder (e.g. Kolb, 1987; van der Kolk, 1987). Drawing on this work, Foa, Zinbarg and Rothbaum (1992) have proposed that the similarity between animals' reactions to aversive stimuli and the reactions of human survivors of traumatic events may reflect a common aetiology. However, although an animal model of PTSD holds considerable theoretical intrigue, by demonstrating the role of unpredictability and uncontrollability, Foa, Zinbarg and Rothbaum (1992) highlight the importance of individual differences in cognitions regarding the traumatic event. From a cognitive perspective, current thinking on stress and coping emphasises the process of stimulus appraisal (Lazarus, 1966, 1991) and there is now considerable agreement that appraisal processes are central to understanding the aetiology of post-traumatic phenomena. For example, one person might construe an event as a lucky escape from which he or she has benefited in some way, whereas another might construe the same event as a catastrophic misfortune which has left him or her feeling that life is meaningless (Joseph, Williams & Yule, 1993). It might be expected that the emotional reactions of these two people will reflect these different appraisals. Appraisal is very much an idiosyncratic process which does not lend itself easily to empirical study. Nevertheless, much work has attempted to investigate these issues with a variety of populations, and there is a growing literature which is beginning to clarify some of the basic mechanisms of appraisal. One aspect of appraisal is

*University of Essex, Colchester

Post-Traumatic Stress Disorders: Concepts and Therapy. Edited by William Yule.
© 1999 John Wiley & Sons Ltd.

causal attribution and, in the present chapter, various theoretical perspectives on the role of causal attribution in the development and maintenance of post-traumatic reactions will be discussed.

ATTRIBUTIONAL PERSPECTIVES

The reason why the constructs of uncontrollability and unpredictability are important rests on the general theoretical viewpoint that people have a need to predict the future and control events (Harvey & Weary, 1985; Heider, 1958; Jones & Davis, 1965; Kelley, 1967; Rotter, 1966) and will operate on a day-to-day basis as if the world was predictable and controllable. The consequence of this is that people who are exposed to uncontrollable and unpredictable events are strongly motivated to understand why the event occurred (Weiner, 1985, 1986; Wong & Weiner, 1981) in an attempt to re-establish perceptions of the world as predictable and controllable (Janoff-Bulman, 1985, 1992). This has been demonstrated following physical illness (Watts, 1982), cancer (Taylor, 1983) and accidents (Dollinger, 1986), and evidence shows that perceptions of being out of control are predictive of poorer adjustment (e.g. Craig, Hancock & Dickson, 1994).

As well as the need for perceived predictability and controllability, people also have a need for self-esteem (Steele, 1988; Tesser & Campbell, 1980) and will attempt to enhance and maintain their self-esteem through their understanding of why events in their lives have occurred (Brewin, 1988; Steele, 1988). Self-esteem, like perceptions of predictability and controllability, is thought to serve a stress-buffering function (Greenberg, Pyszczynski, Solomon, Pinel, Simon & Jordan, 1993; Greenberg et al., 1992). Causal attribution is the central cognitive mechanism involved in the attempt to establish and maintain self-esteem as well as perceptions of the world as predictable and controllable.

Hopelessness Theory

Various theoretical perspectives exist which can help us to understand the role of causal attribution. The perspective which has attracted most interest, however, is the reformulated theory of learned helplessness (Abramson, Seligman & Teasdale, 1978), which has been revised by Abramson and her colleagues as the hopelessness theory (Abramson, Alloy & Metalsky, 1988; Abramson, Metalsky & Alloy, 1989; Alloy, Abramson, Metalsky & Hartledge, 1988; Alloy, Kelly, Mineka & Clements

1990). The essence of this theory is that stable (the perception of the cause of the event as something which is long lasting) and global (the perception of the cause of the event as something which affects a wide range of life domains) causal attributions for a negative event are likely to lead to an expectation of hopelessness (i.e. that the highly aversive situation is likely to reccur and the belief that no response can change the likelihood of this outcome). The expectation of hopelessness is hypothesised to be the proximal sufficient cause of hopelessness depression, a state of negative affect which is not thought to be isomorphic with any current categories of depression and includes a mixture of anxious and depressive phenomena (Alloy et al., 1990).

Hopelessness and PTSD

Although feelings of hopelessness have been observed to underlie a variety of mental health disorders (MacLeod & Tarbuck, 1994; Stotland, 1969) and the hopelessness theory has been applied to a wide variety of illnesses and injuries (e.g. DeVellis & Blalock, 1992), the hopelessness theory does not make explicit predictions regarding PTSD. However, hopelessness, along with perceptions of helplessness and powerlessness, are common themes expressed by survivors of traumatic events (Harvey, Stein, Olsen, Roberts, Lutgendorf & Ho, 1995; Joseph, Williams & Yule, 1993) and the expectation of hopelessness is a theme echoed throughout Janoff-Bulman's (1985, 1992) theory of shattered assumptions. Many of the new beliefs about the world that survivors develop can be considered under the conceptual umbrella of hopelessness expectation. For example, Janoff-Bulman (1979) suggests that the cognitive schemata of traumatised populations emphasises the randomness and malevolence of the world (beliefs that reflect stable and global perceptions that bad things will continue to happen).

Furthermore, much of the symptomatology for which the hopelessness theory was developed to account for are also common to survivors of traumatic events (Brewin, Joseph & Kuyken, 1993; Farmer, Tranah, O'Donnell & Catalan, 1992; McFarlane & Papay, 1992) and are included within sections C and D of the DSM-IV (APA, 1994) criteria for PTSD: C4, markedly diminished interest or participation in significant activities; C5, feelings of detachment or estrangement from others; C6, restricted affect; C7, sense of foreshortened future; D1, difficulty in falling or staying asleep; D2, irritability or outbursts of anger; D3, difficulty in concentrating. Thus, there is a clear symptom overlap between hopelessness depression and the diagnostic category of PTSD. Hopelessness theory would therefore be able to account for at least some aspects of PTSD. However, survivors also experience a wide range of other emotional and behavioural reactions which lie outside the spotlight of hopelessness theory but which may be accounted for by other attributional processes. The role of blame has received particular attention.

Blame

According to the hopelessness theory, another determinant of reactions to events is the person's understanding of the locus of causality. Locus attributions are thought to play an important role in psychosocial functioning following victimization, and their role has probably been most extensively discussed by Janoff-Bulman (1992). Janoff-Bulman's typology of blame will be reviewed in the following section, followed by a discussion of how locus attributions can lead to specific emotional states which, in turn, may lead to particular coping activities.

Self-blame

It has been suggested that there are two types of self-blame that need to be considered: behavioural self-blame and characterological self-blame (Janoff-Bulman, 1979). The term "behavioural self-blame" has largely been used to refer to internal, unstable and specific causal attributions whereas the term "characterological self-blame" has largely been used to correspond to internal, stable and global causal attributions. Characterological self-blame, consistent with the predictions of the hopelessness theory, is predicted to lead to poorer psychological outcome and reduced self-esteem (Janoff-Bulman, 1992). Behavioural self-blame, in contrast to characterological self-blame, has been hypothesised to be adaptive as it allows the person to develop a sense of control; the belief that there is a response that can influence the avoidability of the event in the future.

Although some evidence has been found to support the association between behavioural self-blame and positive outcome among accident victims (Brewin, 1984; Bulman & Wortman, 1977), rape victims (Janoff-Bulman, 1979), cancer patients (Timko & Janoff-Bulman, 1985), mothers of acutely ill infants (Affleck, McGrade, Allen & McQueeney, 1985) and children with diabetes (Tennen, Affleck, Allen, McGrade & Ratzen, 1984), the evidence is inconsistent (see Downey, Silver & Wortman, 1990) with some studies finding an association between greater behavioural self-blame and poorer adjustment following rape (Frazier, 1990; Frazier & Schauben, 1994; Hill & Zautra, 1989; Meyer & Taylor, 1986), accidents (Frey, Rogner, Schuler & Korte, 1985; Nielson & MacDonald, 1988) and bereavement (Frazier & Schauben, 1994). Although the distinction between characterological self-blame and behavioural self-blame is an intriguing one, Frazier and Schauben (1994) suggest that survivors do not seem to make the distinction between these two types of self-blame and that it is difficult to blame one's behaviour without also blaming one's character. Although there are situations in which a person might feel that he or she is to blame it is generally the case that the objective cause for the occurrence of a traumatic event is external to the person (see March, 1993) and often attributable to human agency.

Other-blame

Although the relationship between mental health and other-blame has not been addressed in as much detail as that for self-blame, there is evidence from a variety of studies that other-blame is associated with impaired emotional well-being (see Tennen & Affleck, 1990). Tennen and Affleck (1990) argue that this finding is inconsistent with the revised helplessness and hopelessness theories in which it is predicted that external attributions should buffer the effect on self-esteem of a negative event. However, it might instead be predicted that external attributions contribute to an expectation of hopelessness. Tennen and Affleck (1990) suggest, on the basis of excuse theory (see Higgins & Snyder, 1990), that when someone else is blamed for a threatening event, the victim "unlinks" from the outcome and thus does not believe that he or she can control its sequelae. The role of other-blame deserves greater attention and, following Janoff-Bulman's (1979) distinction between behavioural and characterological self-blame, it might be suggested that the stability and globality of the cause is also central to determining the outcome of other-blame and that it should be possible to distinguish between behavioural other-blame and characterological other-blame—for example, the distinction between perceiving an event as arising from carelessness on the part of someone else as opposed to their malevolence.

Survivors of rape have been found to be particularly prone to the development of post-traumatic reactions (e.g. Rothbaum, Foa, Riggs, Murdock & Walsh, 1992), supporting the prediction that attributions of malevolence lead to higher levels of distress than do attributions of carelessness which, in contrast, might be adaptive in some circumstances. For example, Mikulincer, Solomon and Benbenishty (1988) investigated how battle events contribute to the formation of PTSD. It was shown that the experience of particular battle events, notably officers' errors during battle, and problems in unit functioning were associated with fewer long-term disturbances. One possible explanation for this, they suggested, was that soldiers who experience such events can attribute their Combat Stress Reaction (CSR) to external factors beyond their control. In contrast, those who did not experience such events were less able to fall back on situational attributions and therefore tended to attribute their CSR to personal weakness. Mikulincer, Solomon and Benbenishty (1988) argue that the attribution of CSR to personal weakness would have negative consequences for self-image and long-term mental health. A similar explanation was offered by Solomon, Benbenishty and Mikulincer (1988) for their finding that soldiers who experienced physical deprivations such as hunger, or who suffered the consequences of error such as coming under fire by their own forces, exhibited less severe psychological symptoms than those who did not have such experiences.

Costs and Benefits of Blame

These studies highlight the complex role of attributional processes. It has been suggested that other-blame is driven by the need to maintain self-esteem and that self-blame is driven by the need to maintain controllability. The cost of other-blame might be in fostering a sense of the world as uncontrollable, whereas the cost of self-blame might be in reducing self-esteem. Clearly, the survivor, in attempting to explain events in a way that both serves to maintain self-esteem and perceptions of controllability, is faced with a formidable cognitive task. The processes involved in resolving this conflict of needs has received scant attention. However, there is evidence that people will often attribute causes to several sources simultaneously (Fletcher, Danilovics, Fernandez, Peterson & Reeder, 1986; Flett, Blankstein & Holloway, 1990; Weinberg, 1994), suggesting that those survivors who adapt best are able to understand the cause of an event in a way which meets both the needs for self-esteem and control. There is a need for research into attributional complexity.

Temporal Context

Horowitz (1976, 1980, 1982) has proposed that, following the experience of a traumatic event, there is an initial crying out or stunned reaction followed by a period of information overload in which the thoughts, memories and images of the event cannot be reconciled with current schemata. A variety of psychological defence mechanisms are employed to keep the traumatic information unconscious and the person experiences a period of numbing and denial. However, there is a need for the new information to be integrated with existing cognitive schemata. This completion tendency helps to maintain the trauma-related information in active memory, causing it to break through and intrude into consciousness. Thus, there are alternating phases of intrusive and avoidant phenomena as the person gradually assimilates the new information and struggles to make sense of the experience and to find a sense of meaning.

As de Silva and Marks (see Chapter 8 in this volume) note, intrusive activity can be concerned with thoughts about the meaning of the trauma, e.g. "Why did it happen?". Although such cognitive activity in the initial days, weeks and months following an event might be expected to be part of a normal adaptation process (such as that described by Horowitz), it is likely that the presence of such intrusive activity becomes, over time, increasingly pathological and indicative of a failure to work through the experience and find a sense of meaning. Furthermore, although such attributional processes can be conceptualised as a form of intrusive activity within Horowitz's framework, such activity might also serve avoidant functions; for example, other-blame might be used to avoid taking responsibility for one's own actions or self-blame might be used to protect and shield others from responsibility.

Thus, consistent with Horowitz, who views the phenomenology of post-traumatic reactions within a temporal framework, as well as current perspectives on coping as a dynamic and unfolding process (Folkman & Lazarus, 1980, 1985, 1988), causal attributions must be viewed within their temporal context (e.g. Hanson, Buckelew, Hewitt & O'Neal, 1993). For example, attributions to the self may be harmful early on when needs for self-esteem are greatest; but later, when the person is trying to rebuild his or her life, self-blame may foster the necessary sense of control. However, the temporal aspects of causal attribution remain relatively unexplored and a focus for future investigation.

Emotional Consequences

Although the literature on blame helps to clarify some of the possible attributional processes that are driven by the need to maintain feelings of self-worth and perceptions of personal control which are thought to promote emotional processing, there are also specific emotional consequences of these attributions. Weiner (1986) suggests that there are links between causal attributions and specific emotional states. For example, feelings of anger and guilt are generally experienced in the context of a cause perceived as internal to the target of emotion. The emotional target given anger is another person, while the target given guilt is the self. Weiner's (1986) theory helps to extend the work on blame to account for specific emotional states such as anger and guilt, which are commonly reported in survivors of traumatic events and which may be involved in the development and maintenance of PTSD phenomena (e.g. Joseph, Hodgkinson Yule & Williams, 1993; Riggs, Dancu, Gershuny, Greenberg & Foa, 1992). It has been suggested that specific emotional states such as anger and guilt mediate between causal attributions and post-traumatic phenomena. Whereas the hopelessness theory might provide an appropriate model for conceptualising the consequences of causal attributions for the occurrence of an event, Weiner's (1986) theory provides a useful framework for understanding the role of the causal attributions that are made for what takes place during the event. Two studies, based on Weiner's (1986) work, have investigated the causal attributions made by survivors about the events that took place during disaster and their relationship to subsequent post-traumatic reactions.

In the first, Joseph, Brewin, Yule and Williams (1991) investigated the relationship between causal attributions and psychiatric symptoms in civilian survivors of a shipping disaster in which 193 people died: the *Herald of Free Enterprise* disater. For purposes of legal assessment, 20 survivors provided a detailed account of their experiences during the disaster. From these, causal attributions were extracted and rated along external—internal and uncontrollable—controllable dimensions using the attributional coding system developed by Stratton and his colleagues (Stratton, Heard, Hanks, Munton, Brewin & Davidson, 1986). For example, some of the survivors provided accounts of their attempts to climb up a rope to safety: "I had several attempts to climb the rope but was unable to do so. There were no knots in it and it was very slippy." This was rated as external and uncontrollable, whereas the statement "I was unable to climb the rope because my legs had gone numb" was rated as internal and uncontrollable. It was found that the more internal and controllable the causal attributions, the higher the subsequent levels of depression, anxiety and intrusive thinking.

A second study by Joseph, Brewin, Yule and Williams (1993) replicated the above study with 16 adolescents who survived the *Jupiter* cruise ship disaster. In this study, however, causal attributions were overwhelmingly uncontrollable and so only the externality—internality dimension was rated. For example, the statement "It was not easy swimming because I had my jeans and sweater on" was rated as external, whereas the statement "I found it very hard to swim out of the suction as I am not a strong swimmer" was rated as internal. The results confirmed that, for adolescents, the more attributions were made to internal causes, the higher the subsequent level of intrusive thinking and depressive symptomatology. However, whereas it was hypothesised that the results with the *Herald* survivors reflected the operation of guilt, the virtually complete absence of personally controllable attributions in the *Jupiter* adolescents suggested that it might be shame that provides the link with symptomatology. Although both of these studies have emphasised the possible maladaptive role of self-attributions, it is not known to what extent the results might extend to other situations.

Coping

Work on the role of guilt and shame in psychopathology suggests that these specific emotional states may have a differential relationship to coping which, in turn, might influence the course of post-traumatic reactions. Tangney, Wagner & Gramzow (1992) note that although both shame and guilt involve negative affect, each has a distinct focus (similar to the distinction between behavioral and characterological self-blame made by Janoff-Bulman, 1979) which is related to unique symptom clusters.:

> In guilt, the object of concern is some specific action (or failure to act). There is remorse or regret over the "bad thing that was done" and a sense of tension that often serves as a motivation for reparative action. The tension, remorse, and regret engendered by guilt can be quite uncomfortable, particularly when reparation is blocked for one reason or another . . . In shame, the object of concern is the entire self. The "bad thing" is experienced as a reflection of a "bad self", and the entire self is painfully scrutinized and negatively evaluated. With this painful scrutiny of the self is a corresponding sense of shrinking, of being small, and of being worthless and powerless. (Tangney, Wagner & Gramzow, 1992, p. 469)

One important phenomenological difference between guilt and shame is that shame motivates us to hide, whereas guilt motivates us to take reparative action (Tangney, Wagner & Gramzow, 1992). Thus, it might be expected that shame leads to avoidant or emotion-focused coping (denial, distancing, etc.) whereas guilt leads to approach or problem-focused coping (planning, seeking support, etc.) (see Folkman & Lazarus, 1980, 1985, 1988, for a discussion on coping typology) in order to take reparative action. However, where reparative action cannot be taken, the person will be obliged to relive the events in his or her mind. This might also be true for anger when there is no appropriate outlet. It is suggested, therefore, that these specific emotional states of shame and guilt can lead to the use of coping strategies that resemble aspects of the intrusive and avoidant phenomena characteristic of PTSD, respectively. Furthermore, both shame and guilt involve counterfactual thinking in which cognitions about shame situations involve trying to alter qualities of the self, whereas cognitions about guilt situations involve trying to alter actions. The use of these cognitive coping strategies might serve to amplify feelings of shame and guilt respectively (Niedenthal, Tangney & Gavanski, 1994).

PERSONALITY

Attributional Style

Although the nature of traumatic events is such that the most powerful determinant of causal attribution is likely to be the nature of the event itself, there is evidence that people have relatively stable ways of explaining events (Burns & Seligman, 1989) which, according to the hopelessness theory (Abramson, Alloy & Metalsky, 1988; Abramson, Metalsky & Alloy, 1989; Alloy et al., 1988), help to determine the type of causal attributions that are actually made following negative events and constitute a vulnerability factor for the development of disorder. Evidence, supporting the attributional vulnerability hypothesis of the hopelessness theory using a retrospective behavioural high-risk paradigm has been provided by Alloy, Lipman and Abramson (1992). However, most of the evidence for the relationship between attributional style and depressive symptoms is correlational (Sweeney, Anderson & Bailey, 1986) and alternative relationships between attributional style and outcome remain feasible (Brewin, 1988). Nevertheless, attributional style has been hypothesised to act as a vulnerability factor for the development of PTSD, although the evidence for this also remains correlational in nature (McCormick, Taber & Kruedelbach, 1989; Mikulincer & Solomon, 1988). However, the use of attributional rating techniques which can be used with written or spoken material (e.g. Stratton et al., 1986) promise to provide a useful methodology for the assessment of pre-existing personality in future studies.

But, as already mentioned, the causal relationship between attributional style and disorder remains unclear and it is likely that disorder may also influence attributional style. Indeed, consistent with Janoff-Bulman's (1985, 1992) predictions it might be hypothesised that the experience of trauma has a shattering effect on attributional style (conceptualised as underlying cognitive schemata). However, even if post-trauma attributional style is a function of the event, its role in predicting future psychological adjustment remains of much interest. Attributional style is concerned with subjective perceptions of hypothetical future events. Frazier and Schauben (1994) make the distinction between control over the past (corresponding to causal attribution) and control over the future (corresponding to attributional style) and suggest that it may be more useful to help survivors gain control over future events rather than focus on the adaptiveness of various attributions about why the event occurred. In addition, it may be useful for researchers to investigate sphere-specific beliefs about control in relation to types of stressors. For example, the distinctions between personal, interpersonal and sociopolitical control drawn by Paulhus (1983) provide a useful typology for guiding research into stressor-specific vulnerability. The perception of control over future events might be hypothesised to be one important determinant of adaptive coping activity.

However, in conceptualising the role of subjective perceptions of hypothetical future events it is further necessary to distinguish between positive and negative outcomes. Attributional style has been conceptualised as being either pessimistic (internal, stable, global for negative events and external, unstable and specific for positive events) or optimistic (internal, stable and global for positive events and external, unstable and specific for negative events). Although most theorists have emphasised the role of pessimistic attributional style for negative events as a possible vulnerability factor in relation to actual negative events, it has also been suggested that an optimistic attributional style for positive events might be important in determining how people respond to stress (Craig & Curryhead, 1990; Needles & Abramson, 1990) possibly because of its influence on coping behaviour (Anderson, 1977; Solomon, Mikulincer & Avitzur, 1988) and the seeking of social support (Joseph, Williams & Yule, 1992).

Locus of Control

Evidence suggests that attributional style for positive events corresponds closely to the locus of control concept developed by Rotter (1966) (Brewin & Shapiro, 1984) and other research has utilised this construct in investigating the cognitive determinants of PTSD. Evidence from this tradition of research shows that a more external locus of control is associated with poorer adjustment in combat veterans (Frye & Stockton, 1982; Orr, Claiborn, Altman, Forgue, de Jong & Pitman, 1990; Solomon, Mikulincer & Benbenishty, 1989) which suggests that an optimistic attributional style for positive outcomes is associated with better psychological adjustment. However, these correlational data do not provide evidence in support of a vulnerability model and it is possible that a more external locus of control is simply symptomatic of disorder. One longitudinal study by Solomon, Mikulincer and Avitzur (1988) investigated the relationship between locus of control, coping, social support and PTSD in Israeli veterans at two and three years following combat, finding that, as the intensity of PTSD declined, locus of control became more internal, there was less use of emotion-focused coping and greater social support which might suggest this to be the case.

However, if locus of control is a determinant of post-traumatic stress reactions, the strength of the association would seem to be moderated by the intensity of exposure. Although Solomon, Mikulincer and Benbenishty (1989) found an association between locus of control and trauma-related distress with soldiers who had experienced low battle intensity, no association was found for those soldiers who had experienced high battle intensity. They suggest that the moderating effect of battle intensity was due to its informational value in helping the soldier explain his behaviour to himself. High-intensity battle, they argue, leads the soldier to explain his combat stress reaction entirely by the stressful events, whereas low-intensity battle leads to explanations affected by locus of control.

Self-efficacy

Whereas locus of control is concerned with perceptions of control over an outcome, this must be distinguished from the person's conviction of whether or not he or she is able to exercise that control (see Litt, 1988). This general conviction was defined by Bandura (1977, 1986) as self-efficacy and it has been suggested that self-efficacy mediates between causal attributions and coping behaviour (e.g. Chwalisz, Altmaier & Russell, 1992). Although this remains to be investigated with survivors of trauma, it would help to explain some of the conflicting findings mentioned earlier regarding the role of behavioural self-blame.

SOME IMPLICATIONS AND DIRECTIONS

Methodological Considerations

Attention has been drawn to the need to study attributional complexity in survivors. However, existing methodologies which ask respondents to rate statistically bipolar dimensions (e.g. internality–externality) can miss the richness of people's spontaneous causal attributions by their imposition of logical rigidity. Although people can think about causes in dimensional terms when presented with them, there is evidence that standard attributional dimensions are not represented in people's typical thoughts about causes (Anderson, 1991). Methodologies that are able to recognise attributional complexity are called for.

Also, it is suggested that it is useful to differentiate between causal attributions for: (1) the occurrence of an event; (2) what happens during the event; (3) subsequent emotional reactions; and (4) the recovery process. A particular type of attribution might be helpful when considered in one context but harmful in another. For example, whereas self-blame might be harmful in the context of the occurence of the event, it might be helpful in the context of the recovery process. However, these suggestions remain a focus for research.

Furthermore, blame has been operationally defined in a variety of ways in the literature, and future research should clarify this construct to facilitate greater integration of research findings. It has been suggested that blame must be distinguished from judgements of responsibility and causality (Shaver & Drown, 1986). Shaver and Drown suggest that when causal attributions for an event are made to another person, there may also be an attribution of responsibility if the person is perceived as: (1) having been able to foresee the outcome; (2) having engaged in actions which were not justifiable by the situation; and (3) having acted under free choice. Furthermore, if the person is seen as both causal and responsible, an attribution of blame may be made if that person is also thought to have intended to produce the outcome. However, the role of these other dimensions has received scant attention.

Intervention

Milgram (1986) has noted that the framework within which helping takes place is itself important and has suggested that efficacious treatment of PTSD requires the patient to take responsibility for the progress of his or her own therapy. This would involve fostering perceptions of control as well as self-efficacy. The role of self-efficacy as a mediator of causal attributions has received little attention. However, it has been suggested that the inclusion of self-efficacy in attributional models might help to clarify some of the inconsistent findings. This might be most evident in relation to the work on behavioural self-blame. Janoff-Bulman (1992) has advocated behavioural self-blame as a way of fostering the perception of control. However, the evidence for the role of behavioural self-blame is inconsistent and it would seem that behavioural self-blame is difficult to untangle from characterological self-blame, which the evidence more consistently shows to lead to poorer outcome. But even if victims are able, with the help of a therapist, to make the distinction between behavioural self-blame and characterological self-blame, other people in the person's social network might not be able to make this distinction as easily, and evidence suggests that victims who blame themselves are perceived by others as less adjusted and as more responsible for the attack (Thornton, Ryckman, Kirchner, Jacobs, Kaczor & Kuehnel, 1988) and, consequently, will be seen as less deserving of social support.

Nevertheless, attributional variables, however defined, have proved to be a rich source of ideas and there is growing evidence that attributional processes are involved in the development and maintenance of post-traumatic stress disorders. Consequently, attributional therapy promises to be useful in the treatment of post-traumatic reactions and there may be considerable scope for alleviating distress following exposure to traumatic events. This might be focused at changing cognitions about the cause of the event to reduce expectations of hopelessness, or by altering perceptions of what took place during the event to reduce feelings of guilt or shame. Causal attributions do not necessarily reflect realistic perceptions of events, and the role of therapy, it has been argued, should aim to encourage realistic attributions in the patient (Försterling, 1988). However, it has also been noted that maintaining an illusion which satisfies the need for meaning may be more adaptive than a reality-based explanation (Lyons, 1991; Taylor & Brown, 1988). For example, much of the literature that this review has drawn upon has concerned single events which are unlikely to reccur, as opposed to multiple recurring events, such as political conflict, which may be ongoing in the person's life. In such circumstances, realistic causal attributions may necessarily reflect the stable and global characteristics of the situation rather than an underlying and modifiable belief system. It is ethically dubious for the therapist to encourage non-realistic attributions, and it might even be argued that the therapist has a responsibility to the patient to encourage realistic perceptions even if they are not as seemingly comforting as non-realistic perceptions.

Other forms of intervention are also likely to affect the person's attributions, and it has been suggested that exposure therapy provides the patient with information which allows him or her to reappraise the experience and adopt more adaptive causal attributions. However, there remains a need for systematic investigation into cognitive changes during the course of exposure therapy to assess whether this is the case.

In conclusion, the research does suggest that attributional processes are central to understanding how survivors react to extreme events. There may be conflicting tension between the need to maintain self-esteem and the need to perceive the world as controllable. It is suggested that these needs drive attributional processes. Much research has demonstrated the negative consequences of self-blame and, as a result, it has often been assumed that other-blame will have positive consequences. However, other-blame would also appear to be associated with negative psychological adjustment. An explanation for this is that both types of blame may lead to specific emotional states such as guilt and anger which, in turn, are associated with coping strategies which impede emotional processing. The theoretical spotlight cast by the hopelessness theory is able to encompass a range of psychological reactions commonly observed in survivors, and perceptions of stability and globality are important attributional dimensions which predict the development of an expectation of hopelessness which, it was suggested, may lead to an identifiable syndrome of post-traumatic hopelessness. However, these ideas remain to be tested.

Further research along the lines discussed here will likely be most fruitful in providing insight into the nature of the cognitive struggle survivors are engaged in as they attempt to come to terms with their experiences.

Acknowledgements

The author expresses his grateful thanks to David Richards for helpful comments on an earlier version of this chapter.

REFERENCES

APA (1994). *Diagnostic and Statistical Manual of Mental Disorders* (4th Edition). Washington, DC: American Psychiatric Association.

Abramson, L.Y., Alloy, L.B. & Metalsky, G.I. (1988). The cognitive diathesis-stress theories of depression: Toward an adequate evaluation of the theories' validities. In L.B. Alloy (Ed.), *Cognitive Processes in Depression*, pp. 3–30. New York: Guilford Press.

Abramson, L.Y., Metalsky, G.I. & Alloy, L.B. (1989). Hopelessness depression: A theory based subtype of depression. *Psychological Review*, **96**, 358–372.

Abramson, L.Y., Seligman, M.E. & Teasdale, J.D. (1978). Learned helplessness in humans; critique and reformulation. *Journal of Abnormal Psychology*, **87**, 49–74.

Affleck, G., McGrade, B.J., Allen, D.A. & McQueeney, M. (1985). Mothers' beliefs about behavioural causes for their developmentally disturbed infants' condition: What do they really signify? *Journal of Paediatric Psychology*, **10**, 293–303.

Alloy, L.B., Abramson, L.Y., Metalsky, G.I. & Hartledge, S. (1988). The hopelessness theory of depression: Attributional aspects. *British Journal of Clinical Psychology*, **27**, 5–21.

Alloy, L.B., Lipman, A.J. & Abramson, L.Y. (1992). Attributional style as a vulnerability factor for depression: Validation by past history of mood disorders. *Cognitive Therapy and Research*, **16**, 391–407.

Alloy, L.B., Kelly, K.A., Mineka, S. & Clements, C.M. (1990). Comorbidity in anxiety and depressive disorders: A helplessness–hopelessness perspective. In

J.D. Maser & C.R. Cloninger (Eds.), *Comorbidity in Anxiety and Mood Disorders*, pp. 499–543. Washington, DC: American Psychiatric Press.

Anderson, C. (1977). Locus of control, coping behaviours, and performance in a stress setting: A longitudinal study. *Journal of Applied Psychology*, **62**, 446–451.

Anderson, C.A. (1991). How people think about causes: Examination of the typical phenomenal organization of attributions for success and failure. *Social Cognition*, **9**, 295–329.

Bandura, A. (1977). Self-efficacy: Toward a unifying theory of behaviour change. *Psychological Review*, **84**, 191–215.

Bandura, A. (1986). *Social Foundations of Thought and Action: A Social Cognitive Theory*. Englewood Cliffs, NJ: Prentice Hall.

Brewin, C.R. (1984). Attributions for industrial accidents: Their relationship to rehabilitation outcome. *Journal of Social and Clinical Psychology*, **2**, 156–164.

Brewin, C.R. (1988). *Cognitive Foundations of Clinical Psychology*. Hove and London: Lawrence Erlbaum.

Brewin, C.R., Joseph, S. & Kuyken, W. (1993). PTSD and depression: What is their relationship? Paper presented at a meeting on traumatic stress organised by the Northern Ireland Branch of the British Psychological Society, Belfast, 15 April 1993.

Brewin, C.R. & Shapiro, D.A. (1984). Beyond locus of control: Attributions of responsibility for positive and negative outcomes. *British Journal of Psychology*, **75**, 43–49.

Bulman, R. & Wortman, C.B. (1977). Attributions of blame and coping in the "real world": Severe accident victims react to their lot. *Journal of Personality and Social Psychology*, **35**, 351–363.

Burns, M.O. & Seligman, M.E.P. (1989). Explanatory style across the lifespan: Evidence for stability over 52 years. *Journal of Personality and Social Psychology*, **56**, 471–477.

Chwalisz, K., Altmaier, E.M. & Russell, D.W. (1992). Causal attributions, self-efficacy cognitions, and coping with stress. *Journal of Social and Clinical Psychology*, **11**, 377–400.

Craig, A.R., Hancock, K.M. & Dickson, H.G. (1994). Spinal cord injury: A search for determinants of depression two years after the event. *British Journal of Clinical Psychology*, **33**, 221–230.

Craig, J.F. & Curryhead, W.E. (1990). Attributional style in clinically depressed and conduct disordered adolescents. *Journal of Consulting and Clinical Psychology*, **58**, 109–115.

DeVellis, B.M. & Blalock, S.J. (1992). Illness attributions and hopelessness depression: The role of hopelessness expectancy. *Journal of Abnormal Psychology*, **101**, 257–264.

Dollinger, S.J. (1986). The need for meaning following disaster: Attributions and emotional upset. *Personality and Social Psychology Bulletin*, **12**, 300–310.

Downey, G., Silver, R.C. & Wortman, C.B. (1990). Reconsidering the attribution-adjustment relation following a major negative event: Coping with the loss of a child. *Journal of Personality and Social Psychology*, **59**, 925–940.

Farmer, R., Tranah, T., O'Donnell, I. & Catalan, J. (1992). Railway suicide: The psychological effects on drivers. *Psychological Medicine*, **22**, 407–414.

Fletcher, G.J.O., Danilovics, P., Fernandez, G., Peterson, D. & Reeder, G.D. (1986). Attributional complexity: An individual differences measure. *Journal of Personality and Social Psychology*, **51**, 875–884.

Flett, G., Blankstein, K.R. & Holloway, L.S. (1990). Depression and complex attributions of blame in self and others. *Journal of Personality and Social Behaviour*, **5**, 175–188.

Foa, E.B., Zinbarg, R. & Rothbaum, B.O. (1992). Uncontrollability and unpredictability in post-traumatic stress disorder: An animal model. *Psychological Bulletin*, **112**, 218–238.

Folkman, S. & Lazarus, R. (1980). An analysis of coping in a middle aged community sample. *Journal of Health and Social Behaviour*, **21**, 219–239.

Folkman, S. & Lazarus, R. (1985). If it changes it must be a process: A study of emotion and coping during three stages of a college examination. *Journal of Personality and Social Psychology*, **48**, 150–170.

Folkman, S. & Lazarus, R. (1988). Coping as a mediator of emotion. *Journal of Personality and Social Psychology*, **54**, 466–475.

Försterling, F. (1988). *Attribution Theory in Clinical Psychology*. Chichester: Wiley.

Frazier, P. (1990). Victim attributions and postrape trauma. *Journal of Personality and Social Psychology*, **59**, 298–304.

Frazier, P. & Schauben, L. (1994). Causal attributions and recovery from rape and other stressful life events. *Journal of Social and Clinical Psychology*, **13**, 1–14.

Frey, D., Rogner, O., Schuler, M. & Korte, C. (1985). Psychological determinants in the convalescence of accident patients. *Basic and Applied Social Psychology*, **6**, 317–328.

Frye, J. & Stockton, R.A. (1982). Discriminant analysis of posttraumatic stress disorder among a group of Vietnam veterans. *American Journal of Psychiatry*, **139**, 52–56.

Greenberg, J., Pyszczynski, T., Solomon, S., Pinel, E., Simon, L. & Jordan, K. (1993). Effects of self-esteem on vulnerability-denying defensive distortions: Further evidence of an anxiety-buffering function of self-esteem. *Journal of Experimental Social Psychology*, **29**, 229–251.

Greenberg, J., Solomon, S., Pyszczynski, T., Rosenblatt, A., Burling, J., Lyon, D., Simon, L. & Pinel, E. (1992). Why do people need self-esteem? Converging evidence that self esteem serves an anxiety-buffering function. *Journal of Personality and Social Psychology*, **63**, 913–922.

Hanson, S., Buckelew, S.P., Hewitt, J. & O'Neal, G. (1993). The relationship between coping and adjustment after spinal cord injury: A 5 year follow up study. *Rehabilitation Psychology*, **38**, 41–52.

Harvey, J.H., Stein, S.K., Olsen, N., Roberts, R.J., Lutgendorf, S.K. & Ho, J.A. (1995). Narratives of loss and recovery from a natural disaster. *Journal of Social Behaviour and Personality*, **10**, 313–330.

Harvey, J.H. & Weary, G. (1985). *Attribution: Basic Issues and Applications*. Orlando, FL: Academic Press.

Heider, F. (1958). *The Psychology of Interpersonal Relations*. New York: Wiley.

Higgins, R.L. & Snyder, C.R. (1990). Reality negotiation and excuse making: The health connection. In C.R. Snyder & D.R. Forsyth (Eds.), *Handbook Social and Clinical: The Health Perspective*, pp. 79–95. New York: Pergamon.

Hill, J. & Zautra, A. (1989). Self-blame attributions and unique vulnerability as predictors of postrape demoralization. *Journal of Social and Clinical Psychology*, **8**, 368–375.

Horowitz, M.J. (1976). *Stress response syndromes*. New York: Aronson.

Horowitz, M.J. (1980). Psychological response to serious life events. In V. Hamilton & D. Warburton (Eds.), *Human Stress and Cognition*. New York: Wiley.

Horowitz, M.J. (1982). Stress response syndromes and their treatment. In L. Goldberger & S. Breznitiz (Eds.), *Handbook of Stress*. New York: Free Press.

Janoff-Bulman, R. (1979). Characterological versus behavioral self-blame: Inquiries into depression and rape. *Journal of Personality and Social Psychology*, **37**, 1798–1809.

Janoff-Bulman, R. (1985). The aftermath of victimization: Rebuilding shattered assumptions. In C.R. Figley (Ed.), *Trauma and its Wake*, pp. 15–35. New York: Brunner/Mazel.

Janoff-Bulman, R. (1989). Assumptive worlds and the stress of traumatic events: Applications of the schema construct. *Social Cognition*, **7**, 113–136.

Janoff-Bulman, R. (1992). *Shattered Assumptions: Towards a New Psychology of Trauma*. New York: Free Press.

Jones, E.E. & Davis, K.E. (1965). From acts to dispositions: The attribution process in person perception. In L. Berkowitz (Ed.), *Advances in Experimental Social Psychology*, vol. 2, pp. 220–266. New York: Academic Press.

Joseph, S., Brewin, C.R., Yule, W. & Williams, R. (1991). Causal attributions and psychiatric symptoms in survivors of the Herald of Free Enterprise disaster. *British Journal of Psychiatry*, **159**, 542–546.

Joseph, S., Brewin, C.R., Yule, W. & Williams, R. (1993). Causal attributions and psychiatric symptoms in adolescent survivors of disaster. *Journal of Child Psychology and Psychiatry*, **34**, 247–253.

Joseph, S., Hodgkinson, P., Yule, W. & Williams, R. (1993). Guilt and distress 30 months after the capsize of the Herald of Free Enterprise. *Personality and Individual Differences*, **14**, 271–273.

Joseph, S., Williams, R. & Yule, W. (1992). Crisis support, attributional style, coping style, and post-traumatic symptoms. *Personality and Individual Differences*, **13**, 1249–1251.

Joseph, S., Williams, R. & Yule, W. (1993). Changes in outlook following disaster: The preliminary development of a measure to assess positive and negative responses. *Journal of Traumatic Stress*, **6**, 271–279.

Kelley, H.H. (1967). Attribution theory in social psychology. In D. Levine (Ed.), *Nebraska Symposium on Motivation*, vol. 15, pp. 192–240. Lincoln: University of Nebraska Press.

Kolb, L.C. (1987). A neuropsychological hypothesis explaining post-traumatic stress disorders. *American Journal of Psychiatry*, **144**, 989–995.

Lazarus, R.S. (1966). *Psychological Stress and the Coping Process*. New York: McGraw-Hill.

Lazarus, R.S. (1991). *Emotion and Adaptation*. New York: Oxford University Press.

Lazarus, R.S. & Folkman, S. (1984). *Stress, Appraisal and Coping*. New York: Springer.

Litt, M.D. (1988). Cognitive mediators of stressful experience: Self efficacy and perceived control. *Cognitive Therapy and Research*, **12**, 241–260.

Lyons, J.A. (1991). Strategies for assessing the potential for positive adjustment following trauma. *Journal of Traumatic Stress*, **4**, 93–111.

March, J.S. (1990). The nosology of post-traumatic stress disorder. *Journal of Anxiety Disorders*, **4**, 61–82.

March, J.S. (1993). What constitutes a stressor? The criterion A issue. In J.R.T. Davidson & E.B. Foa (Eds.), *Posttraumatic Stress Disorder: DSM-IV and Beyond*. Washington, DC: American Psychiatric Press.

MacLeod, A.K. & Tarbuck, A.F. (1994). Explaining why negative events will happen to oneself: Parasuicides are pessimistic because they can't see any reason not to be. *British Journal of Clinical Psychology*, **33**, 317–326.

McFarlaue, A.C. & Papay, P. (1992). Multiple diagnoses in posttraumatic stress disorder in the victims of a natural disaster. *Journal of Nervous and Mental Disease*, **180**, 498–504.

Metalsky, G.I. & Abramson, L.Y. (1981). Attributional styles: Toward a framework for conceptualization and assessment. In P.C. Kendall & S.D. Hollon (Eds.), *Cognitive-behavioural Intentions: Assessment Methods*. New York: Academic Press.

McCormick, R.A., Taber, J. & Kruedelbach, N. (1989). The relationship between attributional style and post traumatic stress disorder in addicted patients. *Journal of Traumatic Stress*, **2**, 477–487.

Meyer, B. & Taylor, S.E. (1986). Adjustment of rape. *Journal of Personality and Social Psychology*, **50**, 1226–1234.

Mikulincer, M. & Solomon, Z. (1988). Attributional style and combat-related posttraumatic stress disorder. *Journal of Abnormal Psychology*, **97**, 308–313.

Mikulincer, M., Solomon, Z. & Benbenishty, R. (1988). Battle events, acute combat stress reaction and long-term psychological sequelae of war. *Journal of Anxiety Disorders*, **2**, 121–133.

Milgram, N.A. (1986). Attributional analysis of war related stress: Models of coping and help seeking. In N.A. Milgram (Ed.), *Generalizations from the Israeli Experience*, pp. 255–267 New York: Brunner Mazel.

Needles, D.J. & Abramson, L.Y. (1990). Positive life events, attributional style, and hopefulness: Testing a model of recovery from depression. *Journal of Abnormal Psychology*, **99**, 156–165.

Niedenthal, P.M., Tangney, J.P. & Gavanski, I. (1994). "If only I weren't" versus "if only I hadn't": Distinguishing shame and guilt in counterfactual thinking. *Journal of Personality and Social Psychology*, **67**, 485–595.

Nielson, W.R. & MacDonald, M.R. (1988). Attributions of blame and coping following spinal cord injury: Is self-blame adaptive? *Journal of Social and Clinical Psychology*, **7**, 163–175.

Orr, S.P., Claiborn, J.M., Altman, B., Forgue, D.F., de Jong, J.B. & Pitman, R.K. (1990). Psychometric profile of posttraumatic stress disorder, anxious, and healthy Vietnam veterans: Correlations with psychophysiological responses. *Journal of Consulting and Clinical Psychology*, **58**, 329–335.

Paulhus, D. (1983). Sphere-specific measures of perceived control. *Journal of Personality and Social Psychology*, **44**, 1253–1265.

Peterson, C. & Seligman, M.E.P. (1984). Causal explanations as a risk factor for depression: Theory and evidence. *Psychological Review*, **91**, 347–374.

Rachman, S. (1980). Emotional processing. *Behaviour Research and Therapy*, **18**, 51–60.

Riggs, D.S., Dancu, C.V., Gershuny, B.S., Greenberg, D. & Foa, E.B. (1992). Anger and post-traumatic stress disorder in female crime victims. *Journal of Traumatic Stress*, **5**, 613–625.

Rothbaum, B.O., Foa, E.B., Riggs, D.S., Murdock, T. & Walsh, W. (1992). A prospective examination of post-traumatic stress disorder in rape victims. *Journal of Traumatic Stress*, **5**, 455–476.

Rotter, J.B. (1966). Generalized expectancies for internal versus external control of reinforcement. *Psychological Monographs*, **80** (1, Whole No. 609).

Seligman, M.E.P., Abramson, L.Y., Semmel, A. & Von Baeyer, C. (1979). Depressive attributional style. *Journal of Abnormal Psychology*, **88**, 242–247.

Shaver, K.G. & Drown, D. (1986). On causality, responsibility, and self-blame: A theoretical note. *Journal of Personality and Social Psychology*, **50**, 697–702.

Solomon, Z., Benbenishty, R. & Mikulincer, M. (1988). A follow up of Israeli casualties of combat stress reaction ("battle shock") in the 1982 Lebanon war. *British Journal of Clinical Psychology*, **27**, 125–135.

Solomon, Z., Mikulincer, M. & Avitzur, E. (1988). Coping, locus of control, social support, and combat related posttraumatic stress disorder: A prospective study. *Journal of Personality and Social Psychology*, **55**, 279–285.

Solomon, Z., Mikulincer, M. & Benbenishty, R. (1989). Locus of control and combat related post-traumatic stress disorder: The intervening role of battle intensity, threat appraisal and coping. *British Journal of Clinical Psychology*, **28**, 131–144.

Steele, C.M. (1988). The psychology of self-affirmation: Sustaining the integrity of the self. In L. Berkowitz (Ed.), *Advances in Experimental Social Psychology*, vol. 21, pp. 261–302. San Diego, CA: Academic Press.

Stotland, E. (1969). *The Psychology of Hope*. San Francisco, CA: Jossey Bass.

Stratton, P., Heard, D., Hanks, H.G.I., Munton, A.G., Brewin, C.R. & Davidson, C. (1986). Coding causal beliefs in natural discourse. *British Journal of Social Psychology*, **25**, 299–313.

Sweeney, P.D., Anderson, K. & Bailey, S. (1986). Attributional style in depression: A meta-analytic review. *Journal of Personality and Social Psychology*, **50**, 974–991.

Tangney, J.P., Wagner, P. & Gramzow, R. (1992). Proneness to shame, proneness to guilt, and psychopathology. *Journal of Abnormal Psychology*, **101**, 469–478.

Taylor, S. (1983). Adjustment to threatening life events: A theory of cognitive adaptation. *American Psychologist*, **38**, 1161–1173.

Taylor, S. & Brown, J. (1988). Illusion and well-being: A social psychological perspective on mental health. *Psychological Bulletin*, **103**, 193–210.

Tennen, H. & Affleck, G. (1990). Blaming others for threatening events. *Psychological Bulletin*, **108**, 209–232.

Tennen, H., Affleck, G., Allen, D.A., McGrade, B.J. & Ratzen, S. (1984). Causal attributions and coping with insulin-dependent diabetes. *Basic and Applied Social Psychology*, **5**, 131–142.

Tesser, A. & Campbell, J. (1980). Self-definition and self-evaluation maintenance. In J. Suls & A.G. Greenwald (Eds.), *Psychological Perspectives on the Self*, vol. 2. Hillsdale, NJ: Erlbaum.

Thornton, B., Ryckman, R., Kirchner, G., Jacobs, J., Kaczor, L. & Kuehnel, R. (1988). Reaction to self-attributed victim responsibility: A comparative analysis of rape crisis counsellors and lay observers. *Journal of Applied Social Psychology*, **18**, 409–422.

Timko, C. & Janoff-Bulman, R. (1985). Attributions, vulnerability and psychological adjustment: The case of breast cancer. *Health Psychology*, **4**, 521–546.

van der Kolk, B.A. (1987). *Psychological Trauma*. Washington, DC: American Psychiatric Press.

Watts, F.N. (1982). Attributional aspects of medicine. In C. Antaki & C. Brewin (Eds.), *Attributions and Psychological Change*, pp. 1135–155. London: Academic Press.

Weinberg, N. (1994). Self-blame, other blame, and desire for revenge: Factors in recovery from bereavement. *Death Studies*, **18**, 583–593.

Weiner, B. (1985). Spontaneous causal thinking. *Psychological Bulletin*, **97**, 74–84.

Weiner, B. (1986). *An Attributional Theory of Motivation and Emotion*. New York: Springer-Verlag.

Wong, P.T.P. & Weiner, B. (1981). When people ask "why" questions, and the heuristics of attributional search. *Journal of Personality and Social Psychology*, **40**, 650–663.

Chapter 4

SOCIAL SUPPORT AND MENTAL HEALTH FOLLOWING TRAUMA

*Stephen Joseph**

Social support refers to the complex and dynamic interpersonal processes that help to protect against the development of problems in physical and mental health. In the present chapter, work that my colleagues and I have carried out into the relationship between social support and post-traumatic reactions will be reviewed. Following this, some theoretical perspectives on social support will be discussed. In particular, a sequential model of adaptation that emphasises the type and timing of social support following exposure to traumatic stressors will be reviewed. Finally, implications for research and clinical practice are discussed. Social support, unlike the traumatic event itself, may be modifiable and so there are important implications for therapeutic intervention.

CRISIS SUPPORT

Within the traumatic stress literature, several writers, for example Raphael (1986), have noted that survivors often have compelling needs to talk about their experiences. Indeed, Stiles (1987) argues that the relationship between self-disclosure and psychological distress is analogous to the relationship between fever and physical infection (see also Stiles, Shuster & Harrigan, 1992). Thus, it is necessary to have others who are simply willing to listen, to provide support in emotional and practical ways when necessary, and who do not make the person feel worse in some way. These are the core aspects of crisis support as operationally defined by Brown and his colleagues (Andrews & Brown, 1988; Brown, Andrews, Harris, Adler & Bridge, 1986). Based on the work of Brown and his

*University of Essex, Colchester.

Post-Traumatic Stress Disorders: Concepts and Therapy. Edited by William Yule.
© 1999 John Wiley & Sons Ltd.

colleagues, the Crisis Support Scale was developed (Joseph, Andrews, Williams & Yule, 1992). This is a respondent-based questionnaire developed from the Crisis Support Instrument—a semi-structured interview employing investigator-based ratings (Andrews & Brown, 1988; Brown et al., 1986). The Crisis Support Scale is a six-item self-report measure of received support which is anchored to the traumatic event and a specified time frame.

The *Jupiter* Cruise Ship Disaster

Joseph et al. (1992) administered the Crisis Support Scale (see Appendix) to 23 adult survivors of the *Jupiter* cruise ship disaster. This was a shipping disaster which took place in October 1988 when a party of over 400 British schoolchildren, accompanied by over 90 teachers and other adults, set sail from Piraeus harbour in Greece for an educational cruise of the Eastern Mediterranean. Twenty minutes out of harbour, an oil tanker collided amidships, the *Jupiter* was holed and rapidly began taking in water. Many, fearing that they would drown, had to jump into the oil and debris strewn water to reach the safety of the rescue boat. The 23 survivors completed several self-report symptom measures within the first three months and again at around 12 months, at which time they also completed the Crisis Support Scale (which contained items asking about the support received during the first three months and in the past three months: see Appendix). Although this was a relatively small sample, the respondents were found to be representative of the total surviving population in terms of symptom severity at three months. It was found that the retrospective ratings of crisis support for the time just after the disaster were significantly higher than those ratings of crisis support at the present time, suggesting that levels of support had declined. It was also found that lower scores on the Crisis Support Scale at both time points were associated with greater psychological distress.

In order to assess the causal relationship between crisis support and trauma-related distress, a postal survey that was carried out 18 months after the disaster included 17 of the 23 survivors who took part in the first study (Joseph, Yule, Williams & Andrews, 1993). At 18 months survivors again completed the six-item Crisis Support Scale (asking about the present time) and the Impact of Event Scale (IES: Horowitz, Wilner & Alvarez, 1979). A regression analysis was carried out with scores on the retrospective Crisis Support Scale and the intrusion subscale of the IES completed at three months entered on the same step to predict scores on the intrusion subscale at 18 months. This analysis was repeated with scores on the Crisis Support Scale and avoidance subscale of the IES at three months entered on the same step to predict scores on avoidance at 18 months. It was found that retrospective crisis support at three months, although not associated with intrusion at 18 months, was associated with avoidance at 18 months. The same set of analyses were carried out to assess whether crisis support at 12 months could predict intrusion and avoidance at 18 months over and above intrusion and avoidance at 12 months, but no significant associations were found, suggesting that it is the crisis support received in the immediate aftermath of trauma which is of most importance to later functioning. Overall, the level of symptomatology decreased between each of the three time points. Scores on the Crisis Support Scale also decreased between each of the three time points. This is interesting as other research has shown social support to increase as symptoms abate (Solomon, Mikulincer & Avitzur, 1988), suggesting that there may have been an increase in other supportive behaviours not assessed.

Herald of Free Enterprise

In March 1987, a Townsend Thoresen "roll-on-roll-off" passenger and freight ferry, the *Herald of Free Enterprise*, capsised shortly after leaving Zeebrugge harbour in Belgium. There were around 600 people on board, and in the ensuing chaos 193 passengers and crew lost their lives. Survivors of the *Herald of Free Enterprise* disaster also completed the Crisis Support Scale (see Appendix) at around three years as part of a postal survey of 73 of the survivors (Joseph, Yule, Williams & Hodgkinson, 1994). It was found that lower scores on the total summated Crisis Support Scale, and more negative life events in the time subsequent to the disaster as assessed using the List of Threatening Experiences (Brugha, Bebbington, Tennant & Hurry, 1985), were associated with greater psychological distress as assessed by the General Health Questionnaire (Goldberg & Hillier, 1979) over and above the other variables used in the study: These included the fact of bereavement and retrospective ratings of helplessness during the disaster. However, the strongest correlates of intrusive re-experiencing were perceptions of helplessness and bereavement. These data suggested that, although event-related variables may give rise to symptoms characteristic of PTSD, crisis support and other life-events in the time subsequent to disaster maintain general psychological distress.

At around six years, 37 of these 73 survivors were again contacted as part of ongoing research at the Institute of Psychiatry, which enabled the association between scores on the IES at six years and scores on the Crisis Support Scale at three years to be examined (Dalgleish, Joseph, Thrasher, Tranah & Yule, 1996). A regression analysis was carried out with scores on the Crisis Support Scale and the intrusion subscale of the IES completed at three years entered on the same step to predict scores on the intrusion subscale at six years. This analysis was repeated with scores on the Crisis Support Scale and avoidance subscale of the IES at three years entered on the same step to predict scores on avoidance at six years. Again, it was found that crisis support at three years, although not associated with intrusion at six years, was associated with avoidance at six years.

In addition, survivors also completed the Beck Depression Inventory (Beck, Rush, Shaw & Emery, 1979) and the Spielberger State Anxiety Inventory (Spielberger, Gorsuch & Lushene, 1970) at six years, which allowed the investigation of the association between scores on these scales and scores on the IES at three years. Survivors had also completed the 28-item General Health Questionnaire (Goldberg & Hillier, 1979) at three years. Scores on the GHQ-28 and the Crisis Support Scale were entered together into a regression equation to predict scores on depression and state anxiety at six years. Greater crisis support at three years was associated with lower depression at six years even with scores on the GHQ-28 at three years partialled out. In addition, greater crisis support at three years was associated with lower state anxiety at six years even with scores on the GHQ-28 partialled out. In accord with the time frame of the *Jupiter* study, there was a decrease in crisis support in the first three years, but between three and six years crisis support showed an increase.

THEORETICAL ISSUES

These results with the survivors of the *Herald of Free Enterprise* disaster replicated those with the survivors of the *Jupiter* cruise ship disaster, showing greater crisis support to be predictive of lower subsequent avoidant behaviour. In addition, these data also showed that lower levels of crisis support are predictive of later feelings of depression and anxiety. Other research has shown greater social support to be associated with lower distress following combat (Escobar, Randolph, Puente, Spivak, Assamen, Hill & Hough, 1983; Foy, Sipprelle, Rueger & Carroll, 1984; Foy, Resnick, Sipprelle & Carroll, 1987; Frye & Stockton, 1982; Keane, Scott, Chavoya, Lamparski & Fairbank, 1985; Solkoff, Gray & Keill, 1986; Solomon, Mikulincer & Avitzur, 1988; Solomon, Mikulincer & Hobfoll, 1986; Stretch, 1985, 1986); disaster (Bartone, Ursano, Wright & Ingraham, 1989; Cook & Bickman, 1990; Green, Grace & Gleser, 1985; Madakasira &

O'Brien, 1987), personal injury (Perry, Difede, Musngi, Frances & Jacobsberg, 1992), rape (Burgess & Holmstrom, 1974, 1978), toxic exposure (Bromet, Parkinson, Schulberg, Dunn & Gondek, 1982; Fleming, Baum, Gisriel & Gatchel, 1982) and HIV (Pakenham, Dadds & Terry, 1994). On the basis of the growing evidence for the protective role of social support, it is generally agreed that the inclusion of social support variables within models of adaptation to traumatic events is helpful in explaining why some survivors go on to develop severe and chronic post-traumatic reactions while others do not (Figley, 1986; Flannery, 1990; Jones & Barlow, 1990; Solomon, 1986; Williams, Joseph & Yule, 1993).

Social Support: A Multifactorial Construct

However, in the above studies, social support has been operationally defined in a variety of ways reflecting the diversity of this concept (Winemiller, Mitchell, Sutliff & Cline, 1993). Although the concept of crisis support was adapted from the work of Brown and his colleagues (Andrews & Brown, 1988; Brown et al., 1986) and largely reflects the need that survivors have to talk about traumatic experiences in an emotionally supportive environment, most existing measures of social support have not been developed for use with traumatised populations and reflect different theoretical orientations. For example, one unique feature of crisis support is that others in the social network have similar experiences to those of the survivor. This might be expected to promote empathy and foster self-disclosure (Erikson, 1976; Jacobs & Goodman, 1989).

Furthermore, crisis support is concerned with the social support actually received in a time of need, as opposed to perceived social support, which is concerned with the perception of support availability if it was needed. This is a basic distinction in the social support literature (see Sarason, Sarason & Pierce, 1990). For example, one alternative operational definition of social support used in trauma research is the Purdue Social Support Scale (see Figley, 1986). In contrast to the crisis support scale which asks about the frequency of support received from others, the Purdue scale asks about how satisfied the respondent would expect to be with the support that various people might provide. Although both the Crisis Support Scale and the Purdue Social Support Scale conceptualise social support from the point of view of the person being supported, these two scales clearly reflect very different conceptualisations of social support. Although there has been some research into the question of whether it is perceived or received support which is most strongly associated with mental health (e.g. Wethington & Kessler, 1986), this has not proved to be a fruitful line of enquiry, with most investigators now accepting that social support is a multifactorial construct and that both perceptions of social support and the support actually received should be assessed. Clearly, both operational definitions are concerned with different issues and both are important in psychological well-being.

Although this discussion has emphasised the causal relationship between greater social support and lower psychological distress, alternative relationships should be noted. One consequence of not being able to process traumatic experiences is a withdrawal from social life leading to isolation and a preoccupation with the self (Titchener, 1986). For this reason, a low level of social support may often be a symptom of trauma-related distress. McFarlane (1987) showed that families who had been exposed to the Australian bushfires were characterised by increased levels of irritability, fighting, withdrawal, and decreased enjoyment from shared activities. For this reason investigators should also include measures which assess the extent to which a person actively seeks out social support or engages in social withdrawal.

Stressor-Support Specificity

Both received and perceived support can be further delineated in terms of types of support. Although the specific terminology varies, social support has generally been viewed as a multidimensional construct (e.g. Cohen & Wills, 1985; Dunkel-Schetter & Bennett, 1990; Jacobson, 1986; Sarason, Sarason & Pierce, 1990) with distinctions being drawn between three types of social support: emotional support, practical support and cognitive support. Emotional support refers to the provision of information that the person is accepted, valued and esteemed. Practical support refers to the provision of material resources such as financial aid. Cognitive support refers to the provision of advice, guidance or information regarding the situation. Most researchers now adopt a stressor-support specificity model (Cohen & McKay, 1984; Cutrona & Russell, 1990). The stressor-support specificity model states that the most effective type of social support will be the one that matches the person's needs in a given situation. Some events might require a high level of practical support whereas other situations might require a high level of emotional support. Cutrona and Russell (1990) examined the types of social support that might be needed following either controllable or uncontrollable events showing that controllable events required greater levels of practical support whereas uncontrollable events required greater levels of emotional support. Similarly, according to the conservation of resources model proposed by Hobfoll (1988), stress occurs when individuals judge their environment as causing a loss of resources. Resources are broadly defined as those objects, personal characteristics, conditions or energies that are valued by the individual or that serve as means for attaining these objects, personal characteristics, conditions or energies. Hobfoll's (1988) model outlines how specific resources such as social support can aid stress resistance by replenishing lost resources (Hobfoll, Freedy, Lane & Geller, 1990).

Temporal Aspects

Others have pointed to the possibility that different types of social support are needed at different times as a stressful situation unfolds. Weiss (1976) distinguished between three types of stressful situations: crisis, transition and deficit. Crisis is defined as a situation of sudden onset and limited duration which is threatening to well-being and marked by emotional arousal. Transition is a period of change that involves a shift in the person's assumptive world. Deficit state is a situation in which an individual's life is defined by chronically excessive demands. Although these three types of stressful situation can occur simultaneously, Weiss (1976) suggests that they may be related temporally, typically occurring in the order of crisis, transition, and deficit.

Drawing upon this work, Jacobson (1986) suggests that, to the extent that stressful situations are sequential, different types of support will be needed at different times. In a crisis the most useful form of help is emotional support. In transitions, the primary type of social support is cognitive support. In deficit states, practical support is needed to replenish resources. Jacobson's (1986) analysis of the type and timing of social support provides a useful framework for conceptualising how traumatic events may unfold over time requiring different types of support at different times. Current theory on the role of coping in relation to stressful events adopts a similar perspective, viewing coping as an unfolding process (Folkman & Lazarus, 1985, 1986, 1988). However, the extent to which these states do follow a clear temporal sequence is uncertain and it is likely that there is much overlap between them.

Cognitive Support

A need for cognitive support would seem to be common to survivors of all these events as these events are transitional states involving massive shifts in assumptive worlds (Janoff-Bulman, 1985, 1992). Janoff-Bulman suggests that there are common psychological experiences shared by victims who have experienced a wide range of traumatic events. The experience of traumatic events presents the individual with information incompatible with his or her pre-existing beliefs, for example, that the world is benevolent and meaningful. Successful, emotional processing involves the person assimilating the powerful new information within his or her cognitive schema. Similarly, Figley (1986) discusses the cognitive struggle of survivors to answer fundamental questions such as, what happened to me?, why me?, what will I do in another catastrophe? and argues that it is the answers to such questions as these that determine adjustment. Figley (1986) discusses how others help the victim to recapitulate on the event and act as facilitators who encourage the person to talk:

> . . . while at the same time "cleaning up after" the victim by (a) clarifying insights, (b) correcting distortions, (c) placing blame and credit more objectively, and (d) offering or supporting new and more "generous" or accurate perspectives on the event that was originally traumatic. (Figley, 1986, p. 47)

Account making: From a social-psychological perspective, it has been argued that adaptation to trauma involves account making (Harvey, Orbuch & Weber, 1990). Account making is defined as the story-like constructions of events that include explanations, descriptions, predictions about relevant future events, and affective reactions. Account making provides a theoretical umbrella under which to consider the various cognitive strategies that are thought to be involved in adaption to threatening events; for example, the perception of benefits, attributions of meaning and blame (e.g. Affleck, Tennen, Croog & Levine, 1987; Silver, Boon & Stones, 1983; Taylor, Lichtman & Wood, 1984).

Harvey and his colleagues, who have examined accounts made by Vietnam veterans (Harvey, Agostinelli & Weber, 1989), elderly people's reactions to the loss of loved ones by death, divorce, and relocation (Weber, Harvey & Stanley, 1987), and survivors of sexual assault (Harvey, Orbuch, Chwalisz & Garwood, 1991), elaborate on Horowitz's (1986) sequential stage-model of reactions to stress by proposing that working through involves intensified account making which begins to be reported in confiding activity. The extent to which a person will confide an account to others may vary as a function of several factors, such as the closeness of the relationship and the account-maker's apprehension about the other person's reactions to the account. Completion of the story is necessary for trauma resolution. A similar perspective is presented by Wigren (1994), who argues that narrative processing is crucial to psychological organization, and by Pennebaker and his colleagues, who have provided evidence for the health-related benefits of confession.

Pennebaker and O'Heeron (1984) found that spouses who had been recently bereaved through suicide or accidents and who talked with friends about the death had a lower rate of illness than those who did not. In another study, Pennebaker and Beall (1986) asked undergraduates to write about either a trivial topic or a personally upsetting event for several consecutive days and then compared groups on the number of visits to the health centre in the following months. What they found was that those who wrote about the upsetting events made fewer visits (see also Greenberg & Stone, 1992). Other work has shown that self-disclosure was associated with better immune functioning (Pennebaker, Kiecolt-Glaser & Glaser, 1988), fewer absentee days and improved liver enzyme function (Francis & Pennebaker, 1992). (see also Pennebaker, Hughes & O'Heeron, 1987). More recently, Pennebaker (1993) has concluded that the construction of a coherent story together with the expression of negative emotions work together to produce benefit (although see Siegman, Anderson & Berger, 1990, who suggest that the expression of emotions might only be beneficial when it is done in a relaxed way).

Social Context

Other writers have emphasised that a full understanding of post-traumatic phenomena also requires taking into account the social context in which personal distress is being played out. Summerfield (1993) draws attention to the Vietnam war following which the US veterans were disowned by their society and contrasts this to the Falklands war in which British veterans returned to popular acclaim. Account making is a social phenomena and the role of the sociocultural context has been extensively discussed by Lebowitz and Roth (1994) who have examined the cultural context of rape and how various beliefs might operate to impede emotional processing in women.

The relationship between emotional states and social context is further illustrated in an interesting study by Bartone and Wright (1990) who investigated group recovery following a military air disaster. A chartered US Army jetliner crashed in 1985 killing all on board. This was the second of three flights carrying soldiers home from the Sinai for Christmas. Bartone and Wright collected monthly data using unstructured interviews over a period of six months following the crash on 140 soldiers from the battalion. Their data indicated four relatively distinct phases, each lasting 4–6 weeks. The first phase was labelled as numb dedication and was characterised by denial, generalised affective detachment and numbness, although various intrusive reminders sometimes triggered periods of uncontrollable crying and dreams about the event. Near the six-week point, Bartone and Wright describe how this first phase of numb dedication shifted to one dominated by anger and feelings of betrayal. What was interesting was that the transition into this phase was marked by the publication of a report indicating poor airline safety practices as contributing to the cause of the crash. At around the tenth week, following the burial of the last soldier, there was another marked turning point characterised by a sense of relief, and expressions of sadness and anger were replaced by an attitude of stoic resolve to continue with work and life. When references to the crash were necessary, indirect or euphemistic terms were used. Week 20 marked the final recovery phase which was characterised as one of integration. Although the extent to which these particular phases might apply to other events is not known, this work is important in drawing attention to how the particular social context surrounding an event might act to influence the type and timing of emotional phases by providing a frame through which the survivor can interpret his or her experiences.

NEGATIVE RESPONSE

Social support is a transactional process and other people's reactions to survivors are not always perceived as helpful. For example, they may feel the need to derogate the survivor in order to maintain their own assumptive beliefs (see Janoff-Bulman, 1992). Wilkinson (1983) reported that 20% of survivors of the Kansas City Hyatt Regency disaster rated their families as not helpful. Furthermore, the effects of traumatic events can be disruptive to the lives of close friends and friends who may become upset themselves (Robinson & Mitchell, 1993) and there may be increased conflict within relationships which could, in turn, serve to maintain distress (Gruen, 1993; McFarlane, 1987).

Victimising events will often lead to conflicting reactions in other people. There may be conflict between aversion/fear and optimism/cheerfulness, producing ambivalence and anxiety towards interaction (Dakof & Taylor, 1990). Thus, the person may attempt to avoid the victim, try not to talk about it, and minimise the victim's circumstances. These reactions may lead to feelings of rejection on the part of the victim. Dakof and Taylor (1990) studied 55 cancer patients. They asked them to state the particular acts that others make that are helpful or harmful. Based on the assumption that the ties of kinship, marriage or friendship all create different obligations and constraints, Dakof and Taylor asked respondents about seven other people: (1) spouse; (2) other family members; (3) friends; (4) support group members; (5) doctors; (6) nurses; and (7) acquaintances. For each of these people, respondents were asked: (1) what is the most helpful thing?; (2) what have they said or done to make you angry?; (3) what have they done that nobody else could have?; and (4) what have you wished they did? Helpful and unhelpful actions were divided into three groups: (1) esteem support; (2) information support; and (3) instrumental support. It was found that 70% said that their spouse, family or friends were most helpful with regard to esteem support and that their inappropriate attempts at esteem support were the most unhelpful. Other cancer patients and doctors were seen as the most helpful regarding information support and the lack of this the most unhelpful. More specifically, partners were seen as helpful for expressing concern and affection, and acceptance of the illness. Being critical about their response to the cancer was seen as particularly unhelpful, as was the failure to express concern. Other family members were most appreciated for expressing concern, being there and providing practical assistance, such as transport. However, criticising and minimising the impact of the cancer was seen as most unhelpful. Other work with Israeli women whose husbands had gone off to war showed that social networks increased distress through the transmission of rumours and news of disasters (Hobfoll & London, 1985) and research with men with HIV found that having a partner was associated with poorer social adjustment (Pakenham, Dadds & Terry, 1994). Pakenham and colleagues suggested that having a partner may encourage dependency and adherence to a sick role and, as a consequence, foster ill health and impaired social functioning.

ATTACHMENT AND LONELINESS

Two alternative models explaining the mechanisms through which social support is linked with adjustment have been proposed. First, the main effects model, which proposes that irrespective of the level of stress experienced, social support has a direct effect on adaptation. Secondly, the stress-buffering model, which proposes that social support serves to buffer the individual against the negative consequences of stress. Cohen and Wills (1985) found evidence in support of both models and suggested that main effects are due to a sense of belonging and integration. Some authors have emphasised that people have needs for social integration and attachment (Weiss, 1974) which are met through their personal relationships. Having these needs met are central to psychological health even in the absence of stressful events, and not having these needs met can lead to social and emotional loneliness. Traumatic events often involve the disruption of existing social relationships, through bereavement for example (Solomon, 1986), leaving the person vulnerable to loneliness. Loneliness has been shown to be associated with serious mental health problems, including depression and suicidal behaviour. Loneliness is thought of as inherently aversive and distinct from social isolation (Russell, Cutrona, Rose & Yurko, 1984). Weiss (1973, 1974) has suggested that two types of loneliness can be delineated. Emotional loneliness, which results from the lack of a close intimate attachment to another person, and social loneliness, which results from the lack of a network of social relationships. As with the stressor-specificity model of social support, different types of relationships meet different needs (Weiss, 1974). Relief from emotional loneliness requires the formation of an intimate relationship whereas relief for social loneliness requires entry into a social network. Empirical work has confirmed that emotional and social loneliness are distinct experiences (Russell et al., 1984). Some people, however, have persistent and stable feelings of loneliness which they will bring into the situation and which results from a discrepancy between desired and achieved levels of social relations.

Other writers, drawing on Bowlby's (1973, 1980) attachment theory, have identified three attachment styles: secure, anxious-avoidant and anxious-ambivalent (Ainsworth, Blehar, Waters & Wall, 1978) which are thought to reflect the infant's internalization of his or her experience with the care-giver and extend into adulthood (Hazan & Shaver, 1987). Hazan and Shaver found that intimacy, closeness, supportiveness and trust were characteristic of secure people's relationships. Avoidant people's relationships were characterised by fear of intimacy and difficulty in depending on others; and ambivalent people's relationships were characterised by worry about being abandoned and jealousy. Similar findings have been reported in a number of studies (Collins & Read, 1990; Feeney & Noller, 1990; Levy & Davis, 1988; Mikulincer & Erev, 1991; Mikulincer & Nachshon, 1991) and it has been suggested that attachment styles might determine people's response to stress. One study has investigated how attachment style influenced coping and adjustment following the Iraqi Scud missile attack on Israeli cities during the Gulf war (Mikulincer, Florian & Weller, 1993). It was found that relative to ambivalent and avoidant persons, secure persons showed higher levels of social support seeking and lower levels of distress. It was suggested that insecure people tend to develop a working model that exaggerates the appraisal of events as threatening and uncontrollable, which impairs their working through.

IMPLICATIONS AND DIRECTIONS

In cases where a low level of social support is identified, intervention aimed at increasing support may be possible. The level of support received is, in part, a function of others' perceptions of the victims' need for help. It has been suggested that the self-presentational coping stance taken by victims can play an important role in the support provider's reaction (Silver, Wortman & Crofton, 1990). Silver and colleagues argue that victims who are able to portray "balanced coping"—conveying that although they are distressed, they are attempting to cope through their own efforts—are most likely to receive support from others. On this basis, behavioural intervention aimed at the self-presentational stance employed by survivors may be appropriate in increasing the available social support network.

The level of support received is also a function of the person's own cognitions regarding the event. For example, there is evidence that individuals who blame themselves for a negative event are more likely to withdraw socially and less likely to seek social support from others (Brewin, MacCarthy & Furnham, 1989). On this basis, cognitive therapies may be useful in helping survivors to make better use of their social support networks. For example, it has been argued elsewhere that attribution therapy may be feasible in helping survivors come to terms with guilt or shame-provoking thoughts which, in turn, might increase their support-seeking behaviour (Joseph, Brewin, Yule & Williams, 1991).

Although therapeutic attempts at increasing the quantity of social support might be appropriate with those survivors who are identified as lacking in social support, the quality of social support provided remains paramount. Other people will often cause further distress to the survivor. The therapist, in attempting to help the person foster social support, must also explore with the client the nature of his or her personal relationships and what other people have provided that has been helpful and what has been unhelpful. It may be that these issues should become a focus for discussion within the therapeutic session in order to help the survivor gain awareness of how his or her condition might be affecting family and friends and the problems that they might also be experiencing. Although this discussion has largely focused on social support as resources which are actually received from others, how the person appraises the support received is important and such intervention might be useful in helping to maintain subjective judgements of satisfaction with support. Although a particular behaviour can be seen as unhelpful, it may still be attributed to kindly motives (Lehman & Hemphill, 1990).

What was particularly interesting about the data obtained with survivors of the *Herald of Free Enterprise* disaster (Dalgleish et al., 1996) was that scores on the Crisis Support Scale at three years were more strongly related to state anxiety at five years than were scores on the GHQ-28 at three years. As the GHQ-28 is widely used by clinicians to screen survivors for risk of later disturbance, these data would suggest that the Crisis Support Scale may also be useful in screening survivors. The concept of crisis support would also seem to be most appropriate as it is concerned with received support rather than perceived support. It provides a framework within which to consider the availability of others, contact with other survivors, confiding in others, emotional support, practical support and negative response. The crisis support measure employed in the studies of the survivors of the *Herald* and the *Jupiter* disasters was deliberately brief for use in a postal survey. Other work could attempt to extend the operational definition of crisis support. For example, it would be useful to investigate those who provide each type of support. Barker, Pistraug, Shapiro and Shaw (1990) carried out a survey of over 1,000 adults representative of the UK population with respect to age, sex and socio-economic status. They asked: If you had a personal problem, who would you talk to about it? The most frequent answer was partner (68%) followed by a close relative (54%), a friend or neighbour (43%), the family doctor (41%), a workmate (20%) and, finally, the priest (17%). Men were more likely to seek help from their partner (71%) compared to women (64%); women were more likely to seek help from a close relative (61%) compared to men (45%), and more likely to seek help from a friend or neighbour (52%) compared to men (34%). Men, however, were more likely to seek help from a workmate (23%) compared to women (18%).

Although it has been suggested that the Crisis Support Scale may be useful in screening survivors, it should be emphasised that crisis support represents only one conceptualisation of social support. Future work should endeavour to use a battery of instruments measuring a wider range of social support variables, including aspects of social and emotional loneliness, administered at several time points. In addition, there is a need to understand the relationship of social support to personality and coping variables. One study by Solomon, Mikulincer and Avitzur (1988) examined the relationship between locus of control, coping, social support and PTSD in Israeli veterans at two and three years following combat. They examined: firstly, the relation between personal and social factors, and PTSD at each point in time; and, secondly, the relation between changes in the course of PTSD and changes in both personal and social factors. As expected, the intensity of PTSD declined between the two points of time, reflecting a process of recovery. In accord with this finding, locus of control became more internal over time, there was less emotion-focused coping and more perceived social support. Associations were found at each point in time between PTSD intensity and personal and social factors. In both years, more intense PTSD was associated with external locus of control, emotion-focused coping style and insufficient social support. Some personality variables, such as locus of control, might be predicted to be associated with greater social support seeking (Joseph, Williams & Yule, 1992). Other variables, such as attitudes towards emotional expression, have also been hypothesised to impede social support seeking (Williams, Hodgkinson, Joseph & Yule, 1995).

Finally, the evidence testifies that greater social support is associated with better psychological adjustment following severe stressors. However, social support has been variously defined and there is a need for future research to use a variety of instruments to capture the multifactorial nature of social support. Furthermore, this discussion has emphasised the need to analyse traumatic events contextually and to take into account both the type and timing of social support. Cognitive support would seem to be a common requirement of survivors as they attempt to assimilate the powerful new traumatic information.

APPENDIX: CRISIS SUPPORT SCALE

We would like to ask you a few questions about your family and friends, the people who have turned to for help, advice, and support since the disaster. Below are various people who may be important in your life. Each question asks about the support you received just after the disaster and at the present time. That is, in the three months following the disaster and in the previous three months. Each question has seven answer choices ranging from Never to Always. As a guide, think of these words as representing the numbers below:

Never	Very seldom	Seldom	Some-times	Often	Very often	Always
1	2	3	4	5	6	7

Now, thinking about those people you have turned to for help, advice, and support . . .

	Never						*Always*
1. Whenever you wanted to talk how often was there someone willing to listen *just after the disaster*?	1	2	3	4	5	6	7
2. Whenever you want to talk how often is there someone willing to listen *at the present time*?	1	2	3	4	5	6	7

3. Did you have personal contact with other survivors or people with a similar experience *just after the disaster*?	1	2	3	4	5	6	7
4. Do you have personal contact with other survivors or people with a similar experience *at the present time*?	1	2	3	4	5	6	7
5. Were you able to talk about your thoughts and feelings *just after the disaster*?	1	2	3	4	5	6	7
6. Are you able to talk about your thoughts and feelings *at the present time*?	1	2	3	4	5	6	7
7. Were people sympathetic and supportive *just after the disaster*?	1	2	3	4	5	6	7
8. Are people sympathetic and supportive *at the present time*?	1	2	3	4	5	6	7
9. Were people helpful in a practical sort of way *just after the disaster*?	1	2	3	4	5	6	7
10. Are people helpful in a practical sort of way *at the present time*?	1	2	3	4	5	6	7
11. Did people you expected to be supportive make you feel worse at any time *just after the disaster*?	1	2	3	4	5	6	7
12. Do people you expected to be supportive make you feel worse at any time *at the present time*?	1	2	3	4	5	6	7

NB: Items 11 and 12 are reverse scored.

REFERENCES

Affleck, G., Tennen, H., Croog, S. & Levine, S. (1987). Causal attribution, perceived benefits, and morbidity after a heart attack: An 8-year study. *Journal of Consulting and Clinical Psychology*, **55**, 29–35.

Ainsworth, M.D.S., Blehar, M.C., Waters, E. & Wall, S. (1978). *Patterns of attachment: A Psychological Study of the Strange Situation*. Hillsdale, NJ: Erlbaum.

Andrews, B. & Brown, G.W. (1988). Social support, onset of depression and personality. *Social Psychiatry and Psychiatric Epidemiology*, **23**, 99–108.

Barker, C., Pistrang, N., Shapiro, D.A. & Shaw, I. (1990). Coping and help seeking in the UK adult population. *British Journal of Clinical Psychology*, **29**, 271–285.

Bartone, P.T., Ursano, R.J., Wright, K.M. & Ingraham, L.H. (1989). Impact of a military air disaster on the health of assistance workers. *Journal of Nervous and Mental Disease*, **177**, 317–328.

Bartone, P.T. & Wright, K.M. (1990). Grief and group recovery following a military air disaster. *Journal of Traumatic Stress*, **3**, 523–540.

Beck, A.T., Rush, A., Shaw, B.F. & Emery, G. (1979). *Cognitive Therapy of Depression*. New York: Guilford Press.

Bowlby, J. (1973). *Attachment and Loss: Separation, Anxiety and Anger*. New York: Basic Books.

Bowlby, J. (1980). *Attachment and Loss: Sadness and Depression*. New York: Basic Books.

Brugha, T., Bebbington, P., Tennant, C. & Hurry, J. (1985). The list of threatening experiences: A subset of 12 life event categories with considerable long-term contextual threat. *Psychological Medicine*, **15**, 189–194.

Brewin, C.R., MacCarthy, B. & Furnham, A. (1989). Social support in the face of adversity: The role of cognitive appraisal. *Journal of Research in Personality*, **23**, 2543–2572.

Bromet, E.J., Parkinson, D.K., Schulberg, H.C., Dunn, L.O. & Gondek, P.C. (1982). Mental health of residents near the Three Mile Island reactor: A comparative study of selected groups. *Journal of Preventive Psychiatry*, **1**, 225–274.

Brown, G.W., Andrews, B., Harris, T., Adler, Z. & Bridge, L. (1986). Social support, self-esteem and depression. *Psychological Medicine*, **16**, 813–831.

Burgess, A.W. & Holmstrom, L.L. (1974). Rape trauma syndrome. *American Journal of Psychiatry*, **131**, 981–986.

Burgess, A.W. & Holmstrom, L.L. (1978). *Rape: Crisis and Recovery*. Bowie, Md.: Brady.

Cohen, S. & McKay, G. (1984). Social support, stress, and the buffering hypothesis: A theoretical analysis. In A. Baum., J.E. Singer. & S.E. Taylor (Eds.), *Handbook of Psychology and Health*, pp. 253–267.

Cohen, S. & Wills, T.A. (1985). Stress, social support, and the buffering hypothesis. *Psychological Bulletin*, **2**, 310–357.

Collins, N.L. & Read, S.J. (1990). Adult attachment, working models, and relationship quality in dating couples. *Journal of Personality and Social Psychology*, **58**, 644–663.

Cook, J.D. & Bickman, L. (1990). Social support and psychological symptomatology following natural disaster. *Journal of Traumatic Stress*, **3**, 541–556.

Cutrona, C.E. & Russell, D.W. (1990). The role of coping in support provision: The self-presentational dilemma of victims of life crisis. In B.R. Sarason, I.G. Sarason & G.R. Pierce (Eds.), *Social Support: An Interactional View*, pp. 319–366. New York: Wiley.

Dakof, G.A. & Taylor, S.E. (1990). Victims' perceptions of social support: What is helpful from whom? *Journal of Personality and Social Psychology*, **58**, 80–89.

Dalgleish, T., Joseph, S., Thrasher, S., Tranah, T. & Yule, W. (1996). Crisis support following the Herald of Free Enterprise disaster: A longitudinal perspective. *Journal of Traumatic Stress*, **9**, 833–845.

Dunkel-Schetter, C. & Bennett, T.L. (1990). Differentiating the cognitive and behavioral aspects of social support. In B.R. Sarason., I.G. Sarason & G.R. Pierce (Eds.), *Social Support: An Interactional View*, pp. 267–296. New York: Wiley.

Erikson, K.T. (1976). *Everything in its Path*. New York: Simon & Schuster.

Escobar, J.I., Randolph, E.T., Puente, G., Spivak, F., Assamen, J.K., Hill, M. & Hough, R.L. (1983). Post traumatic stress disorder in Hispanic veterans: Clinical phenomenology and sociocultural characteristics. *Journal of Nervous and Mental Disease*, **171**, 585–596.

Feeney, J.A. & Noller, P. (1990). Attachment style as a predictor of adult romantic relationships. *Journal of Personality and Social Psychology*, **58**, 281–291.

Figley, C.R. (1986). Traumatic stress: The role of the family and social support system. In C.R. Figley (Ed.), *Trauma and its Wake, vol. II: Traumatic Stress Theory, Research, and Intervention*. New York: Brunner/Mazel.

Flannery, R.B. (1990). Social support and psychological trauma: A methodological review. *Journal of Traumatic Stress*, **3**, 593–611.

Fleming, R., Baum, A., Gisriel, M. & Gatchel, R. (1982). Mediating influences of social support on stress at Three Mile Island. *Journal of Human Stress*, **8**, 14–22.

Folkman, S. & Lazarus, R.S. (1985). If it changes it must be a process: A study of emotion and coping during three stages of a college examination. *Journal of Personality and Social Psychology*, **48**, 150–170.

Folkman, S. & Lazarus, R.S. (1986). Stress processes and depressive symptomatology. *Journal of Abnormal Psychology*, **95**, 107–113.

Folkman, S. & Lazarus, R.S. (1988). Coping as a mediator of emotion. *Journal of Personality and Social Psychology*, **54**, 466–475.

Foy, D.W., Resnick, H.S., Sipprelle, R.C. & Carroll, E.M. (1987). Premilitary, military, and postmilitary factors in the development of combat-related stress disorders. *The Behavior Therapist*, **10**, 3–9.

Foy, D.W., Sipprelle, R.C., Rueger, D.B. & Carroll, E.M. (1984). Etiology of posttraumatic stress disorder in Vietnam veterans: Analysis of premilitary, military, and combat exposure influences. *Journal of Consulting and Clinical Psychology*, **52**, 79–87.

Francis, M.E. & Pennebaker, J.W. (1992). Putting stress into words: The impact of writing on physiological, absentee, and self-reported emotional well-being measures. *American Journal of Health Promotion*, **6**, 280–287.

Frye, J. & Stockton, R.A. (1982). Discriminant analysis of posttraumatic stress disorder among a group of Vietnam veterans. *American Journal of Psychiatry*, **139**, 52–56.

Goldberg, D.P. & Hillier, V.F. (1979). A scaled version of the General Health Questionnaire. *Psychological Medicine*, **9**, 139–145.

Green, B.L., Grace, M.C. & Gleser, G.C. (1985). Identifying survivors at risk: Long-term impairment following the Beverly Hills Supper Club fire. *Journal of Consulting and Clinical Psychology*, **53**, 672–678.

Greenberg, M.A. & Stone, A.A. (1992). Writing about disclosed versus undisclosed traumas: Immediate and long-term effects on mood and health. *Journal of Personality and Social Psychology*, **63**, 75–84.

Gruen, R.J. (1993). Stress and depression: Toward the development of integrative models. In L. Goldberger & S.Breznitz (Eds.), *Handbook of Stress*, pp. 550–569. New York: Macmillan.

Harvey, J.H., Agostinelli, G. & Weber, A.L. (1989). Account-making and formation of expectations about close relationships. *Review of Personality and Social Psychology*, **10**, 39–62.

Harvey, J.H., Orbuch, T.L. & Weber, A.L. (1990). A social psychological model of account making in response to severe stress. *Journal of Language and Social Psychology*, **9**, 191–207.

Harvey, J.H., Orbuch, T.L., Chwalisz, D. & Garwood, G. (1991). Coping with sexual assault: The roles of account-making and confiding. *Journal of Traumatic Stress*, **4**, 515–531.

Hazan, C. & Shaver, P. (1987). Romantic love conceptualised as an attachment process. *Journal of Personality and Social Psychology*, **52**, 511–524.

Hobfoll, S.E. (1988). *The Ecology of Stress*. Washington, DC: Hemisphere.

Hobfoll, S.E., Freedy, J., Lane, C. & Geller, P. (1990). Conservation of social resources: Social support resource theory. *Journal of Social and Personal Relationships*, **7**, 465–478.

Hobfoll, S.E. & London, P. (1985). The relationship of self-concept and social support to emotional distress among women during war. *Journal of Social and Clinical Psychology*, **3**, 231–248.

Horowitz, M.J. (1986). *Stress Response Syndromes* (2nd Edition). Northvale, N.J.: Jason Aronson.

Horowitz, M., Wilner, N. & Alvarez, W. (1979). Impact of Event Scale: A measure of subjective distress. *Psychosomatic Medicine*, **41**, 209–218.

Jacobs, M.K. & Goodman, G. (1989). Psychology and self-help groups: Predictions on a partnership. *American Psychologist*, **44**, 536–545.

Jacobson, D.E. (1986). Types and timing of social support. *Journal of Health and Social Behavior*, **27**, 250–264.

Janoff-Bulman, R. (1985). The aftermath of victimization: Rebuilding shattered assumptions. In C.R. Figley (Ed.), *Trauma and its Wake*, pp. 15–35. New York: Brunner/Mazel.

Janoff-Bulman, R. (1992). *Shattered Assumptions: Towards a New Psychology of Trauma*. New York: The Free Press.

Jones, J.C. & Barlow, D.H. (1990). The etiology of post-traumatic stress disorder. *Clinical Psychology Review*, **10**, 299–328.

Joseph, S., Andrews, B., Williams, R. & Yule, W. (1992). Crisis support and psychiatric symptomatology in adult survivors of the Jupiter cruise ship disaster. *British Journal of Clinical Psychology*, **31**, 63–73.

Joseph, S., Brewin, C.R., Yule, W. & Williams, R. (1991). Causal attributions and psychiatric symptoms in survivors of the Herald of Free Enterprise disaster. *British Journal of Psychiatry*, **159**, 542–546.

Joseph, S., Williams, R. & Yule, W. (1992). Crisis support, attributional style, coping style, and post-traumatic symptoms. *Personality and Individual Differences*, **13**, 1249–1251.

Joseph, S., Yule, W., Williams, R. & Andrews, B. (1993). Crisis support in the aftermath of disaster: A longitudinal perspective. *British Journal of Clinical Psychology*, **32**, 177–185.

Joseph, S., Yule, W., Williams, R. & Hodgkinson, P. (1994) Correlates of post-traumatic stress at 30 months: the Herald of Free Enterprise disaster. *Behaviour Research and Therapy*, **32**, 521–524.

Keane, T.M., Scott, W.O., Chavoya, G.A., Lamparski, D.M. & Fairbank, J.A. (1985). Social support in Vietnam veterans with posttraumatic stress disorder: A comparative analysis. *Journal of Consulting and Clinical Psychology*, **53**, 95–102.

Lebowitz, L. & Roth, S. (1994). "I felt like a slut": The cultural context and women's response to being raped. *Journal of Traumatic Stress*, **7**, 363–390.

Lehman, D.R. & Hemphill, K.J. (1990). Recipients' perception of support attempts and attributions for support attempts that fail. *Journal of Social and Personal Relationships*, **7**, 563–574.

Levy, M.B. & Davis, K.E. (1988). Lovestyles and attachment styles compared: Their relations to each other and to various relationship characteristics. *Journal of social and Personal Relationships*, **5**, 439–471.

Madakasira, S. & O'Brien, K.F. (1987). Acute posttraumatic stress disorder in victims of a natural disaster. *Journal of Nervous and Mental Disease*, **175**, 286–290.

McFarlane, A.C. (1987). Family functioning and overprotection following a natural disaster: The longitudinal effects of post-traumatic morbidity. *Australian and New Zealand Journal of Psychiatry*, **21**, 210–218.

Mikulincer, M. & Erev, I. (1991). Attachment styles and the structure of romantic love. *British Journal of Social Psychology*, **30**, 273–291.

Mikulincer, M., Florian, V. & Weller, A. (1993). Attachment styles, coping strategies, and posttraumatic psychological distress: The impact of the Gulf war in Israel. *Journal of Personality and Social Psychology*, **64**, 817–826.

Mikulincer, M. & Nachshon, O. (1991). Attachment styles and patterns of self-disclosure. *Journal of Personality and Social Psychology*, **61**, 273–280.

Pakenham, K.I., Dadds, M.R. & Terry, D.J. (1994). Relationships between adjustment to HIV and both social support and coping. *Journal of Consulting and Clinical Psychology*, **62**, 1194–1203.

Pennebaker, J.W. (1993). Putting stress into words: Health, linguistic, and therapeutic implications. *Behaviour Research and Therapy*, **31**, 539–548.

Pennebaker, J.W. & Beall, S. (1986). Confronting a traumatic event: Toward an understanding of inhibition and disease. *Journal of Abnormal Psychology*, **95**, 274–281.

Pennebaker, J.W., Hughes, C.F. & O'Heeron, R.C. (1987). The psychophysiology of confession: Linking inhibitory and psychosomatic processes. *Journal of Personality and Social Psychology*, **52**, 781–793.

Pennebaker, J.W., Kiecolt-Glaser, J.K. & Glaser, R. (1988). Disclosures of traumas and immune functioning: Health implications for psychotherapy. *Journal of Consulting and Clinical Psychology*, **56**, 239–245.

Pennebaker, J.W. & O'Heeron, R.C. (1984). Confiding in others and illness rates among spouses of suicide and accidental death victims. *Journal of abnormal Psychology*, **93**, 473–476.

Perry, S., Difede, J., Musngi, G., Frances, A.J. & Jacobsberg, L. (1992). Predictors of posttraumatic stress disorder after burn injury. *American Journal of Psychiatry*, **149**, 931–935.

Raphael, B. (1986). *When Disaster Strikes*. Hutchinson, London.

Robinson, R.C. & Mitchell, J.T. (1993). Evaluation of psychological debriefings. *Journal of Traumatic Stress*, **6**, 367–382.

Russell, D., Cutrona, C.E., Rose, J. & Yurko, K. (1984). Social and emotional loneliness: An examination of Weiss's typology of loneliness. *Journal of Personality and Social Psychology*, **46**, 1313–1321.

Sarason, B.R., Sarason, I.G. & Pierce, G.R. (1990). Traditional views of social support and their impact on assessment. In B.R. Sarason., I.G. Saraston & G.R. Pierce (Eds.), *Social support: An Interactional View*, pp. 9–25. New York: Wiley.

Siegman, A.W., Anderson, R.A. & Berger, T. (1990). The angry voice: Its effects on the experience of anger and cardiovascular reactivity. *Psychosomatic Medicine*, **52**, 631–643.

Silver, R.L., Boon, C. & Stones, M.H. (1983). Searching for meaning in misfortune: Making sense of incest. *Journal of Social Issues*, **39**, 81–102.

Silver, R., Wortman, C.B. & Crofton, A. (1990). The role of coping in support provision: The self-presentational dilemma of victims of life crisis. In B.R. Sarason, I.G. Saraston & G.R. Pierce (Eds.), *Social Support: An Interactional View*, pp. 397–426. New York: Wiley.

Solkoff, N., Gray, P. & Keill, S. (1986). Which Vietnam veterans develop post-traumatic stress disorders. *Journal of Clinical Psychology*, **42**, 687–698.

Solomon, S. (1986). Mobilizing social support networks in times of disaster. In C. Figley (Ed.), *Trauma and its Wake, vol. 2: Traumatic Stress Theory, Research, and Intervention*, pp. 232–263. New York: Brunner/Mazel.

Solomon, Z., Mikulincer, M. & Avitzur, E. (1988). Coping, locus of control, social support, and combat related posttraumatic stress disorder: A prospective study. *Journal of Personality and Social Psychology*, **55**, 279–285.

Solomon, Z., Mikulincer, M. & Hobfoll, S.E. (1986). Effects of social support and battle intensity on loneliness and breakdown during combat. *Journal of Personality and Social Psychology*, **51**, 1269–1276.

Spielberger, C.D., Gorsuch, R.L. & Lushene, R.E. (1970). *Test Manual for the State-Trait Anxiety Inventory*. Palo Alto, CA: Consulting Psychologists Press.

Stiles, W.B. (1987). "I have to talk to somebody": A fever model of disclosure. In V.J. Derlega & J.H. Berg (Eds.), *Self-disclosure: Theory, Research, and Therapy*, pp. 257–282. New York: Plenum Press.

Stiles, W.B., Shuster, P.L. & Harrigan, J.A. (1992). Disclosure and anxiety: A test of the fever model. *Journal of Personality and Social Psychology*, **63**, 980–988.

Stretch, R.H. (1985). Posttraumatic stress disorder among U.S. Army reserve Vietnam and Vietnam-era veterans. *Journal of Consulting and Clinical Psychology*, **53**, 935–936.

Stretch, R.H. (1986). Incidence and etiology of post-traumatic stress disorder among active duty personnel. *Journal of Applied Social Psychology*, **16**, 461–481.

Summerfield, D. (1993). War and posttraumatic stress disorder: The question of social context. *Journal of Nervous and Mental Disease*, **181**, 522.

Taylor, S.E., Lichtman, R.R. & Wood, J.V. (1984). Attributions, beliefs in control, and adjustment to breast cancer. *Journal of Personality and Social Psychology*, **46**, 489–502.

Titchener, J.L. (1986). Post-traumatic decline: A consequence of unresolved destructive drives. In C.R. Figley (Ed.), *Trauma and its Wake, vol. II: Traumatic Stress Theory, Research, and Intervention*. New York: Brunner/Mazel.

Weber, A.L., Harvey, J.H. & Stanley, M.A. (1987). The nature and motivations of accounts for failed relationships. In R. Burnett., P. McGhee & D.C. Clarke. (Eds.), *Accounting for Relationships*, pp. 114–113, London, Methuen.

Weiss, R.S. (1973). *Loneliness. The Experience of Emotional and Social Isolation*. Cambridge, MA: MIT Press.

Weiss, R.S. (1974). The provisions of social relationships. In Z. Rubin (Ed.), *Doing unto Others* pp. 17–26. Englewood Cliffs, NJ: Prentice Hall.

Weiss, R.S. (1976). Transition states and other stressful situations: Their nature and programs for their management. In G. Caplan & M. Killilea (Eds.), *Support systems and mutual help: Multi-disciplinary explorations*, pp. 213–232. New York: Grune & Stratton.

Wethington, E. & Kessler, R.C. (1986). Perceived support, received support, and adjustment to stressful life events. *Journal of Health and social Behaviour*, **27**, 78–89.

Wigren, J. (994). Narrative completion in the treatment of trauma. *Psychotherapy*, **31**, 415–423.

Wilkinson, C.B. (1983). Aftermath of a disaster: The collapse of the Hyatt Regency skywalks. *American Journal of Psychiatry*, **140**, 1134–1139.

Williams, R.M., Hodgkinson, P., Joseph, S. & Yule, W. (1995). Attitudes to emotion, crisis support and distress 30 months after the capsize of a passenger ferry. *Crisis Intervention*, **1**, 209–214.

Williams, R.M., Joseph, S. & Yule, W. (1993). Disaster and mental health. In J. Leff & D. Bhugra (Eds.), *Principles of Social Psychiatry*. Oxford: Blackwell.

Winemiller, D.R., Mitchell, M.E., Sutliff, J. & Cline, D.J. (1993). Measurement strategies in social support: A descriptive review of the literature. *Journal of Clinical Psychology*, **49**, 638–648.

Chapter 5

PERSONALITY AND POST-TRAUMATIC STRESS DISORDER

*Ruth Williams**

INTRODUCTION

Personality theory and research which went through an identity crisis in the 1970s and 1980s with the person–situation controversy and an apparently unending debate between trait-theorists about the number and nature of the necessary factors, has entered a new phase. The 1990s have seen a convergence of thinking and research activity around the "Big 5" personality factors (McCrea & Costa, 1990) fuelled in part by a renewed interest in personality disorders which have been mapped onto the Big 5 dimensions (Widiger & Costa, 1994). It would still, nevertheless, be appropriate to consider our understanding of the term "personality", which has important methodological implications.

Pervin (1993), reviewing the major approaches to personality, considers psychodynamic, person-centred, trait, behavioural, social-cognitive and information-processing models, all of which have their contemporary adherents. Hence, personality can be defined in a great variety of ways: in terms of defence mechanisms, a constellation of traits, a tendency to form conditioned responses, schematic contructs about the self, the world and other people, etc. No one view can be said to dominate the field and Pervin carefully considers their relative advantages and disadvantages. Although the Big 5 is generating support, there are some who have pointed out inadequacies. McAdams (1992) considers that the 5 Factor model is "a 'psychology of the stranger', providing information about persons that one would need to know when one knows nothing else about them" (McAdams,1992, p. 330). The 5 Factor traits give us a *description* of

*Institute of Psychiatry, London

Post-Traumatic Stress Disorders: Concepts and Therapy. Edited by William Yule.
© 1999 John Wiley & Sons Ltd.

a person but no *explanation* about how a person's traits are integrated and organised.

Pervin points out how different theories take up differing implicit philosophical views of the person and, with these views, differing positions on the causes of behaviour and, specifically, on the weight placed upon internal versus external factors in their interaction.

The neurotic disorders have, by definition, been seen to be rooted in personality as an internal and sometimes biologically based concept, with or without important developmental origins. PTSD stands out in the nosology as a disorder that has an explicitly external cause in a traumatic event that has implied for some that internal, "personality" factors have less relevance.

However, as Clark, Watson and Mineka (1994) point out in their review of personality and distress disorders, personality can affect PTSD in various ways and these may not be mutually exclusive:

1. Personality can affect the individual's vulnerability to develop PTSD, although there are relatively few studies that can test this hypothesis directly.
2. Personality characteristics can affect the course or expression of PTSD, i.e. a disorder may be modified or maintained as a result of personality-related factors.
3. Personality can be affected by the experience of PTSD (the "scar" hypothesis, usually conceived of as a negative change but not universally so in the PTSD literature).
4. Personality and PTSD reflect the same underlying process (the "continuity" hypothesis).

The review which follows will be organised under these headings. The view of personality that is taken will reflect an interactionist model of personality, varying between trait and cognitive-behavioural models. There are some suggestions that these two types of model are reconcilable: Marshall, Wortman, Vickers, Kusulas and Hervig (1994) carried out a factor analytic study of the NEO-Five Factor Personality Inventory (NEO-FFI; Costa & McCrea, 1989) with a number of other instruments from Health Psychology purporting to assess specific health-related personality attributes or attitudes (such as Optimism and Self-control) and found the health psychology scales to reflect complex mixtures of the five factors. The authors point to the advantages of a unified network of health personality scales anchored to basic personality factors in guiding future research. They also point out that constructs related to the factors of Openness and Conscientiousness have been little explored in health psychology. The same could be said for the PTSD literature.

PERSONALITY AS VULNERABILITY TO PTSD

It follows from the introduction that there are ideological positions in relation to this issue. In Horowitz's information-processing model (Horowitz, 1986), for instance, emphasis is given to the nature of schemata of the self and the world, existing prior to the experience of trauma and with which novel and traumatic information are incompatible. On the external side of the debate, Keane, Zimmering and Caddell (1985) have described a model for PTSD that relies on conditioning occurring at the time of the trauma with little or no reference to previous personality factors. Ideology is one of a number of influences cogently dissected by McFarlane (1990) (himself an advocate of the vulnerability view) to explain the recent relative neglect of this topic, whereas several earlier reviews (e.g. Andreasen & Noyes, 1972, for burn patients; Worthington, 1978, for combat trauma) have implicated previous personality in the aetiology of PTSD. Other influences include political pressures and the need for social justice in the treatment of Vietnam veterans. Exposing previous vulnerability tends to be interpreted by survivors in terms of self-blame and underplays the supreme importance of the trauma; in studying previous personality, researchers run the risk of alienating the survivor group upon whose collaboration their work depends. The study of soldiers and emergency workers tends to underestimate the influence of personality since the especially vulnerable will have been screened out. Furthermore, McFarlane argues that events are not independent of personality, and traumatic experiences can result from adverse mental states and personality traits as well as vice versa. Finally, there are important methodological problems: the difficulty of prospective studies, the problems of sampling bias and choice of personality measures.

McFarlane's view (1990) is that, even with the most devastating disasters, the incidence of PTSD is rarely greater than 50%, and this has to be explained. However, what this somewhat sweeping statement actually means is not entirely clear. The diagnosis of PTSD requires a certain configuration of symptoms, over a certain duration of time and these criteria have changed over the 15 years since the term was originally introduced. Indeed, PTSD might be considered a socially constructed concept influenced, for instance, by the requirements of the law in settling litigation disputes. Prevalence estimates may vary due to differing criteria used. Many survivors experience subclinical syndromes with some, but not all, categories of symptoms which, although not reaching criteria, may be distressing to a not insignificant degree. Some writers (Creamer, Burgess & Pattison, 1990; Williams, Joseph & Yule, 1994) have suggested that the different groups of symptoms comprising the PTSD syndrome may be functionally distinct. The re-experiencing symptoms often, but not always, co-vary with avoidant symptoms and it has been argued that the former represent the specific hall-marks of the experience of trauma, although survivors who show intrusive thinking without avoidant responses do not reach criteria for disorder. The experience of surviving a trauma, such as a war or a natural disaster, is also not a unitary phenomenon. Just as it is said that every individual has his/her own war, so it is observed when talking to survivors of the same event that each person's experience is unique. Thus an overall percentage for a particular event is not very meaningful. Whereas it is clear that interpersonal variability exists in the severity and particularly in the duration of distress, it is not clear how the "normal" person responds to the experience of the sudden and realistic threat of personal annihilation, and to what extent some or all of the symptoms of PTSD represent a "normal" response to an abnormal event as Horowitz's model would suggest, pathological variations being matters of degree rather than type.

Theory

Jones and Barlow's (1990) review of aetiological models makes plain that some current approaches draw upon ideas of pre-existing vulnerability, e.g. Foa, Steketee and Olasov-Rothbaum (1989) specify the importance of traumatic fear structures generated at the time of the trauma, contravening previously held assumptions of safety, hence implicating a role for previously established knowledge structures. The consequences of this element for individual differences in response, however, are not discussed. The role of previous personality structures is most fully discussed by Horowitz (1986) and Horowitz et al. (1993).

In Horowitz's theory, PTSD is seen as the consequence of the individual's failure to integrate traumatic information with previously held schematic constructions of the self, the world and other people. PTSD arises as a result of a normal process of schematic revision and adaptation becoming blocked. Difficulties in processing may arise in a variety of ways. One of these sources of difficulty is the nature of pre-existing cognitive schemata, described by Horowitz et al. (1993) in relation to abnormal grief, as "person schemas", which organise the selection, processing, retention and behavioural aspects of interpersonal relationships, including information about relative roles and characteristics of self and others and plans for behaviour in interactions. In relation to abnormal grief, although not to PTSD as such, Horowitz et al. (1993) hypothesise that the individual's ability to revise schemas during mourning will depend partly upon the pre-existing ambivalence or contradictions inherent in pre-existing person schemas. The activation of these "latent" schemas will result in alarming contradictory thoughts and feelings (perhaps associated with anger, guilt and dependency issues) that may be perceived as difficult to control and integrate.

Janoff-Bulman (1985) speculates further about the nature of the impact of trauma upon personality structures. Specifically, she hypothesises that core beliefs about the invulnerability and basic moral worth of the self and the world as following meaningful rules may be "shattered" by the experience of trauma. "Shattered" implies that the individual moves from one absolute extreme of a dimension to the opposite pole: from "invulnerable" to "vulnerable", from "good" to "bad", from "meaningful" to "meaningless". It is not clear whether Janoff-Bulman is describing a normal process or an abnormal one. Presumably beliefs which can be shattered are not securely held in the first place. Or they are structured inflexibly in a rigid, black and white way and in an overgeneralised, undifferentiated way such that an instance of, for example, lack of control will lead to a powerful sense of generalised vulnerability.

Beck and Emery (1985) suggest that anxiety states may result from the activation of dysfunctional assumptions, a subtype of schemas which specify the conditions an individual perceives to be necessary to maintain safety and self-esteem. These dysfunctional rules differ from more adaptive ones in being rigid and inflexible, absolute and overgeneralised. Beck and Emery do not discuss PTSD specifically but, if so generalisable, their theory would suggest that one route to PTSD might be the prior development of dysfunctional assumptions relating to vulnerability, which potentiate an automatic conclusion being drawn in extreme and overgeneralised terms and associated with intense affect. Rather than the experience of a trauma disconfirming previously held beliefs, Beck and Emery's theory would suggest that, for some vulnerable individuals, the trauma confirms their worst fears: e.g. if I am not perfectly in control all the time, all hell will let loose.

Controllability is a key element of Jones and Barlow's (1990) model of PTSD. They hypothesise that the origins of anxiety may involve a biological vulnerability to stress that may be genetically transmitted (? neuroticism). But important in the development of a disorder are also the psychological attributions of controllability and predictability made about the biological response, such that a state of alarm that is perceived as uncontrollable and unpredictable will lead to a generalised state of overarousal, overvigilance and selective attention for fear of the alarm recurring. Such attributions will be affected by early learning history, specifically experiences of control or lack of control. Thus, there are two sources of vulnerability within Jones and Barlow's model—i.e. biological and psychological—that could both be described within the rubric of personality. Jones and Barlow make an explicit comparison with the aetiology of other anxiety states, especially Panic Disorder which parallels their model of PTSD.

RESEARCH EVIDENCE

Research with a design powerful enough to test the vulnerability model is sparse, since individuals have rarely been identified for study in advance of a traumatic event. Some less convincing data have been collected retrospectively from traumatised individuals and are subject to biases in recall or report which may result from the passage of time and the state of being a survivor. In many cases the measures used have had to be indirect and their validity as reflections of personality is arguable. Where personality variables have been measured, the personality domain has not been assessed in a systematic way to sample over the full range of the Big 5 factors. Another problem relates to the timing of the study and identification of traumatised individuals: some studies have been so long after the event as to obscure the difference between predisposition and maintenance being made in this chapter. Finally it should be noted that no measures of the key theoretical variables, such as schema involved in the theoretical models outlined above, have been used and their development is proving problematic.

In an attempt to disentangle the influences of personality upon onset and maintenance of PTSD, only studies that have assessed subjects within months of the impact will be considered here.

Retrospective Studies

Still one of the most useful and careful studies of the course of reactions to trauma is the study by Weisaeth (1984) of the entire population of survivors of a paint factory fire in Sweden. Weisaeth carried out a descriptive study of disaster behaviours during impact and in the post-impact period. His study suggests that immediately post-disaster, anxiety was almost universal, 90% experienced a resurgence of anxiety in the hours after rescue or escape; 61% experienced distressing tremor and at least 33% of the most severely exposed reported palpitations, sweating and dysphoria. Weisaeth found that symptoms decreased rapidly over the first four weeks, particularly those that were less severe initially. Initial severity of response was predictive of disorder seven months later, but he found other variables to be predictive including adaptational problems in childhood and adult life, previous psychiatric impairment, high psychosomatic reactivity and character pathology.

McFarlane has carried out a series of studies important for the nature of the population surveyed: a community sample, not a patient group, of relatively well-adjusted professionals exposed to the same type of trauma. In the first study (McFarlane, 1987), a population of firefighters involved in severe and life- and property-threatening bush fires in Australia in 1983, was surveyed four months later to assess the level of exposure, previous life-events and psychiatric symptomatology. Using the GHQ (General Health Questionnaire: Goldberg, 1972) as a measure of psychiatric impairment, not specifically a measure of PTSD, McFarlane found the prevalence of disorder to be 23–30%. Little of the variance in symptomatology, however, could be attributed to either previous life events or degree of traumatic exposure. McFarlane argued that his data suggested that disaster acts as a trigger to psychiatric impairment in individuals who are already vulnerable. The sample was followed up for two further surveys (see below.) A pre-disaster personality factor, Neuroticism, assessed with the EPQ (Eysenck Personality Inventory: Eysenck & Eysenck, 1964)—modified to enquire about personality *before* the disaster and measured *subsequently* by a questionnaire 29 months after the disaster—contributed significantly to the variance of GHQ at four months, adding support to McFarlane's hypothesis about personality vulnerability contributing to the aetiology of psychiatric symptoms after a trauma. McFarlane admits, however, that only 29% of the variance in his sample was accounted for at this first point in his series of studies.

As part of a nationwide general population epidemiology survey of psychiatric disorders, Helzer, Robins and McEnvoy (1987) report that among 2,493 participants, the incidence of PTSD was low (1–3.5%) but higher in Vietnam veterans exposed to combat (20%). Evidence of antisocial behavioural problems before the age of 15 years was predictive of PTSD in veterans and also in survivors of attacks and other forms of trauma. However, such childhood problems were also predictive of combat experience itself in veterans and of the experience of being mugged or assaulted in the preceding 18 months. Such data then would lend support to McFarlane and others' contention that events in life are not independent of personality. Clark, Watson and Mineka (1994) argue that personality traits that lead to repeated experiences of stressors may sensitise the individual, raising the level of trait Neuroticism that acts as a vulnerability factor for anxiety disorders and PTSD.

This interpretation is consistent with the results of another community survey (Breslau, Davis, Andreski & Peterson, 1991) of people in their twenties. They found that a prior history specifically of anxiety disorders, rather than a psychiatric history more generally, predisposed to PTSD, whereas a prior history of antisocial tendencies raised the risk of exposure to trauma.

Prospective Studies

One recent longitudinal study of interest—although the "traumatic" experience in question was combat training and not a specific traumatic event as such and the interval is short—is a study by Florian, Mikulincer and Taubman (1995). They assessed a large group of Israeli Defence Forces recruits ($n = 274$) before and after a four-month period of intensive training in an infantry unit. All were healthy men, aged 18 years and single, most of whom had completed high school education. The researchers found that two components of a measure of "hardiness" (see p. 105 for further description of this variable), commitment and control, before training predicted mental health after training. Furthermore, structural path analyses revealed that these effects were mediated by the choice of coping strategies that reduced threat and increased problem-focused coping and support seeking. This study illustrates some of the problems in selection bias discussed above but is one of the few which demonstrates a predictive role of a specific personality factor.

Another relevant study is by Nolen-Hoeksema and Morrow (1991) who studied reactions to a trauma in a group of college students. However, the researchers assessed not PTSD but depression. They selected out of their depression measure a subset of items which were consistent with diagnostic criteria, to use as a measure of PTSD. Nolen-Hoeksema and Morrow had assessed style of responding to symptoms as well as psychological health 14 days before the 1989 Loma Prieta earthquake in San Francisco, in a group of 250 students. Depressive and PTSD symptoms were reassessed at 10 days and 7 weeks post-earthquake. At 10 days, PTSD was predicted by pre-disaster PTSD scores, disaster experiences and pre-disaster assessed ruminative and distractive responses. Together these variables accounted for 47% variance of 10 day PTSD. At seven weeks, only ruminative style predicted depression, although accounting for only 14% of the variance. Only pre-disaster PTSD predicted seven week PTSD. However, post-disaster 10 day ruminations about the disaster predicted seven week PTSD. This differentiation between style of responding and ruminations about the earthquake disaster raises a question about how general a personality factor the response style measure is. Nevertheless, given the overlap of depression and PTSD, it is interesting that previous ruminative response style can predict post-disaster depression rather than disaster experiences themselves. It is also interesting that predictors change rapidly within the 10 day–7 week interval, given the rarity of immediate aftermath investigations. It may be very important what coping intervenes between impact and the interval at which PTSD can be diagnosed.

Conclusions

The scarcity of research in this area is marked in comparison with the richness of theory. It might tentatively be suggested that trait Neuroticism, which may be inversely related to Hardiness, may predispose to the development of relatively severe and enduring PTSD, as it does to the development of depression and other anxiety disorders (Clark, Watson & Mineka, 1994). It may be that antisocial traits may also give rise to an increased risk of trauma and, thereby increase sensitisation. The relevance of other personality factors has been little explored. How Neuroticism and other personality factors relate to person schemas, dysfunctional assumptions and other theoretical constructs has as yet been little studied. The necessity of identifying populations at risk of subsequent trauma and assessing personality systematically is important to carry this area of great theoretical and practical significance forward.

PERSONALITY FACTORS AFFECT COURSE OR EXPRESSION OF PTSD

This aspect of the impact of personality has been given less theoretical attention than vulnerability but, in view of the high prevalence of population distress in the immediate aftermath found in those few studies available (Weisaeth, 1984), it would seem an important area for further work. This review will consider recent theory (Williams, 1989; Horowitz et al., 1993; Joseph, Williams & Yule, 1995) and related research; retrospective and prospective studies of vulnerability to chronic PTSD.

There is a potential overlap between "personality" and concepts of coping style such as locus of control and attributional style. Work within the coping framework, often considered as more flexible than the personality construct suggests, will be excluded from this discussion as it is reviewed elsewhere in this Volume (Joseph, Chapter 3).

A neglected area of considerable interest is the delineation of personality characteristics that help an individual to adapt to challenge. Some interesting ideas are suggested by Flach (1990) and Lyons (1991).

Theory

Williams (1989) advanced a cognitive-behavioural theory of chronic PTSD which focused on factors that maintained disorder in traumatised individuals. Drawing upon Beck's concept of dysfunctional assumptions (Kovacs & Beck, 1978), it was suggested that negative attitudes to emotional states and their expression could lead to strong avoidant tendencies (behavioural, cognitive and emotional) that block processing of traumatic information. This theory, then, is an elaboration of Horowitz's model. Horowitz et al. (1993) in a recent discussion of abnormal grief, make a similar suggestion and draw upon the concepts of information-monitoring versus blunting from health psychology (Miller, 1980) and repressors/sensitisers (Weinberger, Schwartz & Davidson, 1979) to denote personality types vulnerable to the maintainance of chronic dysfunction through overcontrol and avoidance.

Jones and Barlow's (1990) model also highlights an important role for attributional style which may exacerbate biological vulnerability by rendering stressful events or anxiety responses uncontrollable and unpredictable. Clark, Watson and Mineka (1994) link Barlow's model of alarm in panic (Barlow, 1988) and now in PTSD, to Anxious Sensitivity (Reiss, Peterson, Gursky & McNally, 1986) a personality dimension related to Neuroticism, but representing a specific fear of fear factor found to be high in PTSD (Taylor, Koch & McNally, 1992). Fear of fear is consistent with the other views of maintenance reviewed above.

Joseph, Williams and Yule (1995) have recently added to their model incorporating new ideas about obsessional thinking (Salkovskis, 1985) and generalised anxiety and worry (Wells & Matthews, 1994) which has suggested that thoughts and beliefs about cognitions themselves may lead to their repetition or avoidance. It may be that these patterns of thinking are related to background personality variables, such as Conscientiousness, which influence the maintenance of disorder.

Research on Personality in Chronic PTSD

It should be noted that research designs included under this heading do not allow for a distinction to be made between onset and maintenance factors. Studies have been included here since no clear implication about onset mechanisms can be drawn, but both interpretations remain possible.

McFarlane's review (1990) of research on Vietnam veterans concludes that the results are very inconsistent, some finding a contribution from premorbid personality (e.g. Wilson & Krauss, 1982), others not (e.g. Penk, Robinowitz & Roberts, 1981). However, the studies often have major methodological problems associated with sampling, retrospective measures, etc.

One study with Vietnam veterans is worthy of special mention, however, being a prospective study of a representative sample of men studied at age 15 and followed up 21 years later. In the interim some men had experienced combat in Vietnam or other wars, some had been in the military and not seen combat and some had not been enlisted. Card (1987) reports the comparisons between these three groups in incidence of PTSD and in the predictors of PTSD from measures of combat experience and personality at age 15 years. Card concludes that the predictions of PTSD almost exclusively related to battle experiences, with the exception of one measure (out of 10) of premorbid personality (low self-confidence) and one measure of military adjustment (excessive alcohol use). Card uses these data to conclude in favour of assigning most weight to the exogenous event in the aetiology of chronic PTSD in veterans. It is nevertheless of interest that the one adolescent personality variable that was predictive, relates to Horowitz's and cognitive-behavioural theories, which implicate the importance of schema about the self. The other variable, alcohol consumption, is consistent with the importance theoretically ascribed to avoidance in the maintenance of disorder. Both of these factors were measured 21 years prior to the index period.

Elder and Clipp (1989) also report a longitudinal study of a small group of men (n = 149) whose personalities were assessed with the California Q-sort test in adolescence and who were reassessed in adulthood after having served in either World War II or the Korean War. Although the authors emphasise the positive changes in personality, especially in those exposed to heavy combat stress, including marked *increases* in resilience over this long time interval, they found that the least resilient men in adolescence were those most likely to have emotional problems post-war.

Schnurr, Friedman and Rosenberg (1993) have recently reported another prospective study on a group of 131 Vietnam veterans who had taken the MMPI at college as freshmen and were interviewed at age 40 years using the Structured Clinical Interview for DSM-III-R for lifetime PTSD. Twenty subjects received the diagnosis of lifetime PTSD which was predicted by higher scores on the MMPI scales for Hypochondriasis, Psychopathic Deviate, Masculinity–Feminity and Paranoia, although the effect sizes were moderate, and group means were not highly elevated. The authors interpret these scores as suggesting that the premorbid personality of the PTSD veteran is characterised by "self-reports of gloominess, dissatisfaction, impulsivity and irritability . . . inhibition, shyness, withdrawal and conscientiousness" (Schnurr, Friedman & Bosenberg, 1993 p. 483). This study is notable for the nature of the instruments used, both in assessing personality and in diagnosing PTSD. The results are also interesting in view of the preceding theoretical discussion which emphasises the theoretical importance of avoidant strategies in maintaining dysfunction. Although one might criticise the premorbid profile as being a description of symptoms rather than personality attributes, i.e. profile attributes may reflect pre-existing psychological dysfunction rather than personality, this criticism is less easily applied to *normal range* scores as were found in this study. The MMPI scales of Masculinity and Psychopathic Deviate may allow of translation into Big 5 factors such as Extraversion and Conscientiousness. It should be noted that this study failed to show any effect of personality in the prediction of combat experiences.

McFarlane's follow-up studies of firefighters at 11 and 29 months reveal a decreasing contribution to symptomatology provided by trauma experience and more contribution from the pre-disaster variables: Neuroticism (accounting for 26% at 29 months), previously treated psychiatric disorder and a self-reported tendency to avoid thinking about negative events. McFarlane comments, however, that the contribution of N to symptoms is significantly smaller than has been found in other neurotic disorders, reflecting the relatively greater importance of the precipitating event in PTSD. He also points out that the total variance in symptoms is only very partially explained in his series of studies, suggesting that there are other important unexplained factors, such as social support.

Weisaeth's (1984) study, which included a follow-up of survivors from a Swedish fire up to four years after the disaster, similarly demonstrates an increasing importance of personality and previous psychiatric illness factors with increasing duration of time following the disaster.

Williams, Hodgkinson, Joseph and Yule (1995) tested their hypothesis regarding dysfunctional attitudes to emotion in a group of 73 survivors of a major shipping disaster, two to three years after the event. Higher endorsement of dysfunctional attitudes, asessed by means of a brief questionnaire (Attitudes to Emotional Expression—AEE), were associated with higher scores on some measures of symptomatology as assessed by the GHQ and the Impact of Event Scale (IES: Horowitz, Wilner & Alvarez, 1979). Interestingly, AEE was related to the Avoidance scale of the IES but not to the Intrusion scale. The authors argue that this differentiation supports the contention that their attitude to emotion measure reflects a maintenance factor rather than an onset mechanism. Williams et al. also found that their measure related, as predicted, to measures of received crisis support, survivors with more negative attitudes receiving less social support. Furthermore, Joseph, Dalgleish, Williams, Thrasher, Yule and Hodgkinson (1997) have continued to test for the importance of AEE in an additional follow-up survey in a group of 37 survivors of the same disaster two years later, five years after the disaster. More negative attitudes were associated with greater symptoms even when perceptions of helplessness at the time of the disaster and distress at three years were partialled out. The authors conclude that these data provide evidence of a causal link between AEE and the maintenance of psychological distress in PTSD.

Solomon, Mikulincer and Arad (1991) tested Horowitz's hypothesis regarding the effects of monitoring versus blunting strategies in a group of Israeli combat veterans, two years after suffering combat. Their results bore out the predictions that high monitoring/low blunting style was associated with lower symptomatology and problems in social functioning. An association was also found between information-processing style and choice of coping, monitors using more problem-focused coping and blunters more emotion-focused coping. The authors question whether these strategies represent stable, personality characteristics or whether choice of strategy depends on the nature of the stressor.

Conclusions

The research in this area seems to be more consistent in implicating personality characteristics to be associated with maintenance of disorder. The full range of personality attributes have not been assessed in these studies and it is not possible at present to relate the framework of the Big 5 to specific variables such as negative attitudes emotion and monitoring/blunting style with any certainty. Neuroticism seems implicated here but also, perhaps, other factors such as Extraversion, Conscientiousness and Agreeableness.

Resilience and Hardiness

Recently some increasing interest has appeared in the study of individuals who appear to function well following a trauma. Such an investment would seem promising if we wish to understand more about the influences of personality, particularly how personality can influence coping to aid integration of the meaning of a traumatic experience within the individual's world and self views.

Flach (1990) discusses the concept of "resilience" in relation to surviving a trauma. Resilience is defined as follows:

> Psychobiological resilience is the efficient blending of psychological, bio- ⊬
> logical and environmental elements that permits human beings . . . to transit
> episodes of chaos necessarily associated with significant periods of stress
> and change successfully. (Flach, 1990, p. 40)

Resilience is not therefore viewed exclusively in terms of internal characteristics but in terms of an interactive process.

Concentrating for the purposes of this chapter upon internal attributes, Flach cites a number of attributes which are clinically commonly thought to suggest a good prognosis. These are listed below, allied with an attempt, along with the orientation of this review, to relate these characteristics to the Big 5 factors.

- Insight (*Openness*)
- Flexible self-esteem (*Neuroticism*)
- Ability to learn from experience (*Openness*)
- Tolerance for stress (*Neuroticism*)
- Low tolerance for outrageous behaviour (*Conscientiousness*)
- Openmindedness (*Openness*)
- Courage (*Neuroticism, Conscientiousness*)
- Personal discipline (*Conscientiousness*)
- Creativity (*Openness*)
- Integrity (*Conscientiousness*)
- Sense of humour (*Openness, Neuroticism*)
- Constructive philosophy (*Openness, Conscientiousness*)
- Willingness to dream which inspires hope (*Openness*)

In the above tentative translation, factors familiar from discussion of disadvantageous attributes recur as one would expect. The striking new addition here is the factor of "Openness", associated with originality, artistic and creative interests, intellectual pursuits, fantasy and aesthetics (McCrea & John, 1991). This factor has been little investigated in studies of the effects of trauma and could be worth further exploration.

Lyons (1991) draws upon another concept in discussing personality attributes that predict resilence—that of "Hardiness" (Kobasa & Maddi, 1977). Orr and Westman (1990) describe the hardy personality as arising out of an existential concept of the "Authentic" personality. Hardiness is characterised by commitment, control and challenge.

> Commitment captures the authentic positive state of caring. . . . Control
> and challenge assess another major element of the authentic being:

courage . . . recognising hard facts, the personal belief that one is able to exert control over external and internal events, and attributing to stress the meaning of challenge. (Orr & Westman, 1990, pp. 67–68)

The overlap between Flach's concept of resilience and Hardiness is obvious, as is the overlap with Jones and Barlow's emphasis upon the importance of controllability and the implication of a strong and healthy positive self-schema in other theoretical literature.

Bartone, Ursano, Wright and Ingraham (1989) were the first to study the association of Hardiness and symptoms in a group of 191 assistance workers after a military air disaster. The workers were assessed by questionnaire six months and one year after the disaster. Highly significant associations were found between Hardiness and symptomatology with interactional effects between Hardiness and measures of exposure and social support. Interestingly, the highest symptoms were acknowledged by a low hardiness group with high support.

Hodgkinson and Shepherd (1994) also used a measure of Hardiness in assessing the impact of disaster work on a group of 73 disaster support social workers. Predicted relationships were found between Hardiness and symptom measures, low hardiness being associated with higher symptoms. The same relationship between Hardiness commitment and the diagnosis of PTSD was found in a large study of military personnel ($n = 775$) on return from the Persian Gulf War. Sutker, Davis, Uddo and Ditta (1995) used a discrimant functional analysis within which Hardiness was the strongest predictor, accounting for 26% of the variance. Although these are cross-sectional studies lacking the power to assess causality, Hardiness was a powerful predictor of symptoms in both, and Hodgkinson and Shepherd (1994) go so far as suggesting that considerations of Hardiness could be used in selecting individuals to work with disaster survivors. However, it should be noted that 85% of their sample considered that they had benefited from their work experience. Disaster work could also be a source of personal growth and increase in Hardiness, as suggested by Elder and Clipp's (1989) study. As Lyons (1991) points out, hardy individuals are people with experience of coping with stressors. Such experiences may lead to the acquisition of "complex schematic networks capable of integrating trauma (cf. *cognitive models*), richer learning history allowing for more effective stimulus discrimination and thus restricted generalisation of anxiety (*conditioning models*), and more complex neuronal structures (*psychobiological theories*)" (Lyons, 1991, p. 97; author's comments in parentheses).

(Such an attempted integration of personality, cognitive, behavioural and biological models is rare indeed in the literature and is worth quoting!)

Returning to the relation of Hardiness to the Big 5 factor model, Funk (1992) has suggested that it is equivalent to the inverse of Neuroticism. Florian, Mikulincer and Taubmaw (1995) addressed this issue in their study of Israeli recruits entering combat training. Their study found differential relationships with symptoms within the Hardiness measures of commitment, control and challenge, suggesting that Hardiness is not a unitary concept. They interpret their data as suggesting evidence of a direct link between low commitment and distress, consistent with Funk's hypothesis with regard to the commitment component of Hardiness. However, even after controlling for the commitment-distress link at time 1, the commitment and control elements still predicted symptoms at time 2 via the mediation of coping factors, consistent with the idea that "control" is an element independent of N. The purely speculative discussion above has suggested the importance of Conscientiousness and Openness. In one study which has looked at the five factors in trauma survivors with chronic PTSD, Hyer, Braswell, Albrecht, Boyd Boudewyns, and Talbert (1994) found PTSD symptoms to be largely accountable by high N in their sample of 80 male Vietnam veterans. They found significant associations of low Agreeableness and Conscientiousness with PTSD symptoms and suggest that Openness, A and C are all related to treatment outcome.

Conclusions

The research reviewed in this section seems to suggest a stronger association between some personality factors and maintenance of symptoms. The analysis of the concept of Hardiness or Resilience and the linking in of more specific factors with combinations of 5 Factor dimensions would seem profitable areas for further work. The lack of longitudinal studies, however, still limit the conclusions that can be drawn since personality may be affected by stress and trauma as some such studies have shown.

PTSD AFFECTS PERSONALITY

Such a process whereby trauma can affect personality has been heralded by the comments in the last paragraph, although much of the literature focuses upon negative changes, with studies of PTSD sufferers among Vietnam veterans. The *attribution* of personality change is relatively common among chronic PTSD sufferers and their relatives—more common perhaps than among those suffering from other chronic psychiatric conditions that have debilitating and global impact upon work and social functioning as well as upon the subjective sense of well-being. It is worth pondering upon how the distinction is made between the diagnosis of a chronic disorder and a change in personality. It is extremely likely that such an attribution of changed personality is just one cognitive process that would mitigate against integration of the trauma within the previous personality system and could be explainable in terms of black and white thinking, or the "shattering" of core assumptions about the self and the world, previously described. One of the changes introduced in the DSM-IV is the new category of Personality Change due to a General Medical Condition (310.1) but the criteria lack any critical power to differentiate it from an enduring distress disorder, relying upon persistence in time and a "marked" deviation in "pattern".

Elder and Clipp's (1989) study, previously noted, provide interesting and qualitatively rich descriptions of positive changes in outlook reported by their veterans, including learning to cope with adversity, valuing life more and having a clearer sense of direction. Marked increases in goal direction and resilience were found in their heavy combat subgroup, 25% of which had PTSD.

Sherwood, Funari and Piekarski (1990) see the long-term effects of PTSD as impacting upon personality and argue for intervention to address personality style as much as it does symptoms. In a controlled study of Vietnam veterans with and without PTSD, assessed with Millon's Clinical Multiaxial Inventory (MCMI: Millon, 1983) to measure personality style, Sherwood, Funari and Piekarski (1990) found a significant association between PTSD and Passive-Aggressive, Avoidant, Schizoid and Borderline personality. The most common feature was a combination of Avoidant and Passive-Aggressive patterns. They describe the personality as follows:

> Cognitively, the person has disruptive inner thoughts, a self-image which is alienated, and is beset by feeling misunderstood and unappreciated. The person has an aversive and ambivalent interpersonal adjustment and seeks gratification in fault finding and demoralising others. He is vigilant in looking for threats from others and overinterprets others' behaviour as malicious. He desires affection whilst often reacting to people in a cold (numbed) manner. Essentially, the character adjustment is ambivalent; desires for closeness and affection are frustrated by isolation and avoidance of intimacy based upon the expectation of being hurt and misunderstood. (Sherwood, Funari & Piekarski, 1990, p. 628)

In a second study of inpatient veterans, Piekarski, Sherwood and Funari (1993) used cluster analysis to isolate two personality profiles associated with PTSD. The most common they label as the Aggressive Stress group. A smaller cluster was also distinguished as the Dependent Stress group.

Hyer, Woods and Boudewyns (1991) also used the MCMI with a group of 100 Vietnam veterans with PTSD and found 88% to have the same Passive-Aggressive/Avoidant pattern reported by Sherwood, Funari and Piekarski (1990). Hyer, Woods and Boudewyns (1991) denote this pattern as the "Traumatic Personality" and point out that psychologically the style is similar to, although less severe than, the Borderline personality. Indeed, the ambivalent, needy but suspicious alternation of Borderline psychopathology is highlighted by Beck, Freeman et al. (1990) in their cognitive conceptualisation of Borderline Personality Disorder.

Hyer, McCranie, Boudewyns and Sperr (1996) recently report a further study of Vietnam veterans with chronic PTSD, linking symptoms and personality styles to coping strategies. Predictably, increased scores for PTSD symptoms were linked to increased escape/avoidance and confrontative coping and to less support-seeking and positive reappraisal. Together escape/avoidance, distancing, accepting responsibility and confrontative styles accounted for 75% of coping strategies and were associated with avoidant personality styles as measured by Millon's Multiaxial Inventory.

Talbert, Braswell, Albrecht, Hyer and Boudewyns (1993) (like Hyer et al. (1994) quoted above) employed the NEO Personality Inventory in studying a group of 100 Vietnam veterans, finding highly elevated Neuroticism and very low Agreeableness. Openness was in the low range whereas Conscientiousness was in the average range. The Extraversion scale showed high elevation on the Excitement-Seeking facet in contrast to average to very low scores on other facets such as Warmth, Gregariousness and Positive Emotions.

All of these studies carried out upon chronically disabled Vietnam veterans raise the question of the generalisability of their findings to other trauma and social contexts. One bit of evidence that suggests that some generalisation may be made comes from a study of the personality of burn patients at the point of discharge from physical treatment (Roca, Spence & Munster, 1992.) Patients were given the NEO Personality Inventory and then followed up for the development of PTSD four months later. Aspects of PTSD symptomatology were predicted by personality profiles: low Openness predicted re-experiencing symptoms; low Extraversion predicted avoidant/numbing symptoms; higher Neuroticism predicted increased arousal. The assessment of personality was carried out, in most cases, before the emergence of PTSD, hence the authors argue for aspects of personality being predictive of PTSD. The alternative is that the experience of surviving a severe burn may impact upon personality structures giving rise to a "scar" syndrome. If this is so, however, such changes can take place rapidly, within months of the trauma, rather than being the result of many years of chronic disablement.

Rather than viewing personality change as an exclusively negative outcome, Eberly, Harkness and Engdahl (1991) advance the view that increased Neuroticism may represent an adaptational change. They argue that increases in trait Neuroticism and PTSD symptoms have advantages within the traumatic environment of alerting the individual to danger, promoting rehearsal of escape/avoid strategies and thereby promoting the individual's survival.

Joseph, Williams and Yule (1993) report some preliminary work to develop a scale to assess positive as well as negative consequences of trauma. Items were drawn from a pool of responses given by survivors of a shipping disaster to an open question: Has the disaster changed your outlook on life for the better or for the worse? The resulting 40-item questionnaire was administered to 35 adult survivors of another shipping disaster. Higher responses to the negative items were associated with higher symptomatology, lower self-esteem, weaker just world beliefs and more internal attributions for negative events. Higher positive scale scores were associated with higher self-esteem.

Conclusions

Research and theory in this section suffer from a clear distinction being made between personality change and chronic disorder. However the *patterning* of attributes found in some studies may add weight to the personality argument, although many of these studies with Vietnam veterans need to be replicated with other survivors. Again the absence of good longitudinal studies has to be lamented.

PERSONALITY AND PTSD AS ONE PROCESS

The intimate relationships between personality and PTSD have been the subject of this chapter. The ultimate argument for their inextricability is to assert that PTSD is identical with a personality style. It has been suggested that the distinction between chronic disorder and personality lacks critical features and that, for example, Neuroticism may be largely attributable to symptoms which may be found to change over time or with treatment. Lonie (1993) draws attention to the various similarities between PTSD and Borderline Personality Disorder (BPD) and argues for their equivalence with the difference that, in BPD, the trauma has undergone repression or has occurred in an early, preverbal developmental period and has not been registered in a verbally retrievable form. Specifically she suggests that the BPD symptoms of affective instability result from recollections or cued memories of traumatic themes and self-harming behaviours also represent maladaptive avoidant coping with distressing memorial representations. She cites research revealing a high incidence of childhood abuse in BPD patients (Herman, 1986) and links the formulation to psychological conceptualisations of learned helplessness and underlying changes in brain processes. Gunderson and Sabo (1993), in reviewing the conceptual interface between these two disorders, represented on separate axes of the DSM-IV, argue for their distinctness on the basis of life history considerations. The diagnosis of BPD depends upon a lifetime of designated difficulties rather than symptoms developing in adulthood subsequent to the experience of trauma. This may be a relatively trivial distinction if indeed further research points to important parallels between personality disorganisation originating from trauma in childhood and personality disorganisation resulting from trauma in adulthood.

OVERALL CONCLUSIONS

This chapter has examined the complex relationships that may exist between personality and PTSD. There are many relationships that may co-exist and competing and overlapping theories. It has been argued that mapping specific variables onto a common framework such as the 5 Factor personality model might permit increased understanding and convergence of research. The factors of Openness, Agreeableness and Conscientiousness have not been well researched in relation to trauma, and where they have been, some differences (not entirely consistent) have emerged.

Increased investigation of those individuals who adjust well to trauma rather than further study of chronic dysfunctional groups may shed further light on the critical variables involved.

Further longitudinal research with popoulations at risk of high levels of stress and trauma is clearly needed to cast further light upon vulnerability models and appropriate conceptions of change. It is not clear what constitutes a change in personality, but what is clear is that trauma can be a stimulus to growth as well as to disintegration, and the pathways from personality through coping that may lead to different outcomes need further research. A balanced examination of positive and negative changes may help to overcome the prejudices that have played a part in interpreting research in this area.

REFERENCES

Andreasen, N.C. & Noyes, R. (1972). Factors influencing adjustment of burn patients during hospitalization. *Psychosomatic Medicine*, **34**, 517–525.

Barlow, D.H. (1988). *Anxiety and its Disorders: The Nature and Treatment of Anxiety and Panic*. New York: Guilford Press.

Bartone, P.T., Ursano, R.J., Wright, K.M. & Ingraham, L.H. (1989) The impact of a military air disaster on the health of assistance workers: A prospective study. *Journal of Mental and Nervous Disorders*, **177**, 317–328.

Beck, A.T. & Emery, G. (1985). *Anxiety Disorders and Phobias: A Cognitive Perspective*. New York: Basic Books.

Beck, A.T., Freeman, A., and associates (1990). *Cognitive Therapy of Personality Disorders*. New York: Guilford Press.

Breslau, N., Davis, G., Andreski, P. & Peterson, E. (1991). Traumatic events and post-traumatic stress disorder in an urban population of young adults. *Archives of General Psychiatry*, **48**, 216–222.

Card, J. (1987). Epidemiology of PTSD in a national cohort of Vietnam veterans. *Journal of Clinical Psychology*, **43**, 6–17.

Clark, L.A., Watson, D. & Mineka, S. (1994). Temperament, personality and the mood and anxiety disorders. *Journal of Abnormal Psychology*, **103**, 103–116.

Costa, P.T. & McCrea, R.R. (1985). *NEO Five-Factor Inventory: Form S*. Odessa, FL: Psychological Assessment Resources.

Costa, P.T. & McCrea, R.R. (1989). *The NEO-PI/NEO-FFI Manual Supplement*. Odessa, FL: Psychological Assessment Resources.

Creamer, M., Burgess, P. & Pattison, P. (1990). Cognitive processing in post-trauma reactions: Some preliminary findings. *Psychological Medicine*, **20**, 597–604.

Eberly, R.E., Harkness, A.R. & Engdahl, B.E. (1991). An adaptational view of trauma response as illustrated by the prisoner of war experience. *Journal of Traumatic Stress*, **4**, 363–380.

Elder, G.H. & Clipp, E.C. (1989). Combat experience and mental health: impairment and resilience in later life. *Journal of Personality*, **57**, 311–341.

Eysenck, H.J. & Eysenck, S.B.G. (1964). *Manual of the Eysenck Personality Inventory*. London: London University Press.

Flach, F. (1990). The resilience hypothesis and post-traumatic stress disorder. In M.E. Wolfe & A.D. Mosnaim (Eds.), *Post-traumatic Stress Disorder: Etiology, Phenomenology and Treatment*. Washington, DC: American Psychiatric Press.

Florian, V., Mikulincer, M. & Taubman, O. (1995). Does hardiness contribute to mental health during a stressful real-life situation? The role of appraisal and coping. *Journal of Personality and Social Psychology*, **68**, 687–695.

Foa, E.B., Steketee, G. & Olasov-Rothbaum, B. (1989). Behavioural/cognitive conceptualizations of post-traumatic stress disorder. *Behaviour Therapy*, **20**, 155–176.

Funk, S.C. (1992). Hardiness: a review of theory and research. *Health Psychology*, **11**, 335–345.

Goldberg, D.P. (1972). *The Detection of Psychiatric Illness by Questionnaire*. London: Oxford University Press.

Gunderson, J.G. & Sabo, A.N. (1993). The phenomenological and conceptual interface between borderline personality disorder and PTSD. *American Journal of Psychiatry*, **150**, 19–27.

Helzer, J.E., Robins, L.N. & McEnvoy, L. (1987). Post-traumatic stress disorder in the general population. *New England Journal of Medicine*, **317**, 1630–1634.

Herman, J.L. (1986). Histories of violence in an outpatient population. *American Journal of Orthopsychiatry*, **57**, 137–141.

Hodgkinson, P.E. & Shepherd, M.A. (1994). The impact of disaster support work. *Journal of Traumatic Stress*, **7**, 587–600.

Horowitz, M.J. (1986). *Stress Response Syndromes* (2nd edn.). Northvale, NJ: Aronson.

Horowitz, M.J., Bonanno, G.A. & Holen, A. (1993). Pathological grief: Diagnosis and explanation. *Psychosomatic Medicine*, **55**, 260–273.

Horowitz, M.J., Wilner, N. & Alvarez, W. (1979). The Impact of Events Scale: A measure of subjective distress. *Psychosomatic Medicine*, **41**, 209–218.

Hyer, L., Woods, M.G. & Boudewyns, P.A. (1991). A three tier evaluation of PTSD among Vietnam combat veterans. *Journal of Traumatic Stress*, **4**, 165–194.

Hyer, L., Braswell, L., Albrecht, B., Boyd, S., Boudewyns, P. & Talbert, S. (1994). *Journal of Clinical Psychology*, **50**, 699–707.

Hyer, L., McCranic, E.W., Bondewyns, P.A. & Sperr, E. (1996). Modes of long-term coping with trauma memories: relative use and associations with personality among Vietnam veterans with chronic PTSD. *Journal of Traumatic Stress*, **9**, 299–316.

Janoff-Bulman, R. (1985). The aftermath of victimization: Rebuilding shattered assumptions. In C.R. Figley (Ed.), *Trauma and its Wake*. New York: Brunner/ Mazel.

Jones, J.C. & Barlow, D.H. (1990). The etiology of post-traumatic stress disorder. *Clinical Psychology Review*, **10**, 299–328.

Joseph, S., Williams, R.M. & Yule, W. (1993). Changes in outlook following disaster: The preliminary development of a measure to assess positive and negative responses. *Journal of Traumatic Stress*, **6**, 271–279.

Joseph, S., Williams, R.M. & Yule, W. (1995). Psychological perspectives on post-traumatic stress. *Clinical Psychology Review*, **9**, 1030.

Joseph, S., Dalgleish, T., Williams, R., Thrasher, S., Yule, W. & Hodgkinron, P. (1997). Attitudes towards emotional expression and post-traumatic stress in survivors of the *Herald of Free Enterprise* disaster. *British Journal of Clinical Psychology*, **36**, 133–138.

Keane, T.M., Zimmering, R.T. & Caddell, J.M. (1985). A behavioural formulation of PTSD in Vietnam veterans. *Behaviour Therapist*, **8**, 9–12.

Kobasa, S.C.O. & Maddi, S.R. (1977). Existential personality theory. In R. Corsini (Ed.), *Current Personality Theories*. Itasca, IL: T.F. Peacock.

Kovacs, M. & Beck, A.T. (1978). Maladaptive cognitive structures in depression. *American Journal of Psychiatry*, **135**, 525–533.

Lonie, I. (1993). Borderline disorder and post-traumatic stress disorder: An equivalence? *Australian and New Zealand Journal of Psychiatry*, **27**, 233–245.

Lyons, J.A. (1991). Strategies for assessing the potential for positive adjustment following trauma. *Journal of Traumatic Stress*, **4**, 93–110.

Marshall, G.N., Wortman, C.B., Vickers, R.R., Kusulas, J.W. & Hervig, L.K. (1994). The five-factor model of personality as a framework for personality-health research. *Journal of Personality and Social Psychology*, **67**, 278–286.

McAdams, D.P. (1992). The Five-Factor Model in Personality: A critical appraisal. *Journal of Personality*, **60**, 329–361.

McCrea, R.R. & Costa, P.T. (1990). *Personality in Adulthood*. New York: Guilford Press.

McCrea, R.R. & John, O.P. (1991). An introduction to the Five-Factor Model and its applications. *Journal of Personality*, **60**, 175–215.

McFarlane, A.C. (1987). Life events and psychiatric disorder: The role of a natural disaster. *British Journal of Psychiatry*, **151**, 362–367.

McFarlane, A.C. (1990). Vulnerability to post-traumatic stress disorder. In M.E. Wolfe & A.D. Mosnaim, (Eds.), *Post-traumatic Stress Disorder: Etiology, Phonomenology and Treatment*. Washington, DC: American Psychiatric Press.

Miller, S.M. (1980). When a little information is a dangerous thing: Coping with stressful events by monitoring versus blunting. In S. Levine & H. Ursin (Eds.), *Coping and Health: Proceedings of a NATO Conference*. New York: Plenum, Press.

Millon, T. (1983). *Millon Clinical Multiaxial Inventory*. Minneapolis, MN: Interpretive Scoring Systems.

Nolen-Hoeksema, S. & Morrow, J. (1991). A prospective study of depression and post-traumatic stress symptoms after a natural disaster: The 1989 Loma Prieta earthquake. *Journal of Personality and Social Psychology*, **61**, 115–121.

Orr, E. & Westman, M. (1990). Does hardiness moderate stress and how? A review. In M. Rosenbaum (Ed.), *Learned Resourcefulness: On Coping Skills, Self-control and Adaptive Behaviour*. New York: Springer.

Penk, W.E., Robinowitz, R. & Roberts, W.R. (1981). Adjustment differences among male substance abusers varying in degree of combat experience in Vietnam. *Journal of Consulting and Clinical Psychology*, **49**, 426–437.

Pervin, L.A. (1993). *Personality: Theory and Research* (6th Edition). New York: Wiley.

Piekarski, A.M., Sherwood, R. & Funari, D. (1993). Personality subgroups in an inpatient Vietnam veteran treatment program. *Psychological Reports*, **72**, 667–674.

Reiss, S., Peterson, R., Gursky, D. & McNally, R. (1986). Anxiety sensitivity, anxiety frequency and the prediction of fearfulness. *Behaviour, Research and Therapy*, **24**, 1–8.

Roca, R.P., Spence, R.J. & Munster, A.M. (1992). Post-traumatic adaptation and distress among adult burn survivors. *American Journal of Psychiatry*, **149**, 1234–1238.

Salkovskis, P. (1985). Obsessional-compulsive problems: A cognitive-behavioural analysis. *Behaviour, Research and Therapy*, **27**, 677–682.

Schnurr, P.P., Friedman, M.J. & Rosenberg, S.D. (1993). Premilitary MMPI scores as predictors of combat-related PTSD symptoms. *American Journal of Psychiatry*, **150**, 479–483.

Sherwood, R.J., Funari, D.J. & Piekarski, A.M. (1990). Adapted character styles of Vietnam veterans with Post-traumatic Stress Disorder. *Psychological Reports*, **66**, 623–631.

Solomon, Z., Mikulincer, M. & Arad, R. (1991). Monitoring and Blunting: Implications for combat-related post-traumatic stress disorder. *Journal of Traumatic Stress*, **4**, 209–221.

Sutker, P.B., Davis, J.M., Uddo, M. & Ditta, S.R. (1995) War zone stress, personal resources and PTSD in Persian Gulf war returnees. *Journal of Abnormal Psychology*, **104**, 444–452.

Talbert, F.S., Braswell, L.C., Albrecht, J.E., Hyer, L.A. & Boudewyns, P.A. (1993). NEO-P1 profiles in PTSD as a function of trauma level. *Journal of Clinical Psychology*, **49**, 663–669.

Taylor, S., Koch, W. & McNally, R. (1992). How does anxiety sensitivity vary across the anxiety disorders? *Journal of Affective Disorders*, **6**, 249–259.

Weisaeth, L. (1984). Stress reactions in an industrial accident. Unpublished doctoral dissertation, Oslo University, Norway.

Weinberger, D.A., Schwartz, G.E. & Davidson, J.R. (1979). Low-anxious and re-pressive coping styles: Psychometric patterns of behavioural and physiological responses to stress. *Journal of Abnormal Psychology*, **88**, 369–380.

Wells, A. & Matthews, G. (1994). *Attention and Emotion: A Clinical Perspective*. Hove: Lawrence Erlbaum.

Widiger, T.A. & Costa, P.T. (1994). Personality and personality disorders. *Journal of Abnormal Psychology*, **103**, 78–91.

Williams, R.M. (1989). Towards a cognitive-behavioural model for PTSD. Paper presented at EEC symposium on PTSD, London, UK.

Williams, R.M., Hodgkinson, P., Joseph, S. & Yule, W. (1995). Attitudes to emo-tion, crisis support and distress 30 months after the capsize of a passenger berry. *Crisis Intervention*, **1**, 209–214.

Williams, R.M., Joseph, S. & Yule, W. (1994). The role of avoidance in coping with disasters: A study of survivors of the capsize of the "Herald of Free Enterprise". *Clinical Psychology and Psychotherapy*, **1**, 87–94.

Wilson, J.P. & Krauss, G.E. (1982). Predicting post-traumatic stress disorders among Vietnam veterans. In W.E. Kelley (Ed.), *Post-traumatic Stress Disorder and the War Veteran Patient*. New York: Brunner/Mazel.

Worthington, R.E. (1978). Demographic and preservice variables as predictors of postmilitary adjustment. In C.R. Figley (Ed.), *Stress Disorders among Vietnam Veterans*. New York: Brunner/Mazel.

Chapter 6

CULTURAL ASPECTS OF POST-TRAUMATIC STRESS DISORDER

*Padmal de Silva**

INTRODUCTION

Culture and Mental Health

Much has been written about the impact of culture on mental health. It has been shown that there are specific culture-bound, or culture-specific, psychiatric syndromes, such as Koro and Latah. The presentation of universally found psychiatric disorders can be, and often is, influenced by cultural factors. There are, too, culture-related stresses, which can lead to specific disturbances. A further factor is the precipitation of psychological problems as a result of exposure to a set of cultural of demands that are very different from the culture one grew up in. Equally important are the issues of the indigenous therapies that exist in different cultures for various psychological disorders, and the concepts and explanations of mental illness. The field of transcultural or, cross-cultural, psychiatry has developed over the last several decades with these issues as its domain of interest. Many empirical investigations and theoretical expositions have, in recent years, illuminated the link between culture and psychological health. These and related issues are discussed in some detail in Bhugra (1993a, 1993b) and Leff (1988), among others.

While the term "culture" has been defined by sociologists and anthropologists in different ways, most would agree that it refers, collectively, to a number of things. These include patterns of behaviour and customs, values, beliefs and attitudes, implicit rules of conduct, patterns of family and social organisation, and taboos and sanctions—all of which are commonly

*Institute of Psychiatry, London

Post-Traumatic Stress Disorders: Concepts and Therapy. Edited by William Yule.
© 1999 John Wiley & Sons Ltd.

shared in a group of people that have a common identity, based on ethnic and sometimes territorial unity. In one's development in childhood, one imbibes the culture that is around one, this being the process of acculturation. One grows up, in a very general sense, thinking, believing and behaving in ways which are found in one's culture, adhering to its rules and conforming to its practices. Cultures vary in the degree to which the rules, customs, etc., are followed rigidly, and in how pervasive its influence is on the individual's life.

In this chapter, the role of culture on post-traumatic stress disorder (PTSD) will be discussed. As the diagnostic category of PTSD is relatively new, there is only a limited literature addressing the cultural aspects of this disorder, unlike, say, schizophrenia and depression which have been extensively written about from this perspective (see Leff, 1988). However, it is clear that cultural factors have an important role to play in the genesis and presentation of PTSD, and in how it is perceived, responded to and treated. These issues will be considered in some detail.

Post-traumatic Stress Disorder

PTSD is a relatively new diagnostic category, but persistent pathological reactions to traumatic experiences have been recognised for a long time. It is said that a German physician named Eulenberg introduced the concept of psychic trauma in 1878, as a designation for the reaction of outcry and fear following extreme shock (Kleber, Brom & Defares, 1992). This was in the wake of the interest in what was called "Erichsen's disease". According to Keiser (1968), Erichsen had drawn attention to a condition which occurred following railway accidents. In 1866, Erichsen had described this as assuming the form of traumatic hysteria, neurasthenia, hypochondriasis or melancholia, and attributed it to a concussion of the spine resulting from the accident. It was therefore also labelled as "railway spine" (Keiser, 1968; Trimble, 1985). Much debate took place about the causes of the emotional responses to such accidents. In 1883, a British surgeon named Page drew a clear distinction between physical injuries and the symptoms of a psychological nature, and introduced the concept of "nervous shock" to refer to the latter (Trimble, 1981, 1985).

The experiences of soldiers in World War I naturally became the focus of those interested in this area. According to Keiser (1968), Mott had introduced the term "shell shock" as a substitute for traumatic neurosis, previously introduced by the physician Oppenheim ("Schreck Neurose" in German). Mott believed that the effects seen were caused by physical events—specifically, brain damage caused by a displacement of air, an overdose of carbon monoxide, and flying shrapnel. However, during the war, it became clear that many soldiers who had not personally experienced shell fire also displayed shell shock. Also, patients would recover when removed from the trenches. By the end of World War I, the importance of psychological factors and mechanisms in this syndrome had become widely accepted. The work of Kardiner with veterans of the war represents the conceptual developments in the period between the two wars (Kardiner, 1941; Kardiner & Spiegel, 1947). In Kardiner's view, trauma was an alteration of the individual's usual environment in which his habitual adaptive strategies no longer proved adequate. The failure of adaptation led to symptoms. Kardiner observed certain constant symptoms in the war veterans. These included: fixation on the traumatic experience; repeated nightmares; irritability; exaggerated reactions to sudden noises; proneness to explosive aggressive behaviours; and a reduction of the general level of functioning, including intellectual functioning. There was also loss of interest in activities, low self-confidence, and dread of being annihilated.

After World War II, work on trauma-induced stresses flourished, with a variety of subject groups. These included, among others, the following: concentration camp survivors (e.g. Eitinger, 1969); survivors of the atomic bombing in Japan (e.g. Lifton, 1967); survivors of natural disasters (e.g. Lifton & Olson, 1976); veterans of World War II (Futterman & Pumpian-Mindlin, 1951); Vietnam war veterans in the United States (e.g. Horowitz & Solomon, 1975); and victims of personal violence, including rape (e.g. Burgess & Holmstrom, 1974). This large body of work threw considerable light on human reactions to traumatic experiences of all sorts. It highlighted, for example, the fact that, while some developed psychological symptoms immediately, some others became symptomatic only after a period of time. It also highlighted two main aspects of the psychological sequelae of traumata: the first is the tendency to re-experience the anxiety of the event in certain ways; the second is the tendency to numb, withdraw and avoid.

The American Psychiatric Association included PTSD as a diagnostic category in the third edition of the *Diagnostic and Statistical Manual* (DSM-III) in 1980 (APA, 1980). The work on traumatic experiences over the preceding decades formed the basis of this diagnosis and its criteria. The recognition of PTSD as a distinct diagnostic category also acted as a facilitator and impetus for investigators to do further work on a variety of trauma-affected subject groups. The growth of studies and publications in this area in the immediate post-1980 period bears testimony to this (Ahearn & Cohen, 1984; Arnold, 1984). The phenomenal increase in publications on this subject in recent years in psychological journals is also documented by Blake, Albano and Keane (1992). Predictably, the growing body of empirical work on PTSD has also led to the refinement of the conceptualisation of the disorder. The developments in the thinking about, and understanding of, the effects of trauma have, in turn, led to the diagnostic criteria being redrawn in the 1987 revised version of the DSM-III (DSM-III-R; APA, 1987), in the tenth edition of the *International Classification of Diseases* (ICD-10; World Health Organisation, 1992), and in the fourth edition of the DSM (DSM-IV; APA, 1994).

REPORTS OF PTSD ACROSS DIFFERENT CULTURES AND SETTINGS

The large and growing body of literature on the psychological effects of traumatic events in general, and PTSD in particular, contains reports from a diversity of cultures and settings. A selective account is given in the following paragraphs. The bulk of the literature does not specifically address issues relating to cultural background, and this is reflected in the studies reviewed. Where culture-related variables have been studied or commented on in a study, these will be highlighted. The overall importance of culture in the context of traumatic stress will be discussed in the final section of the chapter.

War

The effects of war on combat-exposed soldiers have been reported and extensively described. As noted earlier, the early empirical work on traumatic stress came from World War I (e.g. Kardiner, 1941). This work was based on British and other European soldiers. In World War II, larger numbers of soldiers from a wider range of countries were affected and studied. Swank (1949) published one of the major studies of combat-exposed soldiers in this war. The symptoms he found in these subjects were remarkably uniform. While not everyone agreed with the uniformity observation, Grinker and Spiegel (1945) had also stated that the symptomatology seen in soldiers was rather similar. The commonest symptoms they found in these soldiers included: restlessness, irritability and aggression; fatigue and lethargy; sleep problems; anxiety; startle reactions; tension; depression; personality changes; and memory loss. While much of the work was on American and other Western soldiers, those from other countries were also studied. An interesting report by Williams (1950) included data about Indian soldiers in the British Imperial Army in the Arakan, the northern coastal province of Burma. These were soldiers engaged in the British–Japanese front. This report will be discussed in some detail later.

The most voluminous literature on the effects of war is, of course, that on the soldiers of the Vietnam War. This was the largest war in American history, and over 3 million served in the American army in Vietnam, with fatalities of about 50,000. By 1991, over 500 papers had been published on the psychological effects of war in Vietnam veterans (Kleber, Brom & Defares, 1992). Frye and Stockton (1982) and Kulka, Schlenger, Fairbank, Hough, Jordan, Marmar and Weiss (1991) are examples of informative studies of the Vietnam War veterans' psychological health. The latter study used a sample of 1,600, and it was found that about 15% of all male Vietnam survivors met the criteria of PTSD. There were also significant differences between ethnic categories. Blacks had a higher rate of PTSD than Whites. This was possibly because Blacks were more likely to have been exposed to war-zone stress. The highest rate, however, was among the Hispanic veterans. Their rate was twice as high as that of the Whites. No clear explanation was found for this.

There are also reports on Australian soldiers who fought in the Vietnam War. In a case note study of 126 randomly selected Australian Vietnam veterans who had been voluntary patients at the psychiatric unit of the Veterans Affairs Hospital serving Sydney and New South Wales between 1965 and 1981, it was found that 89 had PTSD (Streimer, Cosstick & Tennant, 1985).

The other major body of literature on the effects of war on soldiers comes from Israel. A number of studies covering the psychological effects in Israeli soldiers in the Six Day War in 1967, the Yom Kippur War in 1973 and the Lebanon Conflict in 1982 have been published (e.g. Solomon, 1990, 1993; Solomon, Mikulincer & Jacob, 1987).

A small number of studies have appeared on the psychological effects of war from Arab countries. Assaf (1990) reported on the effects of the Lebanon Conflict among the Lebanese. In a study of 100 subjects (50 civilians, 25 soldiers and 25 militia men) who had experienced various traumas, it was found that 46% satisfied the diagnostic criteria for PTSD. Jalili (1989) has provided a report on PTSD in Iranian soldiers in the Iran–Iraq War.

The effects of combat experience in an Asian country forms the focus of a study carried out in Sri Lanka (de Silva, 1995). Since 1983, Tamil separatist guerrillas have been fighting with the government army in Sri Lanka, in the northern and eastern parts of the island. Large numbers of young soldiers have been recruited and sent to the combat zone by the Sri Lankan army. The psychological effects of combat experience on these soldiers have been investigated by the present author, in collaboration with Professor Nandadasa Kodagoda. An interview schedule based on the DSM-III-R criteria was developed, and a set of self-report instruments, including the Impact of Event Scale (Horowitz, Wilner & Alvarez, 1979), were translated into Sinhalese. In a pilot run, a sample of police officers injured while on duty were assessed. The majority satisfied the criteria for the diagnosis of PTSD. In the first stage of the main study, 33 combat-exposed soldiers who also had physical injuries and were in a military hospital were seen for assessment. Prevalence of psychological effects, including PTSD, was high, as predicted. Depression scores, however, were on the whole not very high, probably due to the fact that the subjects were living in the same setting together and therefore enjoyed cohesiveness and solidarity. It is also possible that depression was expressed more in somatic symptoms and less in psychological symptoms tapped by an instrument designed in the West (cf. Bhugra, 1993a). The assessment of a comparable group of 46 combat-exposed, but physically uninjured, soldiers has shown a similar pattern of symptoms.

Data have also begun to emerge from the former Soviet Union about combat stress among the Soviet soldiers who saw action in Afghanistan. About 400,000 Soviet soldiers fought in Afghanistan; 15,000 died and twice that number were wounded. The psychological effects of the traumatic experience in many of those who survived are now being recognised, with some specialist services made available for further treatment (den Welde & Weisaeth, 1991).

The effects of the Afghan War on the indigenous population have also been studied. Studies of Afghan refugees have been carried out by Daadfar (1988) and Wardak (1993). They showed a range of symtoms, not very different from those reported in other countries ravaged by war. However, there was a high degree of somatic symptoms. Wardak (1993) commented that Afghans, like many other peoples from Oriental cultures, tend to somatise emotional problems (cf. Bhugra, 1993a).

Natural Disasters

The psychological effects of natural disasters have also been studied in some detail. The Swiss physician Stierelin studied the effect of the large mining disaster of Courrieres in 1906, and the earthquake of Messina in 1909 (Kleber, Brom & Defares, 1992). Interestingly, William James (1911) recorded his observations on the effects of the San Francisco earthquake in 1906. More recently, several major disasters have been studied. The most famous is perhaps the Buffalo Creek disaster, in West Virginia, in 1972.

Prolonged rainfall caused the collapse of a dam in a valley, causing 125 deaths and enormous damage (Erikson, 1976; Lifton & Olson, 1976). The survivors showed various psychological effects, including fears and phobias, particularly regarding water and rain, depression, memories and images of the event, increased sweating, drinking, a change in eating habits, and loss of interest in sex, social activities and pastimes. Clear psychological effects were found to persist over two years after the event. It has been suggested that sociocultural factors contributed to these long-term effects (e.g. Erikson, 1976). Buffalo Creek was a highly traditional and isolated community, controlled by mining companies. The people had little opportunity for other work or activities, even after the disaster. They were housed in emergency accommodation, which had the effect of disrupting relationships and ties.

Other natural disasters studied for their psychological effects include: the Xenia Tornado in Ohio in 1974 (Taylor, 1977); the Mount St Helens volcanic eruption in 1980 (Shore, Tatum & Vollmer, 1986); the mining disaster near Lengede in West Germany (Ploeger, 1977); various earthquakes in Peru and Nicaragua (Cohen, 1976; Janney, Masuda & Holmes, 1977); the mining disaster in Aberfan, Wales (Williams & Parkes, 1975); the cyclone in Sri Lanka (Patrick & Patrick, 1980); and the earthquake in Armenia (Giel, 1991). There are also reports from the Netherlands (Ellemers, 1956, cited by Kleber, Brom & Defares, 1992); Italy (Veltro, Lobrace, Starace, Maj & Kemali, 1990; Greece (Soldatos, Bergiannaki, Syrengelas, Economou, Botsis, Sofia, Koumoula & Theodorou, 1989); Norway (Herlofsen, 1990) and Australia (Abrahams, Price, Whitlock & Williams, 1976; McFarlane, 1988; Raphael, 1986). A recent report details the effects of the severe flash floods that hit Puerto Rico in October 1985 (Escobar, Canino, Rubio-Stipec & Bravo, 1992); and Lima, Chavez, Samaniego & Pai (1992) have reported on the psychological effects of the earthquakes that struck the province of Imbabura in Ecuador in 1987.

Other Disasters

Non-natural disasters and their effects have also been studied, including industrial disasters in Norway (Weisaeth, 1989); sea tragedies (e.g. Friedman & Linn, 1957; Joseph, Brewin, Yule & Williams, 1991; Leopold & Dillon, 1963; Yule & Udwin, 1991); air crashes (e.g. Marks, Yule & de Silva, 1995; Sloane, 1988); and technological disasters. Of the last mentioned, the most famous one is, of course, the Chernobyl nuclear reactor explosion in the Soviet Union. Giel (1991) reported that the psychological effects of this on the population included worries about health, worries about the future of the children, plans to move, and so on, rather than the typical post-traumatic responses. However, intrusive cognitions were found in those affected by the averted nuclear accident in Three Mile Island in Pennsylvania in 1979 (Davidson & Baum, 1986).

Violence

The psychological effects of being a victim of violence have also been documented, and it is clear that many violence victims display PTSD symptomatology. This seems particularly so in rape victims (Rothbaum, Foa, Riggs, Murdock & Walsh, 1992; Symonds, 1980). While most of this work comes from the United States, reports from the Netherlands have given details of the psychological effects of being taken hostage (Kleber, Brom & Defares, 1992). Violence victims' psychological reactions are generally similar to those who have faced other traumatic events, but they also tend to have other effects. One factor that seems to be present is self-blame. A further factor, especially in rape victims, is shame. Depressed mood is also commonly found. Another aspect of the reaction to personal violence derives from the fact that the experience is, in most cases, a personal or individual one, unlike mass disasters or warfare. In the latter, there is a group feeling and a sharing, whereas in personal violence the victim does not have this solidarity and support.

Accidents

Psychological effects of personal accidents, such as burns, and motor traffic accidents, can also include PTSD, and there is a small but growing literature on these (e.g. Blanchard, Hickling, Taylor, Loos & Gerardi, 1994; Kuch, Swinson & Kirby, 1985; Perry, Difede, Musngi, Frances & Jacobsberg, 1992; Roca, Spence & Munster, 1992; Taylor & Koch, 1995).

Concentration Camp Experience

Another group of victims of traumatic experiences, with resultant PTSD in many, needs mentioning. These are concentration camp survivors. Much has been written about the Nazi concentration camp survivors during World War II (Cohen, 1953; Dimsdale, 1974; Friedman, 1949; Luchterhand, 1980). Many survivors not only showed symptoms of chronic PTSD, but they also developed additional effects, including survivor guilt and what has been called the "death imprint", i.e. indelible images of death and destruction, based on the repeated and inescapable experience of being a witness of these horrific events.

The survivors of Nazi concentration camps were mainly German and other European Jews. After the war, they have lived in the United States, Europe and Israel. The studies of the long-term traumatic effects of their experience have come from both the United States and Israel (e.g. Dor-Shav, 1978; Levan & Abramson, 1984; Russell, 1980), as well as European centres (Bastiaans, 1974, cited by Kleber, Brom & Defares, 1992). A recent paper from Canada reported on the presence and frequency of PTSD in 78 survivors of Nazi concentration camps who are now living in the Toronto area (Kuch & Cox, 1992). Of these, a subgroup of 20 had been in the Auschwitz extermination camp, and identification numbers, beginning with the letter A, were tattooed on their forearms. This particular group were found to be more affected by PTSD, and were clearly more impaired by some of the symptoms.

Torture

Much work has been done recently on the psychological effects of torture. Several reports provide evidence that many torture victims develop PTSD. Paker, Paker and Yuksel (1992), for example, studied a group of 208 tortured prisoners in Turkey. A diagnosis of PTSD was made in 81 (39%) of them. Stress reactions, including PTSD, in torture survivors have also been documented for several other countries, e.g. Argentina, South Africa and Pakistan (see Basoglu, 1992).

Imprisonment During War

Finally, prisoners of war are also often victims of stress reactions. Several studies are available on American prisoners of war taken by the Japanese (e.g. Nardini, 1952). A report by Tennant, Goulston and Dent (1986) provides data on 170 Australian soldiers captured by the Japanese in the Malay peninsula in 1942. Even after 40 years, this group showed more depression than a comparable group of soldiers who were not imprisoned.

Comments

From the essentially selective review given in the above paragraphs, it should be clear that psychological reactions to traumatic events can be severe enough and wide-ranging enough to warrant the diagnosis of PTSD in a variety of subject groups. Both in adults and in children, the experience of catastrophic events can potentially cause PTSD. The actual trauma can range from active combat in a major war to severe personal accidents. From the perspective of the present chapter, equally important is the fact that PTSD has been reliably reported from a wide range of countries and cultures, including the United States, Western Europe, Eastern Europe, Latin America, the Middle East and Asia. It clearly spans over different ethnic and religious groups. It is very clear that the vulnerability to PTSD is not culturally limited. As for the relative frequency of PTSD in different countries and cultures, as the condition is linked necessarily to the experience of a traumatic event, general epidemiological comparisons are of little relevance. Systematic studies of the frequency of PTSD among different groups subjected to comparable catastrophic experiences simply do not exist, and are unlikely to be easy to carry out even if the right situations arose.

An implicit assumption in much of the literature is that PTSD, originating from whatever cause, is essentially the same. In the sense that there are established symptoms and set criteria for diagnosis, this assumption is valid. However, the nature of diverse traumas can be so different that lumping together everyone meeting the diagnostic criteria as a uniform group of patients must be open to question. The diversity within PTSD, and how it is linked to the nature of the trauma and other factors, is only beginning to be addressed (e.g. Rubonis & Bickman, 1991).

PTSD AND CULTURE

There are several issues that need to be addressed with regard to the relevance of culture to the study and understanding of PTSD. Some of these issues, especially those related to therapy and service delivery, are discussed in more detail by Draguns (1996).

Perception of Trauma and the Reactions of Society

As PTSD is essentially related to a traumatic event, the question of what sort of event is experienced as traumatic is of obvious importance. The definition of a trauma is in many ways defined by the individual's socio-cultural background, both directly, and indirectly through the beliefs and attitudes he or she has acquired and internalised. Certain traumas, such as near death or severe injury in the war front, may be seen as catastrophic by almost everyone. This is the assumption found in the DSM-III-R and DSM-IV. Certain others, it may be argued, are more open to cultural construction. Even the former, however, may not be as clear cut as it appears at first glance. The near death experience in the war front, or the witnessing of colleagues' deaths in those circumstances, may well be experienced in a different way if the war itself is seen, for example, as a matter of great religious importance. Thus, the sociocultural meaning of the traumatic event, whatever that event may be, is a crucial variable.

Furthermore, the reaction to the individual's traumatic experience by his or her society is relevant to the way the effects of the event will develop. Is the individual seen as a martyr, an unfortunate victim, or a mere mercenary, to name but a few possibilities? It has been said that one of the reasons for the poor psychological condition of many of the American Vietnam veterans was the hostile attitude that many of their fellow-countrymen took towards the war in the late 1960s and the 1970s (e.g. De Fazio, 1975). So the traumatised soldier returned to a social network which looked upon him as, at worst, another perpetrator of a cruel and abominable imperialist war, or, at best, an insignificant pawn in such a conflict. In Figley's (1978) much-cited volume, the importance of societal attitudes towards Vietnam veterans in their adjustment is fully discussed. In cultures and subcultures where self-determination is highly valued, victims of traumatic events such as violence may have greater difficulty in preserving their self-worth. The victim may be openly or implicitly treated as a failure (cf. Bard & Sangrey, 1979). There is, too, the related phenomenon of society blaming the victim (Ryan, 1971). A rape victim may, for example, be made to feel that it was all her fault that she was attacked and, instead of sympathy, receive blame and even vilification. In societies where sexual violation is seen as a matter of shame as much for the victim as for the family and clan, a rape victim may find it impossible even to talk about the event, let alone seek help. The role of shame in the context of PTSD is discussed by Stone (1992). An example of the role of social stigma attached to rape, and the consequences of this social attitude for the victims, is found in a newspaper report, not at all atypical, from India. On 6 January 1996 *The Asian Age* reported the case of Sameena (not the real name of the person) who had been raped by two men in Malegoan in Maharashtra. She had to admit the incident to her husand when he later found out about it. He was sympathetic to her, and they made a complaint to the police, who arrested the alleged perpetrators of the crime. The newspaper reported that she was the first rape victim ever to report the event to the Malegoan police. The report went on to say: "Local residents know all about Sameena and ostracism has begun a new life for her. 'My father's relatives and friends have pressed upon him to force me to withdraw the case. They say the family's pride is at stake (*ghar ke ijjat ka sawal hai*)', said Sameena" (p. 1). The relatives reportedly threatened her that all ties would be broken. Her parents had not turned up to see her after the incident. One can infer from this how just reporting rape, let alone getting help or counselling for the consequence of the trauma, is almost impossible in cultures where rape means dishonour for the victim's family and clan. This is likely to be an additional psychological burden for the unfortunate victims.

Broadly speaking, the various parameters that go to make up the individual's identity all determine, to some extent, his or her reaction to a significant traumatic event. Social class, race, ethnicity and gender are thus all relevant (McCann & Pearlman, 1990). The significance of these in this role is influenced, to a greater or lesser degree, by the assumptions and attitudes found in individual's society and culture.

Social Support

An equally important variable is the presence or absence, and the extent, of social support that a trauma victim has after his or her experience. The support may come from family and friends, or from a wider network. This has been discussed at some length by Figley (1986) and Green, Wilson and Lindy (1985), among others. There is empirical evidence that demonstrates the value of this support, as for example shown by Barrett and Mizes (1988) for Vietnam veterans. Recent empirical work by Joseph in his study of disaster victims in Britain (e.g. Joseph, Williams, Yule & Andrews, 1992) highlights the importance of social support for trauma victims. This support can contribute to the reduction of the probability of the individual developing full-blown PTSD, and also to the speed of recovery and adjustment. It has been said, in this context, that "social support is the individual's psychological experience of others' helpfulness rather than some objective or observable phenomenon" (McCann & Pearlman, 1990, p. 119). It is certainly the case that the individual's perception of the support given is a critical factor. However, the ready availability or otherwise of a clear support system is a variable that can be objectively tested for its overall efficacy in helping trauma victims. As cultures differ markedly in the extent to which such support systems, such as the extended family, exist, this is an empirical question that can be investigated.

There is a further point that needs to be made about support systems. While the individual trauma victim may be well cared for by such a social support system, in societies affected by war and by mass disasters, the traumatic events and their aftermath can also disrupt and even destroy such support systems. Wardak (1993), in his study of Afghan War refugees, has commented on how the traditional social support systems were no longer functioning or available to many of those traumatised. This clearly added to their difficulties, as a source of support they would normally have taken for granted was no longer there.

Related to this is the effect of mass trauma on the overall sociocultural structures of a country or community. Prolonged war, or major and devastating natural disasters, can disrupt the basic elements of culture. Consequently, the impact of the trauma on the individual may well be exaggerated; not only has he had a traumatic personal experience, but the sociocultural framework he is used to is no longer there to provide him with any sense of safety or continuity. A clear example of this phenomenon is the Buffalo Creek disaster. Erikson (1976), who studied the effects of these floods, maintained that the considerable psychological difficulties and distress still seen in the survivors two years after the event were at least partly related to the total devastation of a "recovery environment". More recently, Wardak (1993) has observed how various key aspects of Afghan culture (e.g. entertainment of guests, provision of food and shelter for strangers, helping the needy and showing generosity) were shattered by the war. This has led, among the people in the affected areas, to a sense of bewilderment and insecurity, in addition to whatever individual traumatic effects some of them had. The sociocultural structures of the population, with the extended family, lineage tribe and so on have been extensively damaged in certain areas. In addition, many have also lost their traditional social status, which is evidently quite important in Afghan culture, due to the effects of war, this being caused by loss of wealth, inability of perform various religious duties as a result of the loss of means or incapacity, and due to disruption of family networks and hierarchies.

Role of the Military Culture in War

With regard specifically to soldiers in combat situations, it has been argued that the prevailing culture in the military organisation as well as the national culture can have an effect on the soldier's vulnerability to stress reactions—and thus to PTSD. Labuc (1991) has highlighted how morale in the army correlates with the incidence of combat stress reactions. Analysing a number of campaigns by Israeli and British soldiers, he says: "It can be seen that when morale is high stress casualties are low, and vice versa" (Labuc, 1991, p. 485). Unit cohesion and support are among the factors that have been shown to determine morale.

Cultural and National Differences in Responses to Trauma

As for national, cultural and ethnic differences in the vulnerability to, and manifestation of, traumatic stress reactions, the available empirical evidence is not extensive. It was noted in a previous section that Kulka et al. (1991) found ethnic differences among the American Vietnam War veterans. It will be recalled that the most affected group were the Hispanics, with a rate which was about twice as high as that for Whites. The early work by Williams (1950), also referred to previously, provides a fascinating study of Indian and British soldiers in World War II, in the battles in Burma against the Japanese. Williams was a field psychiatrist to the 26th Indian Division in the Arakan from February 1944 to May 1945. He found that, among these soldiers, "psychiatric illness was proportionally $2\frac{1}{2}$ times more frequent in all British than in all Indian troops" (Williams, 1950, p. 131). When a comparison was made for the troops who were actually fighting, the ratio rose to $3\frac{1}{2}$ to 1. The British troops were vastly more affected by anxiety states than their Indian counterparts. Psychosomatic reactions were also much commoner among the British, while it was the opposite for hysterical reactions. Williams's report provides further details, and also offers various speculations about the differences he had observed, and comments on the "different kinds" of Indians. One interesting comment he makes is that the Indians showed far fewer anxiety states, because "to exhibit anxiety meant great loss of face" (p. 165). So some of them terminated an anxiety-laden situation with a self-inflicted wound. In contrast, "British soldiers did not need to deny anxiety as fear was socially acceptable" (p. 165). Williams (1950) also commented on other sociocultural factors (e.g. extended family) that he considered relevant.

While Williams's (1950) paper is of historical interest, it is not possible to generalise from his findings and observations. The kind of empirical, up-to-date, information needed for any conclusions to be drawn about national differences in vulnerability to stress, and in the manifestation of stress reactions, is limited. It remains a challenging area to investigate, but one fraught with numerous problems for the researcher.

Some interesting data relevant to this issue has recently been provided by Daadfar (1988) and Wardak (1993) working with Afghan War victims and refugees. Wardak (1993, p. 360) states:

> Certain symptoms reported by Afghans, such as severe dysphoria, sleep disturbances, and loss of appetite, are similar to those reported in Western countries. Other symptoms (e.g. crying spells, feeling of guilt, suicidal thoughts and acts) are largely inhibited by sociocultural factors. Men and

young boys are not supposed to cry; this is believed to be appropriate only for girls and women.

Wardak (1993) has also commented on the extremely low figures of suicidal ideation, let alone suicidal acts, in the traumatised population he studied. He attributes this to the fact that Islam strongly prohibits the act of suicide and regards it as a criminal act.

It is relevant, at this point, to refer to the notion of "shattered assumptions" that has been postulated by Janoff-Bulman (1985, 1992). According to Janoff-Bulman, the experience of a major trauma shatters the individual's assumptions about the universe and self. She proposes that there are three fundamental assumptions: (i) the world is benevolent; (ii) the world is meaningful; and (iii) the self is worthy. A major catastrophe can cause these assumptions to be shattered. One feels that the world is not safe, is not benevolent, and that one is not invulnerable. Part of the psychological reaction to a major trauma is this shattering of one's assumptions. Janoff-Bulman's views have clear implications for the role of culture in PTSD. The world view, including the core assumptions, of an individual can be expected to be largely determined by the beliefs in his or her culture, including religion. The core assumptions identified by Janoff-Bulman (1992) are, at best, those of Western industrialised cultures, with a Christian outlook. What of people of very different cultures, where, for example, the traditional religious beliefs, and indeed history, do not promote notions of a meaningful word or a benevolent world, or an invulnerable self? If Janoff-Bulman's position is correct, then people from cultures very different from that of the industralised, Christian West, should respond to traumatic and catastrophic events in a different way. Is this really so? The literature on the effects of trauma in various parts of the world, reviewed earlier in this chapter, shows that people tend to develop stress reactions, including PTSD, as a result of major traumatic events, irrespective of place or culture. It is indisputable that, even in countries where the predominant world view accepts hardships and disasters as entirely in the nature of things (e.g. the concept of *karma* in some Indian religions), those who experience major traumatic events are no more protected against PTSD than their Western counterparts. Other, less obvious, differences that may be predicted from the Janoff-Bulman model may of course emerge in future research specifically geared to such investigations.

Issues Related to Therapy

An important issue related to the role of culture in PTSD is what is available, in a given cultural setting, to help the traumatised individual in the healing process. Wilson (1989) has provided an illuminating discussion of this. He points out that historically, in many cultures and societies, rituals were performed to welcome home those who went to war. This eased the return of the soldier to civilian life. An implication is that these rituals may contribute to the psychological well-being of the individuals concerned. Wilson cites the example of the Sweat Lodge purifications ritual (*inipi onikare*) of the Native Americans. It is a religious event of thanksgiving and forgiveness which is typically conducted by a "medicine person" in the tribe.

> It is regarded as a serious and sacred occasion in which spiritual insights, personal growth, and physical and emotional healing may take place. The process of purification is experienced on many levels of awareness, including the physical, psychological, social and spiritual. (Wilson, 1989, p. 44)

He analyses the elements found in the Sweat Lodge ritual and goes on to examine how it may function as a form of treatment for PTSD. The elements of the Sweat Lodge ritual include extreme heat, sensory deprivation, singing, restricted mobility, self-disclosure, and a sense of collectiveness. These, Wilson argues, can bring about changes in the various symptoms and symptom clusters that are part of PTSD. It is well known that many tribes and cultures do have similar rituals and healing ceremonies, and some of them may be effective in helping trauma victims to reintegrate and heal. Wilson (1989) reports on his experimental treatment programme for patients with PTSD where a number of elements, including daily Sweat Lodge exercises, were used. This was a six-day-long event, which utilised a number of treatment modalities. The results were impressive. More recently, Johnson, Feldman, Lubin and Southwick (1995) reported on a similar application of ritual and ceremony in treating PTSD. In their paper, they described four ceremonies which were used, with some success, in this way.

Whether indigenous cultural rituals and ceremonies can usefully be incorporated into the treatment programmes of PTSD cases in different cultures is an open question. There is, no doubt, recourse to local agents and techniques among many trauma-affected individuals in many cultures, either as an alternative or as an adjunct to general psychiatric services (Torrey, 1986; Ward, 1989). There is, at present, a lack of firm evidence as to whether they are of any demonstrable use or not. The need for systematic evaluation is the most important concern, and any cultural procedure used in the context of present-day therapy should be tested empirically (see Lloyd & Bhugra, 1993).

A related issue is whether Western psychiatric treatment techniques are suitable for use with PTSD cases in cultures which are markedly different.

There is already a large body of literature that draws attention to the problems inherent in using therapeutic techniques developed in one setting with patients from a markedly different culture (e.g. d'Ardenne & Mahtani, 1989; Kareem & Littlewood, 1992; Lloyd & Bhugra, 1993; Summerfield, 1995). Van der Veer (1992) has provided an illuminating discussion of many of the issues involved, based on his experience working with refugees of non-European origin in the Netherlands. A psychological therapy reflects a particular world view, and acceptance of therapy as well as compliance with therapeutic instructions is enhanced if the patient finds this to be harmonious with his other beliefs. The principles of cognitive and behavioural therapy have been used, with suitable modifications, in a variety of cultures (e.g. de Silva & Samarasinghe, 1985, 1998; Yamagami, Okuma, Morinaga & Nakao, 1982). They have been used most commonly and successfully for neurotic disorders such as phobias and obsessive-compulsive problems, although other types of disorder have also been treated with these. In the case of PTSD, a range of behavioural and cognitive techniques have been shown as useful in treating patients with this disorder in the West (Keane, Gerardi, Quinn & Litz, 1992: Resick & Schnike, 1992; Veronen & Kilpatrick, 1983). These techniques have been used, on a small scale, with PTSD victims in non-Western cultures with some promise (Samarasinghe, 1995, pers. comm.). It appears that these techniques may have wider use in non-Western societies for the treatment of trauma victims, but culturally suited additions and modification may profitably be made. It is equally important to maximise the effects of social support available in the patient's own setting.

REFERENCES

Abrahams, M.J., Price, J., Whitlock, F.A. & Williams, G. (1976). The Brisbane floods, January 1974: Their impact on health. *Medical Journal of Australia*, **2**, 936–939.

Ahearn, F.L. & Cohen, R.E. (1984). *Disasters and Mental Health: An Annotated Bibliography*. Rockville, MD: National Institute of Mental Health.

APA (1980). *Diagnostic and Statistical Manual of Mental Disorders* (3rd Edition). Washington, DC: American Psychiatric Association.

APA (1987). *Diagnostic and Statistical Manual of Mental Disorders* (3rd Edition, revised). Washington, DC: American Psychiatric Association.

APA (1994). *Diagnostic and Statistical Manual of Mental Disorders* (4th Edition). Washington, DC: American Psychiatric Association.

Arnold, A.L. (1984). *Selected Bibliography: Post-traumatic Stress Disorder With Special Attention to Vietnam Veterans*. Phoenix, AZ: Veterans Administration Medical Centre.

Assaf, J. (1990). War neurosis and post-traumatic stress disorder in Lebanon. In C.N. Stefanis, A.D. Rabvilas & C.R. Soldatos (Eds.), *Psychiatry: A World Perspective*, vol. 1. Amsterdam: Elsevier.

Bard, M. & Sangrey, D. (1979). *The Crime Victim Book.* New York: Basic Books.

Barrett, T.W. & Mizes, J.S. (1988). Combat level and social support in the development of post-traumatic stress disorder in Vietnam veterans. *Behavior Modification*, **12**, 110–115.

Basoglu, M. (Ed.) (1992). *Torture and Its Consequences.* Cambridge: Cambridge University Press.

Bhugra, D. (1993a). Influence of culture on presentation and management of patients. In D. Bhugra & J. Leff (Eds.), *Principles of Social Psychiatry.* Oxford: Blackwell.

Bhugra, D. (Ed.) (1993b). *Cross-Cultural Psychiatry: Special Issue of International Review of Psychiatry*, vol. 5, nos 2 and 3.

Blake, D.D., Albano, A.M. & Keane, T.M. (1992). Twenty years of trauma: *Psychological Abstracts* 1970 through 1989. *Journal of Traumatic Stress*, **5**, 477–484.

Blanchard, R., Hickling, E.J., Taylor, A.E., Loos, W.R. & Gerardi, R.J. (1994). Psychological morbidity associated with motor vehicle accidents. *Behaviour Research and Therapy*, **32**, 283–290.

Boudewyns, P.A. & Hyer, L. (1990). Physiological response to combat memories and preliminary treatment outcome in Vietnam Veteran PTSD patients treated with direct therapeutic exposure. *Behavior Therapy*, **21**, 63–87.

Burgess, A.W. and Holmstrom, L.L. (1974). Rape trauma syndrome. *American Journal of Psychiatry*, **31**, 981–986.

Cohen, E.A. (1953). *Human Behaviour in the Concentration Camp.* New York: Norton.

Cohen, R.E. (1976). Post-disaster mobilization of a crisis intervention team: The Managua experience. In H.J. Parad, H.L.P. Resnik & L.G. Parad (Eds.), *Emergency and Disaster Management.* Bowie, MD: Charles Press.

Daadfar, M.A. (1988). *Psychiatry Centre for Afghan Refugees Annual Report.* Peshawar, Pakistan: PCAR.

d'Ardenne, P. & Mahtani, A. (1989). *Transcultural Counselling in Action.* London: Sage.

Davidson, L.M. & Baum, A. (1986). Chronic stress and post-traumatic disorders. *Journal of Consulting and Clinical Psychology*, **54**, 303–308.

De Fazio, V.J. (1975). The Vietnam era veteran: Psychological problems. *Journal of Contemporary Psychotherapy*, **7**, 9–15.

den Welde, W.O. & Weisaeth, L. (1991). What have they done to the pigeons? A review of the Moscow Conference on Traumatic Stress, 18–19 September 1990. *Journal of Traumatic Stress*, **4**, 445–450.

de Silva, P. (1995). Post-traumatic stress reactions in combat-exposed soldiers in Sri Lanka. Paper presented at the Fourth European Conference on Traumatic Stress, Paris (April).

de Silva, P. & Samarasinghe, D. (1985). Behavior therapy in Sri Lanka. *Journal of Behavior Therapy and Experimental Psychiatry*, **16**, 95–100.

de Silva, P. & Samarasinghe, D. (1998) Behavior therapy in Srihanka. In T.P.S. Oei (Ed.) *Behavior Therapy and Cognitive Behavior Therapy in Asia.* Glebe, NSW: Edumedia.

Dimsdale, J.E. (1974). The coping behavior of Nazi concentration camp survivors. *American Journal of Psychiatry*, **131**, 792–797.

Dor-Shav, N.K. (1978). On the long-range effects of concentration camp internment of Nazi victims: 25 years later. *Journal of Consulting and Clinical Psychology*, **46**, 1–11.

Draguns, J.G. (1996). Ethnocultural considerations in the treatment of PTSD: Therapy and service delivery. In A.J. Marsella, M.J. Friedman, E.T. Gerrity &

R.M. Scurfield (Eds.), *Ethnocultural Aspects of Post-traumatic Stress Disorder: Issues, Research and Clinical Applications*. Washington, DC: American Psychological Association.

Eitinger, L. (1969). Psychosomatic problems in concentration camp survivors. *Journal of Psychosomatic Research*, **13**, 183–189.

Erikson, K.T. (1976). *Everything in Its Path: Destruction of Community in the Buffalo Creek Flood*. New York: Simon & Schuster.

Escobar, J.I., Canino, G., Rubio-Stipec, M. & Bravo, M. (1992). Somatic symptoms after a natural disaster: A prospective study. *American Journal of Psychiatry*, **149**, 965–967.

Figley, C.R. (Ed.) (1978). *Stress Disorders among Vietnam Veterans: Therapy, Research and Treatment*. New York: Brunner/Mazel.

Figley, C.R. (1986). Traumatic stress: The role of the family and social support. In C.R. Figley (Ed.), *Trauma and Its Wake: The Study and Treatment of Post-traumatic Stress Disorder*, vol. 2. New York: Brunner/Mazel.

Frank, E., Anderson, B., Stewart, B.D., Dancu, C., Hughes, C. & West, D. (1988). Efficacy of cognitive behaviour therapy and systematic desensitization in the treatment of rape trauma. *Behavior Therapy*, **19**, 403–420.

Friedman, P. (1949). Some aspects of concentration camp psychology. *American Journal of Psychiatry*, **105**, 601–605.

Friedman, P. & Linn, L. (1957). Some psychiatric notes on the Andrea Doria disaster. *American Journal of Psychiatry*, **114**, 426.

Frye, J.S. & Stockton, R.A. (1982). Discriminant analysis of post-traumatic stress disorder among a group of Vietnam Veterans. *American Journal of Psychiatry*, **139**, 52–56.

Futterman, S. & Pumpian-Mindlin, E. (1951). Traumatic war neurosis five years later. *American Journal of Psychiatry*, **108**, 401–408.

Giel, R. (1991). The psychosocial aftermath of two major disasters in the Soviet Union. *Journal of Traumatic Stress*, **4**, 381–392.

Green, B.L., Wilson, J.P. & Lindy, J.D. (1985). Conceptualizing post-traumatic stress disorder: A psychosocial framework. In C.R. Figley (Ed.), *Trauma and its Wake: The Study and Treatment of Post-traumatic Stress Disorder*. New York: Brunner/Mazel.

Grinker, R.R. & Spiegel, J.P. (1945). *Men Under Stress*. Philadelphia: Blakiston.

Herlofsen, P.H. (1990). Psychosocial support services for bereaved families after disasters. In C.N. Stefanis, C.R. Soldatos & A.D. Rabavilas (Eds.), *Psychiatry: A World Perspective*, vol. 4. Amsterdam: Elsevier.

Horowitz, M.J. and Solomon, G.F. (1975). A prediction of delayed stress response syndromes in Vietnam Veterans. *Journal of Social Issues*, **31**, 67–80.

Horowitz, M.J., Wilner, N. & Alvarez, W. (1979). Impact of Event Scale: A measure of subjective stress. *Psychosomatic Medicine*, **41**, 209–218.

Jalili, S.A. (1989). Fifty-four cases of post-traumatic stress disorder. Paper presented at the Eighth World Congress of Psychiatry, Athens, October 1989.

James, W. (1911). On some mental effects of the earthquake. *Memories and Studies*. New York: Longman Press.

Janney, J.G., Masuda, M. & Holmes, T.H. (1977). Impact of a natural catastrophe on life events. *Journal of Human Stress*, **3**, 22–24.

Janoff-Bulman, R. (1985). The aftermath of victimization: Rebuilding shattered assumptions. In C.R. Figley (Ed.), *Trauma and Its Wake: The Study and Treatment of Post-traumatic Stress Disorder*. New York: Brunner/Mazel.

Janoff-Bulman, R. (1992). *Shattered Assumptions: Towards a New Psychology of Trauma*. New York: The Free Press.

Johnson, D.R., Feldman, S.C., Lubin, H. & Southwick, S.M. (1995). The therapeutic use of ritual and ceremony in the treatment of post-traumatic stress disorder. *Journal of Traumatic Stress,* **8**, 283–298.

Joseph, S., Brewin, C.R., Yule, W. & Williams, R. (1991). Causal attributions and psychiatric symptomatology in survivors of the Herald of Free Enterprise disaster. *British Journal of Psychiatry,* **15**, 542–546.

Joseph, S., Williams, R., Yule, W. & Andrews, B. (1992). Crisis support and psychiatric symptomatology in adult survivors of the Jupiter Cruise ship disaster. *British Journal of Clinical Psychology,* **31**, 63–73.

Kardiner, A. (1941). *The Traumatic Neuroses of War*. New York: Hoeber.

Kardiner, A. & Spiegel, H. (1947). *War Stress and Neurotic Illness*. New York: Hoeber.

Kareem, J. & Littlewood, R. (1992). *Intercultural Therapy: Theory and Practice*. Oxford: Blackwell.

Keane, T.M., Gerardi, R.J., Quinn, S.J. & Litz, B.T. (1992). Behavioral treatment of post-traumatic stress disorder. In S.M. Turner, K.S. Calhoun & H.E. Adams (Eds.), *Handbook of Clinical Behavior Therapy* (2nd Edition). New York: Wiley.

Keiser, L. (1968). *The Traumatic Neurosis*. Philadelphia: Lippincott.

Kleber, R.J., Brom, D. & Defares, P.B. (1992). *Coping with Trauma: Therapy, Prevention and Treatment*. Amsterdam: Swets & Zeitlinger.

Kuch, K. & Cox, B.J. (1992). Symptoms of post-traumatic stress disorder in 124 survivors of the Holocaust. *American Journal of Psychiatry,* **149**, 337–340.

Kuch, K., Swinson, R.P. & Kirby, M. (1985). Post-traumatic stress disorder after car accidents. *Canadian Journal of Psychiatry,* **30**, 426–427.

Kulka, R.A., Schlenger, W.A., Fairbank, J.A., Hough, R.L., Jordan, B.K., Marmar, C.R. & Weiss, D.S. (1991). *Trauma and the Vietnam War Generation*. New York: Brunner/Mazel.

Labuc, S. (1991). Cultural and societal factors in military organizations. In R. Gal & D. Mangelsdorff (Eds.), *Handbook of Military Psychology*. New York: Wiley.

Leff, J. (1988). *Psychiatry Around the Globe: A Transcultural View* (2nd Edn) London: Gaskell.

Leopold, R.L. & Dillon, H. (1963). Psycho-anatomy of a disaster: A long-term study of post-traumatic neuroses in survivors of a marine explosion. *American Journal of Psychiatry,* **111**, 913–921.

Levan, I. & Abramson, J.H. (1984). Emotional distress amongst concentration camp survivors: a community study in Jerusalem. *Psychological Medicine,* **14**, 215–218.

Lifton, R.J. (1967). *Death in Life: The Survivors of Hiroshima*. New York: Random House.

Lifton, R.J. & Olson, E. (1976). Death imprint in Buffalo Creek. In H.J. Parad, H.L.P. Resnik & L.G. Parad (Eds.), *Emergency and Disaster Management*. Bowie, MD: Charles Press.

Lima, B.R., Chavez, H., Samaniego, N. & Pai, S. (1992). Psychiatric disorders among emotionally distressed disaster victims attending primary mental health clinics in Ecuador. *Bulletin of the PAHO,* **26**, 60–66.

Lloyd, K. & Bhugra, D. (1993). Cross-cultural aspects of psychotherapy. *International Review of Psychiatry,* **5**, 291–304.

Luchterhand, E.G. (1980). Social behavior of concentration camp prisoners: Continuities and discontinuities with pre- and post-camp life. In J.E. Dimsdale (Ed.),

Survivors, Victims, and Perpetrators: Essays on the Nazi Holocaust. Washington, DC: Hemisphere.

Marks, M., Yule, W. & de Silva, P. (1995). Post-traumatic stress disorder in aeroplane cabin crew attendants. *Aviation, Space and Environmental Medicine,* **66,** 264–268.

McCann, I.L. & Pearlman, L.A. (1990). *Psychological Trauma and the Adult Survivor: Theory, Therapy and Transformation.* New York: Brunner/Mazel.

McFarlane, A.C. (1988). The aetiology of post-traumatic stress disorders following a natural disaster. *British Journal of Psychiatry,* **15,** 116–121.

Nardini, J.E. (1952). Survival factors in American prisoners of work of the Japanese. *American Journal of Psychiatry,* **109,** 241–248.

Paker, M., Paker, O. & Yuksel, S. (1992). Psychological effects of torture: An empirical study of tortured and non-tortured non-political prisoners. In M. Basoglu (Ed.), *Torture and its Consequences.* Cambridge: Cambridge University Press.

Patrick, V. & Patrick, W.K. (1980). Cyclone '78 in Sri Lanka: The mental health trail. *British Journal of Psychiatry,* **138,** 210–216.

Perry, S., Difede, J., Musngi, G., Frances, A.J. & Jacobsberg, L. (1992). Predictors of post-traumatic stress disorder after burn injury. *American Journal of Psychiatry,* **149,** 931–935.

Ploeger, A. (1977). A ten year follow up of miners trapped for two weeks under threatening circumstances. In C.D. Spielberger & I.G. Sarason (Eds.), *Stress and Anxiety,* vol. 4. New York: Wiley.

Raphael, B. (1986). *When Disaster Strikes.* London: Hutchinson.

Resick, P.A. & Schnike, M.K. (1992). Cognitive processing therapy for sexual assault victims. *Journal of Consulting and Clinical Psychology,* **60,** 748–756.

Roca, R.P., Spence, R.J. & Munster, A.M. (1992). Post-traumatic adaptation and distress among adult burn survivors. *American Journal of Psychiatry,* **149,** 1234–1238.

Rothbaum, B.O., Foa, E.B., Riggs, D.S., Murdock, T. & Walsh, W. (1992). A prospective examination of post-traumatic stress disorder in rape victims. *Journal of Traumatic Stress,* **5,** 455–475.

Rubonis, A.V. & Bickman, L. (1991). Psychological impairment in the wake of disaster: The disaster–psychopathology relationship. *Psychological Bulletin,* **109,** 384–399.

Russell, A. (1980). Late effects—influence on the children of the concentration camp survivor. In J.E. Dimsdale (Ed.), *Survivors, Victims, and Perpetrators: Essays on the Nazi Holocaust.* Washington, DC: Hemisphere.

Ryan, W. (1971). *Blaming the Victim.* New York: Pantheon Books.

Samarasinghe, D.S. (1995). Personal communication.

Shore, J., Tatum, E. & Vollmer, W. (1986). Psychiatric reactions to disaster: The Mount St Helens experience. *American Journal of Psychiatry,* **143,** 590–595.

Sloane, J.R. (1988). Post-traumatic stress disorder in survivors of an airplane crash landing: A clinical and exploratory research intervention. *Journal of Traumatic Stress,* **1,** 222–229.

Soldatos, C., Bergiannaki, J., Syrengelas, M., Economou, M., Botsis, A., Sofia, K., Koumoula, A. & Theodorou, C. (1989). Psychosocial effects of a disaster: The early and later post-impact periods. Paper presented at the Eighth World Congress of Psychiatry, Athens October 1989.

Solomon, Z. (1990). PTSD in Israeli soldiers in the Lebanon war. In C.N. Stefanis, A.D. Rabavilas & C.R. Soldatos (Eds.), *Psychiatry: A World Perspective,* vol. 1. Amsterdam: Elsevier.

Solomon, Z. (1993). *Combat Stress Reaction: The Enduring Toll of War.* New York: Plenum Press.

Solomon, Z., Mikulincer, M. & Jacob, B.R. (1987). Exposure to recurrent combat stress: Combat stress reactions among Israeli soldiers in the 1982 Lebanon war. *Psychological Medicine,* **17**, 433–440.

Solomon, Z., Bleich, A., Shoham, S., Nardi, C. & Kotler, M. (1992). The "Koach" project for treatment of combat-related post-traumatic stress disorder: Rationale, aims and methodology. *Journal of Traumatic Stress,* **5**, 175–193.

Stone, A.M. (1992). The role of shame in post-traumatic stress disorder. *American Journal of Psychiatry,* **62**, 131–136.

Streimer, J.H., Cosstick, J. & Tennant, C. (1985). The psychological adjustment of Australian Vietnam Veterans. *American Journal of Psychiatry,* **142**, 616–618.

Summerfield, D. (1995). Addressing human response to war and atrocity: Major challenges in research and practices and the limitations of Western psychiatric models. In R.J. Kleber, C.R. Figley & B.P.R. Gersons (Eds.), *Beyond Trauma: Cultural and Societal Dynamics.* New York: Plenum, Press.

Swank, R.L. (1949). Combat exhaustion. *Journal of Nervous and Mental Disease,* **109**, 475–508.

Symonds, M. (1980). The second injury to victim: Acute responses to victims of terror. *Evaluation and Change, Special Issue,* 36–41.

Taylor, S. & Koch, W.J. (1995). Anxiety disorders due to motor vehicle accidents: Nature and treatment. *Clinical Psychology Review,* **15**, 721–738.

Taylor, V. (1977). Good new about disaster. *Psychology Today,* **11**, 93–94, 124–126.

Tennant, C.C., Goulston, K.J. & Dent, O.F. (1986). The psychological effects of being a prisoner of war: Forty years after release. *American Journal of Psychiatry,* **143**, 618–621.

The Asian Age, **2**, 322, 6.01.1996.

Torrey, E.F. (1986). *Witchdoctors and Psychiatrists.* New York: Harper & Row.

Trimble, M.R. (1981). *Post-traumatic Neurosis: From Railway Spine to the Whiplash.* Chichester: Wiley.

Trimble, M.R. (1985). Post-traumatic stress disorder: History of a concept. In C.R. Figley (Ed.), *Trauma and Its Wake: The Study and Treatment of Post-traumatic Stress Disorder.* New York: Brunner/Mazel.

Van der Veer, G. (1992). *Counselling and Therapy with Refugees.* New York: Wiley.

Veltro, F., Lobrace, S., Starace, F., Maj, M. & Kemali, D. (1990). Prevalence of mental disorders among subjects exposed to seismic phenomena in Naples province. In C.N. Stefanis, C.R. Soldatos & A.D. Rabavilas (Eds.), *Psychiatry: A World Perspective,* vol. 4. Amsterdam: Elsevier.

Veronen, L.J. & Kilpatrick, D.G. (1983). Stress management for rape victims. In D. Michenbaum & M.E. Jaremko (Eds.), *Stress Reduction and Prevention.* New York: Plenum Press.

Ward, C.A. (Ed.) (1989). *Altered States of Consciousness and Mental Health: A Cross-cultural Perspective.* Newbury Park: Sage.

Wardak, A.W.H. (1993). The psychiatric effects of war stress on Afghan society. In J.P. Wilson & B. Raphael (Eds.), *International Handbook of Traumatic Stress Syndromes.* New York: Plenum Press.

Weisaeth, L. (1989). A study of behavioural responses to an industrial disaster. *Acta Psychiatrica Scandinavica,* **80**, 13–24.

Williams, A.H. (1950). Psychiatric study of Indian soldiers in the Arakan. *British Journal of Medical Psychology,* **24**, 130–181.

Williams, R. & Parkes, C.M. (1975). Psychosocial effects of disaster: Birth rate in Aberfan. *British Medical Journal*, **2**, 303.

Wilson, J.P. (1989). *Trauma, Transformation, and Healing: An Integrative Approach to Theory, Research, and Post-traumatic Therapy*. New York: Brunner/Mazel.

World Health Organisation (1992). *The International Classification of Diseases* (10th rev. edn.). Geneva: WHO.

Yamagami, T., Okuma, H., Morinaga, Y. & Nakao, H. (1982). Practice of behavior therapy in Japan. *Journal of Behavior Therapy and Experimental Psychiatry*, **13**, 21–26.

Yule, W. & Udwin, O. (1991). Screening child survivors for post-traumatic stress disorder: Experience from the "Jupiter" sinking. *British Journal of Clinical Psychology*, **30**, 131–138.

Chapter 7

PSYCHOBIOLOGY OF POST-TRAUMATIC STRESS DISORDER

Hassan Hagh-Shenas*, Laura Goldstein*
and William Yule*

This chapter examines recent ideas and theories regarding information processing and its neural correlates in people with post-traumatic stress disorder (PTSD). In this context we shall review two main approaches: neuropsychological and neurochemical/neuroanatomical. Both of these can be explored to explain the nature of the cardinal symptoms of PTSD, namely the re-experiencing of the traumatic event, hypervigilance, exaggerated startle responses, sleep disturbances and memory and concentration difficulties.

NEUROPSYCHOLOGICAL STUDIES OF PTSD

Neuropsychological methods try to correlate human behaviour with the functioning of the brain. Neuropsychological studies of PTSD have adopted at least two approaches. In the first, researchers have adopted a neuropsychological test battery or have applied a selection of neuropsychological tests, in order to elicit deficits in a particular group of subjects. The tests used in this area are mainly those that have been standardised on brain-damaged individuals. Any abnormality found on these tests could be explained as either a direct or indirect effect of dysfunction of particular brain structures. In the second approach, researchers have undertaken hypothesis-driven experiments.

Neuropsychologists have shown particular interest in studying disturbances of memory and attention in PTSD patients. Poor memory and

*Institute of Psychiatry, London

Post-Traumatic Stress Disorders: Concepts and Therapy. Edited by William Yule.
© 1999 John Wiley & Sons Ltd.

concentration are common symptoms among PTSD sufferers (Archibald & Tuddenham, 1965; White, 1983; Burstein, 1985; Bleich, Grab & Kottler, 1986), and a number of authors have reviewed the memory impairments elicited in people with PTSD (e.g. Bremner, Krystal, Southwick & Charney, 1995a). Thus, for example, Bremner et al. (1993) compared memory performance of a group of Vietnam veterans with PTSD to that of a group of healthy subjects on the story and figure recall subtests from the Wechsler Memory Scale. The results showed poorer performance by the PTSD group in terms of verbal free recall and this could not be accounted for by between groups differences in IQ. In addition PTSD patients were poorer on the Selective Reminding Test in terms of recall of verbal and visual elements (Bremner et al., 1993; see also Yehuda et al., 1995). Uddo, Vasterling, Brailey & Sutker (1993) reported verbal learning deficits in Vietnam veterans with PTSD as compared to National Guards without PTSD. Bremner et al. (1995a) also discuss unpublished data indicating poorer verbal recall on the Wechsler Memory Scale Logical Memory stories for adult survivors of child abuse. However, when performance of PTSD patients was compared to that of a group of other psychiatric patients, rather than non-psychiatric patients as in the above studies, it was not significantly different (Gill, Calev, Greenberg, Kugelmass & Bernard, 1990).

In contrast to this approach, the theoretically based studies which focused on the specific sensitivity of PTSD patients to memory of the trauma and its reminders, have perhaps been more informative.

Research studies dealing with the specific memory of traumatic experiences explored whether PTSD patients exhibited a memory bias for trauma-related information. The paradigms used in this area are the implicit and explicit testing of memory (Zeitlin & McNally, 1991). Explicit memory is revealed when the task performance requires conscious recollection of a previous experience; it is usually assessed by tests involving recognition, free recall, and cued recall. Implicit memory indicates the effect of past experiences on subsequent performance on a memory task and it is usually assessed by indirect tests such as word-stem completion, lexical decision and tachistoscopic word identification.

Thus, for example, when PTSD subjects were requested to learn groups of words with different emotional content (positive, neutral and PTSD-related words), and had to retrieve them in a stem completion task (implicit memory), they showed a tendency to recall more trauma related words than other words (Zeitlin & McNally, 1991; Vrana, Roodman & Beckham, 1995). McNally, Litz, Prassas, Shin and Weathers (1994) used an explicit memory test to explore autobiographical disturbance in PTSD patients. Vietnam veterans with and without PTSD and a group of normal subjects were requested to retrieve a specific personal memory associated with cue words with different emotional content (positive and negative). The results showed that PTSD patients had difficulties retrieving specific autobiographical memories, especially in response to positive trait cue words. They were found to be poorer in producing specific memories than control subjects.

McNally, Lasko, Mackin and Pitman (1995) replicated this study with Vietnam veterans with and without PTSD and confirmed the poorer ability of PTSD sufferers in retrieving specific memories. Furthermore, the investigators asked the subjects to retrieve a memory of events that had occurred 10 years previously, in response to positive and negative cue words. In this part of their study, the control subjects (Vietnam veterans without PTSD) produced 20% of memories in response to positive cues and 24% in response to negative cues. In contrast, these percentages for PTSD patients were 50 and 75% respectively. More interestingly, these investigators noticed that a group of Vietnam veterans with PTSD who wore Vietnam regalia (e.g. combat medals, fatigues, POW/MIA buttons) to the interview, were worst at producing specific memories but they produced the most Vietnam-related memories. For these subjects, 43% of memories produced in response to positive cues and 90% produced in response to negative cues were related to the Vietnam war. These findings suggest that PTSD patients were less able to produce specific autobiographical memories, and, when asked to produce earlier memories, they were more likely to recall memories of war. The findings of these studies should be viewed cautiously, because the PTSD related to specific circumstances that had occurred at least 20 years previously. Furthermore, the effect of prolonged involvement in a war that could produce multiple traumatic experiences must be taken into consideration. In addition, information likely to be gained about the Vietnam war from the media or other sources (repeatedly talking about the war and self-exposure to various sources of information related to the war, especially for those wearing regalia) might overshadow the personal experiences of a particular event. Replication of these findings with civilian accident trauma sufferers (e.g. car accident, personal violence)—especially for those sufferers experiencing more recent traumas—would certainly increase our knowledge of this issue. If replicated successfully in future, these findings could confirm that memories of traumatic experiences can persist for years and that they have both an intrusive capacity and enhanced accessibility characteristics.

A group of studies has focused on the attentional bias of PTSD patients. These studies used an adaptation of the Stroop test (Stroop, 1935), which is often called the "emotional Stroop test". In this paradigm, subjects are shown words of different emotional impact that are printed in different colours. The subjects are then required to name quickly the colour in which the word is printed while ignoring the meaning of the word. Reaction times for colour naming of neutral words can be subtracted from the reaction times of colour naming for the target words. In this way an interference effect can be measured and it is possible to determine whether the emotional content of the words in some way delays the colour-naming process. It is also possible to use computerised or paper-and-pencil versions of the test. The computerised version of the test allows presentation of the different groups of words singly and inter-spersed in a random order. In the paper and pencil version each group of words shown is presented on the same page; therefore, there may be some contamination from the cumulative effect of a group of words upon attention or emotional reaction. The interference effect arises because, despite the subject's effort to focus on the colour in which the word is printed, the emotional significance of the word captures the attention of the subject and produces a delay in colour naming, in contrast to the words that are not emotionally significant for them. Stroop experiments have consistently shown that words closely associated with the subject's traumatic experiences produce greater interference than other word groups. These studies are summarised in Table 7.1.

These findings with PTSD patients support Horowitz's (1976) view that incompletely processed material (trauma-related memories) remains "in an active form" in memory. It seems that the information about traumatic events is readily accessible and readily interferes with patients' ongoing activities even when they make a conscious attempt to avoid it.

Studies that have used the emotional Stroop test with Vietnam veterans have mostly shown a significant interference effect for trauma-related material only, while other studies using anxiety disorder patients showed that the Stroop interference effect can be generated by positive words, as well as general threat words. In addition to the significant interference of PTSD-related words, a considerable interference effect of positive words and general threat words has also been observed (Thrasher, Dalgleish & Yule, 1994, Hagh-Shenas, 1996). Samples used in these studies differ from studies of Vietnam veterans in various ways. They had experienced civil accidents, most of them were not taking any medication for their psycho-logical problems and, finally, the time interval between the traumatic event and assessment was shorter than for the Vietnam veterans. If future replications support these findings this might indicate that PTSD sub-jects are more responsive to all kinds of emotional stimuli (positive or

Table 7.1 Stroop Interference Effect As A Measure of Intrusive Thought in Post-Traumatic Stress Disorder

Authors	Subjects	Word groups	Procedure
McNally et al. (1990)	Combat PTSD, $n = 15$ Combat non-PTSD, $n = 15$	PTSD-related words Positive OCD*-related words Neutral words	Each category of words presented on a single single card
Cassiday et al. (1992)	Rape victims with PTSD, $n = 12$ Without PTSD, $n = 12$ Normal control, $n = 12$	High-Low PTSD rape-related words Positive words Neutral words	Computerised presentation
Foa et al. (1991)	Rape victims with PTSD, $n = 15$ Without PTSD, $n = 14$ Normal, $n = 16$	Rape-related words General threat words Neutral words Non-words	Computerised presentation
Kaspi et al. (1991)	Combat PTSD and medical students before national board medical examination	Different stress-related words for each group	Computerised presentation
Thrasher et al. (1994)	Survivors of the Zeebrugge ferry disaster with Low PTSD, $n = 10$ High PTSD, $n = 13$ Normal, $n = 12$	PTSD-related General threat Semantically related/unrelated Neutral, Positive	Each category of words on a single piece of paper
McNally et al. (1993)	Combat PTSD, $n = 24$	PTSD-related words Positive words OCD-related words Neutral words	Each category of words on a single piece of paper
Kaspi et al. (1995)	Combat PTSD Without PTSD Healthy	Neutral Positive Negative Combat related	Random and block computerised presentation

*OCD = Obsessive-compulsive disorder

negative). Whether this emotionality predisposes to, or is a byproduct of, the psychopathology, requires further investigation.

Other studies, suggesting that PTSD patients have altered selective attention processes, have studied brain event-related potentials (e.g. Attias, Bleich & Gilat, 1996a; Attias, Bleich, Furman & Zinger, 1996b). In these studies Israeli combat veterans showed prolonged P3 latencies in response to combat-related pictures, with increased latencies correlating positively with measures of intrusiveness and negatively with measures of avoidance using the Impact of Event Scale (Attias, Bleich & Gilat, 1996a). In addition, other event-related potential components (N1, N2 and P2) were measured in response to pictures of non-threatening domestic animals, domestic furnishings and flowers or combat-related stimuli (Attias et al., 1996b). PTSD patients responded more slowly to the target stimuli than controls, and demonstrated other differences in P3 and N1 components for the combat-related pictures and animal pictures in comparison to the controls. Attias et al. (1996b) interpret their results as indicative of accentuated information processing occurring in the PTSD patients before stimulus classification took place. They suggest that alterations in early and late selective attention co-exist with a general state of hypersensitivity in PTSD patients, with this being particularly apparent in the case of trauma-related stimuli, and they relate this to the apparent difficulty experienced by PTSD patients in avoiding trauma-related memories. It is possible that such neurophysiological measures could be used to chart recovery from PTSD following treatment.

NEUROCHEMICAL AND NEUROANATOMICAL FEATURES OF PTSD

The studies reviewed above indicate that individuals with PTSD may show altered patterns of cognitive processing, both of relatively neutral clinical neuropsychological test material and of information more specifically related to their own traumatic experience. Why should this be the case?

A number of recent reviews have discussed the likely involvement of a number of neurochemical systems in stress and, particularly, in PTSD (see, for example, Charney, Deutch, Krystal, Southwick & Davis, 1993; Bremner, Krystal, Southwick & Charney, 1995a, 1996a, 1996b; McIvor, 1997). These reviews have all broadly set out to examine how the main symptom of PTSD are related to mechanisms of fear conditioning, extinction and sensitisation that are influenced by altered functions of neurochemical systems which, in turn, have an effect on the functioning of different brain regions.

Psychophysiological Studies on PTSD

PTSD sufferers have consistently been found to be highly psychophysiologically reactive to reminders of their trauma, and this has been explained on the basis of PTSD patients having undergone behavioural sensitisation to stressful stimuli (see Charney et al., 1993). A range of stressful stimuli may produce increases in brain noradrenergic function in the locus coeruleus, hypothalamus, hippocampus and amygdala, as well as in the cerebral cortex. Charney et al. (1993) suggest that many of the enduring symptoms of PTSD are reflective of increased noradrenergic function. Although there is inconsistent evidence about whether PTSD patients show higher basal noradrenergic function, there is evidence overall that PTSD patients may show greater responsivity of this neurochemical system than non-PTSD patients (see Bremner et al., 1996b). Bremner et al. (1996a) also suggest that early exposure to stress, presumably accompanied by increased norepinephrine release in the locus coeruleus, may sensitise the person in terms of his or her later responsiveness to subsequent stressors, thus providing a tentative explanation of why some individuals develop PTSD while others do not.

Studies on memory consolidation suggest that with increased levels of arousal the level of norepinephrine increases. Norepinephrine has been shown to have an inverted U-shaped relationship with memory consolidation. Both very low and very high levels of norepinephrine activity in the central nervous system interfere with memory storage. The release of excessive norepinephrine at the time of trauma probably plays a significant role in creating hyperamnesia or an oversensitivity to trauma-related information. As Gold and Zorenetzer (1983) and McGough (1983) suggested, emotional state has a strong influence in imprinting memories, and a stimulus–response association learned in a state of extreme emotion is never forgotten.

To demonstrate the heightened psychophysiological responsiveness of PTSD patients, it is possible to produce taped audio-visual cues related to the trauma using video films or a script that can be replayed in a psychophysiological laboratory. Changes in physiological indices such as blood pressure (BP), heart rate (HR) and skin conductance response (SCR) can then be observed. Studies using these techniques with PTSD sufferers (Vietnam veterans or civil-accident sufferers) have shown that PTSD patients can be successfully differentiated from non-PTSD patients, with considerable elevation on measures of BP, HR and SCR when presented with reminders of the original trauma (see Orr, 1994, for review). Furthermore, it has been shown that these heightened psychophysiological responses tend to decrease after successful psychotherapeutic intervention (Keane & Kaloupek, 1982; Shalev, Orr & Pitman, 1992; Boudewyns & Hyer, 1990). These laboratory findings confirm clinical observations that trauma memories are always associated with strong emotion.

One of the main neural components of emotional reaction, and linked to noradrenergic production, is the activation of the sympathetic nervous system (SNS), and McIvor (1997) suggests that the noradrenergic changes during stress underlie the autonomic conditioning hypothesis of PTSD proposed by Keane, Zimmering and Caddell (1985). A behavioural explanation for fear reaction is based on Mowrer's two-factor theory; this is used to explain the physiological arousal of PTSD patients in the presence of trauma cues (Becker, Skinner, Able, Axelrod & Cichon, 1984; Kilpatrick, Veronen & Best, 1985; Keane, Zimmering & Caddell, 1985). According to this theory, two types of learning (classical and instrumental) occur in the acquisition of fear and avoidance. In the first stage, via temporal contiguity, a previously neutral stimulus becomes associated with an unconditional stimulus (e.g. autonomic nervous system activation) that innately evokes discomfort or fear. The neutral stimulus then acquires aversive properties such that its presence elicits anxiety; it now becomes a conditional stimulus for a fear response.

This simple explanation shows how heightened physiological arousal to a particular stimulus might develop in these patients. Furthermore, the aversive character of trauma memories (Mowrer's second factor) may act to inhibit the rehearsal of these memories and keep patients away from any activity that would allow them to become habituated or desensitised to these memories. According to Rachman (1980), the failure of "emotional processing" results in emotional disturbance and efficient emotional processing occurs when these memories are absorbed and decline to the extent that other experiences and behaviour can proceed without disruption. The factors that prevent efficient emotional processing fall within the domain of the psychotherapist. McIvor (1997) and Bremner et al. (1996a), on the other hand, suggest that, with extreme noradrenergic activation, some brainstem structures, including the locus coeruleus, come under reduced inhibitory cortical control and may undergo synaptic changes that result in reduced capacity for habituation, as well as for new learning and discrimination.

Other neurochemicals have been discussed in relation to PTSD. Dopamine release and metabolism is increased in a number of specific brain areas under conditions of acute stress (see Charney et al., 1993; Bremner et al., 1996a). In particular, medial prefrontal cortical dopamine innervation is increased during stress, and this shows an increased response to repeated stress as well as to the effect of repeated exposure to substances such as amphetamines. Charney et al. (1993) indicate that the dopamine prefrontal system is involved in a number of high-level cognitive functions such as working memory and attention, and this system may also be involved in the hypervigilant state seen in PTSD, via its connections to other brain regions such as the amygdala, entorhinal cortex and the locus coeruleus.

The Limbic System, Emotion and Memory

Papez (1937) suggested that a set of interconnected brain structures formed a circuit whose primary function is motivation and emotion. This system included several regions of the limbic cortex and interconnected structures surrounding the core of the forebrain. The system has subsequently been expanded to include other structures and named the limbic system. The most important parts of the limbic system are the hippocampus and amygdala, located in the medial regions of the temporal lobe.

Of all the central nervous system structures the amygdala is most clearly implicated in the evaluation of the emotional meaning of incoming stimuli. Charney et al. (1993) indicate the importance of the amygdala in the conditioning and also the extinction of sensory and cognitive associations in relation to the original trauma; it must be appreciated, however, that all of the findings related to emotional functions of the amygdala, derived from animal studies, are based on avoidance-training procedures (Gold, 1995). In addition, the amygdala has extensive connections with cortical sensory systems, and Charney et al. (1993) suggest the possibility that many memories associated with traumatic events will ultimately be stored in the cortex. Charney et al. suggest that the amygdala may play a crucial role in the ability of specific sensory stimuli to elicit traumatic memories because of its rich interconnections.

Lesions of the amygdala interfere with a wide range of emotional memories, including inhibitory avoidance, fear-potentiated startle, and conditioned fear (e.g. Davis 1992; Helmestetter, 1992; Kesner, 1992; LeDoux, 1992). Charney et al. (1993) indicate that NMDA receptors are involved in these processes, since NMDA antagonists applied to the amygdala, as well as NMDA lesions of the amygdala, render impossible the development of fear-conditioned responses, and the extinction of fear-potentiated startle. According to LeDoux (1992), thalamo-amygdala connections provide rapid reactions to fear-conditioned stimuli, while thalamo-cortico-amygdala circuits are assumed to have a slower processing speed and possibly subserve more elaborated kinds of fears.

The hippocampus is implicated in a variety of types of mental functioning. One of the earliest functions recognised for this brain structure was its role in spatiotemporal processing. This notion formed the core of the cognitive map theory of O'Keefe and Nadel (1978). The septohippocampal system (hippocampus, and other structures including the septum, ventral thalamus and cingulate cortex) is believed to be involved in the evaluation of spatially and temporally related events, comparing them with previously stored information and determining whether and how they are associated with each other and with reward, punishment, novelty, or non-reward (Gray, 1987). The slow maturation of the hippocampus, which is not fully myelinated until after the third or fourth year of life, is believed to be the cause of infantile amnesia (Nadel & Zola-Morgan, 1984; Schacter & Moscovitch, 1984).

In stressful situations the sympathetic branch of the autonomic nervous system is active, and the adrenal glands secrete epinepherine, norepinepherine and steroid stress hormones. The activation of the sympathetic nervous system (SNS) is highly related to the activity of the amygdala (see Davis, 1992, for a comprehensive review). In view of the knowledge that acute trauma can lead to great increases in glucocorticoid levels (see Charney et al., 1993) studies have begun to emphasise the adverse effect of cortisol on the hippocampus.

In essence, the hippocampus has two kinds of neuroreceptors: mineralocorticoid and glucocorticoid receptors. In neutral conditions the level of cortisol is low, whereas in stressful conditions it increases. In the rest condition cortisol has a tendency to occupy 70% of mineralocorticoid receptors and 10% of glucocorticoid receptors. In highly stressful situations, however, with increased levels of cortisol, glucocorticoid receptors are almost completely occupied by cortisol (70% of mineralocorticoid and 80% of glucocorticoid receptors). The occupation of glucocorticoid receptors by cortisol interferes with hippocampal functioning by suppressing the excitability of hippocampal neurons. Suppression of hippocampal neurons means interference with long-term potentiation (LTP) which is found to be relevant for memory formation; LTP disrupts or suppresses the normal activity of that part of the brain responsible for encoding a spatiotemporal frame of reference. According to the formulation suggested by Nadel and Jacob (in press), memories of traumatic experiences are timeless and frameless, as if they are free floating, and can enter consciousness as a result of internal or external triggers. When these memories, which are likely to have visual characteristics, are triggered they have a very "live" and fresh quality and for the PTSD sufferer it is as if they are happening in the "here and now", rather than belonging to a specific time and place in the past. McIvor (1997) indicates that van der Kolk et al. (1985) had viewed the connections between the locus coeruleus and hippocampus, amygdala and temporal neocortex as a "neurophysiological analogue of memory"; increased noradrenergic innervation, due to extreme stress, thereby creating long-term potentiation of these pathways, might therefore be the biological correlate of flashbacks and nightmares.

Charney et al. (1993) propose a neural model for the development of PTSD that invokes the clear assumption that a number of brain regions are involved both at the time of the original trauma and subsequently (see Charney et al, 1993, p. 301). The original trauma leads to activation of norepinephrine, involving the locus coeruleus, hippocampus, amygdala, hypothalamus and cerebral cortex, accounting for the anxiety, fear, hypervigilance, autonomic hyperarousal, fight or flight readiness, encoding of traumatic memories and facilitation of sensori-motor responses. Increased dopamine release in the frontal cortex and nucleus accumbens, together with activation of mesocortical dopamine neurones, also occurs. Increased opiate release occurs in the cortex and amygdala and produces the analgesia that may be seen at the time of trauma perhaps facilitating survival at that time, as well as the subsequent emotional blunting seen in PTSD; McIvor (1997) notes that self-medication with opiates is the preferred form of drug abuse in many PTSD patients, suggesting that an addiction to opiates may arise from the condition. In addition, activation of the hypothalamic-pituitary-adrenal axis, leading to greatly elevated glucocorticoid levels and elevation of corticotrophin-releasing factor, affecting the hippocampus, amygdala and locus coeruleus, may lead to changes in metabolism, learned behaviour responses and anxiety and fear. Finally, McIvor (1997) reviews evidence concerning sleep disturbance in PTSD patients, indicating the role of the locus coeruleus in normal sleep regulation, and the possibility that the abnormal control of rapid eye movement may play a role in the exaggerated startle response seen in PTSD.

Summary

The above review indicates that it may be possible to find neurochemical explanations for many of the clinical and experimental findings in PTSD.

These findings have led to tentative models for the development of the symptom constellation that is well documented (see Charney et al., 1993; McIvor 1997). McIvor (1997) indicates that there remains much further to be understood about the biological underpinnings of PTSD. Further research in this area may further the rational use of psychopharmacological as well as psychotherapeutic treatments of this disorder.

CEREBRAL HEMISPHERES AND LATERALISATION OF EMOTIONAL PROCESSING: ARE THERE HEMISPHERIC DIFFERENCES IN PTSD?

There is a body of evidence of psychology literature indicating brain hemispheric specialisation, especially for emotion. Lateralised brain lesion studies (e.g. Heilman, Scholes & Watson, 1974) and various unimodal stimulus presentation methods (e.g. tachistoscopic presentation, dichotic listening, single nostril presentation of odours), document greater sensitivity of the right hemisphere in emotional information processing. There is also evidence of hemispheric differences in positive (pleasant) and negative (unpleasant) emotional states. For example, Davidson and Tomarken (1990), in a series of studies, have shown right hemisphere activation in negative and left hemisphere activation in positive emotional states. His findings are derived from power spectral analysis of EEG recordings. On the other hand, Ehrlichman (1986), using EEG recordings with pleasant and unpleasant smells, and Bradley, Cuthbert and Lang (1991), using right and left ear presentation of startle stimuli during pleasant and unpleasant slide presentations, have shown that the dichotomy of right/left hemisphere in emotions can be misleading. The results of their studies showed that right hemisphere activity increases in pleasant mood states but there is no evidence of change in left hemisphere activation in pleasant and unpleasant emotional states.

A few experimental studies exist which show right hemisphere involvement in fear conditioning. For example, in Hugdahl and Johnsen's (1991) experiment, subjects who had a picture of an angry face as a conditional stimulus (CS) were conditioned with electric shock (unconditioned stimulus). During the extinction stage of the experiment, which was carried out with right hemisphere presentation of CS, subjects showed a more persisting effect of learning and a greater skin conductance response in contrast to the other group, who had a happy face as the CS and left hemisphere presentation during extinction stage. In addition, the fear-potentiated startle paradigm has been useful for delineating the mechanisms of fear conditioning because fear is measured by a change in a simple reflex mediated by a defined neural pathway (Lang, 1994). However, it has been found that the startle probe to the right and left ear while the subjects are in pleasant or unpleasant mood states produces a different magnitude of eye blink (Bradley, Cuthbert & Lang, 1991). The investigators found significant increases in the magnitude of the eye blink reflex when the subjects were in an unpleasant mood state and startle probes were presented to the left ear (right hemisphere).

As mentioned earlier, the amygdala has been known to mediate fear conditioning (LeDoux, 1989) and the fight and flight system (Gray, 1994). This brain structure has a critical role in the fear-potentiated startle response because it projects directly to one of the brainstem nuclei necessary for startle (Rosen et al., 1991). Lesioning this pathway blocks the ability of conditioned or unconditioned fear stimuli to elevate the startle response (Hitchcock, Sananes & Davis, 1989; Hitchcock & Davis, 1991). Examining this brain structure with electrophysiological recording, Lloyd and Kling (1991) showed that monkeys which acquired fear conditioning in an ambiguous situation (without cue) when placed in that situation in the absence of US, have lateralised right amygdala power delta band activity. This wave was found to be specific for the fear conditioned response in their earlier study (Kling, Lloyd & Perryman, 1987).

With specific reference to PTSD, Bremner et al. (1995b) examined lateralised asymmetries in the hippocampi of 26 Vietnam combat veterans and in 22 control subjects matched for age, gender, race, years of education socioeconomic status, body size and years of alcohol abuse. They found that the PTSD patients had right hippocampi that were 8% smaller in volume compared to the right hippocampi of the control subjects, whereas the 3.8% smaller left hippocampal volume was not significant. In addition, there were no between-group differences in the size of two other brain regions measured for reference. In addition to the structural differences, the PTSD patients performed more poorly on standardised tests of verbal, and, for the PTSD patients, a positive correlation was found between right (but not left) hippocampal volume and percent retention of verbal material. The authors raise the possibility either that a small right hippocampus from birth might have predisposed towards the development of PTSD, or that extreme stress, with the release of glucocorticoids and other neurotransmitters, could have been associated with hippocampal damage. Bremner et al. (1995b) are unclear about why hippocampal asymmetries occur as a result of steroid production, although other neurotransmitters may act asymmetrically. They also raise the possibility that bilateral changes may occur which, in this study, were only significant on the right side. They speculate that there may be pathological processes affecting both hippocampi with perhaps greater magnitude on the right. However, Bremner et al. (1995a) report having found a 12% reduction in left hippocampal volume in 17 adult survivors of childhood sexual abuse in comparison to closely matched controls, and so this is an area requiring further investigation.

The fact that asymmetry of cortisol secretion under conditions of stress may have some role to play in the hippocampal asymmetry reported by Bremner et al. (1995b), and discussed above, receives some support from Wittling and Pfluger (1990). Right-handed normal subjects were shown either an emotionally aversive or neutral film in either their right or left visual fields via univisual field contact lenses. Film-related changes of cortisol secretion relative to baseline were determined by salivary cortisol radio-immunoassay. The aversive film led to significantly higher cortisol increases than the neutral film, and right hemisphere presentation of the emotionally aversive film produced significantly higher increases in cortisol secretion than left hemisphere film presentation. No between-hemisphere differences were noted for the neutral film.

To explore further the implication of the limbic system in memories of traumatic experiences, Rauch and colleagues (1996) used a Positron Emission Tomography (PET) scanning with eight PTSD patients. They used a script-driven imagery provocation technique. A script relevant to each subject's traumatic experience was recorded and replayed during PET scanning. They reported significant increases in regional cerebral blood flow (rCBF) in right-sided limbic and paralimbic structures. The amygdala, and secondary visual cortex (Brodmann's area 18) of the right hemisphere, were found to be highly activated. Interestingly, Rauch et al. found significant decreases in rCBF in the left inferior temporal cortex. The result of this study shows that traumatic memories are encoded differently from memories of ordinary events, possibly because of the high degree of emotional arousal at the time of consolidation. Increased rCBF in the secondary visual cortex during traumatic imagery suggests that activation of sensory brain structures might underlie the visual re-experiencing phenomena in PTSD. Decreased rCBF in the left-sided cortical area, Broca's area (a territory thought to be responsible for constructing semantic representations of experiences), was also found.

Our own studies (Hagh-Shenas, 1996) have thrown additional light on the lateralisation of trauma-related stimulus processing in PTSD patients. The use of an emotional Stroop test (see above) indicated that our sample of PTSD patients showed greater sensitivity to trauma-related words presented to their right hemisphere in contrast to a group of neutral words. However, they were more sensitive overall to words with an emotional content (positive or negative) than controls, thus suggesting that the right hemisphere was contributing to general processing of emotionality of the stimuli in these patients. In a further study, investigating brain EEG activity during the processing of trauma-related information, right temporal activation was observed when the PTSD patients were listening to trauma-related words, whereas left temporal activation was observed for control subjects who were listening to words related to an unpleasant event that had occurred to them. The PTSD group also showed greater activation of bilateral parieto-occipital regions than the control group; this would appear to be related to the observation that the PTSD subjects reported seeing a visual image of the trauma in response to the words, whereas the control subjects did not. Thus our studies provide some support for the disproportionate involvement of right hemisphere structures in the processing of trauma-related information.

Thus, there is some, although by no means incontrovertible, evidence that right hemisphere structures may be implicated in the mediation of PTSD-related stimuli. The following section will review whether the nature of the PTSD symptoms themselves might support such right hemisphere involvement; in so doing it is necessary to bear in mind the usual association between the left hemisphere and verbal memory processes and the right hemisphere and non-verbal, visual and emotional memory processes. Moreover, when one hemisphere learns, has certain experiences, and/or stores information in memory, this information is not always available to the opposite hemisphere; one hemisphere cannot always gain access to memories stored in the other half of the brain (Joseph, 1988). However, available information in this area suggests that, in the intact brain, some memory traces appear to be stored unilaterally rather than laid down in both hemispheres.

Trauma images and memories

Janet (1889) suggested that intense emotional reactions to a traumatic event resulted in memories related to the event being dissociated from consciousness and being stored as visceral sensations or visual images. At a later stage, visceral sensations presented themselves as feelings of anxiety and panic and visual images emerged as flashbacks and nightmares. In less intense emotional states, memories may yet have a vivid and fresh quality, for example in "flashbulb" memories. Brown and Kulik (1977) coined the term "flashbulb" to convey the notion that memories of highly surprising events retain their freshness and vividness over a long period of time. They found that personal importance and the consequences of the event for the subject were important factors determining the formation of the flashbulb memories. However, their hypothesis emphasised that both public and personal events that produce a high level of surprise, and are shocking, are associated with a high likelihood of the establishment of flashbulb memories. They proposed that, in cases of extreme surprise, the whole memory system may be destabilised resulting in amnesia for the event. In contrast, when an event conveys no surprise, there would be no detailed memory of it. In the case of a surprise value falling between the two extremities, flashbulb memory formation is more likely to occur. More interestingly, Brown and Kulik (1977) and Conway (1995) suggested that flashbulb memories have increased non-verbal characteristics; with respect to our current consideration it may be that they are mediated by right hemisphere structures. By further processing and elaboration, mainly by discussing these memories with other people, accounts or descriptions of these memories are likely to be consolidated in long-term memory. Flashbulb memories may still retain their own identity (with non-verbal characteristics) and come to mind when triggered by cues.

Van der Kolk (1994) argued that the memory of a traumatic event resides in our memory system as a pure visual image; this might again implicate right hemisphere structures. Brewin, Dalgleish and Joseph (1996) proposed two levels in memory in which trauma information might be represented. At the level of "verbal accessible memories" a verbal description or account of a traumatic experience is available to our conscious mind and can be manipulated in this way, and implicates the involvement of left hemisphere structures, while at the level of "situationally accessible memories", traumatic experiences are not accessible to our conscious mind in the way they are in the first level. Furthermore, these memories are unlikely to lead themselves to editing or manipulation. It seems that the flashback phenomena observed in PTSD patients represent the extreme form of these latter type of memories.

The visual characteristics of memories of traumatic scenes depicted in flashback phenomena—which, in their extreme form, happens in a dissociative state—have been reported by various researchers and clinicians (Mellman & Davis, 1985; Lansky & Bley, 1991; Brockway, 1988; Solursh, 1988; see Frankel, 1994 for a comprehensive review).

Findings by Rauch et al. (1996) and Kosslyn et al. (1996) have suggested that imagining aversive stimuli involves the activation of the visual cortex; in Rauch et al.'s study, the right-sided secondary visual cortex was activated, whereas in Kosslyn et al.'s study of non-PTSD subjects, right area 17 and bilateral area 18 were found to be activated. Increased rCBF in the secondary visual cortex during traumatic imagery suggests that activation of sensory brain structures might underlie visual re-experiencing phenomena in PTSD. The decrease in rCBF in Broca's area—a left hemisphere region thought to be responsible for constructing semantic experiences—is consistent with the notion that PTSD patients have difficulties in cognitively restructuring their traumatic experiences. It seems that, when people are traumatised, they are more likely to experience "speechless terror" (Rauch et al., 1996); the emotional impact of the event may interfere with the capacity to capture the experience in words or symbols. Recurrent thoughts and images related to the event often evoke extreme levels of fear and stress that may thwart any natural process of relating this information to resources producing symbolic accounts. It seems that a cycle of flow of information configured within the right hemisphere emerges through recollections, nightmares and flashbacks. As a result of these, the events become verbalisable, and thereby permit further processing of the information.

CONCLUSIONS

Current knowledge concerning the neuropsychology and neurochemical and anatomical underpinnings of PTSD allows a rational explanation of the cardinal symptoms of the disorder to be made. Understanding the neurochemical changes that occur during conditions of extreme stress and trauma, and the brain systems affected by these changes, renders it easier to understand why, for example, hyperarousal, attention and memory impairments and sensitivity to re-exposure to stresses might be found. It also begins to lead to rational suggestions about possible pharmacological treatments.

Current research is also suggestive of specific hemispheric involvement in the processing of trauma-related as opposed to simply unpleasant information; this may in part be related to the known bias of the right hemisphere in processing emotionally laden material, and may suggest that, in circumstances where a traumatic event occurs without the opportunity for any ongoing consideration of its nature, the right hemisphere preferentially mediates the information, with the result that it is stored in a predominantly non-verbal form. It is then the role of therapy to translate these into verbal structures that are then amenable to treatment.

REFERENCES

Archibald, H. & Tuddenham, R. (1965). Resistant stress reaction after combat: A 20-year follow-up. *Archivs of General Psychiatry*, **12**, 475–481.

Attias, J., Bleich A. & Gilat, S. (1996a). Classification of veterans with post-traumatic stress disorder using visual brain evoked P3s to traumatic stimuli. *British Journal of Psychiatry*, **168**, 110–115.

Attias, J., Bleich, A., Furman, V. & Zinger, Y. (1996b) Event-related potentials in post-traumatic stress disorder of combat origin. *Biological Psychiatry*, **40**, 373–381.

Becker, J.V., Skinner, L.J., Able, G.G., Axelrod, R. & Cichon, J. (1984). Sexual problems of sexual assault survivors. *Women and Health* **9**, 5–20.

Blake, D., Weather, F., Nagy, K., Kaloupek, D., Klauminzer, G., Charney, D. & Keane, T. (1990). *Clinician-Administered PTSD Scale (CAPS)*. National Centre for Post-Traumatic Stress Disorder.

Bleich, A., Grab, R. & Kottler, M. (1986). Treatment of prolonged combat reaction. *British Journal of Psychiatry*, **148**, 493–496.

Boudewyns, P.A. & Hyer, L. (1990). Physiological response to combat memories and preliminary treatment outcome in Vietnam veteran PTSD patients treated with direct therapeutic exposure. *Behavior Therapy*, **21**, 63–87.

Bradley, M.M., Cuthbert, B.N. & Lang, P.J. (1991). Startle and Emotion: Lateral acoustic probes and bilateral blink. *Psychophysiology*, **28** (3), 285–295.

Bremner, J., Tammy, M., Delaney, R., Southwick, S., Mason, J., Johnson, D., Innis, R., McCarthy, G. & Charney, D. (1993). Deficit in short-term memory in post-traumatic stress disorder. *American Journal of Psychiatry*, **150** (7), 1015–1019.

Bremner, J.D., Krystal, J.H., Southwick, S.M. & Charney, D.S. (1995a). Functional neuroanatomical correlates of the effects of stress on memory. *Jourual of Traumatic Stress*, **8**, 527–553.

Bremner, J.D., Randall, P., Scott, T.M., Bronen, R.A., Seibyl, J.P., Southwick, S.M., Delaney, R.C., McCarthy, G., Charney, D.D. & Innis, R.B. (1995b). MRI-based measurement of hippocampal volume in patients with combat-related posttraumatic stress disorder. *American Journal of Psychiatry*, **152**, 973–981.

Bremner, J.D., Krystal, J.H., Southwick, S.M. & Charney, D.S. (1996a). Noradrenergic mechanism in stress and anxiety: I. Preclinical studies. *Synapse*, **23**, 28–38.

Bremner, J.D., Krystal, J.H., Southwick, S.M. & Charney, D.S. (1996b). Noradrenergic mechanism in stress and anxiety: II. Clinical studies. *Synapse*, **23**, 39–51.

Brewin, C.R., Dalgleish, T. & Joseph, S. (1996). A dual representation theory of posttraumatic stress disorder. *Psychological Review*, **103**, 670–686.

Brockway, S. (1988). Case report: Flashback as a post-traumatic stress disorder (PTSD symptoms in a world war II veteran). *Military-medicine*, **153**, 372–373.

Brown, R. & Kulik, J. (1977). Flashbulb memories. *Cognition*, **5**, 73–99.

Burstein, A. (1985). Post-traumatic flashback, dream disturbance, and mental imagery. *Journal of Clinical Psychiatry*, **46**, 374–378.

Cassiday, K.L., McNally, R.J. & Zeitlin, S.B. (1992). Cognitive processing of trauma cues in victims with post-traumatic stress disorder. *Cognitive Therapy and Research*, **16** (3), 283–295.

Charney, D.S., Deutch, A.Y., Krystal, J.H., Southwick, S.M. & Davis, M. (1993). Psychobiologic mechanisms of posttraumatic stress disorder. *Archives of General Psychiatry*, **50**, 294–305.

Conway, M. (1995). *Flashbulb Memories*. Hillsdale, NJ: Lawrence Erlbaum.

Davidson, R.J. & Tomarken, A.J. (1990). Laterality and emotions: An electrophysiological approach. In F. Boller and J. Grafman (Eds.), *Handbook of Neuropsychology*, vol. 3, pp. 419–441. Amsterdam: Elsevier.

Davis, M. (1992). The role of amygdala in fear and anxiety. *Annual Review of Neuroscience*, **15**, 353–375.

Ehrlichman, H. (1986). Hemispheric asymmetry and positive-negative affect. In: A. Dottson (Ed.), *Duality and Unity of the Brain*. London: Macmillan.

Foa, E.B., Feske, U., Murdock, T.B., Kozak, M.J. & McCarthy, P.R. (1991). Processing of threat-related information in rape victims. *Journal of Abnormal Psychology*, **100** (2), 156–162.

Frankel, F.H. (1994). The concept of flashback in historical perspective. Special issue: Hypnosis and delayed recall: I. *International Journal of Clinical and Experimental Hypnosis*, **42**, 321–336.

Gill, T., Calev, A., Greenberg, D., Kugelmass, S. & Bernard, L. (1990). Cognitive functioning in Post-Traumatic Stress Disorder. *Journal of Traumatic Stress*, **3**, 29–45.

Gold, P.E. (1995). Modulation and emotional and nonemotional memories: Same pharmacological system, different neuroanatomical system. In J.L. McGaugh, N.M. Weinberger & G. Lynch (Eds.), *Brain and Memory: Modulation and Mediation of Neuroplasticity*. New York: Oxford University Press.

Gold, P.E. & Zorenetzer, S.F. (1983). The mnemon and its juices: Neuromodulation of processes. *Behavioral and Neural Biology*, **38**, 151–189.

Gray, J.A. (1987). *The Psychology of Fear and Stress* (2nd Edition). Cambridge: Cambridge University Press.

Gray, J.A. (1994). Framework for taxonomy of psychiatric disorder. In, S.H.M. Vam Goozen, N.E. Van de Poll & J.A. Sergeant (Eds.), *Emotions: Essays on Emotion Theory*. Hillsdale, NJ: Lawrence Erlbaum.

Hagh-Shenas, H. (1996). Cerebral lateralisation in processing of trauma-related information in post traumatic stress disorder (PTSD). Unpublished PhD thesis, University of London.

Heilman, K.M., Scholes, R. & Watson, R.T. (1974). Auditory affective agnosia. *Journal of Neurological and Neurosurgical Psychiatry*, **38**, 69.

Helmestetter, F.G. (1992). Contribution of amygdala to learning and performance of conditional fear. *Physiological Behaviour*, **51**, 1271–1276.

Hitchcock, J.M., Sananes, C.B. & Davis, M. (1989). Sensitisation of the startle reflex by footshock: Blockade by lesion of the central nucleus of the amygdala or its efferent pathway to the brainstem. *Behavioural Neuroscience*, **103** (3), 509–518.

Hitchcock, J.M. & Davis, M. (1991). Efferent pathway of the amygdala involved in conditioned fear as measured with the fear-potentiated startle paradigm. *Behavioural Neuroscience*, **105** (6), 826–842.

Horowitz, M. (1976). *Stress Response Syndromes*. New York: Jason Aronson.

Hugdahl, K. & Johnsen, B.H. (1991). Brain asymmetry and human electrodermal conditioning. *Integrative Physiological and Behavioral Science*, **26** (1), 39–44.

Janet, P. (1889). *L'automatisme Psychologique*. Paris: Alcan.

Joseph, R. (1988). The right cerebral hemisphere: Emotion, music, visual-spatial skills, body -image, dreams and awareness. *Journal of Clinical Psychology*, **44**, 630–673.

Kaspi, S.P. & McNally, R.J. (1991). Selective processing of idiographic emotional information in PTSD. Paper presented at the meeting of the Association for Advancement of Behaviour Therapy, New York.

Kaspi, S.P., McNally, R.J. & Amir, N. (1995). Cognitive processing of emotional information in post-traumatic stress disorder. *Cognitive Therapy and Research*, **19**, 319–330.

Keane, T.M. & Kaloupek, D.G. (1982). Imaginal flooding in the treatment of a post-traumatic stress disorder. *Journal of Consulting and Clinical Psychology*, **50**, 138–140.

Keane, T.M., Zimmering, R.T. & Caddell, J.M. (1985). A behavioural formulation of post-traumatic stress disorder in Vietnam veterans. *Behaviour Therapist*, **8**, 9–12.

Kesner, R.P. (1992). Learning and memory in rats with emphasis on the role of amygdala. In J.A. Aggelton (Ed.), *The Amygdala: Neurobiological Aspects of Emotion, Memory, and Mental Dysfunction*, New York: Wiley-Liss.

Kilpatrick, D.G., Veronen, L.J. & Best, C.L. (1985). Factors predicting psychological distress among rape victims. In C.R. Figley (Ed.), *Trauma and its Wake*. New York: Brunner/Mazel.

Kosslyn, S., Shin, L.M., Thompson, W.L., McNally, R.J., Rauch, S.L., Pitman, R.K. & Alpert, N.M. (1996). Neural effects of visualizing and perceiving aversive stimuli: a PET investigation. *Neuroreport*, **10**, 1569–1576.

Kling, A.S., Lloyd, R.L. & Perryman, K.M. (1987). Slow wave changes in amygdala to visual, auditory and social stimuli following lesions of the inferior temporal cortex in Squirrel monkey (*S. sciureus*). *Behavioral and Natural Biology*, **42**, 54–72.

Lang, P.J. (1994). The motivational organisation of emotion: Affect–reflex connection. In VanGoozen (Ed.), *Emotions: Essays on Emotion Theory*. Hillsdale, NJ: Lawrence Erlbaum.

Lansky, M.R. & Bley, C.R. (1991). Flashback as screen memory. *Bulletin of the Menninger Clininc*, **55**, 104–110.

LeDoux, J.E. (1989). Cognitive-emotional interactions in the brain. *Cognition and Emotion*, **3**, 267–289.

LeDoux, J.E. (1992). Emotion and amygdala. In J.A. Aggelton (Ed.), *The Amygdala: Neurobiological Aspects of Emotion, Memory, and Mental Dysfunction*. New York: Wiley-Liss.

Lloyd, R.L. & Kling, A.S. (1991). Delta activity from amygdala in squirrel monkeys (*Saimiri sciureus*): Influence of social and environmental context. *Behavioural Neuroscience*, **106** (2), 223–229.

McGough, J.L. (1983). Hormonal influences on memory. *Annual Review of Psychology* **34**, 297–323.

McIvor, R. (1997). Physiological and biological mechanisms. In D. Black, M. Newman, G. Mezey & J. Harris Hendricks (Eds.), *Psychological Trauma: A Developmental Approach*, pp. 55–60. London: Gaskell.

McNally, R.J., Kaspi, S.P., Riemann, B.C. & Zeitlin, S.B. (1990). Selective processing of threat cues in post-traumatic stress disorder. *Journal of Abnormal Psychology*, **99**, 4398–4402.

McNally, R.J., English, G.E. & Howard, J.L. (1993). Assessment of intrusive cognition in post-traumatic stress disorder. *Journal of Traumatic Stress*, **6**, 33–41.

McNally, R.J., Litz, B.T., Prassas, A., Shin, L.M. & Weathers, F.W. (1994). Emotional priming of autobiographical memory in post-traumatic stress disorder. *Cognition and Emotion*, **8**, 351–367.

McNally, R.J., Lasko, N.B., Mackin, M.L. & Pitman, R.K. (1995). Autobiographical memory disturbance in combat-related post-traumatic stress disorder. *Behaviour Research and Therapy*, **33**, 619–630.

Mellman, T.A. & Davis, G.C. (1985). Combat related flashbacks in post-traumatic stress disorder: phenomenology and similarity to panic attack. *Journal of Clinical Psychiatry*, **46**, 379–382.

Nadel, L. & Jacob, W.J. (in press). The role of the hippocampus in PTSD, panic and phobia. In N. Kato (Ed.), *Hippocampus: Functions and Clinical Relevance*. Amsterdam, Elsevier.

Nadel, L. & Zola-Morgan, S. (1984). Infantile amnesia: A neurobiological perspective. In M. Moscovitch (Ed.), *Infant Memory*. New York: Plenum Press.

Orr, S.P. (1994). An overview of psychophysiological studies of PTSD. *PTSD Research Quaraterly*, **5**, 1.

O'Keefe, J. & Nadel, L. (1978). *The Hippocampus as a Cognitive Map*. Oxford: Clarendon Press.

Papez, J.J.W.A. (1937). A proposed mechanism of emotion. *Archives of Neurology and Psychiatry*, **38**, 725–744.

Rachman, S. (1980). Emotional processing. *Behaviour Research and Therapy*, **8**, 15–60.

Rauch, S.L., van der Kolk, B.A., Fisler, R.E., Alpert, N.M., Orr, S.P., Savage, C.R., Fischman, A.J., Jenike, M.A. & Pitman, R.K. (1996). A symptom provocation study of post-traumatic stress disorder using Positron Emission Tomography and script-driven imagery. *Archives of General Psychiatry*, **53**, 380–387.

Rosen, J.B., et al. (1991). Direct projection from the central nucleus of the amygdala to the acoustic startle pathway: Anterograde and retrograde tracing studies. *Behavioural Neuroscience*, **105**, 817–825.

Schacter, D.L. & Moscovitch, M. (1984). Infants, amnesia: A neurobiological perspective. In M. Moscovitch (Ed.), *Infant Memory*. New York: Plenum Press.

Shalev, A.Y., Orr, S.P. & Pitman, R.K. (1992). Psychophysiologic response during script-driven imagery as outcome measure in post-traumatic stress disorder. *J. Clinical Psychiatry*, **53**, 324–326.

Solursh, L. (1988). Combat addiction post-traumatic stress disorder re-explored. *Psychiatric Journal of the University of Ottawa*, **13**, 17–20.

Stroop, J.R. (1935). Studies of interference in serial verbal reactions. *Journal of Experimental Psychology*, **18**, 643–662.

Thrasher, S.M., Dalgleish, T. & Yule, W. (1994). Information processing in post-traumatic stress disorder. *Behaviour Research and Therapy*, **32**, 247–254.

Uddo, M., Vasterling, J.T., Brailey, K. & Sutker, P.B. (1993). Memory and attention in posttraumatic stress disorder. *Journal of Psychopathology and Behaviour Assessment*, **15**, 43–52.

van der Kolk, B.A. (1994). The body keeps the score: Memory and the evolving psychobiology of post-traumatic stress. *Harvard Review of Psychiatry*, **1**, 253–265.

van der Kolk, B.A., Greenberg, M.S., Boyd, H., *et al.* (1995). Inescapable shock, neurotransmitters and addictions to trauma: Towards a psychobiology of posttraumatic stress. *Biological Psychiatry*, **20**, 314–325.

Vrana, S.A., Roodman, A. & Beckham, J.C. (1995). Selective processing of trauma-relevant words in post-traumatic stress disorder. *Journal of Anxiety Disorders*, **9**, 515–530.

White, N.S. (1983). Post-traumatic stress disorder. *Hospital and Community Psychiatry*, 34, 1061–1062.

Wittling, W. & Pfluger, M. (1990). Neuroendocrine hemisphere asymmetries: Salivary cortisol secretion during lateralised viewing of emotion related and neutral films. *Brain and Cognition*, **14**, 243–265.

Yehuda, R., Keefe, R., Harvey, P., Levengood, R., Gerber, D., Geni, J. & Siever, L.J. (1995). Learning and memory in combat veterans with Post-traumatic Stress Disorder. *American Journal of Psychiatry*, **152**, 137–139.

Zeitlin, S.B. & McNally, R.J. (1991). Implicit and explicit memory bias for threat in post-traumatic stress disorder. *Behaviour Research and Therapy*, **29**, 451–457.

Chapter 8

INTRUSIVE THINKING IN POST-TRAUMATIC STRESS DISORDER

Padmal de Silva* and Melanie Marks*

INTRODUCTION

Intrusive thinking is one of the main characteristics of post-traumatic stress disorder (PTSD). Ever since PTSD was officially recognised as a psychiatric disorder, intrusive thinking has been regarded as a major feature in its phenomenology (see DSM-III; APA, 1980). Even prior to the official acceptance of PTSD as a diagnostic category, accounts of traumatic stress reactions (e.g. war neurosis) often included vivid descriptions of intrusive thoughts and images (e.g. Kardiner, 1941).

In this chapter, we shall examine the nature and presentation of intrusive thinking in PTSD. In order to place this phenomenon in context, we shall begin with a discussion of intrusive thinking in general, including such thinking in non-clinical subjects. In our analysis of intrusive thinking in PTSD, we shall focus on the form, content, consequences and correlates of such experiences. An attempt will be made to examine the relationship of intrusive thoughts with other cognitions in PTSD patients. Finally, the intrusive thinking in PTSD patients will be compared with such thinking in other psychiatric disorders, mainly obsessive-compulsive disorder.

A note on terminology is needed at this point. The term "intrusive thinking" usually refers to both intrusive thoughts and intrusive images—i.e. intrusive cognitions in general. In the body of this chapter, to avoid any ambiguity, we shall use the term "intrusive cognitions" as a generic term to refer to both thoughts and images; the term "thoughts" will be used specifically to refer to what one might call "lexical cognitions" or "verbal thoughts", and the term "images" will be used to refer to imagery

*Institute of Psychiatry, London

Post-Traumatic Stress Disorders: Concepts and Therapy. Edited by William Yule.
© 1999 John Wiley & Sons Ltd.

cognitions—i.e. cognitions that take the form of mental images. The problems arising from the common use of the terms "thinking" and "thought" to refer to both lexical cognitions and imagery cognitions are well known (e.g. de Silva, 1986), and we hope that our clarification of terms will avoid any ambiguity. There are, of course, more serious difficulties related to the definition of cognition itself, with cognitions often comprising both lexical and imagery elements with varying degrees of dominance and prominence. These create difficulties for the clinician and the researcher, as the elicitation of accurate reports of cognitions from patients and subjects needs to take account of this feature. We shall comment on this problem in a later paragraph.

WHAT ARE INTRUSIVE COGNITIONS?

Intrusive cognitions have been discussed in the literature in some depth and detail since the work of Rachman and his colleagues over 20 years ago (e.g. Rachman, 1971, 1978, 1981; Rachman & de Silva, 1978; Parkinson & Rachman, 1981). The early work was focused on *unwanted* intrusive cognitions, which Rachman and de Silva called "normal obsessions" in their 1978 paper. The term was suggested as the nature and formal properties of unwanted, intrusive cognitions in normal subjects were not very different from clinical obsessions in obsessive-compulsive patients. Obsessions in obsessive-compulsive disorder are essentially intrusive phenomena, and this quality is shared by normal obsessions. While the early work concentrated on unwanted intrusive cognitions of a negative kind (e.g. thoughts of blasphemy, thoughts of violent acts, images of unpleasant scenes), it was recognised even at that stage that there are also intrusive cognitions that are not negative or unpleasant, and indeed many of which are not unwanted at all despite their intrusiveness (e.g. daydreams, romantic fantasies). Rachman (1981) referred to "a wide range of welcome forms of intrusive activity, up to and including what artists sometimes describe as inspiration" (p. 89).

How, then, might one define intrusive cognitions? Salkovskis (1990, p. 91) has offered the following definition:

> Intrusive cognitions are mental events which are perceived as interrupting a person's stream of consciousness by capturing the focus of attention. These cognitive events can take the form of "verbal" thoughts, images or impulses or some combination of the three.

By definition, intrusive cognitions intrude into, and therefore interrupt, a person's ongoing mental activity. They are not merely "perceived as interrupting a person's stream of consciousness", as stated by Salkovskis (1990, cited above); they in fact *do* interrupt the stream of consciousness. The cognition *happens* to the person; that is, it is not a voluntary event. We concur with Rachman's statement (1981, p. 89) that

> the necessary and sufficient conditions for defining a thought, image or impulse as intrusive are as follows: the subjective report that it is interrupting an ongoing activity; the thought, image or impulse is attributed to an internal origin; and it is difficult to control.

The reason why internal attribution is specified arises from the need to distinguish intrusive cognitions from certain other experiences that patients with psychotic disorders commonly report. These, while sometimes appearing similar to intrusive cognitions, are perceived by the person as caused by some external agency—e.g. a thought has been put into one's head by aliens.

POSITIVE AND NEGATIVE INTRUSIVE COGNITIONS

Intrusive cognitions occur in both clinical and non-clinical populations. In the original study of intrusions in normal subjects, Rachman and de Silva (1978) found that nearly 80% of non-clinical subjects experienced intrusive cognitions of a negative type, similar to obsessions in clinical obsessive-compulsive patients. Many other investigators have since confirmed that normal subjects commonly experience intrusive cognitions (Salkovskis & Harrison, 1984; Edwards & Dickerson, 1987; Freeston, Ladouceur, Thibodeau & Gagnon, 1991). What has also been shown in some of these later empirical studies is that these intrusive cognitions are not always experienced as negative. The work of Edwards and Dickerson (1987) particularly emphasises this. Intrusive cognitions can be negative or positive; memories of a pleasant event that intrude into one's mind exemplify the latter. They can, of course, also be neutral in terms of emotional tone.

INTRUSIVE COGNITIONS AND STRESS

There is a relatively large literature which demonstrates that intrusive cognitions of a negative nature tend to occur repeatedly as a result of stress. Some of the early work of Mardi Horowitz was aimed at investigating the appearance of intrusions following a stressful experience. Essentially, Horowitz found that subjects who were exposed to a stressful event reported numerous repetitive cognitions, mainly images, in the hours that followed (Horowitz, 1969). While Horowitz clearly established the occurrence of intrusive cognitions following a contrived stress, such as seeing a film that showed war, killing and injuries, Parkinson and Rachman (1981) demonstrated the links between uncontrived stress and intrusive cognitions. In a study of mothers whose children were hospitalised for tonsillectomy, they found that these mothers experienced many more intrusive cognitions than a similar group of mothers whose children were not in hospital. There was a particularly high level of occurrence of images, more than three times that the control mothers had. Some of the intrusions experienced by the mothers whose children were in hospital for tonsillectomy were as follows:

> "I have been worrying about it in case anything went wrong with the operation or the anaesthetic."
>
> "I have this repeated image of K on a trolley, and they put him in a bed and then I see blood everywhere."
>
> "I have seen him lying there like a vegetable and not coming round from an operation."
>
> (Parkinson & Rachman, 1981, p. 115)

The ability of stressful experiences to generate repetitive intrusive cognitions of a negative kind is now firmly established. There are numerous studies in the literature that show this. To cite but one example, McFarlane (1992) documented the development of intrusive cognitions in a group of firefighters in Australia who were exposed to devastating bushfires. As PTSD is by its very definition a disorder emanating from a severe stress experience, the occurrence of a high degree of intrusive cognitions in patients with PTSD is only to be expected.

INTRUSIVE COGNITIONS IN PTSD

In the diagnostic criteria for PTSD given in the American Psychiatric Association's *Diagnostic and Statistical Manual*, Fourth Edition (DSM-IV; APA, 1994), several requirements are stipulated for this diagnosis to be given. The first is, of course, the experience of a genuinely traumatic event. The second is that there has to be evidence of persistent re-experiencing of the traumatic experience. The third is that there has to be evidence of avoidance and/or numbing of responsiveness. Fourth, it is stated that the above three should have a duration of at least a month. Finally, it is stipulated that these symptoms cause significant distress and/or impairment of the person's functioning. It is the second of these requirements that is of relevance to the present context: the requirement that the person has to have persistent re-experiencing of the trauma reflects the re-cognition that such re-experiencing is a major and significant feature of PTSD. Of the several ways listed in the DSM-IV in which such re-experiencing can occur, the first is the recurrent and intrusive distressing recollections of the event, including images, thoughts and perceptions. The others are recurrent, distressing dreams; acting/feeling as if the traumatic event were recurring; intense distress at exposure to cues that resemble or symbolise the trauma; and, physiological reactivity upon such exposure.

The clinical literature provides a wealth of evidence for the occurrence of these, in varying combinations, in persons with PTSD. "Recurrent and intrusive distressing recollections of the event" which can take the form of images or thoughts are indeed very common. These represent the major intrusive cognitions that occur in PTSD. They are far more common than dreams or acting/feeling as if the trauma were recurring. To give an example, Solomon's study (1993) of Israeli soldiers who took part in the war in Lebanon showed that nearly all of them had what the author described as "recurrent scenes and thoughts" in the first year after their traumatic experience. These included vivid memories of being shot at and images of bloated and charred bodies. Similar data were reported by de Silva (1995) from his study of Sri Lankan soldiers exposed to combat. One soldier, whose foot had been badly injured by a land mine, reported his intrusive recollections in the following way:

> "It kept coming back to me. My foot was in pieces. There was blood every-where. I was half-sitting. My friends were trying to lift me on to a stretcher."

We give below a few other examples of intrusive recollections of the traumatic event reported by some patients with PTSD seen by us:

- Image of accident, especially lying on the road, with leg at an angle, blood around him.
- Memory of accident, with recollections of how he felt as the collision occurred.
- Memory of loud bang and commotion around him, and memory of thinking "This is the end, I'm going to die".
- Recollection of her body shaking, with the electric cable stuck to her hand, trying to scream but no sound coming.
- Vivid memory of his jacket ablaze, and his frantic movements as he tries to take it off.

It is clear that intrusive recollections can be either thoughts or images or both. The evidence suggests that images are more common than thoughts, or purely lexical cognitions (Ehlers & Steil, 1995). As noted in an earlier paragraph, the reporting and elicitation of intrusive cognitions have not always clarified whether the experience takes the form of a thought or an image. Many investigators tend to treat the two phenomena as one. For example, Wells and Davies (1994), in their Thought Control Questionnaire, instruct the respondents to lump verbal thoughts and mental images together. Their instructions begin as follows: "Most people experience unpleasant and/or unwanted thoughts (in verbal and/or picture form) which can be difficult to control" (Wells & Davies, 1994, p. 873). This issue has been discussed at some length by Brett and Ostroff (1985) and, in the context of obsessive-compulsive disorder, by de Silva (1986). Cognitive experiences can sometimes be a blend of thoughts and images, and in such instances the classification of the experience as one or the other is misleading. One way round this is to ask the subject about the dominant form of the intrusive cognition; another is to record the intrusive cognition as a combination of a thought and an image. Accurate assessment is important because the nature of the cognitive experience may be relevant to treatment choice. For example, exposure-based treatments may be more suited to dealing with intrusive images while a cognitive approach may be more appropriate for lexical cognitions.

It is worth noting, at this point, that the most widely used instrument for the measurement of the impact of traumatic events (The Revised Horowitz Impact of Event Scale: Horowitz, Wilner & Alvarez, 1979), does have some items which refer to thoughts (e.g. "I thought about it when I didn't mean to") and others which specifically refer to images ("Pictures about it popped into my mind"). However, as many understand by the words "thoughts", "thinking", etc., a whole range of cognitive activities, including images, even this instrument does not help fully to differentiate between thoughts and images in these patients.

A further observation needs to be made about images that appear as intrusive recollections. The vast majority of these are visual images, as highlighted by the item, noted above, in the Revised Horowitz Impact of Event Scale—"Pictures about it popped into my mind". There are, however, a small but significant minority of instances where the imagery is in a modality other than visual. Patients with war trauma often refer to "hearing" loud explosions, the sound of gunfire, etc. Several patients with road traffic accidents that we have seen have reported intrusive cognitions including very clear auditory images of the sound of the collision ("I hear the loud bang, and then the sound of crunching metal"). Less common, but no less interesting, are tactile, olfactory and gustatory images. An example is the intrusive experience of a man who had suffered a serious road traffic accident: "It all comes back to me. The smell of oil . . . The taste of oil in my mouth . . ."

Intrusive recollections in PTSD can be triggered by stressful stimuli (e.g. "Every time I see a knife, the whole incident comes back to me"; "When I see any pictures of war on television, I get vivid memories of how I was wounded"), and sometimes the trigger is an internal event, like a related memory. In many instances, the intrusive recollection may occur with no apparent trigger at all.

These intrusions are repetitive and persistent, especially in the initial stages of PTSD.

Responses to Intrusive Recollections

Intrusive recollections in PTSD are, mostly, quite distressing to the person. Occasionally, a patient may report such recollections with no associated negative affect; in these cases, clearly a numbing/dissociative reaction has taken place. It is also clear from the clinical evidence that the degree of distress felt by the patient, even when there is no numbing or dissociation, is variable. Some express very high distress, even to the point of finding their intrusive recollections almost unbearable, while others report less acute distress. In some cases, the distress caused by the intrusive cognition causes the person to terminate the activity or behaviour which triggers the intrusion. Nowhere is this clearer than in those with the experience of sexual trauma (e.g. rape, sex abuse in childhood). The person may suddenly "freeze" during the activity and/or attempt to get away. Sometimes the distress causes inconsolable crying, or aggressive outbursts.

How does the person respond to the intrusive recollection? The commonest reaction seems to be to try to dismiss the cognition. Many say that they try to "shut it out". Many also resort to distraction as a way of getting rid of the distressing cognition. Distracting thoughts and distracting activities are both reported. Spitzer, Gibbon, Skodol, Williams and First (1989) refer to a 7-year-old girl who had been held by a sniper in the playground, with many other children. One child died and several were injured.

> Leah described a recurring image of the injured girl lying bleeding on the playground. She said thoughts of the event sometimes disrupted her attention, though she would try to think about something else. (p. 286)

Equally common are attempts to avoid, or ward off, the intrusive recollections from occurring as far as possible. The person will avoid all possible stimuli and cues that may trigger the intrusive recollections. Some activities (e.g. driving the car in the area where the accident occurred) may be completely avoided. Equally, television programmes which show accidents, disasters or violence may be avoided. Many do not talk about the trauma, for fear that talking about the event will bring distressing intrusive recollections.

There is a general diminution of the distress with the passage of time since the event (Solomon, 1993). In most cases, there is also an overall reduction over time in the frequency of the intrusions themselves (McFarlane, 1992).

Intrusive Cognitions that are not Recollections of the Traumatic Event

So far, we have discussed intrusive cognitions in PTSD which are recollections of the traumatic event. While these are clearly the commonest type of intrusive cognitions in PTSD, there are also other intrusive cognitions which some report, and which many find quite distressing. Solomon (1993, p. 75), writing about the intrusive cognitions experienced by the Israeli soldiers in the Lebanon war, states:

> Vivid memories of being strafed and shot at, images of bloated and charred bodies, the faces of fallen friends, and sometimes questions (e.g. "Did it have to happen this way?") assail them.

Cognitions such as the questions referred to in the above sentence, which are not really part of the recollections of the trauma, are reported by a proportion of patients with PTSD. In terms of their intrusiveness, and their generally distressing quality, they are similar to the more common intrusive recollections. They are, also, equally persistent and repetitive, and may be especially distressing as they have no answer and endlessly plague the sufferer. Such unanswerable intrusive questions may be similar to worries reported by patients with generalised anxiety disorder (Borkovec & Inz, 1990).

Some examples, from our own clinical experience, of such intrusive cognitions in PTSD which are not direct recollections of the trauma are given below. These fall into different categories, those relating to (a) threat and danger, (b) negative thoughts about the self, and (c) thoughts about the meaning of the event.

(a) "Am I safe?"
    "Is it okay to go out?"
    "What will happen to my children if I die?"
    "Did I check all the windows?"
(b) "I am a dirty person."
    "I am filthy."
    "I am jinxed."
(c) "Why did it have to happen?"
    "It is my fault that it happened like this."

In some PTSD patients, intrusive cognitions such as these are quite prominent among the symptoms that distress them and impair their functioning. It is our view that these intrusions are under-reported, mainly because many clinicians do not specifically ask about such experiences, perhaps because they are not part of the diagnostic criteria for PTSD. In a review of the records of 60 cases of PTSD seen by us for detailed assessment, we found that 21 had such non-recollective intrusive cognitions. We have also come across cases where these non-recollective intrusive cognitions occur in the absence of intrusive recollections. In one example, a young woman who suffered a horrific road traffic accident, in which she was severely injured and her partner was killed, had no recollection of the event at all, let alone intrusive cognitions depicting the event. Despite this amnesia, she did meet the diagnostic criteria for PTSD, as she had other symptoms of re-experiencing the trauma (e.g. severe anxiety when exposed to cues). She did, however, have very persistent, recurrent intrusive cognitions which clearly were linked to the trauma. One of these was a visual image of her partner, on an occasion several months prior to his death. She also had the thoughts: "Will I ever be able to lead a normal life again?" and "Why did it have to happen?"

Compulsive Cognitions: A Related Phenomenon

There is a further type of cognition that is sometimes reported by patients with PTSD which merits mention. Some patients refer to what can only be described as "compulsive cognitions", very much like the covert compulsions that many patients with obsessive-compulsive disorder report, which have also been termed "cognitive rituals" (de Silva & Rachman, 1992; Rachman, 1971; Salkovskis & Westbrook, 1989). Again, we believe that this phenomenon is under-reported, as most clinicians do not routinely enquire about such experiences. Typically, this experience is reported by patients as something they find they "have to do". In other words, there is a subjectively felt compulsive urge which leads to these cognitive acts being performed. One patient "had to go over the details of what happened", including conjuring up various mental images in a strict sequence. Another patient reported that she had the urge—to which she yielded—to think through what might have happened if the traumatic event (a road traffic accident) had caused her death. This included what specific effects it would have had on her family. Another example is the patient who was involved in a serious collision and who silently said to herself, repeatedly, that it was not her fault. One patient had to have "good thoughts" to cancel out images of a dying friend. Finally, a soldier who was suffering from PTSD compulsively repeated the sentence, "He had a good life", the "he" being a fellow-soldier who had perished in battle.

We have also seen cases where patients cannot remember a traumatic event but try to create a mental picture to make sense of the experience: "I try to imagine what people told me happened"; "I wish I could remember, then I could understand and let go of it"; "It bothers me that other people know what happened but I don't".

These cognitive compulsions are carried out with a sense of resistance in some cases and without any resistance in others. They have all the qualities of compulsions in obsessive-compulsive behaviour. The key experience is the strong subjective urge to engage in the behaviour, the form and content of which are predetermined. It often interferes with the person's thinking, and sometimes patients complain about this phenomenon as a major problem. These urges, in most instances, occur immediately following intrusive recollections of the traumatic event; but they can also happen in response to other triggers, such as an external cue (e.g. a similar event or behaviour; someone's enquiry about the event), without being mediated by an intrusive recollection.

In our review of 60 patients with PTSD, we found 10 cases that had compulsive cognitions as described above. This is a small but significant proportion (16%). We believe that such compulsive cognitions are, in some cases of PTSD, an integral part of the psychopathology, and that efforts should be made to elicit these experiences during clinical examination.

INTRUSIVE COGNITIONS IN PTSD AND OTHER PSYCHIATRIC DISORDERS

We noted in an earlier section that unwanted intrusive cognitions are a major feature of obsessive-compulsive disorder. For someone to be diagnosed as suffering from obsessive-compulsive disorder, he or she has to have obsessions or compulsions, or both (APA, 1994). Obsessions are, of course, unwanted, repetitive and persistent intrusions, and they can take the form of thoughts, images or impulses; they often are a combination of two or more of these (de Silva & Rachman, 1992). We noted above that intrusions in PTSD show many of the properties of those in obsessive-compulsive disorder. Are there ways in which the intrusions in these two disorders can be distinguished? Despite the commonalities, there are certain clear differences which are worth noting.

Firstly, intrusive cognitions that take the form of impulses (which are not uncommon in obsessive-compulsive disorder, e.g. an obsessive-compulsive patient may report an intrusive, recurrent impulse to shout blasphemies; another may report an impulse to harm her child) are relatively rare in PTSD. Nonetheless, they are not entirely absent in PTSD. We have seen at least two patients with PTSD who reported such impulses. One felt an impulse to shout abuse at drivers of vehicles of a certain description; she never acted on this impulse. Secondly, intrusions in obsessive-compulsive disorder are often senseless, inappropriate and ego-dystonic (de Silva & Rachman, 1992; Rachman & Hodgson, 1980). This is not generally the case with PTSD. Intrusions in PTSD are as unwanted as those in obsessive-compulsive disorder, but they are never senseless or inappropriate, and the patient usually identifies with the cognition. Thirdly, intrusions in obsessive-compulsive disorder in most instances lead to a compulsive behaviour; while, in PTSD, in a minority of cases the intrusive recollections, or other intrusions, may lead to a compulsive cognition or another form of compulsive behaviour, in general they do not lead to compulsions. Fourthly, intrusions in obsessive-compulsive disorder are in most instances not linked to a specific past experience. In PTSD, the intrusions are generally firmly derived from, and based on, specific past experiences. Fifthly, the physiological arousal that is connected with intrusions in obsessive-compulsive disorder is due to the distress about the occurrence of the intrusion. It is the fact that an intrusion has occurred that makes the patient agitated. In PTSD, the physiological arousal connected with an intrusion is part of the memory of the past trauma.

Although these differences are significant, one must not lose sight of the considerable overlap that exists between the intrusions in PTSD and those in obsessive-compulsive disorder. We noted, too, in an earlier section that, in some PTSD cases, there are compulsive cognitions which are comparable to the cognitive rituals in obsessive-compulsive disorder. There are reports in the literature which suggest that PTSD and obsessive-compulsive disorder may be more closely related than is generally assumed. Pitman (1993), for example, has reported a case which he describes as "posttraumatic obsessive-compulsive disorder". And Lipinksi and Pope (1994) have argued that "flashbacks" in PTSD may be seen to represent obsessional imagery. In our own view, traumatic experiences may have a clear aetiological role in the development of obsessive-compulsive disorder, and we have seen clinical cases where this is clearly inferrable from the history. It is an interesting question whether, in these cases, the obsessive-compulsive disorder is always preceded by PTSD. The possible links between the two disorders are a topic which warrants investigation in its own right, and we shall not attempt to discuss it here.

Intrusive cognitions also occur in generalised anxiety disorder, as they do in non-pathological worry (Borkovec & Inz, 1990; Wells & Morrison, 1994). Indeed, persistent worry occurring for at least six months, about a number of topics, and difficulty controlling worry are the central defining features of general anxiety disorder (APA, 1994). How similar are the intrusive cognitions in generalized anxiety disorder to those in PTSD? The basic feature of intrusiveness, and the general aversiveness of the intrusions, are common to both. We noted earlier that intrusions that take the form of unanswerable questions that some PTSD patients report are similar to such experiences in generalised anxiety disorder. However, there are major differences. In generalised anxiety disorder, the patient has repeated intrusive cognitions about a number of matters not confined to one theme, and there is no evidence that the content of worries is related to a trauma within the specific worry domain. In addition, the intrusions in generalised anxiety disorder are mostly lexical—i.e. they take verbal form rather than imagery form. While it is indeed possible that a PTSD patient may later develop generalised anxiety disorder, the evidence of any significant link between these two disorders is at present not strong.

WHY DO INTRUSIVE COGNITIONS OCCUR FOLLOWING TRAUMA?

It is beyond the scope of this chapter to theorise at length about the reasons why traumatic experiences tend to lead to recurrent, persistent intrusive cognitions. There are many theoretical views about this issue. One influential theory is that of Rachman (1980), who argued that stressful experiences need to be fully processed and absorbed by the individual if they are not to cause any malfunctioning. When such emotional processing does not happen satisfactorily, either because of the severity of the trauma or due to other factors, the memory of the stress tends to reappear in several ways, including nightmares, fear reactions and—commonly—

intrusive cognitions. As intrusions are aversive, the person usually tries to dismiss them, thus further preventing the processing of the emotional material in question. This to us appears to be a plausible model of the aetiology and persistence of intrusive cognitions in PTSD. The evidence on the efficacy of exposure-based treatments, and especially cognitive-processing therapy, for PTSD provides strong support for this position (Keane, Albano & Blake, 1992; Resick & Schnicke, 1992).

Another, not dissimilar, model is that offered by Creamer (Creamer, 1995; Creamer, Burgess & Pattison, 1992). In his view, naturally occurring intrusions can also be conceptualised as a form of "processing" the trauma. The occurrence of an intrusive experience indicates that the trauma-related memory network has been activated, allowing for revision of the network in an adaptive way. Thus, in this model some intrusive experiences are seen as essentially adaptive. Such experiences, over a period of time, can lead to symptom reduction. Creamer (1995) stresses that only some intrusions act in this way. Others are dysfunctional, in that they result in very high arousal and prompt the patient to escape or shut out the traumatic recollections. This explains why some patients with PTSD continue to experience intrusive cognitions for years after the trauma.

Recent experimental work has thrown useful light on this last point. The attempt to suppress a cognition often leads, paradoxically, to its repeated reappearance subsequently (Trinder & Salkovskis, 1994; Wegner, 1989). It appears that, in PTSD, attempts at suppressing the distressing, intrusive cognitions often have the effect of promoting their persistence over time, frequency and repetitiveness. This phenomenon appears to be a relevant consideration in accounting for the repeated experience of trauma-related intrusions over long periods of time.

REFERENCES

APA (1980). *Diagnostic and Statistical Manual of Mental Disorders* (3rd Edn.). Washington, DC: American Psychiatric Association.

APA (1984). *Diagnostic and Statistical Manual of Mental Disorders* (4th Edn.). Washington, DC: American Psychiatric Association.

Borkovec, T. & Inz, J. (1990). The nature of worry in Generalized Anxiety Disorder: a predominance of thought activity. *Behaviour Research and Therapy*, **28**, 153–158.

Brett, E.A. & Ostroff, R. (1985). Imagery and post-traumatic stress disorder: An overview. *American Journal of Psychiatry*, 142.

Creamer, M. (1995). A cognitive processing formulation of posttrauma reactions. In R.J. Kleber, C.R. Figley & B.P.R. Gersons (Eds.), *Beyond Trauma: Cultural and Societal Dynamics*. New York: Plenum Press.

Creamer, M., Burgess, P. & Pattison, P. (1992). Reaction to trauma: A cognitive processing model. *Journal of Abnormal Psychology*, **101**, 452–459.

de Silva, P. (1986). Obsessional-compulsive imagery. *Behaviour Research and Therapy*, **24**, 333–350.

de Silva, P. (1995). Post-traumatic stress reactions in combat-exposed soldiers in Sri Lanka. Paper presented at the Fourth European Conference on Traumatic Stress, Paris, May 1995.

de Silva, P. & Rachman, S. (1992). *Obsessive-Compulsive Disorder: The Facts*. Oxford: Oxford University Press.

Edwards, S. & Dickerson, M. (1987). Intrusive unwanted thoughts: A two stage model of control. *British Journal of Medical Psychology*, **60**, 317–328.

Ehlers, A. & Steil, R. (1995). Maintenance of intrusive memories in posttraumatic stress disorder: A cognitive approach. *Behavioural and Cognitive Psychotherapy*, **23**, 217–249.

Freeston, M.H., Ladouceur, R., Thibodeau, N. & Gagnon, F. (1991). Cognitive intrusions in a non-clinical population. I. Response style, subjective experience and appraisal. *Behaviour Research and Therapy*, **29**, 585–597.

Horowitz, M. (1969). Psychic trauma: Return of images after a stress film. *Archives of General Psychiatry*, **20**, 552–559.

Horowitz, M., Wilner, N. & Alvarez, W. (1979). Impact of Event Scale: A measure of subjective stress. *Psychosomatic Medicine*, **41**, 209–218.

Kardiner, A. (1941). *The Traumatic Neuroses of War*. New York: Hoeber.

Keane, T.M., Albano, A.M. & Blake, D.D. (1992). Current trends in the treatment of post-traumatic stress symptoms. In M. Basoglu (Ed.), *Torture and Its Consequences*. Cambridge: Cambridge University Press.

Lipinski, J.F. & Pope, H.G. (1994). Do "flashbacks" represent obsessional imagery? *Comprehensive Psychiatry*, **35**, 245–247.

McFarlane, A.C. (1992). Avoidance and intrusion in posttraumatic stress disorder. *Journal of Nervous and Mental Disease*, **180**, 439–445.

Parkinson, L.A. & Rachman, S. (1981). Intrusive thoughts: The effects of an uncontrived stress. *Advances in Behaviour Research and Therapy*, **3**, 111–118.

Pitman, R.K. (1993). Posttraumatic obsessive-compulsive disorder: A case study. *Comprehensive Psychiatry*, **34**, 102–107.

Rachman, S. (1971). Obsessional ruminations. *Behaviour Research and Therapy*, **9**, 229–235.

Rachman, S. (1978). An anatomy of obsessions. *Behavior Analysis and Modification*, **2**, 253–278.

Rachman, S. (1980). Emotional processing. *Behaviour Research and Therapy*, **18**, 51–60.

Rachman, S. (1981). Unwanted intrusive cognitions. *Advances in Behaviour Research and Therapy*, **2**, 89–99.

Rachman, S. & de Silva, P. (1978). Abnormal and normal obsessions. *Behaviour Research and Therapy*, **16**, 233–248.

Rachman, S. & Hodgson, R. (1980). *Obsessions and Compulsions*. Englewood Cliffs, NJ: Prentice Hall.

Resick, P.A. & Schnicke, M.K. (1992). Cognitive processing therapy for sexual assault victims. *Journal of Consulting and Clinical Psychology*, **60**, 748–756.

Salkovskis, P.M. (1990). Obsessions, compulsions and intrusive cognitions. In D.F. Peck & D.M. Shapiro (Eds.), *Measuring Human Problems*. Chichester: Wiley.

Salkovskis, P.M. & Harrison, J. (1984). Abnormal and normal obsessions: A replication. *Behaviour Research and Therapy*, **22**, 549–552.

Salkovskis, P.M. & Westbrook, D. (1989). Behaviour therapy and obsessional ruminations: Can failure be turned into success? *Behaviour Research and Therapy*, **27**, 149–160.

Solomon, Z. (1993). *Combat Stress Reaction: The Enduring Toll of War*. New York: Plenum Press.

Spitzer, R.L., Gibbon, M., Skodol, A.E., Williams, J.B. & First, M.B. (1989). *DSM-III-R Casebook*. Washington, DC: American Psychiatric Press.

Trinder, H. & Salkovskis, P.M. (1994). Personally relevant intrusions outside the laboratory: Long term suppression increases intrusion. *Behaviour Research and Therapy*, **33**, 833–842.

Wegner, D.M. (1989). *White Bears and Other Unwanted Thoughts: Suppression, Obsession and the Psychology of Mental Control*. New York: Viking.

Wells, A. & Davies, M. (1994). The Thought Control Questionnaire: A measure of individual differences in the control of unwanted thoughts. *Behaviour Research and Therapy*, **33**, 871–878.

Wells, A. & Morrison, T. (1994). Qualititative dimensions of normal worry and normal intrusive thoughts: A comparative study. *Behaviour Research and Therapy*, **32**, 867–870.

Chapter 9

THE USE OF INFORMATION-PROCESSING PARADIGMS TO INVESTIGATE POST-TRAUMATIC STRESS DISORDER: A REVIEW OF THE EVIDENCE

Sian Thrasher* and Tim Dalgleish[†]

In recent years, researchers have turned to paradigms from experimental cognitive psychology in order to try to isolate the dysfunctional processes underlying emotional disorders (McNally, 1990; Williams, Watts, MacLeod & Mathews, 1988). A variety of experimental paradigms have been used in this way to test hypotheses about cognitive biases associated with symptoms of depression (Gotlib & Cane, 1987; Williams & Nulty, 1986), anxiety (MacLeod, Mathews & Tata, 1986), eating disorders (Channon, Hemsley & de Silva, 1988), and, most recently, PTSD (Cassiday, McNally & Zeitlin, 1992; Foa, Feske, Murdock, Kozak & McCarthy, 1991; Kaspi & McNally, 1991; McNally, Kaspi, Riemann & Zeitlin, 1990; Thrasher, Dalgleish & Yule, 1994; Zeitlin & McNally, 1991). The advantage of such laboratory-based paradigms is that they circumvent the limitations of subjective report methodologies and allow inferences about cognitive processes that are not available to conscious introspection. For example, Mathews and MacLeod (1986) used a dichotic listening paradigm (see below) to show that patients with Generalised Anxiety Disorder (GAD) exhibit attentional shifts towards threat cues of which they are not aware. Such attentional biases are inaccessible to subjective report. The rationale behind such a research programme is that the onset, maintenance and remission of emotional disorders may be intimately associated with biases in basic cognitive processes

---

*Private Practice, London, and [†]MRC Cognition and Brain Sciences Unit, Cambridge

---

Post-Traumatic Stress Disorders: Concepts and Therapy. Edited by William Yule.
© 1999 John Wiley & Sons Ltd.

(Beck et al., 1979) and, therefore, a greater understanding of these proc-esses can potentially inform management and treatment of psychological problems.

While the use of information-processing paradigms in other emotional disorders has been illuminating, a shift of focus to PTSD is particularly compelling because (a) a number of symptoms of this disorder are sugges-tive of basic cognitive distortions; for example, intrusive memory reactivations, hypervigilance, and concentration problems; and (b) there are two groups from any trauma—one group with symptoms of post-traumatic stress, and one group without. This situation provides a unique opportunity to disentangle variables such as familiarity with the stimuli being processed (common to both groups) and the emotiveness of the stimuli for the individual (predominant in the former group).

In this chapter we review the research which has investigated attention, memory and judgement processes in PTSD and discuss briefly the possi-ble implications of this approach for understanding the nature of the disorder.

Research in Attention

Research into attentional processes associated with PTSD has utilised three information-processing methodologies: the modified Stroop para-digm; the dichotic listening paradigm; and the attentional deployment paradigm. We shall consider each approach in turn.

THE MODIFIED STROOP TASK

One of the oldest and more robust information-processing tasks is the Stroop paradigm (Stroop, 1935). In the original version of the task the subject is required to name the colour in which a word is printed while ignoring the word itself. The essential variable is the congruence between word and colour; that is, subjects consistently take longer to name colours when the words are antagonistic colour names (e.g. the word "blue" written in red-coloured ink). This difference between the reaction times for congruent and incongruent stimuli is known as the Stroop effect.

In the emotional Stroop the experimental stimuli are emotional words and the control stimuli are neutral words. The words can either be presented singly on a computer screen, or all together on large cards. Using the emotional Stroop task, Gotlib and Cane (1984) found that response latency was far greater for negative emotional words than for neutral words in emotionally disturbed subjects. In other words, the emotional content of the word interfered with the subject's ability to name the ink colour in which it was written. This difference was not found in controls.

The emotional Stroop effect has been demonstrated in people with generalised anxiety (Dalgleish & Power, 1995; Martin, Williams & Clark, 1991; Mathews & MacLeod, 1985; Mogg, Mathews & Weinman, 1989; Mogg & Marden, 1990; Richards & Millwood, 1989; Richards & French, 1990), phobias (Ehlers & Breuer, 1995; Hope & Heimberg, 1993; Mattia, Heimberg & Hope, 1993; McNeil, Reis, Taylor, Boone, Carter, Turk, & Lewin, 1995; Watts, McKenna, Sharrock & Tresize, 1986), panic disorder (Ehlers & Breuer, 1995; Ehlers, Margraf, Davies & Roth, 1988; McNally et al., 1990), obsessive-compulsive disorder (McCarthy, Foa, Murdock & Ilia, 1990) and, more recently, in PTSD (Foa et al., 1991; see below).

There are several competing explanations of the mechanism underlying the Stroop interference effect. The most popular of these (Glaser & Glaser, 1982) invokes some form of competition at the response output stage between the signal to generate the name of the ink colour (the task instructions) and a signal to generate the word itself (the automatic tendency to read the word). In the case of the emotional Stroop effect with anxiety-related material, there may be increased competition at the response output stage because representations of these stimuli are initially more active or activeatable in long-term memory. Alternatively, it may be more difficult for anxious people to inhibit the signal to generate the word response for an anxiety-related word. Finally, the effect may be predominantly attentional rather than one of response competition. In this analysis interference occurs because the meaning of the emotional words automatically attracts the subject's attentional resources despite efforts to focus on the colour of the word (Williams et al., 1988). This possibility has led McNally (1993, p. 77) to suggest that, in PTSD:

> . . . interference produced by the trauma-related words may provide a quantitative index of intrusive cognitive activity—the hallmark of PTSD.

To investigate this, McNally, Kaspi, Riemann & Zeitlin (1990) compared colour-naming latencies of Vietnam veterans with and without PTSD for combat-related words (e.g. "bodybags"), positive words (e.g. "love"), words related to OCD (e.g. "germs"), and neutral words (e.g. "input"). The words were blocked together and presented on large cards. Also, the groups of words were matched for frequency of usage. The PTSD subjects took significantly longer to colour-name combat-related words than other words, and took significantly longer to name combat-related words than non-PTSD controls. The effect was specific for trauma-related words. Stroop interference scores were related to severity of PTSD but not to the extent of combat exposure. In fact the correlation between interference for trauma words and severity of PTSD remained significant even when the effects of combat exposure were partialled out.

Thrasher, Dalgleish and Yule (1994) compared the Stroop performance of normal control subjects with that of survivors of the *Herald of Free Enterprise* ferry sinking with either high levels of PTSD symptomatology, or with few PTSD symptoms. Five types of card-presented words were used: ferry disaster words (e.g. "ship"); general threat words (e.g. "danger"); neutral, semantically unrelated words (e.g. "cat"); neutral semantically related words musical instrument (e.g. "tambourine"); and positive words (e.g. "smile"). The pattern of findings was similar to those of McNally et al. (1990): survivors with high levels of PTSD symptoms evidenced significantly longer colour-naming latencies for disaster-related words than for other word-types. The results for the low-PTSD survivors and the non-traumatised controls showed no difference between response latencies for general threat words and disaster words, although all three groups showed increased colour-naming delay for general threat words compared to neutral words.

Foa et al. (1991) developed a computerised version of the emotional Stroop paradigm which allows the accurate measurement of colour-naming times for single words appearing on a screen, as opposed to the time to colour-name blocks of words in the card version. Foa et al. used three groups of subjects: rape victims with PTSD; rape victims without PTSD; and non-traumatised controls. They were asked to colour-name four types of words: rape-related words; general threat words; neutral words; and nonsense words (e.g. "scrome"). As with the studies reviewed above, the PTSD group exhibited greater interference for trauma-related (rape) words than for other word groups, and greater interference for rape words compared with the other subject groups. The non-PTSD rape victims showed no interference effects for the rape words.

Cassiday, McNally and Zeitlin (1992) also investigated the processing of rape words in rape victims. In Cassiday et al.'s study, three groups of subjects—rape victims with PTSD; rape victims without PTSD, and non-traumatised normal controls—were asked to colour-name high-threat rape-related words (e.g. "rape"), moderate-threat rape-related words (e.g. "crime"), positive words, and neutral words. The degree of threat associated with the rape-related words had been rated by rape survivors who did not participate in the study. Cassiday et al. hypothesised that if Stroop interference is a function of the threat-relevance of the word then high-threat words should produce more interference than moderate-threat words. Indeed, the PTSD group were slower to colour-name high-threat words compared with low-threat words. No such pattern of interference was seen in the non-PTSD rape survivors, although, in contrast to Foa et al.'s results, they were slower to colour-name high-threat rape-related words compared with non-traumatised controls. Furthermore, the degree of interference for high-threat words correlated with the severity of PTSD symptoms remaining in this group. A possible reason for this discrepancy is that Foa's non-PTSD group had recently undergone successful cognitive-behavioral treatment for their PTSD while Cassiday's group had had no treatment and suffered some residual symptoms. The degree of interference shown by this untreated group was intermediate between that of the full-blown PTSD groups, and the non-traumatised controls.

The computerised Stroop has been modified to investigate the effects of personal relevance, threat and emotionality on selective processing in a group of Vietnam veterans with PTSD (Kaspi & McNally, 1991). The PTSD group and a group of medical students just about to undergo a stressful medical examination, were asked to rate (on a 7-point scale from-3 to +3, i.e. from very negative to very positive through neutral 0) the personal emotional significance of a list of positive, negative and neutral words. The student group also rated a list of words associated with academic failure, and the PTSD group words related to Vietnam. Five words with a 0 rating, five words with a +3 rating and five with a −3 rating were selected for each subject, and used as neutral, positive and general threat words respectively. Similarly, five Vietnam (or academic) words rated −3 were used as the personal threat words. PTSD subjects exhibited Stroop interference for Vietnam words, but no differential Stroop effect was found for the students on any word groups. The researchers concluded that Stroop interference is strongest for self-referent threatening information, but that this result is specific to individuals with severe anxiety problems such as PTSD.

In a recent study at the Institute of Psychiatry, the use of a computerised version of the modified Stroop has been extended to investigate hemispheric differences in visual processing in PTSD (see Hagh-Shenas et al., Chapter 7 in this volume). Twenty PTSD subjects and 20 controls were asked to colour-name five types of words presented to each visual field. The stimuli were semantically unrelated neutral words, positive words, general threat words, semantically-related words (musical instruments) and individualised trauma-related words. Consistent with previous findings, the PTSD subjects exhibited longer colour-naming latencies overall, with the greatest interference effect being seen for trauma-related words.

In PTSD subjects, trauma-related and positive emotion words (but not neutral words) produced greater interference when presented to the left visual field. No such effect was seen in normal controls. The results are taken by the authors as support for lateralisation of emotions, and suggest that in PTSD the right hemisphere is involved in the processing of emotional information.

Further work at the Institute of Psychiatry (Moradi, Neshat, Taghavi & Yule, 1995a) has investigated performance on the modified Stroop task in children with PTSD and non-symptomatic children whose parents have PTSD. On a computerised version of the task with general threat, sadness, trauma, positive and neutral words, it was revealed that children with PTSD exhibited greater Stroop interference for trauma-related words relative to other words and to normal controls. Non-symptomatic children of parents with PTSD exhibited increased Stroop interference for both general threat and PTSD words relative to other words and to normal controls.

In summary, a number of researchers have shown that survivors of trauma with PTSD are distinguished from survivors of the same trauma who do not have PTSD, in terms of the degree of interference produced by trauma-related and threat-related words on the modified Stroop task. The greatest interference in PTSD sufferers is associated with trauma-related words, suggesting an information-processing bias in these subjects towards stimuli directly associated with their traumatic experience. Furthermore, the absence of clear interference effects in non-symptomatic trauma survivors suggests that aspects of the stimuli, over and above their familiarity, underlie the Stroop effect.

The Dichotic Listening Paradigm

In the dichotic listening task, subjects are required to repeat (shadow) a message presented to one ear (the attended message) while ignoring a message presented simultaneously to the other ear (the unattended message). The variable of interest is the amount of processing of the items in the unattended message. This task is designed to measure attentional bias with the assumption being that the processing of items in the unattended message is an index of the amount of attentional resources those items recruit.

This task has been used with General Anxiety Disorder (GAD) patients (Mathews & MacLeod, 1986), phobic patients (Burgess, Jones, Robertson, Radcliffe & Emerson, 1981; Foa & McNally, 1986) and PTSD patients

(Trandel & McNally, 1987). In Mathews and MacLeod's study, anxious subjects shadowed stories presented to the unattended channel while ignoring lists of threat-related or neutral words on the unattended channel. At the same time, subjects were required to press a button as quickly as possible when the word "PRESS" appeared on the screen (timed to coincide with either a threat-related or neutral word in the unattended channel). The researchers found that anxious patients were slower than controls on the reaction time task when "PRESS" coincided with a threat-related word in the unattended channel, but not for neutral words. There were no differences in shadowing errors, or in performance on a recognition memory task given immediately after the dichotic listening. Mathews and MacLeod concluded that the threat-related information was being selectively processed by the anxious subjects outside of their awareness, and that this could be due to a pre-attentional bias towards threat, or to an additional demand on processing resources in order to inhibit awareness of the threat-related words.

In the case of PTSD, Trandel and McNally (1987) used the dichotic listening paradigm with a group of Vietnam veterans with this disorder. Their results were negative; however, only seven PTSD-related target stimuli were used in the unattended message. Given the considerable error variance associated with this task, seven stimuli are unlikely to have been sufficient to pick up any effects. Hence this task may have potential in the study of attentional bias in PTSD, but requires further study.

The Attentional Deployment Task

The finding that anxious subjects are likely to divert their attentional resources to threat-related stimuli and away from simultaneous task demands is further supported by work using the attentional deployment task. In the prototypical study anxious patients were asked to read a threat word appearing at the top of a screen while ignoring another threat word presented in the lower part of the screen, and to subsequently detect the presence of a small dot that appeared in the space previously occupied by one of the words (MacLeod, Mathews & Tata, 1986). The time to detect the probe dots was taken to be a measure of attentional deployment. On the experimental trials, one of the two words was always threat-related and the other neutral. Anxious subjects were quicker to detect the dot probe following presentation of threat words compared with non-threat words. No such difference was demonstrated by non-anxious subjects. Hence, generalised anxiety was taken to be associated with a shift in attentional resources towards threat-related information.

In the only study to date using the dot probe task in a PTSD population, Moradi, Neshat, Taghavi and Yule (1995) showed that children with PTSD tended towards an attentional deployment bias for social-threat stimuli relative to controls, but that no other effects were significant.

In summary, the investigation of biased attentional processing in PTSD has produced mixed results. The modified Stroop paradigm has revealed strong effects in PTSD subjects when processing trauma-related materials. However, such effects have been marginal or even absent when other methodologies have been employed. Clearly, it is too early to draw any firm conclusions concerning these data; although broadly attentional, the three tasks measure different aspects of cognition and the results may reflect biases in some aspects of attention-like processing but not in others. Alternatively, the relative paucity of data from tasks other that the modified Stroop might indicate that more research is required before we can state with any conviction that PTSD subjects exhibit no biases on attentional deployment or dichotic listening methodologies.

MEMORY PROCESSES

PTSD is characterised by the experience of frequent involuntary intrusions of traumatic memories, either spontaneously or in response to a wide range of cues (APA, 1994). This suggests that in PTSD, traumatic memories are readily accessible, or "primed" in some individuals. In contrast, PTSD is sometimes associated with partial or complete psychogenic amnesia for the event. These varying and sometimes contradictory symptoms mean that the investigation of memory processes in PTSD had been a particular attraction for researchers.

Explicit and Implicit Memory

Again researchers have turned to experimental cognitive psychology tasks in order to investigate memory for trauma related information. In one such experiment, Vietnam veterans with PTSD were exposed to combat words (e.g. "bodybags"), social threat words (e.g. "humiliated"), positive words and neutral words, followed by a recall test and a word completion task (Zeitlin & McNally, 1991). The former is a test of explicit memory (or conscious recollection) in which subjects are presented with a list of words and then given a word stem which they are told is the first part of one of the words presented previously. The word completion task is a test of implicit memory, believed to be a relatively automatic process rather than one relying on elaborate encoding or conscious recollection. In this task subjects are told to complete a word stem with the first word that comes to mind.

In the explicit memory task, PTSD patients demonstrated a greater tendency to generate combat words, compared with controls. They also exhibited implicit memory bias for combat words, while no such bias was seen in controls. Furthermore, in contrast with controls, the PTSD group showed poorer memory for non-threat words—further evidence that, in PTSD, trauma-related information is primed in memory (McNally, 1993).

In work at the Institute of Psychiatry, Moradi, Neshat, Taghavi and Yule (1995) looked at explicit recall and recognition for trauma-related material in children with PTSD, non-symptomatic children of parents with PTSD and controls. The results revealed some evidence of biased memory processing in PTSD subjects for trauma-related words relative to neutral words and also relative to the other two groups.

Autobiographical Memory

A number of PTSD researchers report that trauma can alter self-representations with the result that in PTSD sufferers, negative attributes or traits dominate schematic representations of the self (Eells, Horowitz, Stinson & Fridhandler, 1993; Janoff-Bulman, 1985, 1992; McNally, 1993). McNally et al. (1994) found that, unlike controls, Vietnam veterans with PTSD have difficulties retrieving specific personal memories in response to positive and neutral words, especially after exposure to reminders of traumatic events. Deficits in retrieving specific autobiographical memories were also found in depressed women with histories of sexual abuse, but not in women without abuse histories (Kuyken & Brewin, 1994). On the basis of findings such as these, McNally et al. (1995) predicted that specific autobiographical memories exemplifying negative traits ought to be easier to access in people with PTSD, but not in those without PTSD. As predicted, Vietnam veterans with PTSD had greater difficulty retrieving specific autobiographical memories compared with veterans with no PTSD. This effect was most evident when the PTSD veterans were asked to retrieve autobiographical episodes exemplifying positive traits (McNally et al., 1995). Despite the small subject numbers and the lack of control for level of depression (higher in the PTSD group), these results indicate that there may be significant memory differences in people with PTSD. However, it is unclear exactly what a difficulty in accessing specific memories means with respect to questions of the onset, maintenance and overall course of the disorder.

THE DIRECTED FORGETTING TASK

In contrast with depressed people, generally anxious subjects consistently fail to demonstrate an explicit memory bias for negative material (see Dalgleish & Watts, 1990, for a review) although, as we saw above, the studies which have examined this question in PTSD do provide evidence of a processing bias in this group. One explanation of the relative paucity of findings in generalised anxiety states is that

> depression may enhance deployment of mood-congruent cues at retrieval, enhancing recall of negative material . . . By contrast, if the material to be recalled involves an element of threat (as it may do in phobic or anxious patients), then mood-congruent recall may be inhibited and consequently never elaborated in long term memory. (Williams et al., 1988)

In this case "inhibition" refers to "a process whereby the response of interest is directly suppressed in some way" (Power, Dalgleish, Claudio, Tata & Kentish, submitted). Cognitive psychology has examined this putative process of inhibition using the directed forgetting paradigm. In this task, subjects are presented with a number of to-be-remembered (TBR) items, and at some point in this presentation they are instructed that the items presented so far are now to-be-forgotten (TBF) and will not be tested; that is, they are directed to forget them (see Johnson, 1994, for a review). Typically, the level of recall of TBR items after the forget cue is compared with the level of recall of TBR items in two conditions—one in which only the TBR items are presented, and one in which the subjects are not given a forget cue. The standard result is that the forget cue almost completely eliminates the interference from the TBF items (Geiselman, Bjork & Fishman, 1983). This is taken as evidence for some kind of inhibition in which the subject is successfully forgetting items such that they do not interfere with subsequent remembering. Power et al. (submitted) used the directed forgetting task with threat-related items in normals and in a group of mildly depressed students. Subjects were asked to rate 20 positive and 20 negative adjectives in terms of the extent to which they described the self. These words were then used in a directed forgetting procedure as described above. A substantial directed forgetting effect was shown, with the healthy group recalling significantly more positive adjectives than negative on both TBR and TBF items. In contrast, the depressed group recalled equal numbers of positive and negative adjectives. This finding is consistent with the interpretation that in normal subjects there is increased inhibition of negative material in memory, but that this bias is not present in depressed subjects.

In PTSD subjects, one might predict that they will fail to show a positive bias towards negative words, and that subjects may in fact show a negative bias towards trauma-related material; that is, there will be greater inhibition of this type of information. This prediction is currently being investigated in an ongoing study at the Institute of Psychiatry, involving survivors of a range of traumas who go on to develop chronic PTSD. Preliminary results suggest a stronger directed forgetting effect for trauma-related material in PTSD subjects (Thrasher & Dalgleish, in prep.).

Overall. there has been relatively less work using information-processing methodologies to investigate memory processes in PTSD. At present it is difficult to draw any firm conclusions from the existing data without further replication and research.

SUBJECTIVE PROBABILITY JUDGEMENTS

When estimating the probability of an event's occurrence, it has been suggested that in certain circumstances people will tend to adopt an availability heuristic; that is, the probability of occurrence accorded a given event is a function of the availability in memory of instances and scenarios similar to that event (Tversky & Kahneman, 1974). For example, subjects who have recently read newspaper reports vividly describing a death, showed increases in the estimated probability of occurrence of death (Johnson & Tversky, 1983). Butler and Mathews (1983) found that anxious individuals made higher predictions for threat-related events, particularly when these events referred to themselves. The explanation given was that:

> memories of threatening events associated with anxiety are . . . organized and stored together in long-term memory (. . .). When an individual becomes anxious again this material should be relatively easy to bring to mind (. . .) and may therefore influence estimates of self-rated unpleasant events. (Butler & Mathews, 1983, pp. 582–583)

When a person experiences a traumatic event—that is, an event with a low objective probability of occurrence—it is predicted that people with PTSD will make higher probability estimates of the occurrence of future trauma-related events relative to controls (Foa et al., 1989). These estimations should be higher when the events refer to themselves because blurring of the safety/danger boundary occurs principally with respect to self. The extension of the fear network, to include information about situations previously perceived as benign (Foa et al., 1989) would predict that this bias in probability estimates will be extended to all types of threatening event.

In order to test these hypotheses, Dalgleish (1993) asked 35 survivors of a ferry disaster, and 33 normal controls, to complete a questionnaire requiring them to rate the probability of occurrence of a number of incidents, a proportion of which were transport related. Each item referred either to the self or to another person. In accordance with an availability model, the results indicated that, compared with controls, disaster survivors with high levels of PTSD symptoms made higher probability risk estimates across all event types. Normal subjects showed no effects of reference for either type of event. However, neither did disaster survivors with low PTSD symptomatology and this latter finding counsels against a straightforward availability explanation as it would have to be assumed that even low symptom survivors had elevated availability for transport-related events. In the high-PTSD group a significant self-referent bias was indicated for non-transport-related events, and another-referent bias was found for transport-related events. Dalgleish invokes some form of cognitive inhibition in this group with regard to self-referent material, such that the availability process is blocked.

Dalgleish, Neshat-Doost, Taghavi, Moradi, Yule and Canterbury (1997) have investigated subjective probability judgements for general negative events in children with PTSD and the results are broadly similar to the findings with adults, indicating that children with PTSD generate higher estimates for the risk of future negative events relative to controls.

DISCUSSION

Tests of attention, memory and probability estimation clearly demonstrate biases in the processing of information in PTSD subjects compared with controls. Such results have great potential in terms of our understanding of this disorder.

Possibly the greatest potential for this type of research is in the area of vulnerability. Cognitive differences distinguish people who are vulnerable to emotional disorders from those who are not (e.g. Beck, 1976). In terms of cognitive vulnerability to anxiety disorder, so far there is little evidence of a direct causal link between information-processing biases and anxiety disorders such as PTSD. However, it may be the case that certain people are biased towards selectively processing threat-related information; this in turn increases the chance of an anxious appraisal of that information and the onset of an anxious state which in turn could increase the extent of the bias towards threat-related information and so on. A vulnerable person would thus be caught in a vicious circle similar to that proposed as a maintaining factor in depression (Teasdale, 1983). Someone vulnerable to developing PTSD would exhibit processing biases towards a wide range of trauma-related information (which would be picked up in that person's performance on the trauma-related emotional Stroop, for example) which would increase the probability of anxious appraisals of that information and the onset of anxiety, which in turn increases the information-processing bias. Thus the cognitive biases picked up using the experimental paradigms described above may represent a vulnerability to the development of PTSD, and may allow us to predict which people will go on to develop long-term problems.

The study of cognitive biases in PTSD is still in its infancy, but the early work described here points to the importance of continuing this line of investigation. Future research might be fruitfully aimed at investigating which aspects of the cognitive biases are important in the maintenance and onset of PTSD, and which aspects are affected by current therapeutic practice. It might be postulated that one function of exposure therapy (the most widely reported psychological treatment for PTSD) is to act so as to alter the criteria for what is appraised as threat related by repeated feedback that the stimulus (external or internal) appraised as threatening is benign. Cognitive therapy may act at a higher level in the appraisal process, by deliberately showing the patient that what he or she is interpreting as threatening is in fact harmless.

So far there has been very little work using cognitive paradigms in assessment and treatment evaluation. Watts et al. (1986) and Lavy, van den Hout and Arntz (1993) showed a reduction in the emotional Stroop effect in spider-phobics following desensitisation. And in a study which points to the great potential for the use of information-processing tasks for the prediction of outcome in PTSD, MacLeod and Hagan (1992) showed that, in women undergoing screening for cancer, performance on a masked version of the threat-related Stroop task prior to diagnosis consistently and reliably predicted the intensity of emotional distress elicited by a positive diagnosis, over and above any self-report measures. In this study, subjects who showed the greatest degree of colour-naming interference from masked threat words compared to non-masked threat worlds, experienced the most negative emotional reactions to this life event. This points to the potential use of this instrument in the screening of people at risk for developing symptoms either before, or immediately after, a traumatic experience.

REFERENCES

APA (1980). *Diagnostic and Statistical Manual of Mental Disorders* (3rd Edition). Washington, DC: American Psychiatric Association.

APA (1986). *Diagnostic and Statistical Manual of Mental Disorders* (3rd Edition, Revised). Washington, DC: American Psychiatric Association.

APA (1994). *Diagnostic and Statistical Manual of Mental Disorders* (4th Edition). Washington, DC: American Psychiatric Association.

Beck, A.T. (1976). *Cognitive Therapy and the Emotional Disorders*. New York: International University Press.

Beck, A.T., Rush, A.J., Shaw, B.F. & Emery, G. (1979). *Cognitive Therapy of Depression: A Treatment Manual*. New York: Guilford Press.

Burgess, I.S., Jones, L.M., Robertson, S.A., Radcliffe, W.N. & Emerson, E. (1981). The degree of control exerted by phobic and non-phobic verbal stimuli over the recognition behaviour of phobic and non-phobic subjects. *Behaviour Research and Therapy*, **19**, 233–243.

Butler, G. & Mathews, A. (1983). Cognitive processes in anxiety. *Advances in Behaviour Research and Therapy*, **5**, 51–62.

Cassiday, K.L., McNally, R.J. & Zeitlin, S.B. (1992). Cognitive processing of trauma-related cues in rape victims with Post-Traumatic Stress Disorder. *Cognitive Therapy and Research*, 233–295.

Channon, S., Hemsley, D. & de Silva, S.B. (1988). Selective processing of trauma cues in rape victims with post-traumatic stress disorder. *Cognitive Therapy and Research*, **16**, 283–295.

Chemtob, C., Roitblat, H.L., Hamada, R.S., Carlson, J.G. & Twentyman, C.T. (1988). A cognitive action theory of Post-Traumatic Stress Disorder. *Journal of Anxiety Disorders*, **26**, 253–275.

Dalgleish, T. (1993). The judgement of risk in traumatised and non-traumatised disaster survivors. Unpublished MSc Thesis, University of London.

Dalgleish, T., Neshat-Doost, H., Taghavi, R., Moradi, A., Yule, W. & Canterbury, R. (1997). Information processing in clinically depressed and anxious children and adolescents. *Journal of Child Psychology and Psychiatry* **38**, 535–541.

Dalgleish, T. & Power, M.J. (1995). *Theoretical Approaches to post-traumatic stress disorder: The SPAARS model*. Paper presented at the Second International Conference on Mental Health in the State of Kuwait, Kuwait.

Dalgleish, T. & Watts, F.N. (1990). Biases of attention and memory in disorders of anxiety and depression. *Clinical Psychology Review*, **10**, 589–604.

Eells, T.D., Horowitz, M.J., Stinson, C.H. & Fridhandler, B. (1993). Self-representation in anxious states of mind: A comparison of psychodynamic models. In Z.V. Segal & S.J. Blatt (Eds.), *The Self in Emotional Distress: Cognitive and Psychodynamic Perspectives* (pp. 100–122). New York: Guilford Press.

Ehlers, A., Margraf, J., Davies, S. & Roth, W.T. (1988). Selective processing of threat cues in subjects with panic attacks. *Cognition and Emotion*, **2**, 201–209.

Ehlers, A. & Breuer, P. (1995). Selective attention to physical threat in subjects with panic attacks and specific phobias. *Journal of Anxiety Disorders*, **9** (1), 11–31.

Epstein, W. (1972). Mechanisms in directed forgetting. In G.H. Bower (Ed.), *The Psychology of Learning and Motivation*, vol. 6. New York: Academic Press.

Foa, E.B. & McNally, R.J. (1986). Sensitivity to feared stimuli in obsessive-compulsives: A dichotic listening analysis. *Cognitive Therapy and Research*, **10**, 477–485.

Foa, E.B. & Kozak, M.J. (1986). Emotional Processing of fear: Exposure to corrective information. *Psychological Bulletin*, **99**, 20–35.

Foa, E.B., Feske, U., Murdock, T.B., Kozak, M.J. & McCarthy, P.R. (1991). Processing of threat-related information in rape victims *Journal of Abnormal Psychology*, **100**, 156–162.

Foa, E.B., Steketee, G. & Rothbaum, B.O. (1989). Behavioural/cognitive conceptualisation of Post-Traumatic Stress Disorder. *Behaviour Therapy*, **20**, 155–176.

Geiselman, R.E., Bjork, R.A. & Fishman, D.L. (1983). Disrupted retrieval or directed forgetting: A link with post-hypnotic amnesia. *Journal of Experimental Psychology: General*, **112**, 58–72.

Glaser, M.O. & Glaser, W.R. (1982). Time course analysis of the Stroop phenomenon. *Journal of Experimental Psychology: Human Perception and Performance*, **8**, 875–94.

Gotlib, I.H. & Cane, D.B. (1987). Construct accessibility and clinical depression: A longitudinal investigation. *Journal of Abnormal Psychology*, **96**, 199–204.

Horowitz, M.J. (1986). *Stress Response Syndromes*. Northvale, NJ: Aronson.

Hope, D.A. & Heimberg, R.G. (1993). Social phobia. In C.G. Last & M. Hersen (Eds.), *Adult Behaviour Therapy Casebook*. New York: Plenum Press.

Janoff-Bulman, R. (1985). The aftermath of victimisation: rebuilding shattered assumptions. In C.R. Figley (Ed.), *Trauma and Its Wake*, Vol. 1 (pp. 15–35). New York: Brunner/Mazel.

Janoff-Bulman, R. (1989). Assumptive worlds and the stress of traumatic events: Applications of the schema construct. *Social Cognition*, **7**, 113–136.

Janoff-Bulman, R. (1992). *Shattered Assumptions: Towards a New Psychology of Trauma*. New York: Free Press.

Jensen, A.R. & Rohwer, W.D. (1966). The Stroop colour word test: A review. *Acta Psychologica*, **48**, 1413–1426.

Johnson, H.M. (1994). Process of successful intentional forgetting. *Psychological Bulletin*, **116**(2), 274–292.

Kaspi, S.P. & McNally, R.J. (1991, November). Selective Processing of ideographic-emotional information in PTSD. Paper presented at the meeting of the Association for the Advancement of Behaviour Therapy, New York, NY.

Kuyken, W. & Brewin, C. (1994). Intrusive memories of childhood abuse during depressive episodes. *Behaviour Research and Therapy*, **32**, 525–528.

Lang, P.J. (1985). The cognitive psychophysiology of emotion: Fear and anxiety. In A.H. Tuma & J.D. Maser (Eds.), *Anxiety and the Anxiety Disorders* (pp. 131–170). Hillsdale, NJ: Lawrence Erlbaum.

Litz, B.T. & Keane, T.M. (1989). Information processing in anxiety disorders: Application to the understanding of post-traumatic stress disorder. *Clinical Psychology Review*, **9**, 243–257.

Lavy, E., van den Hout, M. & Arntz, A. (1993). Attentional bias and spider phobia: Conceptual and clinical issues. *Behaviour Research and Therapy*, **31**, 17–24.

MacLeod, C. (1991). Half a century of research on the Stroop effect: An integrative review. *Psychological Bulletin*, **190**, 163–203.

MacLeod, C., Mathews, A. & Tata, P. (1986). Attentional bias in emotional disorders. *Journal of Abnormal Psychology*, **95**, 15–20.

MacLeod, C. & Hagan, R. (1992). Individual differences in the selective processing of threatening information, and emotional responses to a stressful event. *Behaviour Research and Therapy*, **30**, 151–161.

March, J.S. (1990). The nosology of post-traumatic stress disorder. *Journal of Anxiety Disorders*, **4**, 61–82.

Martin, M., Williams, R.M. & Clark, D.M. (1991). Does anxiety lead to selective processing of threat-related information? *Behaviour Research and Therapy*, **29**, 147–160.

Mathews, A. & Bradley, B. (1983). Mood and the self-reference bias in recall. *Behaviour Research and Therapy*, **21**, 233–239.

Mathews, A. & Klug, F. (1993). Emotionality and interference with colour-naming in anxiety. *Behaviour Research and Therapy*, **31**, 57–62.

Mathews, A. & MacLeod, C. (1985). Selective processing of threat cues in anxiety states. *Behaviour Research and Therapy*, **122**, 567–572.

Mathews, A. & MacLeod, C. (1986). Discrimination of threat cues without awareness in anxiety states. *Behaviour Research and Therapy*, **23**, 563–569.

Mattia, J.I., Heimberg, R.G. & Hope, D.A. (1993). The revised Stroop colour-naming task in social phobics. *Behaviour Research and Therapy*, **31** (3), 305–313.

McCarthy, P.R., Foa, E.B., Murdock, T. & Ilia, D. (1990). Does anxiety lead to selective processing of threatening information? *Behaviour Research and Therapy*, **29**, 147–160.

McNally, R.J. (1990). Psychological approaches to panic disorder: A review. *Psychological Bulletin*, **108**, 403–419.

McNally, R.J. (1992). Psychopathology of PTSD: Boundaries of the syndrome. In M. Basoglu (Ed.), *Torture and its Consequences: Current Treatment Approaches*. Cambridge: CUP.

McNally, R.J. (1993). Self-representation in Post-traumatic Stress Disorder: A cognitive perspective. In Z.V. Segal & S.J. Blatt (Eds.), *The Self in Emotional Distress*. New York: Guilford Press.

McNally, R.J., English, G.E. & Lipke, H.J. (1993). Assessment of intrusive cognition in Post-Traumatic Stress Disorder: Use of the modified Stroop paradigm. *Journal of Traumatic Stress*, **6** (1), 33–41.

McNally, R.J., Foa, E.B. & Donnell, C.D. (1989). Memory bias for anxiety information in patients with panic disorder. *Cognition and Emotion*, **3**, 27–44.

McNally, R.J., Kaspi, S.P., Riemann, B.C. & Zeitlin, S.B. (1990). Selective processing of threat cues in Post-Traumatic Stress Disorder. *Journal of Abnormal Psychology*, **99**, 398–402.

McNally, R.J., Litz, B.T., Prassas, A., Shin, L.M. & Weathers, F.W. (1994). Emotional priming of autobiographical memory disturbance in post-traumatic stress disorder. *Cognition and Emotion*, **8**, 351–368.

McNally, R.J., Luedke, D.L., Besyner, J.K., Peterson, R.A., Bohm, K. & Lips, O.J. (1987). Sensitivity to stress-relevant stimuli in Post-Traumatic Stress Disorder. *Journal of Anxiety Disorders*, **1**, 105–116.

McNally, R.J., Reimann, B.C. & Kim, E. (1990). Selective processing of threat cues in panic disorder. *Behaviour Research and Therapy*, **28**, 407–412.

McNeil, D.W., Reis, B.J., Taylor, L.J., Boone, M.L., Cater, L.E., Turk, C.L. & Lewin, M.R. (1995). Comparison of social phobia subtypes using Stroop tests. *Journal of Anxiety Disorders*, **9** (1), 47–57.

Mogg, K. & Marden, B. (1990). Processing of emotional information in anxious subjects. *British Journal of Clinical Psychology*, **29**, 277–229.

Mogg, K., Mathews, A. & Weinman, J. (1989). Selective processing of threat cues in anxiety states: A replication. *Behaviour Research and Therapy*, **29**, 317–323.

Moradi, A.R., Neshat, M.R., Taghavi, M.R. & Yule, W. (1995). The performance of children with PTSD on colour naming task (Stroop paradigm). Paper presented at the Fourth European Conference on Traumatic Stress, Paris, May 1995.

Power, M.J., Dalgleish, T. & Claudio, V. (1993). The directed forgetting task: application to emotionally valent material. Unpublished manuscript.

Power, M.J., Dalgleish, T., Claudio, V., Tata, P. & Kentish, J. (submitted). The directed forgetting task: Application to emotionally valenced material.

Rachman, S. (1980). Emotional processing. *Behaviour Research and Therapy*, **18**, 51–60.

Richards, A. & French, C.F. (1990). Central vs peripheral presentation of stimuli in an emotional Stroop task. *Anxiety Research*, **3**, 41–49.

Richards, A. & Millwood, B. (1989). Colour identification of differentially valenced words in anxiety. *Cognition and Emotion*, **3**, 171–176.

Singer, J.L. (Ed.) (1990). *Repression and Dissociation*. Chicago: University of Chicago Press.

Stroop, J.R. (1935). Studies of interference in serial verbal reactions. *Journal of Experimental Psychology*, **18**, 643–662.

Teasdale, J.D. (1983). Negative thinking in depression: Cause, effect or reciprocal relationship. *Advances in Behaviour Research and Therapy*, **5**, 3–25.

Thrasher, S.M., Dalgleish, T. & Yule, W. (1994). Information processing in Post-traumatic Stress Disorder. *Behaviour Research and Therapy*, **32** (2), 247–254.

Thrasher, S.M. & Dalgleish, T. (in prep.) Directed Forgetting in Post-traumatic Stress Disorder.

Trandel, D.V. & McNally, R.J. (1987). Perception of threat cues in post-traumatic stress disorder: Semantic processing without awareness? *Behaviour Research and Therapy*, **25**, 469–496.

Tversky, A. & Kahneman, D. (1974). Judgement under uncertainty: Heuristics and biases. *Science*, **125**, 1124–1131.

Watts, F.N., McKenna, F.P., Sharrock, R. & Tresize, L. (1986). Colour naming of phobia-related words. *British Journal of Psychology*, **77**, 97–108.

Williams, J.M.G. & Nulty, D.D. (1986). Construct accessibility, depression and the emotional Stroop task: Transient mood or stable structure? *Personality and Individual Differences*, **7**, 485–491.

Williams, J.M.G., Watts, F.N., MacLeod, C. & Mathews, A. (1988). *Cognitive Psychology and Emotional Disorders*. Wiley: Chichester.

Zeitlin, S.B. & McNally, R.J. (1991). Implicit and explicit memory biases for threat in Post-Traumatic Stress Disorder. *Behaviour Research and Therapy*, **29**, 451–457.

Chapter 10

COGNITIVE THEORIES OF POST-TRAUMATIC STRESS DISORDER

*Tim Dalgleish**

The experience of trauma raises a number of compelling issues for the theoretician. On the one hand, trauma can happen to any one of us and a cursory content analysis of psychiatric diagnostic manuals reveals post-traumatic stress disorder (PTSD) to be one of the few so-called disorders which has a specific *external* aetiology. On the other hand, the range of reactions which people experience and report following traumatic events is enormous; some individuals appear to come through the most horrendous ordeals psychologically unscathed whereas others exhibit chronic post-traumatic reactions lasting years or even decades and experience profound changes in their personalities (Epstein, 1990). Yet others seem to cope very well for some time following a trauma, only to experience a later, delayed, onset of PTSD (van Dyke, Zilberg & McKinnon, 1985).

In attempting to reconcile these two factors—the indiscriminate nature of traumatic events and the range of individual differences to those events—trauma researchers have investigated a number of variables which might define the nature and extent of the post-traumatic reaction and several chapters in the present volume focus on one or more of these factors. Such variables include aspects of the actual event; for example, whether individuals were bereaved (Joseph, Yule, Williams & Hodgkinson, 1994) or experienced a threat to their own life (Fontana, Rosenheck & Brett, 1992). Prior experience of trauma (Burgess & Holmstrom, 1978) or a premorbid history of psychological problems (McFarlane, 1989) also seem important as do post-event variables such as degree of social support (Kilpatrick, Veronen & Best, 1985; also see Chapter 4 this volume), the attributions

*MRC Cognition and Brain Sciences Unit, Cambridge

Post-Traumatic Stress Disorders: Concepts and Therapy. Edited by William Yule.
© 1999 John Wiley & Sons Ltd.

about the event (Joseph, Brewin, Yule & Williams, 1991; see Chapter 3 this volume) and the individual's ability to express emotions concerning the event (Joseph, Dalgleish, Williams, Thrasher, Yule & Hodgkinson, 1995; see also Chapter 5 this volume). This combination of intra-individual, social and event variables has led to the development of a number of sophisticated psychosocial frameworks within which PTSD can be understood (Green, Wilson & Lindy, 1985; Williams and Joseph, Chapter 15 this volume; Peterson, Prout & Schwartz, 1991).

Such psychosocial frameworks are undoubtedly important in bringing a sense of order to the confusion of trauma research and in generating new ideas and predictions. Nevertheless, at the present time these frameworks remain descriptive and there exists a need for a parallel strand of theoretical work which seeks to provide an explanatory model of *how* the various factors listed above interact with each other and *how* the different reactions to traumatic events come to be manifested. In the present chapter I review a selection of theoretical approaches to PTSD which aspire to such explanatory power, and I endeavour to assess the extent to which these aspirations are fulfilled. In making these assessments it seems that a good theory needs to account satisfactorily for at least the following preconditions:

- *Precondition 1.* To explain the three central constellations of problems in PTSD (DSM-IV: APA, 1994): re-experiencing phenomena; avoidance symptoms; and symptoms of hyperarousal.
- *Precondition 2.* To account for the range of individual reactions to trauma: no apparent emotional sequelae; acute PTSD; chronic PTSD; delayed onset PTSD; and so on.
- *Precondition 3.* To explain the effects of event variables, premorbid history of psychological problems, social support, attributional style and attitudes to emotional expression.
- *Precondition 4.* To account for the efficacy of exposure-based treatments for PTSD (Thompson, Charlton, Kerry, Lee & Turner, 1995).
- *Precondition 5.* To provide a coherent model of mind within which the above four preconditions can be realised.

A number of models in psychology provide theories which seek to meet these five preconditions; for example, the psychodynamic (Freud, 1919), learning theory (Keane, Zimmering & Caddell, 1985), psychobiology (van der Kolk, 1988) and cognitive (Horowitz, 1986). While all of these models encompass approaches which offer interesting insights into the nature of the disorder, it is probably the cognitive approach which is the most fully developed and which provides the most coherent and successful attempts at accounting for the range of factors implicated in PTSD. Consequently, in this chapter I shall restrict my review of theoretical approaches to PTSD to those which sail under the cognitive banner.

Such cognitive theories of PTSD have a certain theoretical family resemblance. They all propose that individuals bring to the traumatic experience a set of pre-existing beliefs and models of the world, of others, and of themselves. These mental representations are a product of the individuals' prior experiences. The occurrence of trauma provides information to the individual which is, on the one hand, highly salient and, on the other hand, incompatible with these pre-existing meaning structures. So, unlike non-salient information which the cognitive system can easily ignore or compatible information which the system can easily assimilate, this salient, incompatible trauma-related information cannot be ignored and must be integrated to avoid psychological "chaos". This attempt to integrate trauma-related information into existing models leads, cognitive theories argue, to the various phenomena which characterise post-traumatic reactions. Successful resolution of the trauma occurs when the new information is integrated into the existing models (often by virtue of changes in those same models). Unsuccessful resolution occurs when individuals are unable to bring the new trauma-related information into accord with their pre-existing conceptualisations of the self and the world. Different cognitive theories focus on different aspects of this disparity between pre-existing mental representations and new trauma-related information. Inevitably, this means that a given theory generally has more explanatory power in some areas than it does in others and few of the theories I shall review are able, satisfactorily, to meet all five of the preconditions outlined above.

THE THEORIES

Horowitz's Formulation of Stress Response Syndromes

The Horowitz (1973, 1976, 1979, 1986; Horowitz, Wilner, Kaltreider & Alvarez, 1980) formulation of stress response syndromes offers perhaps the most influential cognitive model of reactions to trauma to date. Although derived from classical psychodynamic psychology (notably Freud, 1920), Horowitz's theory is principally concerned with discussing such ideas in terms of the cognitive processing of traumatic information such as ideas, thoughts, images, affects and so on. Horowitz has argued that the main impetus within the cognitive system for the processing of trauma-related information comes from a *completion tendency*: the psychological "need to match new information with inner models based on older information, and the revision of both until they agree" (Horowitz, 1986, p. 92). This completion tendency allows the mind to remain in accord with current reality—a necessary requirement for effective decision making and action.

Horowitz (1986) proposed that, subsequent to the experience of trauma, there is an initial "crying out" or stunned reaction followed by a period of information overload in which the thoughts, memories and images of the trauma cannot be reconciled with current meaning structures; that is, there is an initial failure to "complete". As a result, Horowitz suggests that a number of psychological defence mechanisms come into play to keep the traumatic information in the unconscious and the individual then experiences a period of numbing and denial. However, the completion tendency maintains the trauma-related information in what Horowitz calls *active memory*, causing it to break through these defences and intrude into consciousness in the form of flashbacks, nightmares and unwanted thoughts as the individual endeavours to merge the new information with pre-existing models. According to Horowitz, this tension between the completion tendency on the one hand and the psychological defence mechanisms on the other causes individuals to oscillate between phases of intrusion and denial-numbing as they gradually integrate the traumatic material with long-term meaning representations. Failures of such processing can mean that the partially processed traumatic information remains in active memory without ever being fully assimilated, thus leading to chronic post-traumatic reactions.

Horowitz's analysis of the processes underlying completion, intrusion and denial has considerable explanatory power for PTSD phenomenology (Precondition 1) and he also talks extensively about the role and effects of treatment (Precondition 4). Furthermore, his theory indicates clearly the ways in which normal reactions to trauma can become chronic (Precondition 2). See Figure 10.1 for a schematic summary of Horowitz's model.

Horowitz's proposals, however, have a number of limitations which it is important to outline. First, there is little discussion of the central question in trauma research—why some individuals develop PTSD while others, after essentially similar traumatic experiences, exhibit little or no outward signs of being traumatised (Precondition 2). Indeed, there is little detail in Horowitz's writings concerning the nature of existing schema structure and the exact ways in which it fails to accommodate new information from the traumatic experience (Precondition 5). Secondly, Horowitz's formulation struggles to account for epidemiological data regarding the frequency of late onset PTSD (Precondition 2); however, this might be

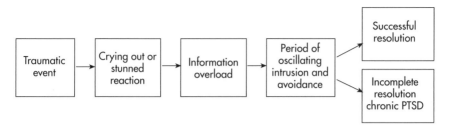

Figure 10.1 Sequence of reactions following trauma according to Horowitz

explained as a long period of denial which later breaks down. Thirdly, while Horowitz provides a clear description of the time course of post-traumatic reactions, it is far from certain that all individuals do experience an initial period of denial, or later oscillations between denial and intrusion. In fact, Creamer, Burgess and Pattison (1992) disagree entirely and argue for an initial episode of intrusive symptoms (see below). Finally, although Horowitz touches briefly on factors such as social support, attributions and so on, there is little explanation of how such factors might operate and interact with processes such as completion (Precondition 3).

Janoff-Bulman's Cognitive Appraisal Theory

The cognitive-appraisal model of Janoff-Bulman (1985, 1992; Janoff-Bulman & Frieze, 1983) centres almost exclusively on the content of the pre-existing beliefs about the self and the world which the individual carries into a traumatic situation. Janoff-Bulman argues that PTSD is the result of certain basic assumptions about self and the world being "shattered". The assumptions which Janoff-Bulman is referring to are: the assumption of personal invulnerability; the perception of the world as meaningful or comprehensible; and the view of the self in a positive light. The proposal is that these assumptions provide structure and meaning in the individual's life but that they cannot be maintained in the face of a traumatic experience and, consequently, they "shatter", plunging the individual into a confusion of intrusion, avoidance and hyperarousal.

Janoff-Bulman's work is important in that it describes the ways in which trauma-related information is incongruent with the usual beliefs and assumptions about the self and world which people possess. There is little attempt, however, to explain how such models are represented or what processes are involved when they are shattered (Precondition 5). Are the assumptions merely sets of *beliefs* about the world and the self which are easy to articulate in natural language, or are they labels for *models* of the self and the world with higher-order meaning which can only be incompletely and clumsily described in natural language? (See the discussion of multi-level theories below.) Moreover, on what basis can it be determined that the three assumptions highlighted by Janoff-Bulman are the important ones? Is it not more conceivable that for each individual the assumptions which are implicated in the reaction to trauma will be many and varied? A related problem is raised by the finding (Kilpatrick, Veronen & Best, 1985) that individuals with a premorbid history of psychological problems are more likely to develop PTSD following a trauma. Such individuals would presumably be characterised within Janoff-Bulman's scheme as having assumptions of personal vulnerability and views of the self in a negative light (Foa & Riggs, 1993). Such premorbid negative assumptions are unlikely to be shattered by a traumatic experience; in fact, they are more likely to be confirmed. Finally, the concept of "shattering" seems problematic. The implication is that certain assumptions are irreparably destroyed and must be replaced with new working models. However, Janoff-Bulman envisages that assumptions once shattered can be "rebuilt" and it seems that the overextension of this metaphor has begun to confuse the theoretical picture. I shall return to this point in the discussion of multilevel theories below.

Foa's Fear Network

Applying Lang's (1977, 1985) theory of fear structures, Foa and her colleagues (Foa & Kozak, 1986; Foa & Riggs, 1993; Foa, Steketee & Rothbaum, 1989; Foa, Zinbarg & Rothbaum, 1992) have outlined an information-processing theory of PTSD which centres on the formation of a so-called fear network in long-term memory. This fear network (cf. Lang) encompasses: stimulus information about the traumatic event; information about cognitive, behavioural and physiological reactions to the event; and information which links these stimulus and response elements together. Activation of the trauma-related fear network by cue stimuli (i.e. reminders of the trauma), according to Foa, causes information in the network to enter conscious awareness (the intrusion symptoms of PTSD). Attempts to avoid and suppress such activation of the network lead to the cluster of avoidance symptoms of PTSD. Foa argues that successful resolution of the trauma can only occur by integrating the information in the fear network with existing memory structures. Such assimilation requires, first, the activation of the fear network so that it becomes accessible for modification and, second, the availability of information that is incompatible with the contents of the fear network so that the overall memory structure can be modified. A number of factors mediate the course of such integration; for example, Foa suggests that the unpredictability and uncontrollability of the traumatic event can make it very difficult to assimilate into existing models in which the world is controllable and predictable. Furthermore, factors such as the severity of the event disrupt the cognitive processes of attention and memory at the time of the trauma and Foa proposes that this disruption can lead to the formation of a disjointed and fragmented fear network which is consequently difficult to integrate with existing, more organised models.

By outlining an architectural framework within which some of Horowitz's and Janoff-Bulman's theoretical suggestions can be modelled, Foa has taken a big step towards a greater understanding of how the processes underlying PTSD might operate within a cognitive system. Moreover, in emphasising factors such as the predictability and controllability of the trauma, Foa highlights one important role of the individual's attributions and interpretations of the traumatic event (Precondition 3). Also, the suggestion that the availability of information incompatible with the trauma is necessary for successful processing provides a framework for understanding both the role of social support as a vehicle for the provision of such incompatible information (Precondition 3) and also the processes underlying the success of exposure-based interventions for PTSD (Precondition 4). What is less clear, however, is whether network theory provides an architecture powerful enough to cope with the range of PTSD phenomenology. A network with a single level of representation struggles to explain how the existing meaning structures and models of the world, which are such a feature of the social-cognitive models (Foa & Riggs, 1993), are represented and how integration of the trauma-related information with such models might take place (Precondition 5). Nor does if explain why fear networks develop in some individuals and not in others (Precondition 2).

Cognitive Action Theory

The cognitive action theory of Chemtob, Roitblat, Hamada, Carlson and Twentyman (1988) is a product of research with veterans of the war in Vietnam. It presents a similar perspective to that of Foa, though with more detailed analysis of the structure of the fear network which is formulated in terms of a localised connectionist architecture (see Figure 10.2). Chemtob et al. argue that, in individuals with PTSD, the fear network is permanently activated causing them to function in a "survival mode"—a

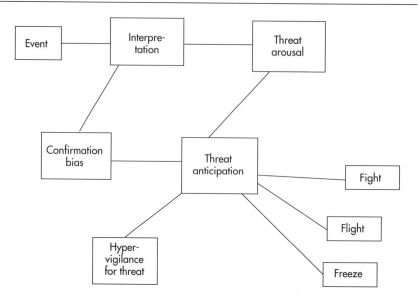

Figure 10.2 A possible cognitive action network for PTSD in Chemtob et al. (1988)

way of functioning that was adaptive during the traumatic incident. This permanent activation of the network, it is suggested, leads to the symptoms of hyperarousal and intrusion. Such symptoms are exacerbated by two further functions of the Chemtob et al. model. First, the increased "gain" of the system in PTSD means that vicious circles of increasing arousal operate more quickly and, secondly, it is suggested that PTSD sufferers have higher limits on the magnitude to which the threat-arousal system can be activated.

Cognitive action theory provides another potential processing framework within which to understand PTSD. It is compromised somewhat by its narrow emphasis on combat-related trauma. In addition, as with the other models discussed above, Chemtob et al.'s approach offers little explanation as to why some individuals remain in "survival mode" while others do not (Precondition 2). Similarly, there is no discussion of other variables of known importance such as attributions and social support (Precondition 3) or of the mechanisms of treatment (Precondition 4).

The Information-Processing Theory

The cognitive-processing model of PTSD of Creamer, Burgess and Pattison (1992) is a derivative approach presented as a "synthesis and reconceptualisation of existing formulations" (p. 453). It combines the core themes of Horowitz's work with the network architecture of Foa et al. (1989) and Chemtob et al. (1988). As with Foa's model, Creamer et al. argue that the fear network must be activated for recovery from trauma to occur and they refer to this as *network resolution processing*. As a concept this is not unlike Horowitz's (e.g. 1986) completion tendency. However, as noted above, Horowitz and Creamer et al. differ in their proposals regarding the course of such resolution or completion. Horowitz argues for an initial period of denial-numbing followed by oscillating experiences of intrusion and denial-numbing. In contrast, Creamer et al. argue for an initial period of intrusion (due to activation of the fear network) with which the individual copes by calling upon a range of defensive and avoidant strategies. Moreover, Creamer et al. suggest that the extent of this initial intrusive experience can be used as an index of the degree of network resolution processing that is occurring. In this analysis, then, high levels of initial intrusion are a predictor of successful recovery whereas low levels of initial intrusion are a predictor of poor outcome and chronic pathology. Indeed, Creamer et al.'s LISREL path analyses of their own longitudinal follow-up data from the victims of an office block shooting support these predictions. However, other data analysed using standard multiple regression techniques (McFarlane, 1989) suggest that prior levels of high intrusion are predictive of a *poorer* outcome.

Creamer et al.'s (1992) work is important in that it is based on longitudinal data and makes clear predictions about outcome. However, it has a number of limitations. First, because it is data driven, the model has limited explanatory value; essentially it is an attempt at presenting some interesting correlational data in a loose theoretical framework. Secondly, the theory gives no indication as to why some individuals develop PTSD and others do not (Precondition 2), nor does it discuss the effects of factors of known importance such as social support or the individual's attributions and interpretations of the event (Precondition 3). Finally, the strong predictions concerning outcome are only partially supported by the literature (Horowitz, 1986; McFarlane, 1989) and this alone provides sufficient reason for caution.

Brewin's Dual Representation Theory

Brewin, Dalgleish and Joseph (1995) have applied Brewin's (1989) dual representation theory to PTSD. This approach endeavours to circumvent the shortcomings of single level theories such as Foa's (see above) by proposing two levels in memory at which trauma-related information can be represented. The first level of representation is of the individual's conscious experience of the traumatic event. This forms what Brewin has called *Verbally Accessible Memories (VAMs)*. VAMs are characterised by their ability to be deliberately retrieved and progressively edited by the traumatised individual. VAM representations, it is argued, as with Foa's fear network, contain sensory, response and meaning information about the traumatic event. The second level of representation proposed by Brewin consists of *Situationally Accessible Memories (SAMs)*. SAMs contain information which cannot be deliberately accessed by the individual and is not available for progressive editing. In fact, SAMs, as the name suggests, are accessed only when aspects of the original traumatic situation cue their activation. Dual representation theory proposes that VAM and SAM representations are encoded in parallel at the time of the trauma and between them account for the range of PTSD phenomenology. For example, wholistic, dissociative memories or "flashbacks" would be considered to be the result of the activation of SAM representations, whereas the person's ability to recount the trauma, for example in a therapeutic situation, would be a function of the accessibility of VAM representations. See Figure 10.3 for a schematic illustration of Dual Representation Theory.

Brewin et al. (1995) propose that the emotional processing of trauma needs to proceed on both the VAM and SAM fronts in order to be successful. It is proposed that individuals need to consciously integrate the verbally accessible information in VAM with their pre-existing beliefs and models of the world and "the end point of this process is to reduce negative affect by restoring a sense of safety and control, and by making appropriate adjustments to expectations about the self and the world". The second emotional processing element, it is suggested, is the activation of information in SAM through exposure to cues concerning the event. In

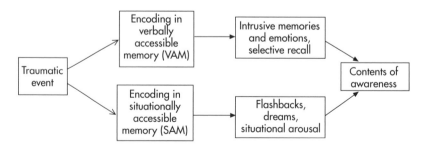

Figure 10.3 A schematic illustration of dual representation theory applied to PTSD (based on Brewin et al., 1995)

fact, as Brewin et al. point out, this would usually happen automatically when the individual begins, progressively, to edit VAM information. Alterations in SAM representations can then occur via the integration of new, non-threatening information into the SAMs (cf. Foa) or by the creation of new SAMs (Brewin, 1989). These two proposed routes to successful emotional processing are clearly derived from the theoretical ideas reviewed earlier. The editing of VAM information to bring it into accord with pre-existing models of the world owes much to the work of Horowitz and Janoff-Bulman, while the requirement of activation and the subsequent integration of new information into SAMs is reminiscent of Foa's implementation of fear networks.

Successful emotional processing of VAM and SAM information concerning the trauma may not always be possible. Brewin et al. suggest that, in some circumstances, for example when the discrepancy between the trauma and prior assumptions is too great, emotional processing of trauma information will become chronic. Alternatively, emotional processing may be prematurely inhibited due to sustained efforts to avoid the reactivation of highly distressing information stored in VAM and SAM. In this situation, Brewin et al. suggest, there may be no active emotional processing but the SAM information should still be accessible in certain circumstances and the individual is hence vulnerable to delayed onset PTSD when those circumstances arise.

Dual Representation Theory offers a coherent account of the phenomenology of PTSD, and makes particularly clear statements concerning the more distinctive experiences such as flashbacks which traumatised individuals report (Precondition 1). There is also considerable discussion of the various outcomes following trauma, what Brewin et al. (1995) call the three endpoints of emotional processing (Precondition 2), and the modi operandi of both cognitive and behaviour-based treatments are outlined in some detail (Precondition 4). Finally, important processes such as attributions, social support and attitudes to emotional expression are considered in tandem with the three endpoints of processing (Precondition 3). On the surface, one strength of Brewin's approach is the application of a coherent cognitive architecture which was developed as a general framework for understanding therapeutic processes (Brewin, 1989) to PTSD (Precondition 5). However, it is important to note that it is perhaps too early to judge how much mileage the concepts of VAM and SAM will turn out to have. Some problems are immediately apparent; first, although credit is due to Brewin et al. for moving away from the single level theories such as Foa's, the proposal of dual representations still leaves it unclear how higher-order models and assumptions about the world and the self might be represented. Are these just one part of the VAM system?

If so, then is it really true to say that the contents of such models are verbally accessible in their entirety? Furthermore, exactly how does the integration of VAM information concerning the trauma into pre-existing representations take place? And what functions do VAMs and SAMs serve in memory generally, or are they merely systems for dealing with memory for emotional material? Overall, Brewin's ideas make considerable progress towards a coherent theory of mind which can account for the known variables of interest in PTSD; however, a number of important questions remain to be answered.

THE SPAARS APPROACH

The SPAARS (Schematic, Propositional, Associative and Analogical Representational Systems) approach to emotions (Dalgleish & Power, 1995; Power & Dalgleish, 1996) is a multi-representational model with four levels/formats of representation in which two routes to the generation of emotions are specified. It is beyond the scope of this chapter to provide a comprehensive overview of the SPAARS model (for a detailed discussion see Power & Dalgleish, 1996). However, the complexity of the model means that it does not lend itself easily to presentation in a cursory form. In this section I try to take a middle line and introduce the main components of the SPAARS approach and show how these interact before discussing the application of SPAARS to PTSD.

SPAARS is a functional theory of emotions. Within SPAARS emotions are functional tools which the cognitive system employs to resolve problems with active, valued goals. So, for example, if a goal is threatened this will be appraised within SPAARS and a fear *module* will be activated. The fear module is essentially a reconfiguration of the cognitive system to deal with the imminent threat and any possible future threats. Such reconfiguration would involve preparation for fight or flight, attentional bias for threat-related information, activation of threat-related concepts in memory and so on. Similarly, if a goal is lost, this will be appraised within SPAARS and the sadness module will be invoked. This might involve the allocation of resources for the elaboration of material associated with the loss in memory in order to enable the individual to replace the goals. Within SPAARS, then, emotions are adaptive processes which reorganise the cognitive system in different ways to deal with changes in the internal or external environment. The suggestion is that the adaptiveness of emotions can sometimes go awry and this can lead to the development and maintenance of so-called emotional disorders and the main thrust of the present section of the chapter is to show how this adaptive nature of the emotion system can lead to profound emotional difficulties in cases of trauma.

An Introduction to the SPAARS Architecture

As the name suggests, the SPAARS model comprises four levels/formats of representation of information (see Figure 10.4).

The *analogical* representational system stores information and memories in analogical form. This information includes visual, olfactory, auditory, gustatory and proprioceptive 'images' which are either episodic or semantic; that is, they are either memories of specific events or fragments of events from an individual's life or they are representations of the properties of objects, smells, sounds etc. in the world. So, for example, a soldier who is the victim of a bombing attack would recognise the sounds of the bombs, the smell of the battlefield, the sights around him, the tension in his body and so on via the representations of this information in the analogical system within SPAARS. Some time later, memories of those sounds, sights, smells and so on might be accessed such that the soldier experiences them as they were when they originally occurred. Within SPAARS this would be due to the activation of episodic representations of those experiences within the analogical system.

In contrast to analogical representations, *propositional* representations within SPAARS are encodings of verbal information, although they represent beliefs, ideas, objects and concepts and the relations between them in

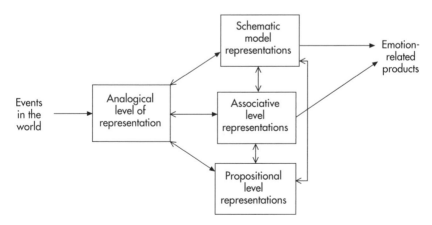

Figure 10.4 The basic architecture of the SPAARS model of emotion (based on Power and Dalgleish, 1996)

a form which is not specific to any language. In other words, propositions are a kind of language of thought, a mental lingua franca, in which different components of the mind communicate. An essential point to grasp about propositional representations is that although they are language free their entire semantic or meaning context can be captured by statements in natural language. So, for example, the propositional information that the capital of France is Paris, although not represented in SPAARS in English or French, is entirely captured by sentences in either language; namely, "Paris is the capital of France"; or "Paris est la capitale de France". Both sentences have the same *propositional* content. The propositional level of representation within SPAARS is responsible for the storage of semantic facts about the world as well as episodic memories of events in the individual's life. So, for example, if we think again of the soldier on the battlefield, semantic information that the bombs which were being dropped were of a certain type or that there was some cover 30 metres to the left would be represented in the propositional system. In addition, episodic memories of the bombing—such as the sequence of events, what the individual did, what they were thinking at the time— would be stored at the propositional level. Propositional representations in SPAARS, then, are the equivalent of VAMs in Dual Representation Theory (Brewin, 1989; Brewin et al., 1995) discussed above.

Propositions refer to thoughts and beliefs which can be expressed in natural language without any corresponding loss of meaning or content. However, as I have argued in the discussion of the work of Foa and Brewin above, there remains a need to propose a mental structure which can represent a higher-order ideational content which cannot readily be expressed in natural language; for instance, the models of the self, the world and others which are so important in understanding PTSD. So, for example, a model of the world as a safe place is likely to contain more complexity than is captured by a simple propositional level statement such as "The world is safe"; rather, a model of the world as safe incorporates all aspects of what the concept of safety means to the individual and is a guiding construct for the way information is processed and organised within the system. In the cognitive psychology literature concepts such as schemas (e.g. Bartlett, 1932), scripts (Schank & Abelson, 1977), frames (Minsky, 1975), mental models (Johnson-Laird, 1983) and the implicational level of Interacting Cognitive Subsystems (ICS: Barnard, 1985; Teasdale & Barnard, 1993) are all concerned with the representation of knowledge at higher levels than that of verbally expressible propositional concepts. Within SPAARS these higher-order representations of ideational content are referred to generically as *schematic models* .

The configuration of schematic models within SPAARS is what provides individuals with their sense of self and of reality and meaning. The proposal is that the self has structure and the world has coherence because of the way they are modelled within this highest level of meaning within SPAARS. In addition to the representation of higher-order meaning, the schematic model level within SPAARS is concerned with the individual's hierarchy of current goals. These goals are utilised in planning action and range from low-level goals such as picking up a cup to the highest level goal in the hierarchy, which is to maintain the current configuration of dominant schematic models; in other words, to maintain the sense of self and a grasp on reality. I shall suggest below that the threat to this highest level goal is one of several powerful aspects of traumatic events.

I have so far outlined three of the four formats of mental representation within the SPAARS model. Before discussing the final representational format, namely the *associative* level, I shall outline the first of two routes to emotion within the SPAARS approach.

The Schematic Model Route to Emotion within SPAARS

As was mentioned in the introduction to this section, SPAARS is an appraisal-based model of emotion. Events and interpretations of events are appraised at the schematic model level of meaning with respect to the individual's active goal structure. In this analysis, then, appraisal is shorthand for the construction of a schematic model representing the implications of any incoming information for the individual's valued goals. So, for example, the emotion of fear is generated when there is an appraisal of threat; that is, a model is constructed which represents the possible future interruption or non-completion of a valued goal. *Anger* would be generated when there is an appraisal that a valued goal has been thwarted or interrupted and when the individual can make an attribution of agency, *sadness* when there is an appraisal of loss and so on. Emotions are activated, as discussed above, in the form of modules which it is suggested imperialistically take over the SPAARS system and reorganise it to deal with the goal discrepancies that have arisen. In the schematic model system, for each emotion there are several levels of appraisal which increase in sophistication; for example, a more sophisticated appraisal for anger, over and above the appraisal of a goal blocked by a recognisable agent, would involve some attribution of blame or intent on the part of that agent. The more sophisticated the appraisal components involved, it is suggested, the more processing resources they take up within SPAARS. So, in the case of anger, when processing resources are at a premium, the more sophisticated "moral" judgements of intent are dispensed with and the individual feels anger when appraisals lacking this component take place.

The Associative Level of Representation and the Second Route to Emotion Generation within SPAARS

I have so far described three of the four representational systems within SPAARS and outlined the first of two routes to emotion generation within the model. In this section I describe the fourth representational system and the second route to emotion generation.

The main thesis of the SPAARS approach with regards to the associative level of representation is that:

1. a useful distinction can be made between controlled and automatic cognitive processes (Shiffrin & Schneider, 1977);
2. automised processes of emotion generation are possible and frequent;
3. such automised emotion generation occurs via an *associative* level of representation and requires *no* concurrent access to the schematic model level of representation as outlined above.

Essentially, then, automatised emotions are generated in a way which does not involve appraisal with respect to the individual's goals at the time of the event's occurrence; rather, automatically generated emotions are a function of the individual's emotional responses in the *past*. So, if we consider the example of Peter, whose father terrified him as a child with his shouting (Power & Dalgleish, 1996), then when Peter's father raises his voice at him 30 years later, Peter might experience the automatic generation of the fear he had as a child. This automatised emotional reaction is akin to what Logan has called (1988) "single step direct-access retrieval of past solutions from memory". It is conceived of as a relatively inflexible and unmodifiable process once activated.

Within SPAARS, it is proposed that the generation of emotions can become automatised in two ways: (1) through repetition of the event-emotion pairing as in the example of Peter's father and his shouting; or (2) when the event is biologically "prepared" in some way as, for example, in specific animal phobias (Seligman, 1971).

In summary, the proposal is that there is a second, *automatic* route to emotion generation which differs from the generation of emotions via schematic models. This automatic generation of emotion, it is suggested, occurs via the associative level of representation within SPAARS.

In this section I have presented a brief summary of the architecture of the SPAARS model of emotion. SPAARS was developed as a model of normal everyday emotions which can also be applied to so-called emotional disorders and in the following section I will discuss the application of this framework to understanding PTSD.

PTSD within SPAARS

At the time of the trauma, it is proposed that information about a traumatic event is appraised at the schematic model level within SPAARS in a threat-related way leading to an experience of intense fear. Furthermore, it is suggested that trauma-related information is encoded and represented at the analogical, propositional and schematic model levels of meaning.

So, if we consider an example: Suzanne is involved in a terrible industrial accident. As the accident is happening, Suzannes's interpretation of the sequence of events (e.g. machinery going wrong, people being injured) is appraised at the schematic model level within SPAARS as highly threatening with respect to several valued goals within Suzanne's goal hierarchy such as personal survival and also to the highest goal of all—the maintenance of the existing configuration of dominant schematic models (see above). That is, the traumatic event threatens Suzanne's maintenance of a sense of reality and of how the world "should" be. Perhaps not surprisingly, therefore, Suzanne experiences intense fear as the trauma occurs. Furthermore, information concerning the trauma—the images, sounds, what Suzanne was thinking, the sense of danger—is encoded within SPAARS at the various levels of the model (analogical, propositional and schematic model). See Figure 10.5.

Such representations of trauma-related information are highly incompatible with the individuals' schematic models of themselves, the world and others. This very incompatibility, it is suggested, means that the trauma-related material threatens the person's very sense of self and reality, which are a function of these models. Consequently, trauma-related information is poorly integrated into existing representations at encoding.

Following a traumatic event, then, the individual possesses representations of trauma-related information in memory at the analogical, propositional and schematic model levels. Within SPAARS, however, this information is unintegrated with the individual's dominant schematic models of the self, world and other. It is proposed that this pattern of representation within SPAARS accounts for the constellation of

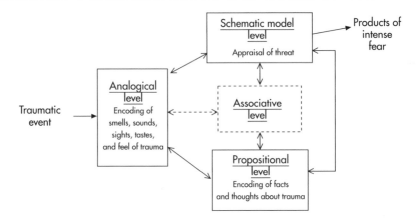

Figure 10.5 The experience of a traumatic event as conceptualised within SPAARS

symptoms which characterise PTSD and related problems following the trauma, and we shall turn to a discussion of these issues next.

Re-experiencing Phenomena

It is suggested that within SPAARS the dominant schematic models of self, world and other constantly seek to organise and provide a meaning structure for the information represented in memory at the different levels within the system and seek to preserve that meaning structure by allocating processing resources to incompatible information in an attempt to assimilate it. This continual appraisal process is similar to Horowitz's completion tendency (see above). Following a traumatic event, it is suggested that the appraisal system at the schematic model level will endeavour to process the unintegrated trauma-related information and, as a consequence, will continue to appraise it as incompatible and as a threat to the existing configuration of schematic models of the world and of the self. The continual appraisal of the incompatibility and threatening nature of the trauma-related information in memory means that the individual experiences constant activation and reactivation of the fear module. This ensures that traumatised individuals are in an almost continuous existential state of "being in danger", even though they will not always be explicitly experiencing intrusive thoughts or images. In addition, information related to the trauma which is the object of such appraisals will intrude, by virtue of its activated state, into consciousness in a variety of ways ranging from intrusive thoughts to nightmares.

A second route to the generation of intrusion phenomena depends on the fact that the chronic activation of the fear module and consequent reconfiguration of SPAARS means that the traumatised individual will exhibit a number of cognitive-processing biases for information related to the trauma (see Chapter 9, this volume) as that information is represented in memory as (a) danger-related and (b) related to current concerns because it has not been successfully integrated into the individual's models of the self, world and other. This means that any cues in the environment which are related to the traumatic information are likely to be selectively processed and will themselves activate the trauma-related information in memory, thereby increasing the probability of intrusions.

Because the trauma-related information across the different levels of representation within SPAARS remains unintegrated, it retains high levels of internal cohesion within memory. In other words, the representational links between different aspects of the traumatic memory are far stronger than the links between the traumatic memory representations and pre-existing memory structures. Furthermore, the representations of the trauma are very "true to life" as there has been little assimilation or blending with other information in memory. As a result of this high level of cohesion, external cues are able to activate the entire trauma memory much more easily than if the trauma-related information had been intermeshed with existing information in memory. This results in such phenomena as flashbacks in which stimuli representing fragments of the traumatic experience are able to trigger intrusive phenomena which involve re-experiencing the whole. Flashbacks can involve reactivation of unintegrated information at all levels within SPAARS . Clearly, analogical level images and sounds are predominant, but propositional thought patterns and the "sense" of danger of schematic model representations can also be re-experienced. Finally, as well as experiencing the generation of fear via repeated appraisal in these ways at the schematic model level, the longer the PTSD lasts the more will the individual who has been traumatised experience the automatic activation of fear via the associative level of meaning as a function of the repetition during intrusions of the link between trauma-related information and fear. Consequently, external or internal trauma-related cues will come to lead to the generation of fear "out of the blue". This suggestion of dual routes to emotion in PTSD is also reflected in work investigating the neuropsychology of the disorder (van der Kolk, 1988).

Avoidance Phenomena

The magnitude of the intrusive phenomena, it is suggested, leads the individual to recruit a number of protective mechanisms and processes. He or she is likely to consciously endeavour to avoid any reminders of the trauma and will try not to think about the trauma or talk about it. In addition, individuals may minimise their interaction with the world generally by socially withdrawing in order to reduce the number of putative triggering stimuli. Other extreme avoidance symptoms of PTSD, such as psychogenic amnesia, are considered below.

Hyperarousal Phenomena

The process of dealing with the existence of unintegrated traumatic information in memory can lead to the various manifestations of hyperarousal in different ways. First, as we have suggested above, the fear module within SPAARS is continuously being activated and reactivated by both the direct appraisal of the unintegrated representations of trauma-related information within memory and also via multiple cueing from the environment; secondly, such continual appraisals utilise executive processing resources and the resultant lack of available resources means that the more sophisticated levels of appraisal which would normally be used in the mediation of emotions via the schematic model level are less likely to operate. So, for example, in the case of anger it was suggested above that when processing resources are limited a higher level of moral appraisal is less likely to be invoked. Consequently, individuals whose processing resources are continually being utilised by appraising the incompatibility of unintegrated trauma-related information in memory, are likely to be irritable and to get angry at actions even when those actions were *not* deliberate or could *not* be helped.

Individual Differences at the Schematic Model Level

It is important to elaborate on the types of models of self, world and other which the individual holds at the schematic model level within SPAARS and the ways in which these models relate to the individual's prior emotional and developmental history in order to understand the enormous range of individual differences in the way people respond to traumatic events. An individual's models of the self, world and others can vary considerably along the dimensions highlighted by authors such as Janoff-Bulman (see above). So, some individuals might hold schematic models in which the world is conceptualised as *reasonably* safe or the self as *generally* invulnerable, whereas others might hold models in which the self is seen, to all intents and purposes, as *completely* invulnerable. In addition to these variations in the models of self, world and other, it is proposed that individuals will have developed very different ways of dealing with information which is incompatible with these models thoughout their emotional histories. Some people may have become highly practised at repressing or denying such incompatible information in the past such that it has rarely actually been integrated with the models of the self, world and other but instead has been isolated in memory—swept under the emotional carpet. Other individuals will have learnt to deal with information incompatible with their models of the world, self and other and to emotionally process it (Rachman, 1980) such that there is a rapprochement between the models and the information.

If we consider these two broad issues together—namely, individual differences in the content of the models of self, world and other and the different histories of dealing with incompatible information—a number of combinations emerge which seem important in the understanding of trauma.

Most individuals, it is suggested, will possess schematic models of the world, self and others in which the world is a reasonably safe place, the individual is reasonably safe and in which there is a high concordance between the individual's actions in the world and their consequences. In most cases, such models are not 'overvalued' in the sense that, for example, the individual holds an assumption of *complete* invulnerability. Furthermore, such models are not rigid and inflexible because they are usually the product of a learning history in which the individual has had to process information which is at odds with extant models and has had to integrate that information in adapting those same models; for example, when goals have not been fulfilled. Consequently, these persons' models of the self, world and other—the structures which provide the sense of meaning and reality- have a certain flexibility and potential to adapt to incorporate disparate information. It is argued that, following a traumatic event, individuals such as these, namely the majority, will most usually experience an initial period of post-traumatic reactions (though some will be able to integrate the trauma-related information almost immediately) but would normally be able to integrate the traumatic information into their models of the self, world and others within weeks or months, either within therapy or within their social support networks (and we discuss these processes below). Such individuals would be unlikely to develop chronic PTSD reactions.

In contrast, it is argued that other people will possess what one might call *overvalued* models and assumptions about the self, world and others at the schematic model level in which, for example, the world is conceptualised as *completely* safe, or as somewhere where *nothing* really bad will ever happen to the individual, only to others, and so on. Individuals might hold such models of the world for two very different reasons: they may have led a very predictable, controllable, safe life in which things have rarely gone wrong and goals have invariably been fulfilled; that is, the schematic models of self, world and other, might be a valid reflection of the life that the individuals have experienced. Alternatively, in order to maintain the overvalued models which they hold, some people may have evolved a way of dealing with emotional events which has involved the repression and denial of any information which is incompatible with those models (see Singer, 1990). A characteristic of these overvalued models of the self, world and other, whether they are maintained through repression and denial or are a function of the individual's relatively un-scathed past, is that they are likely to be *inflexible*. In neither case will such individuals have a history of adapting their schematic models in order to accommodate incongruent information.

It is suggested that both of these types of supposedly invulnerable indi-vidual *are* highly vulnerable to extreme emotional distress following a traumatic event but in different ways. Individuals whose pre-trauma life has been safe, controllable and predictable will have no way of beginning to integrate the trauma-related information into their relatively inflexible schematic models of the self, world and other; furthermore, they will have no way of defending against its impact. Consequently, these people are likely to be most at risk of suffering severe and chronic PTSD. This is unlike individuals who, over a period of months, are able to adapt their schematic models to eventually assimilate the trauma-related information through "emotional processing" (Rachman, 1980) in therapy or within their social support network. People with inflexible models will be unable to resolve this tension and are likely to *abandon* their models of self, world and other. It is really only these individuals, it is argued, who experience Janoff-Bulman's "shattered assumptions". Most other trauma survivors seem to cling desperately to the models of self, world and other in order to retain some sense of meaning and some grasp of reality in the face of what has happened. Such abandonment of the inflexible, overvalued schematic models of self and reality which, until the trauma, had served so well, can lead to severe and chronic personality changes which prove destructive for individuals and their families. In contrast, those individu-als who have employed a repressive coping style in order to maintain their overvalued models are likely to be able to continue to employ these coping processes fairly effectively in dealing with the new trauma-related information. In these people, then, there will be few outward signs of post-traumatic reactions in most cases (although in the extreme case they may suffer severe dissociative reactions and psychogenic amnesia). Most usually, it is proposed, they will be able to lock the trauma-related infor-mation away in memory and throw away the key. Such individuals are likely to be characterised in a number of ways:

1. They will still experience some automatically generated emotions via the associative level within SPAARS.
2. Cognitive processing systems will still be biased towards the processing of trauma-related information, and such people will consequently exhibit processing biases as measured by standard information processing tasks (see also Brewin et al., 1995).
3. They will be vulnerable to late onset PTSD when either later life changes shift the way that their schematic models of self, world and other are organised, or when situations similar to the original trauma occur. Life events such as these may be sufficient to overwhelm the system which is already trying to repress the information related to the previous trauma; late-onset PTSD is then likely to occur.
4. Such individuals are likely to suffer from increased rates of psychosomatic problems as the effects of repressing the traumatic information take their toll on the rest of the system (Pennebaker, 1982).

Finally, there are individuals who have premorbidly damaged models of the self, world and others; that is, they already have schematic model representations that the world is not safe, they are vulnerable and so on. Such individuals may even have a premorbid psychiatric history. These people are likely to have their models confirmed by the new traumatic information and it is proposed that they are likely to experience increases in their associated feelings of anxiety and depression concerning the trauma rather than severe PTSD symptomatology.

Emotional Processing and Treatment within SPAARS

It has been suggested above that, following a traumatic event, the majority of people are able to integrate the trauma-related information over time into their schematic models of self, world and other within SPAARS. In this section, I discuss how this assimilation might occur.

The integration of trauma-related information, or *emotional processing* as Rachman (1980) has called it, normally occurs as a function of exposure to the information either within a therapeutic context (Thompson et al., 1995) or within a supportive social network (see Chapter 4, this volume). Such exposure can take many forms; for example, systematically recounting the event, returning to the place that it happened or just talking about it in more general ways. Within the SPAARS analysis, it is suggested that this exposure serves to reduce post-traumatic symptomatology in two main ways. First, it allows the individual to re-experience the trauma-related information (which is incompatible with higher-order models) in a safe context—an environment in which the higher-order models of safety, controllability, predictability and so on to which the person clings do still hold. This process allows the individual to begin to conceptualise the event as something anomalous and unusual in a world where the models of meaning and reality which had served for so long do still have a significant place. Foa talks of this process as an integration of non-danger-related information into the fear network (see above). However, it is proposed that it can be more readily understood in terms of the higher level of meaning represented by schematic models.

The second means by which various forms of exposure to the trauma-related information operate, we propose, is by weakening the links between that information and the automatic generation of fear via the associative level within SPAARS. This weakening depends on the individual experiencing a reduction in fear during the exposure session. Such exposure-based emotional processing serves to enable the individual to integrate the trauma-related information in memory. Consequently, it is argued, this approach is likely to have little benefit for those individuals with chronic PTSD as they are unlikely as a consequence of their very inflexible models of the self, world, and others to be able to modify those models to integrate the trauma-related information, regardless of how many times that information is re-presented through exposure. For these individuals, their sense of reality and meaning have been "shattered" (Janoff-Bulman, 1985) and it seems likely that cognitive-oriented treatments would be more efficacious in replacing the abandoned, overvalued, inflexible models with more adaptable, functional ones.

In this final theoretical section of the chapter I have outlined the SPAARS model of emotions and considered its application to PTSD. In doing so I have endeavoured to illustrate how it is the adaptive nature of the emotional system which is the individual's undoing following a traumatic event. Attempts by the emotional system, on the one hand, to integrate information which does not fit the current models of reality while, on the other hand, seeking to preserve those self-same models at whatever cost, leads, it has been suggested, to the constellations of difficulties experienced in PTSD (Precondition 1). Furthermore, the various ways in which this process can be played out, it has been proposed, are a function of the content *and* structure of the higher-order meaning representations, or schematic models, which the individual brings to the traumatic event (Precondition 2) and these have different implications for both therapy (Precondition 4) and for processes such as social support (Precondition 3). Finally SPAARS provides a coherent cognitive architecture in which PTSD can be understood (Precondition 5). Perhaps, more importantly, this architecture does not stand or fall by virtue of the account it is able to provide of PTSD; rather, it is a model of both normal everyday emotions and of all types of so-called emotional disorders.

CONCLUSION

In this chapter I have reviewed a number of cognitive theories of PTSD. Consideration of the various approaches together reveals a clear evolutionary pattern. Early models of PTSD focused on a description of the conflict between experiencing a trauma and trying to hold on to beliefs about the world and the self which are unable to account for the details of the traumatic events. Later models offered relatively simple cognitive architectures, such as a single-level network, in which these kinds of ideas might be instantiated. Finally, later dual- and multilevel theories have provided coherent frameworks within which all aspects of the experience of trauma and the individuals' premorbid understanding of the world and of themselves can be incorporated. These latter approaches represent a movement away from a consideration of PTSD as a stand-alone "disorder" towards a conceptualisation in which emotional reactions to trauma are one more way in which we interact with our worlds. Thus, the problems which characterise PTSD are seen as the result of a *functional* response to circumstances. Intense trauma, until it is resolved, is represented as a continuing threat and intrusion, avoidance and hypervigilance are highly adaptive ways of dealing with such circumstances. PTSD, then, is not a disorder of the cognitive system but a function of its efficiency. Consequently, it is the dual- and multilevel theories of PTSD which provide a contextual theory of mind which currently offer the best response to the five preconditions laid down at the beginning of the chapter. At the present time, the explanatory utility and predictive power of such multilevel approaches is unknown, not only in the case of trauma but also for other so-called disorders such as depression (Teasdale & Barnard, 1993). The arguments in this chapter represent the case for the defence but, for the present, the jury is still out.

REFERENCES

APA (1994). *Diagnostic and Statistical Manual of Mental Disorders* (4th Edition). Washington, DC: American Psychiatric Association.

Barnard, P.J. (1985). Interacting cognitive subsystems. A psycholinguistic approach to short-term memory. In A. Ellis (Ed.), *Progress in the Psychology of Language*, vol. 2. Hove: Erlbaum.

Bartlett, F.C. (1932). *Remembering: A Study in Experimental and Social Psychology.* Cambridge: Cambridge University Press.

Brewin, C.R. (1989). Cognitive change processes in psychotherapy. *Psychological Review*, **96**, 379–394.

Brewin, C.R., Dalgleish, T. & Joseph, S. (1995). A dual representation theory of post-traumatic stress disorder. Manuscript submitted for publication.

Burgess, A.W. & Holmstrom, L.L. (1974). Rape trauma syndrome. *American Journal of Psychiatry*, **131**, 981–986.

Burgess, P. & Holmstom, L.L. (1978). Recovery from rape and prior life stress. *Research in Nursing and Health*, **1**, 165–174.

Creamer, M., Burgess, P. & Pattison, P. (1992). Reaction to trauma: A cognitive processing model. *Journal of Abnormal Psychology*, **101**, 452–459.

Chemtob, C., Roitblat, H.L., Hamada, R.S., Carlson, J.G. & Twentyman, C.T. (1988). A cognitive action theory of post-traumatic stress disorder. *Journal of Anxiety Disorders*, **2**, 253–275.

Dalgleish, T. & Power, M.J. (1995). Theoretical approaches to Post-traumatic Stress Disorder: The SPAARS model. Paper presented at the Fourth European Conference on Traumatic Stress, Paris, France, 7–11 May.

Epstein, S. (1990). Beliefs and symptoms in maladaptive resolutions of the traumatic neurosis. In D. Ozer, J.M. Healy & A.J. Stewart (Eds.), *Perspectives on Personality*, vol. 3. London: Jessica Kingsley.

Foa, E.B. & Kozak, M.J. (1986). Emotional processing of fear: Exposure to corrective information. *Psychological Bulletin*, **99**, 20–35.

Foa, E.B. & Riggs, D.S. (1993). Post-traumatic stress disorder in rape victims. In J. Oldham, M.B. Riba & A. Tasman (Eds.), *American Psychiatric Press Review of Psychiatry*, vol. 12. Washington, DC: American Psychiatric Press.

Foa, E.B., Steketee, G. & Rothbaum, B.O. (1989). Behavioral/cognitive conceptualisation of post-traumatic stress disorder. *Behavior Therapy*, **20**, 155–176.

Foa, E.B., Zinbarg, R. & Rothbaum, B.O. (1992). Uncontrollability and unpredictability in post-traumatic stress disorder: An animal model. *Psychological Bulletin*, **112**, 218–238.

Fontana, A., Rosenheck, R. & Brett, E. (1992). War zone traumas and post-traumatic stress disorder symptomatology. *Journal of Nervous and Mental Disease*, **180**, 748–755.

Freud, S. (1919). *Introduction to the Psychology of the War Neuroses* (Standard edn., vol. 18). London: Hogarth Press.

Freud, S. (1920). *Beyond the Pleasure Principle* (Standard edn., vol. 18). London: Hogarth Press.

Green, B.L., Wilson, J.P. & Lindy, J.D. (1985) Conceptualizing post-traumatic stress disorder: A psychosocial framework. In C.R. Figley (Ed.), *Trauma and its Wake: The Study and Treatment of Post-Traumatic Stress Disorder*. New York: Brunner/Mazel.

Horowitz, M.J. (1973). Phase-oriented treatment of stress response syndromes. *American Journal of Psychotherapy*, **27**, 506–515.

Horowitz, M.J. (1976). *Stress Response Syndromes*. New York: Jason Aronson.

Horowitz, M.J. (1979). Psychological response to serious life events. In V. Hamilton & D.M. Warburton (Eds.), *Human Stress and Cognition*, pp. 235–263. New York: Wiley.

Horowitz, M.J. (1986). *Stress Response Syndromes* (2nd Edition). Northvale, NJ: Jason Aronson.

Horowitz, M.J., Wilner, N., Kaltreider, N. & Alvarez, W. (1980). Signs and symptoms of post-traumatic stress disorder. *Archives of General Psychiatry*, **37**, 85–92.

Janoff-Bulman, R. (1985). The aftermath of victimisation: Rebuilding shattered assumptions. In C.R. Figley (Ed.), *Trauma and its Wake: The Study and Treatment of Post-Traumatic Stress Disorder*, pp. 15–35. New York: Brunner/Mazel.

Janoff-Bulman, R. (1992). *Shattered Assumptions: Towards a New Psychology of Trauma*. New York: The Free Press.

Janoff-Bulman, R. & Frieze, I.H. (1983). A theoretical perspective for understanding reactions to victimisation. *Journal of Social Issues*, **39**, 1–17.

Johnson-Laird, P.N. (1983). *Mental Models*. Cambridge: Cambridge University Press.

Joseph, S.A., Brewin, C.R., Yule, W. & Williams, R. (1991). Causal attributions and psychiatric symptoms in survivors of the Herald of Free Enterprise disaster. *British Journal of Psychiatry*, **159**, 542–546.

Joseph, S.A., Brewin, C.R., Yule, W. & Williams, R. (1993). Causal attributions and post-traumatic stress in children. *Journal of Child Psychology and Psychiatry*, **34**, 247–253.

Joseph, S.A., Dalgleish, T., Thrasher, S. & Yule, W. (1995). Crisis support and emotional reactions following trauma. *Crisis Intervention*, **1**, 203–208.

Joseph, S.A., Dalgleish, T., Williams, R., Thrasher, S., Yule, W. & Hodgkinsion, P. (1996). Chronic emotional processing in survivors of the *Herald of Free Enterprise* disaster: The relationship of intrusion and avoidance at 3 years to distress at 5 years. *Behaviour Research and Therapy*, **34**, 357–360.

Joseph, S.A., Yule, W., Williams, R. & Hodgkinson, P. (1994). The *Herald of Free Enterprise* disaster: Correlates of distress at thirty months. *Behaviour Research and Therapy*, **32**, 521–524.

Keane, T.M., Zimmering, R.T. & Caddell, R.T. (1985). A behavioural formulation of PTSD in Vietnam veterans. *Behaviour Therapist*, **8**, 9–12.

Kilpatrick, D.G., Veronen, L.J. & Best, C.L. (1985). Factors predicting psychological distress among rape victims. In C.R. Figley (Ed.), *Trauma and its wake*. New York: Brunner/Mazel.

Lang, P.J. (1977). Fear imagery: An information processing analysis. *Behavior Therapy*, **8**, 862–886.

Lang, P.J. (1985). The cognitive psychophysiology of emotion: Fear and anxiety. In A.H. Tuma & J.D. Maser (Eds.), *Anxiety and the Anxiety Disorders*. Hillsdale, NJ: Erlbaum.

Logan, G.D. (1988). Toward an instance theory of automatisation. *Psychological Review*, **95**, 492–527.

McFarlane, A.C. (1989). The aetiology of post-traumatic morbidity: Predisposing, precipitating and perpetuating factors. *British Journal of Psychiatry*, **154**, 221–228.

Minsky, M. (1975). A framework for representing knowledge. In P.H. Winston (Ed.), *The Psychology of Computer Vision*. New York: McGraw-Hill.

Pennebaker, J.W. (1982). *The Psychology of Physical Symptoms*. New York: Springer-Verlag.

Peterson, K.C., Prout, M.F. & Schwartz, R.A. (1991). *Post-Traumatic Stress Disorder: A Clinician's Guide*. New York: Plenum Press.

Power, M.J. & Dalgleish, T. (1997). *Cognition and Emotion: From Order to Disorder*. Hove: Psychology Press.

Rachman, S. (1980) Emotional processing. *Behaviour Research and Processing*, **18**, 51–60.

Schank, R.C. & Abelson, R.P. (1977). *Scripts, Plans, Goals and Understanding*. Hillsdale, NJ: Erlbaum.

Shiffrin, R.M. & Schneider, W. (1977). Controlled and automatic human information processing: II Perceptual learning, automatic attending and a general theory. *Psychological Review*, **84**, 127–190.

Singer, J.L. (Ed.). (1990). *Repression and Dissociation: Implications for Personality Theory, Psychopathology and Health*. Chicago: University of Chicago Press.

Teasdale, J.D. & Barnard, P.J. (1993) *Affect Cognition and Change: Re-Modelling Depressive Thought*. Hove: Erlbaum.

Thompson, J.A., Charlton, P.F.C., Kerry, R., Lee, D. & Turner, S.W. (1995). An open trial of exposure therapy based on deconditioning for post-traumatic stress disorder. *British Journal of Clinical Psychology*, **34**, 407–417.

van der Kolk, B.A. (1988). The biological response to trauma. In F. Ochberg (Ed.), *Posttraumatic Therapy and Victims of Violence*. New York: Brunner/Mazel.

van Dyke, C., Zilberg, N.J. & McKinnon, J.A. (1985). Posttraumatic stress disorder: A thirty year delay in a WWII veteran. *American Journal of Psychiatry*, **142**, 1070–1073.

Chapter 11

DEBRIEFING AND CRISIS INTERVENTION

Rachel Canterbury* and William Yule*

It is now widely accepted that a significant proportion of people exposed to traumatic events go on to develop severe and prolonged psychological reactions. Although much research in this field has been on survivors of major disasters (e.g. Raphael, 1986; Green et al., 1990) and combat survivors (Kulka et al., 1990), who have been subjected to prolonged periods of exposure to stressful and life-threatening situations, severe post-traumatic stress reactions are being increasingly recognised in survivors of relatively brief traumas, such as road traffic accidents (Mayou, Bryant & Duthie, 1993) and violent crime (Taylor, 1989). A recent US epidemiological survey estimated the lifetime prevalence of post-traumatic stress disorder (PTSD) to be 7.8% (Kessler, Sonnega, Bromet, Hughes & Nelson, 1995) but PTSD is by no means the only consequence of exposure to trauma. Other disorders, including depression, alcohol and substance abuse, dissociative disorders and profound personality change, have been reported, and rates of co-morbidity are high.

In this context, it is perhaps not surprising that increasing attention has been paid to strategies aimed at reducing the risk of chronic post-traumatic stress reactions. As well as the possibility of reducing long-term suffering among those exposed to a traumatic event, preventive approaches have a broader appeal. The immediate distress associated with exposure to trauma is a powerful motivator to act. As Raphael et al. (1995) points out, early intervention strategies may serve a variety of needs simultaneously, including: the need for workers to provide assistance and show concern; the need of survivors to talk about and understand what has happened and to gain control; and the need of those not directly

---

*Institute of Psychiatry, London

Post-Traumatic Stress Disorders: Concepts and Therapy. Edited by William Yule.
© 1999 John Wiley & Sons Ltd.

affected to overcome feelings of helplessness, guilt at having survived and to experience and master vicariously the traumatic encounter with death. Furthermore, treatment of chronic disorders is often lengthy and expensive, and in a world where health care resources are scarce, brief preventive interventions are attractive. The question remains, however, as to what form such interventions should take and their effectiveness in reducing long-term psychopathology.

Among the preventive procedures described in the trauma literature, psychological debriefing has been the most widely accepted and applied. Debriefing has its origins in the military (Salmon, 1919; Marshall, 1944) but more recently procedures have been refined and adapted for use with other groups exposed to trauma. Despite its popularity, however, the efficacy of the technique has yet to be demonstrated and to date knowledge is derived largely from clinical experience. This chapter will review the current status of debriefing in the psychological literature and suggest directions for future research.

THE NATURE OF TRAUMATIC EXPERIENCE

Before discussing psychological debriefing in more detail it is necessary to consider the nature of traumatic experience and the contexts in which it can occur. Post-traumatic stress reactions can develop following exposure to a wide variety of traumatic events. Such events may involve individuals, groups or whole communities. Those affected may be survivors; workers, such as disaster and emergency services personnel; or other occupational groups who are exposed to trauma in the course of their work.

In planning any form of preventive intervention, consideration needs to be given to the circumstances of the traumatic event and the corresponding needs of the individuals involved. For example, in the case of a major disaster involving the destruction of a community, the impact and implications of the event will be different for survivors and rescue workers. Survivors may be faced with massive losses and, in the short term, may need to focus on establishing a place of safety and attending to basic physical needs. The full psychological impact of the event may only be felt later, and thus interventions that are offered too early might be perceived as intrusive rather than helpful. Rescue workers, on the other hand, will be expected to return rapidly to their previous roles, and preventive interventions offered shortly after their involvment with the disaster has ended may be of considerable benefit.

Different traumatic events are likely to elicit differing levels of support and sympathy for those affected. Natural or technological disasters are headline news and subsequent offers of help are often overwhelming. In contrast, individual traumas such as road traffic accidents, assaults or rape, often receive little interest and in some cases give rise to hostility and victim blaming. The role and timing of preventive interventions clearly needs to take account of these complexities. Interventions offered by "professionals" should not interfere with or undermine the natural coping responses of a community affected by disaster, but nor should it be assumed that help will not be needed in the future even if it is not appropriate immediately. In this context, the community needs to be made aware of the help available and how to access it. This is more problematic when disasters involve large groups who just happen to be together, for example transport accidents or at sporting events, when those affected may come from a large geographical area. In these circumstances there may be no natural groupings towards whom interventions could be targeted. The task then becomes the enormously complicated one of providing adequate follow-up and intervention to individuals in different localities with different health care provision. Similarly, traumatic events involving one or only a few people are unlikely to come to the attention of those in a position to offer preventive interventions, and the individuals concerned may also be less likely to receive support from the community. This is of particular concern, given that the total number of people involved in such events is greater than those involved in large-scale disasters and is thus likely to represent a greater demand on health care resources. If preventive interventions are of benefit in reducing long-term psychopathology, finding ways of making such interventions accessible to all these groups is clearly a priority.

Unfortunately, at present, our understanding of the aetiology and natural course of post-traumatic stress disorders is limited and many questions about what interventions may be of benefit, when they should be offered and to whom, remain unanswered. These questions apply as much to psychological debriefing as to any other form of intervention.

APPROACHES TO PSYCHOLOGICAL DEBRIEFING

Among the debriefing procedures most frequently described in the literature is Critical Incident Stress Debriefing (CISD). Originally developed by Mitchell (1983) for use with emergency services personnel, the model has since been adapted for use with other groups exposed to traumatic incidents. These include survivors of disasters and near disasters, helpers in disasters, groups of colleagues following accidents or suicide in the workplace and, increasingly with children following a variety of traumatic experiences (Dyregrov, 1989, 1991).

Mitchell observed that while most emergency personnel were able to deal effectively with repeated exposure to a wide range of traumatic events, some "critical incidents" gave rise to unusually strong emotional reactions which had the potential to interfere with their ability to function either at the scene or later. Examples of such incidents include line of duty deaths, multiple or child fatalities, or identification with the victim. The original goals of CISD were to protect and support emergency personnel following such incidents and to minimise the development of abnormal stress response syndromes which may cause lost time, reduced effectiveness at work and problems within the family. Mitchell originally suggested that the debriefing should take place 24–72 hours after the incident, but now acknowledges that the time frame may need to be more flexible. He advocates that the meeting should be led by a skilled mental health professional together with a number or peer support personnel.

CISD is a seven-stage process usually lasting for 2–3 hours. In the *introductory phase*, the rules and rationale for the debriefing are discussed. Group members are encouraged to participate and confidentiality is emphasised. It is also stressed that the meeting is not intended to be a critique of procedural aspects of the incident but rather a supportive experience during which members have the opportunity to express feelings and to learn from others. The second phase is the *fact phase*, in which each member of the group is asked briefly to describe his or her role and experiences during the incident. Sharing information in this way can help to clarify the nature and sequence of events and to clear up misconceptions about what took place. During the *thought phase*, each member of the group is asked to relate his or her first or most prominent thought during the incident. The fourth phase, the *reaction phase*, is the most emotionally powerful. Group members are asked about the elements of the situation that caused them the most distress and that have been most difficult to cope with since the incident ended. In the *symptom phase*, participants are asked about any symptoms of distress, physical or psychological, they may have encountered during the incident or since. This provides a natural lead into the *teaching phase* during which the team leaders teach the group about normal stress reactions and techniques that may be helpful in reducing stress and promoting recovery. The final phase is called the *re-entry phase* during which any unanswered questions are addressed and summary comments made.

Mitchell argues that CISD should be used in the context of a comprehensive traumatic stress management programme which includes: pre-incident education on the causes, effects and management of stress; on scene support services; individual consultations; follow-up services; and family support services.

Raphael (1986) describes a debriefing approach for mental health workers involved in disaster rescue operations. Raphael emphasises the need to integrate the disaster experience and to deal with the inevitable stresses so that problems do not subsequently arise. She advocates formal group sessions during which a number of aspects of the disaster experience are explored. Participants are encouraged to discuss their introduction to, and first knowledge of, the disaster. Time is given to the participants' personal experiences of the disaster, both negative and positive, together with the feelings those experiences engender. Relationships with other workers and family are also discussed as well as issues of empathy or identification with other workers and victims. Finally, disengagement from the disaster role and the return to normal routines are discussed. Raphael (1986, p. 286) concludes:

> This discusson promotes the processes of integration and mastery of the disaster, by actively defining, both concretely and at a feeling level, the experience and its consequences. The experience is given a cognitive structure, and the emotional release of reviewing it helps the worker to a sense of achievement and distancing. He will not forget the experience but neither is he likely to retain an ongoing stressful burden from it.

Raphael's model therefore places greater emphasis on a review of the work undertaken, the relationships of workers and integration of the experience.

Recognition that disaster relief workers are often faced with multiple stressors over a prolonged period led Armstrong, O'Callahan and Marmar (1991) to develop the Multiple Stressor Debriefing Model (MSDM). As a result of their work with Red Cross disaster personnel following the 1989 San Francisco earthquake, the authors identified a number of aspects of the disaster situation which put workers at particular risk of developing stress reactions. These included: multiple contacts with trauma victims; long hours and a poor work environment; the threat of further quakes; administrative and policy changes; being away from home; recent exposure to trauma; inexperience of some personnel; and other situation-specific factors. In considering the format for a debriefing procedure, Armstrong et al. also had to take account of the large number of personnel involved and the wide range of job roles undertaken.

MSDM is based on Mitchell's model but also draws upon Raphael's debriefing approach. The model involved four stages: (1) disclosure of events, which may involve several incidents for each person; (2) feelings and reactions; (3) coping strategies; (4) termination, in which relationships are acknowledged and goodbyes said as well as preparing for the transition home and the return to usual roles.

The debriefing procedures described have a number of features in common. The debriefing usually takes place shortly after exposure to a traumatic event. It is a group procedure involving individuals exposed to the same traumatic event. The debriefing includes a sharing of factual information about the event and of emotional responses to it. It also provides an opportunity to learn from others and to reframe existing views of the experience. However, the fact that the procedures described also differ somewhat in their structure, content and goals suggests a lack of agreement about the critical components of an early intervention. It might be that these differences simply reflect differences in the perceived needs of the trauma populations to which they were applied, but rigorous evaluation is needed if firm conclusions are to be drawn.

GROUP PROCESSES IN PSYCHOLOGICAL DEBRIEFING

While the stages and structure of psychological debriefing have been described in detail, little has been written about the possible group processes involved (Dyregrov, 1996). Based on the structure outlined by Mitchell (1983), Dyregrov has adapted the psychological debriefing procedure for use with a wide variety of trauma-exposed groups including survivors of natural and man-made disasters, accidents, hostage and hijack situations, armed robbery, and to mediate organisational crisis and change. Drawing upon the group psychotherapy literature (Rohde & Stockton, 1994; Aveline, 1993), Dyregrov delineates a model which incorporates an understanding of group processes. Active participation by group members, mobilisation of group support, the normalisation of reactions by other group members, and the use of the group as a resource are seen as essential components of the debriefing procedure. Dyregrov suggests that an understanding of these group processes and the factors which influence them is essential if the debriefing is to be sucessful. He nevertheless maintains that debriefing is a crisis intervention, and not group therapy, with the need to complete the work in a single session if possible.

Dyregrov identifies a number of factors which may enhance or impede the debriefing process. In particular, he emphasises the structure of the meeting; leader and co-leader training and interaction; the nature, culture, cohesion and conflict within the group; organisational issues; exposure variables; and the physical setting in which the debriefing takes place. It is beyond the scope of this chapter to review all these factors in detail, but some of the main points will be summarised.

In examining the stages of the debriefing process, Dyregrov focuses particularly on the introduction phase. The way in which the debriefing team introduce themselves, the stated purpose of the meeting and the rules outlined are considered vital in establishing a climate and structure that will enhance the group process. Dyregrov suggests that the introduction should be used to define boundaries, build trust, reduce anxiety and hence increase the likelihood of active participation by group members. The rules then serve as tools for regulating the process later.

The role of the leader is seen as crucial throughout the debriefing process. Dyregrov argues that, in view of the limited time available, the group leader must ensure that the meeting is paced appropriately, that adequate attention is given to all members of the group and that potentially destructive processes are minimised. Ideally, leader activity should reduce over the course of the debriefing as participants become more actively involved, only increasing again at the end. Dyregrov suggests that communication and teaching skills are essential and that an outgoing, directive and active leadership style that is not too authoritarian is needed. The way in which the debriefing team interact is also seen as important in providing a model of interaction for the rest of the group.

Dyregrov identifies a number of group and organisational factors that might affect the debriefing process. He suggests that the culture of the group will often be reflected in the acceptance of debriefing within an organisation. When there is resistance to the use of debriefing, particularly at management level, there is also likely to be resistance at group level. In organisations with a strict hierarchical structure, members may be reluctant to share personal experiences for fear that they will be used negatively in the future by someone present who is senior to them. The type of group to be debriefed might also influence the aims of the debriefing. With regard to natural work groups, a major focus might be to stimulate group cohesion and mutual support that can have a beneficial effect beyond the debriefing meeting. However, with stranger groups, group cohesiveness may be less important compared with the normalisation of experiences.

Dyregrov suggests that pre-existing group cohesion often provides the opportunity to activate previously used group coping mechanisms. Prior conflict, on the other hand, is seen as potentially destructive to the group process and is likely to be managed better if the debriefing team have some prior knowledge of the conflict. Conflict that arises during the debriefing also threatens group cohesion and the group process. Dyregrov argues that the leader needs experience in handling such conflicts, but also needs to use the structure and rules established at the beginning of the meeting in order to manage the situation effectively.

The nature of the group can also vary in terms of gender, occupation and previous experience of trauma. Different groups may respond to the debriefing process differently and have slightly different needs. Dyregrov suggests, for example, that psychosocial support staff may spend more time reflecting on role issues involved in their work, while other groups may find too much self-reflection stressful as they have to face threatening situations on a regular basis.

The nature of the group can also be considered in terms of exposure to the trauma. In general, Dyregrov advocates homogeneous groups that are logical within a given situation. Groups could be defined according to profession, usual working group, stressor exposure or geographical loca-tion. Taking account of sensory exposure is important to allow detailed description without the risk of traumatising others in the group. When this is not possible, individual sessions can be offered to those most severely affected.

Dyregrov's comments on the group processes involved in a debriefing are based on his extensive experience of conducting debriefings and of train-ing debriefers. To this extent they are speculative but they suggest that the debriefing process is more complex than it might at first appear and that more detailed description and operationalisation will be needed if the mechanisms of debriefing are to be understood and evaluated.

EVALUATION OF PSYCHOLOGICAL DEBRIEFING

Despite the widespread use of, and considerable anecdotal support for, psychological debriefing procedures there has been little formal evalua-tion of their effectiveness in reducing psychological distress following trauma.

Robinson and Mitchell (1993) reported a descriptive study of 172 emer-gency service, welfare and hospital personnel who had taken part in 31 debriefings. Participants were asked to complete an evaluation questionnaire two weeks post-debriefing. The majority of respondents rated the debriefings as valuable, and those who experienced stress at the time of the incident attributed a reduction in symptoms, at least in part, to the debriefing. Aspects of the debriefing that were most commonly described as helpful included: talking to others who had shared the same experience; talking about the incident; improved self-understanding; and improved between-agency cohesion. It should be noted, however, that those who responded to the study represent only 60% of the total participants in the 31 debriefings. It is possible that those who viewed the debriefings less positively were also less likely to respond.

Griffiths and Watts (1992) followed up emergency services personnel involved in bus crashes. They found that those who had attended debriefing had significantly higher levels of intrusive and avoidance symptoms, as measured by the Impact of Event Scale (IES) (Horowitz, Wilner & Alvarez, 1979), than those who did not. They also report that there was no relationship between the perceived helpfulness of the debriefing and symptoms. However, those who experienced greatest distress at the time of the crash were likely to have attended more debriefing sessions and to have perceived them as more helpful.

In a study of firefighters involved in the Ash Wednesday bushfires in Australia, MacFarlane (1988) found that those who received debriefing shortly after the incident were less likely to develop acute post-traumatic stress symptoms. However, he also found that those who developed delayed-onset post-traumatic stress reactions were more likely to have attended a debriefing than those who did not.

Kenardy, Webster, Lewin, Carr, Hazell and Carter (1996) reported on the effects of stress debriefing on the rate of recovery of 195 helpers (e.g. emergency service personnel and disaster workers) following an earthquake in Newcastle, Australia. Sixty-two debriefed helpers were compared with 133 who were not debriefed on measures of post-traumatic stress reactions (IES) and general psychological morbidity (General Health Questionnaire, GHQ-12: Goldberg, 1972) on four occasions over the first two years post-earthquake (six months after the earthquake and then at intervals of 6–8 months). Perceived helpfulness of debriefing was also assessed.

No significant differences were found between the two groups on the basis of age, marital status, exposure to threat, exposure to disruption experiences or the proportions helping in threat situations. However, those in the debriefed group had higher educational levels, were more likely to be helping in non-threat situations and were more likely to be counsellors or coordinators of services. Kenardy et al. found that there was a significant reduction in IES scores over time, with the greatest change occurring between assessments 2 and 3. Higher scores on both the IES and the GHQ-12 were found to be associated with greater exposure to threat and disruption. However, a more rapid reduction in GHQ-12 scores was found in the group that were not debriefed. On the basis of their results, Kenardy et al. conclude that there was no evidence of a more rapid recovery rate for those who were debriefed compared to those who were not. The researchers point out that this was a naturalistic study and, therefore, that those who were debriefed may have been in some way self-selected because they were most at risk. They also point out that there was no standardisation of debriefing procedures and, consequently, the quality and appropriateness of the debriefings was unclear. It has been suggested that the Mitchell (1983) model of CISD may not be appropriate following disasters which involve a series of stressors and should be adapted as, for example, in the Multiple Stressor Debriefing Model (Armstrong, O'Callaghan & Marmar, 1991).

Hytten and Hasle (1989) compared debriefed and non-debriefed groups of firefighters involved in a hotel fire in Norway. While most who attended the debriefing reported it as helpful and said that it had increased their self-confidence, there was no significant difference in IES scores between those who had been debriefed and those who had talked informally to colleagues.

A study reported by Deahl, Gillham, Thomas, Searle and Srinivasan (1994) comes closer to the desired model of a controlled trial. It concerned troops serving with the Army War Graves Service during the Gulf War. For operational reasons, some troops (69%) were debriefed on completion of their duties while others were not. The debriefings were conducted in small groups by two welfare professionals using the Dyregrov (1989) model. At nine months, 50% of the study sample had evidence of psychological disturbance suggestive of post-traumatic stress disorder (as indicated by scores on the IES and General Health Questionnaire, GHQ-28: Goldberg & Hillier, 1979). Neither prior training nor the psychological intervention appeared to make any difference to subsequent psychiatric morbidity. Morbidity was more likely in those with a history of psychological problems and in those who believed their lives had been in danger in the Gulf.

Lee, Slade and Lygo (1996) attempted one of the first randomised controlled trials of psychological debriefing in women following early miscarriage. Women were assessed using the Hospital Anxiety and Depression Scale (HADS) (Zigmond & Snaith, 1983) and the IES, at one week and four months post-miscarriage. Half the women received an hour-long session of psychological debriefing, by a female psychologist, in their own homes at approximately two weeks post-miscarriage. The debriefing process was based on the formats described by Dyregrov (1989) and Mitchell (1983). Intrusion and avoidance scores on the IES were initially as high as those of post-trauma victims, but had significantly decreased by four months. Depression was not detected at any time point, but anxiety was significantly higher than community sample estimates at one week and four months.

Psychological debriefing was perceived as helpful, but did not influence emotional adaptation. The authors put forward a number of hypotheses to account for the apparent ineffectiveness of the debriefing intervention. These included: sample sizes that were too small to detect significant differences; the passage of time allowing the emotional adaptation of women who did not receive the intervention to "catch up" with those who were debriefed; the intervention could have been helpful for some, but not all, and may have had an adverse effect on some people, cancelling out any benficial effect; and continued high levels of anxiety may reflect anticipation of future events, for example, future pregnancies (Prettyman, Cordle & Cook, 1993), which were not a focus of the debriefing intervention. In terms of the content of the intervention, some women commented that they would have liked more medical information as well as emotional support. This raises questions about the application of fairly standardised debriefing procedures to specific trauma populations. Outcome scores at one week significantly predicted outcome at four months, suggesting that early assessment would be important in determining which women were most in need of psychological follow-up.

A second randomised controlled trial is reported by Hobbs, Mayou, Harrison and Worlock (1996). Road accident victims admitted to hospital consecutively were allocated randomly to receive a debriefing intervention or to act as controls, who were assessed but not debriefed. Initial screening involved a semi-structured interview and two self-report measures, the IES and the brief symptom inventory, which generates a global emotional distress score. Each person was debriefed within 24–48 hours of the accident and sessions lasted about an hour. The debriefings were said to have involved a review of the traumatic experience, encouragement of emotional expression, and promotion of cognitive processing of the experience. Advice was also given about common emotional reactions, the value of talking about the experience, and early graded return to normal road travel. There were no significant differences between the groups in baseline post-traumatic or other psychiatric symptoms. Both groups were reassessed at four months. Neither group showed a significant reduction in symptoms either on the self-report measures or as assessed clinically by the interviewer. The intervention group had a significantly worse outcome on two subscales of the brief symptom inventory. Hobbs et al. offer a number of explanations for the apparent failure of the intervention. They suggest that the debriefing may have been too early; that it may not have seemed relevant to people expecting an unproblematic recovery; that it may not have been adequate to address major emotional problems; and that early interventions may disturb natural psychological defenses against anxiety and distress. In light of the above, they favour later psychological intervention which targets emerging problems rather than generalised debriefing.

Bisson, Jenkins, Alexander and Bannister (1997) investigated the effectiveness of debriefing in acute burn trauma victims. Consecutive admissions to a Regional Burns Unit were randomly allocated to receive a debriefing intervention or to serve as controls, who received no intervention. Following admission all participants completed the Hospital Anxiety and Depression Scale (HADS) and the IES. These measures were repeated at three and 13 month follow-up together with the Clinician Administered PTSD Scale (Blake, Weathers & Nagy, 1990). The debriefing intervention was based on the Mitchell (1983) model, adapted for use with individuals or couples, and was supplemented with written information. The debriefings were conducted 2–19 days post-trauma, lasted 30–120 minutes and were facilitated by a nurse or psychiatrist trained and supervised by one of the authors. The results indicated that, at 13-month follow-up, those who received the debriefing intervention scored significantly higher compared with the controls on both the anxiety and depression subscales of the HADS and the IES. The prevalence of PTSD was also significantly higher among those who had received the intervention.

There are, however, a number of features of this study which suggest the need for caution in interpreting the results. Although not statistically significant, the intervention group were found to have higher initial questionnaire scores and more severe dimensions of burn trauma than the controls, both of which were associated with a poorer outcome. Indeed, a higher initial IES score was associated more strongly with poorer outcome as measured by the IES at 13 months than were debriefing status or percentage burn. In addition, although the sample size of the study is greater than in many PTSD and burn trauma studies, the rates of PTSD are low, which affects the level of power of the results (in this case below 60%). Nevertheless, the possibility that debriefing can be harmful clearly needs to be considered. It is interesting to note that Bisson et al. found that the closer the temporal relationship of the debriefing to the burn, the worse the outcome. They suggest that individuals may not be ready to consider psychological sequelae within a few days of burn trauma. Such findings point to the need to consider debriefing procedures in more detail and to investigate systematically the various components of these procedures in order to identify aspects which might be of benefit as well as potential risk factors. Finally, as the authors point out, the results of a trial using a debriefing procedure with individuals or couples may not be directly comparable with results of trials of group debriefing or with debriefing following other kinds of trauma. We should, therefore, be cautious about drawing general conclusions about the status of psychological debriefing from single studies of this kind.

A somewhat different approach to psychological debriefing is described by Chemtob, Thomas, Law and Cremniter (1997). Two groups of disaster workers were debriefed at separate times following Hurricane Iniki which struck the Hawaiian Island of Kauai in 1992. All the participants were Kauai residents who themselves had been exposed to the hurricane. The first group was debriefed six months after the hurricane. Prior to debriefing they were asked to complete the IES and this measure was repeated 90 days later. The second group was debriefed in the same week that the first group was retested. They also completed the IES prior to the debriefing and the measure was repeated a further 90 days later. There was no significant difference between the two groups with respect to pre-intervention IES scores. The goals of the intervention are reported to have been normalisation, education and psychological support. Participants were encouraged to describe their experience, touching on its cognitive, affective and behavioural components. Following approximately three hours of group work, a two-hour lecture on post-disaster recovery was provided. The facilitator in charge of the psychological debriefing also gave the lecture.

At follow-up, both groups showed a significant reduction in reported levels of distress, as indicated by a decrease in IES scores. The authors argue that the replication of this finding across both groups suggests that the reduction in distress can, at least in part, be attributed to the intervention. They acknowledge the limitations of the study and accept that the intervention used diverged somewhat from others that have been reported. In particular, they stress the timing of the intervention, which at six and nine months is considerably later than is usually recommended but may be of greater benefit. In conclusion, they argue that studies of this kind should encourage attempts at randomised controlled trials of debriefing in post-disaster contexts.

There have been even fewer studies evaluating debriefing with children. Yule and Udwin (1991) describe their use of CISD with girls from one school who survived the sinking of the *Jupiter*. Self-report data five months after the incident indicate that, compared with a group from another school who had not received debriefing, the debriefed group showed much lower scores on a version of the Fear Survey Schedule for Children (Ollendick, Yule & Ollier, 1991) and on the Impact of Event Scale. There were no significant differences between the groups on measures of anxiety and depression (Yule, 1992). It is important to note, however, that some of the girls who were debriefed went on to receive group treatment and thus it is not possible to isolate the effects of debriefing from subsequent therapy.

Stallard and Law (1993) show more convincing evidence that debriefing greatly reduced the distress of girls who survived a school minibus crash. They used the same battery of self-report measures as used by Yule and Udwin (1991) before, and three months after, two sessions of debriefing. At follow-up, significant reductions were found on all measures. Given the stability of scores prior to the intervention, the authors argue that the improvement was related to the intervention.

OTHER FORMS OF CRISIS INTERVENTION

Models of crisis intervention other than psychological debriefing have been found to be effective in studies of bereavement (Raphael, 1977; Parkes, 1980) and other crises (Viney, Clark, Bunn & Benjamin, 1985). These models typically involve a fixed number of focused counselling sessions offered in the first weeks or months after the event. However, these studies did not assess post-traumatic symptomatology, nor were the interventions designed with the intention of preventing it.

Brom, Kleber and Hofman (1993) investigated both post-traumatic symptomatology and the impact of a brief (3–6 sessions) therapeutic intervention in victims of moderately serious to serious road accidents. Participants were assessed at one month and six months post-accident using a Dutch version of the IES. In both groups, intrusion and avoidance subscale scores decreased significantly. However, while more than 90% of people in the intervention group indicated that they were satisfied with the intervention, the group was more symptomatic to begin with and the intervention could not be shown to be more effective than the passage of time.

CONCLUSIONS AND DIRECTIONS FOR FUTURE RESEARCH

At present, the evidence that psychological debriefing has a substantial effect in reducing morbidity following trauma is sadly limited. Indeed a number of studies (e.g. Hobbs et al., 1996; Bisson et al., 1997) raise the possibility that, in some circumstances at least, early interventions of this kind may result in poorer outcomes. Despite this, many who participate report debriefing as helpful and many professionals are committed to extending the availability of debriefing. While existing studies do little to support this movement they are, to date, inadequate to reject the notion of debriefing altogether. In view of the resources and training being devoted to debriefing there is clearly a need for more systematic evaluation of the procedure, particularly in the form of randomised controlled trials.

Before embarking on such trials, however, there is a need to consider further what is meant by psychological debriefing and whether standardised procedures (e.g. Mitchell, 1983) can be meaningfully applied across a range of trauma situations. One might reasonably expect that the needs of victims of a large-scale disaster are different from workers involved in rescue operations. Similarly, the needs of those involved in single traumatic events such as road traffic accidents or assaults are likely to be different to those involved in prolonged traumatic situations such as natural disasters or ongoing trauma such as warfare.

These perceived differences in need are reflected in the range of debriefing procedures described in the literature. Indeed, the authors themselves often highlight the limitations of debriefing and stress the need for flexibility in the application of such techniques. Mitchell (1983), for example, argues that CISD should be part of an ongoing and comprehensive stress management package, and Dyregrov (1996) emphasises the complexities of the group debriefing process and the need to take account of the particular circumstances surrounding a given traumatic event. These words of caution do not, however, seem to be reflected in the current evaluation literature.

There are clearly a number of possible explanations for this. Traumatic events and, in particular, large-scale disasters generate a sense of urgency to act which may override more considered evaluation of the situation. Protocols for the evaluation of preventive interventions are unlikely to be in place, resources are unpredictable and there are ethical concerns about withholding assistance that might be of benefit. Large populations of traumatised individuals who might be the subject of systematic investigation are not available on demand. As a result, researchers have turned to those who are victims of individual trauma such as burns victims or victims of road traffic accidents. While it is clearly important to evaluate the role of debriefing interventions in these populations, the result has been that the existing randomised controlled trials (Hobbs et al., 1996; Bisson et al., 1997) have used individual rather than group debriefing procedures. At present, it is far from clear whether or not these procedures can be considered to be equivalent.

It is interesting to note that studies which lend greatest support to debriefing interventions (Chemtob et al., 1997; Stallard and Law, 1993) use debriefing procedures that are longer and that are offered many months after the traumatic event. The suggestion that debriefing may make some people worse may, in part, be due to the use of procedures that are too short, resulting in exacerbation of symptoms rather than habituation. Equally, if interventions are offered too soon after a traumatic event, those involved may not be "ready" psychologically to make use of such interventions.

In view of the above, psychological debriefing should be used with caution. Adequate training in the use of such techniques is essential and needs to be updated as knowledge increases. The lack of empirical support for the procedure suggests that scarce resources should only be targeted at those at greatest risk. The possible mechanisms by which debriefing may effect change have yet to be elucidated and may be important in informing future practice (Shalev, 1994; Busuttil & Busuttil, 1997).

REFERENCES

Armstrong, K., O'Callahan, W. & Marmar, C.R. (1991). Debriefing Red Cross disaster personnel: The multiple stressor debriefing model. *Journal of Traumatic Stress*, **4**, 581–593.

Aveline, M.O. (1993). Principles of leadership in brief training groups for mental health care professionals. *Group International Journal of Psychotherapy*, **43**, 107–129.

Busuttil, W. & Busuttil, A. (1997). Debriefing and crisis intervention. In D. Black, M. Newman, J. Harris-Hendricks & G. Mezey (Eds.), *Psychological Trauma: A Developmental Approach*. London: Royal College of Psychiatrists.

Bisson, J.I., Jenkins, P., Alexander, J. & Bannister, C. (1997). Randomised controlled trial of psychological debriefing for victims of acute burn trauma. *British Journal of Psychiatry*, **171**, 78–81.

Blake, D.D., Weathers, F.W. & Nagy, L.N. (1990). A clinician administered rating scale for assessing current and lifetime PTSD: the CAPS-1. *Behaviour Therapist*, **18**, 187–188.

Brom, D., Kleber, R.J. & Hofman, M.C. (1993). Victims of traffic accidents: Incidence and prevention of post-traumatic stress disorder. *Journal of Clinical Psychology*, **49** (2), 131–140.

Chemtob, C.M., Tomas, S. Law, W. & Cremniter, D. (1997). Postdisaster psychosocial intervention: A field study of the impact of debriefing on psychological distress. *American Journal of Psychiatry*, **154** (3), 415–417.

Deahl, M.P., Gillham, A.B., Thomas, J., Searle, M.M. & Srinivasan, M. (1994). Psychological sequelae following the Gulf War: Factors associated with subsequent morbidity and the effectiveness of psychological debriefing. *British Journal of Psychiatry*, **165**, 60–65.

Dyregrov, A. (1989). Caring for helpers in disaster situations: psychological debriefing. *Disaster Management*, **2**, 25–30.

Dyregrov, A. (1991). *Grief in Children: A Handbook for Adults*. London: Jessica Kingsley.

Dyregrov, A. (1996). The process in critical incident stress debriefings. Paper presented at the European Conference on Traumatic Stress in Emergency Services, Peacekeeping Operations and Humanitarian Aid Organisations. University of Sheffield, England, 17–20 March 1996.

Goldberg, D.P. (1972). *The Detection of Psychiatric Illness by Questionnaire*. London: Oxford University Press.

Goldberg, D.P. & Hillier, V.F. (1979). A scaled version of the GHQ. *Psychological Medicine*, **9**, 139–145.

Green, B.L., Lindy, J.D., Grace, G.C., Leonard, A.C., Korol, M. & Winget, C. (1990). Buffalo Creek survivors in the second decade: Stability of stress symptoms. *American Journal of Orthopsychiatry*, **1**, 43–45.

Griffiths, J. & Watts, R. (1992). *The Kempsey and Grafton Bus Crashes: The Aftermath*. East Lismore, Australia: Instructional Design Solutions.

Hobbs, M., Mayou, R., Harrison, B. & Worlock, P. (1996). A randomised controlled trial of psychological debriefing for victims of road traffic accidents. *British Medical Journal*, **313**, 1438–1439.

Horowitz, M.J., Wilner, N. & Alvarez, W. (1979). Impact of event scale: A measure of subjective distress. *Psychosomatic Medicine*, **41**, 209–218.

Hytten, K. & Hasle, A. (1989). Fire fighters: A study of stress and coping. *Acta Psychiatrica Scandinavica*, **80** (Suppl. 355), 50–55.

Kenardy, J.A., Webster, R.A., Lewin, T.J., Carr, V.J., Hazell, P.L. & Carter, G.L. (1996). Stress debriefing and patterns of recovery following a natural disaster. *Journal of Traumatic Stress*, **9** (1), 37–49.

Kessler, R.C., Sonnega, A., Bromet, E., Hughes, M. & Nelson, C.B. (1995). Posttraumatic stress disorder in the national comorbidity survey. *Archives of General Psychiatry*, **52**, 1048–1060.

Kulka, R.A., Schlenger, W.E., Fairbank, J.A., Hough, R.L., Jordan, B.K., Marmar, C.R. & Weiss, D.S. (1990). *Trauma and the Vietnam War generation*. New York: Brunner/Mazel.

Lee, C., Slade, P. & Lygo, V. (1996). The influence of psychological debriefing on emotional adaptation in women following early miscarriage: A preliminary study. *British Journal of Medical Psychology*, **69**, 47–58.

McFarlane, A.C. (1988). The longitudinal course of posttraumatic morbidity: The range of outcomes and their predictors. *Journal of Nervous and Mental Disease*, **176**, 30–39.

Mayou, R., Bryant, B. & Duthie, R. (1993). Psychiatric consequences of road traffic accidents. *British Medical Journal*, **307**, 647–651.

Mitchell, J. (1983). When disaster strikes . . . The critical incident stress debriefing process. *Journal of the Emergency Medical Services*, **8**, 36–39.

Marshall, S.L.A. (1944). *Island Victory*. New York: Penguin Books.

Ollendick, T.H., Yule, W. & Ollier, K. (1991). Fears in British children and their relation to manifest anxiety and depression. *Journal of Child Psychology and Psychiatry*, **32**, 321–331.

Parkes, C.M. (1980). Bereavement counselling: Does it work? *British Medical Journal*, **281**, 3–6.

Prettyman, R.J., Cordle, C.J. & Cook, G.D. (1993). A three month follow-up of psychological morbidity after early miscarriage. *British Journal of Medical Psychology*, **66**, 363–372.

Raphael, B. (1977). Preventive intervention with the recently bereaved. *Archives of General Psychiatry*, **34** (12), 1450–1454.

Raphael, B. (1986). *When Disaster Strikes*. New York: Basic Books.

Raphael, B., Meldrum, L. & McFarlane, A.C. (1995). Does debriefing after psychological trauma work? *British Medical Journal*, **310**, 1479–1480.

Robinson, R.C. & Mitchell, J.T. (1993). Evaluation of psychological debriefings. *Journal of Traumatic Stress*, **6** (3), 367–382.

Rohde, R. & Stockton, R. (1994). Group structure: A review. *Journal of Group Psychotherapy, Psychodrama and Sociometry*, **46**, 151–158.

Salmon, T. (1919). The war neurosis and their lesson. *New York State Journal of Medicine*, **59**, 933–944.

Shalev, A.I. (1994). Debriefing following traumatic exposure. In R.J. Ursano, B.G. McCaughey & C.S. Fullerton (Eds.), *Individual and Community Responses to Trauma and Disaster*. Cambridge: Cambridge University Press.

Stallard, P. & Law, F. (1993). Screening and psychological debriefing of adolescent survivors of life-threatening events. *British Journal of Psychiatry*, **163**, 660–665.

Taylor, A. (1989). Victims of crime as victims of disaster. *Australian and New Zealand Journal of Psychiatry*, **23**, 403–406.

Viney, L.L., Clark, A.M., Bunn, T.A. & Benjamin, Y.N. (1985). Crisis intervention counselling: An evaluation of long and short term effects. *Journal of Counselling Psychology*, **32** (1), 29–39.

Yule, W. (1992). Post traumatic stress disorder in child survivors of shipping disasters: The sinking of the "Jupiter". *Psychotherapy and Psychosomatics*, **57**, 200–205.

Yule, W. & Udwin, O. (1991). Screening child survivors for post traumatic stress disorders: Experiences from the "Jupiter" sinking. *British Journal of Clinical Psychology*, **30**, 131–138.

Zigmond, A.S. & Snaith, R.P. (1983). The hospital anxiety and depression scale. *Acta Psychiatrica Scandinavia*, **67**, 361–370.

Chapter 12

BEHAVIOURAL AND COGNITIVE BEHAVIOURAL INTERVENTIONS IN THE TREATMENT OF PTSD

David Richards* and Karina Lovell†

BEHAVIOURAL AND COGNITIVE-BEHAVIOURAL THERAPIES

During the last 40 years there has been a revolution in our understanding and treatment of emotional disorders. Most anxiety disorders now respond very well to psychological treatments based on cognitive and behavioural principles. Affect is seen as a combination of three linked systems—autonomic, behavioural and cognitive (Lang, 1979). Behavioural and cognitive-behavioural treatments attempt to modify the responsivity of these systems.

Initially treatments were developed which were closely modelled on learning theory, in particular Wolpe's *systematic desensitisation* (Wolpe, 1958). This procedure, drawn from work on classical conditioning, pairs fear stimuli with a competing non-fearful stimuli—usually relaxation—leading to a reduction in the fearful response. However, while this is certainly effective, it is a long and complex treatment. We now know that fear will reduce without the presence of a competing stimuli. Instead, *exposure* to a feared situation or object will lead eventually to a reduction in fear, a process termed *habituation*.

Exposure, the therapeutic confrontation with a feared stimulus, is now the treatment of choice for many anxiety disorders such as phobias and obsessive-compulsive disorder (Marks, 1987). More recently, cognitive

*Leeds Community Mental Health Services NHS Trust, Leeds and †University of Manchester, Manchester

Post-Traumatic Stress Disorders: Concepts and Therapy. Edited by William Yule.
© 1999 John Wiley & Sons Ltd.

therapy has been developed where cognitive aspects of the arousal mechanism are the target for treatment (Beck, Rush, Shaw & Emery, 1979). Cognitive therapy has been particularly useful in the treatment of depression, panic and eating disorders and is being widely applied to many other areas.

The translation of behavioural and cognitive techniques into workable therapies has been based on the following key ethical principles (Hackman, 1993, p. 8):

1. The empirical validation of treatment.
2. A treatment focus on the "here and now".
3. The use of explicit, agreed and operationally defined treatment strategies.
4. The specification of treatment goals (usually chosen by the client) to bring about desired changes in the client's life.
5. The use of collaborative therapeutic strategies between client and therapist.

TREATMENT OF PTSD

Three principal treatment approaches have been outlined in the behavioural and cognitive treatment literature for PTSD. These are: (1) exposure (live and imaginal), which aims to evoke anxiety and promote habituation; (2) cognitive restructuring, which aims to modify dysfunctional thoughts, beliefs and assumptions; (3) anxiety management techniques, including stress inoculation training (SIT), which aim to teach the individual a variety of coping skills in order to manage anxiety and other symptoms.

In this chapter we have taken the emotional-processing model (Foa, Steketee & Rothbaum, 1989) as the basis for our understanding of PTSD and as the rationale for treatment. This builds on simpler stimulus–response models, e.g. Mowrer's (1960) two-stage theory of fear acquisition and maintenance. This model, which combines initial classical learning to explain the genesis of fear together with instrumental learning maintaining it, is ideally suited to explain much PTSD phenomena. A sudden traumatic event which leads to individuals purposefully avoiding any situation or object which reminds them of the event results in a memory which is "unprocessed".

Avoidance may be behavioural or cognitive (just not thinking about the traumatic event). However, such avoidance, whether cognitive or behavioural, is rarely 100% successful. Environmental reminders cause intrusive cognitions, images and associated physiological arousal, resulting in a continuous vicious circle of intrusion and avoidance.

The emotional-processing model postulates that the reason traumatised individuals avoid thinking about a traumatic event is because of the meaning the trauma has for them. Specific attributions impede cognitive processing and may underly psychological states of guilt, shame, anger and depression (see Joseph, this volume).

Certainly, the now undoubted efficacy of exposure and cognitive restructuring can be understood from an emotional-processing point of view. If avoidance is the key to maintaining problems, exposure is clearly most likely to be effective. However, cognitive factors (the meaning of the event in particular) are so central to PTSD that any treatment must address these too.

Anxiety management, by contrast however, is a symptom management package assisting individuals to cope with their current distress. A consensus is beginning to emerge that anxiety management techniques are best seen as adjunctive techniques which should be used to aid emotional processing of traumatic memories by prolonged exposure or cognitive restructuring techniques (Keane, 1995). We will use examples of anxiety management to illustrate this point later.

Exposure

Exposure is a highly effective treatment for many anxiety disorders where avoidance is a key maintaining factor (Marks, 1987). Along with other disorders, phobias, panic and obsessive-compulsive disorder all respond very well to an exposure treatment approach. Exposure is usually to real-life feared stimuli and is prolonged, repeated and undertaken by the client as self-help "homework" (Al-Kubaisy Marks, Logsdale, Marks, Lovell, Sungar & Araya, 1992).

Variants of exposure have been used to treat PTSD and include systematic desensitisation (Muse, 1986), flooding (Keane, Fairbank, Caddell & Zimmering, 1989), image habituation training (Vaughan & Tarrier, 1992) and prolonged exposure (Foa, Rothbaum, Riggs & Murdock, 1991). Currently, the preferred international term is prolonged exposure.

Prolonged exposure involves the planned therapeutic confrontation to a feared situation, object or memory so that arousal is increased but manageable. Exposure is prolonged and repeated until the arousal levels reduce to acceptable levels, at least 50% below the peak level—a process called habituation.

Unlike phobias and other anxiety disorders, where the feared stimuli are present in the real world, people with PTSD are scared to think about their past traumatic experiences. Although, real-life exposure to phobic stimuli is the preferred option for other anxiety disorders, this poses problems for PTSD sufferers. We would not, for example, normally wish to expose them to repeated traumatic experiences.

Most PTSD treatments, therefore, use imaginal exposure to assist the client to confront his or her disturbing memory. This requires the client to relive the trauma by bringing up imaginal scenes. The most usual approach is to instruct the client to replay the whole event in his or her imagination and recount it out loud to the therapist. This should be done in the

- *first person* and the
- *present tense* with the therapist checking that the client uses a rich variety of
- *stimuli,*
- *response* and
- *meaning* elements in his or her account.

Treatment sessions normally last $1^1/_2$ hours, of which at least one hour should be exposure. The therapist should monitor the clients' account and, after each run through, feedback to the clients, prompting them to use more and more detail. Because the events being recalled may be quite short lived it may be necessary to run through the account many times in a session.

It is usual to ask clients to repeat the session daily as *homework*. This maximises the therapeutic input by the therapist. A useful way of assisting clients in their homework practice is to audiotape the session and ask the clients to take the tape home, using it to structure their homework. Importantly, therapists and clients should ensure that the tape is there as an aid to imaginal recreations of the event. Care must be taken that clients do not merely listen to the tape in a superficial way, thereby dissociating from or cognitively avoiding the exposure itself.

After 1–3 session of imaginal exposure most clients can identify specific "hot-spots" in their traumatic memory which cause them most distress. In fact, by this stage most of the account may be causing them little distress at all. A technique called *rewind and hold* is useful here. The therapist and client select a "hot-spot", bring up the image and try to concentrate on it without letting the memory roll on. The images are frozen and described by the client in ever-increasing detail, prompted by the therapist.

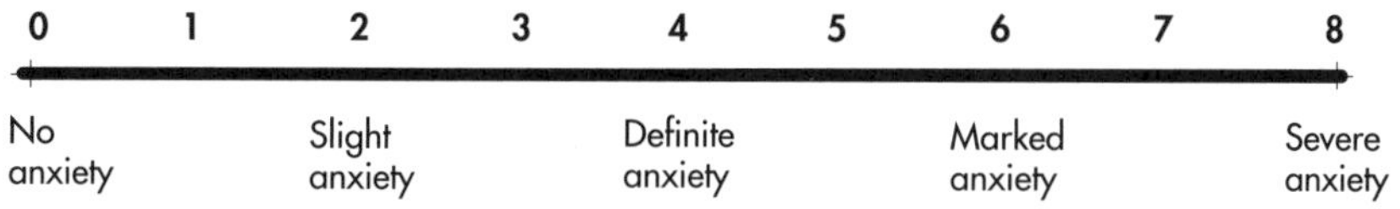

0	1	2	3	4	5	6	7	8
No anxiety		Slight anxiety		Definite anxiety		Marked anxiety		Severe anxiety

Figure 12.1 Simple anxiety self-rating scale

In order to monitor arousal and subsequent habituation during exposure, clients and therapist agree a simple anxiety rating scale (0–8 is usual, see Figure 12.1) where the more anxiety-provoking the image, the higher the rating. After each run through of the image, or each rewind and hold, the clients rate their anxiety using this scale. They also do this during exposure homework exercises. By examining these records of within session exercises and homework, therapist and clients can work together to decide the pacing and development of the treatment programme.

Although imaginal exposure is the most commonly reported mechanism for delivering exposure, other techniques may be equally useful. If one remembers that the purpose of exposure is to effect the therapeutic confrontation with the feared stimuli so that emotional processing can occur, it is clear that writing about one's experiences may have the same effect, provided the client fully engages in the task. Often writing is used as a way of grading exposure, although on occasions it may be sufficient in its own right, as seen later in case example 1.

Despite our cautious comments earlier, real-life exposure to relevant stimuli can be a part of treatment. Many PTSD clients avoid environmental triggers for their intrusions. Such triggers can be used in therapy to elicit memories and allow them to be processed—for example, touching and looking at a mask or balaclava may be a useful technique with a robbery victim. Real-life cues are particularly useful where a client has difficulty with imaginal exposure.

Real-life exposure should also be used where the client has developed secondary avoidances which are persisting despite the resolution of the intrusive symptoms. The presentation of these symptoms is often more akin to agoraphobia than traumatic avoidances in that they are maintained by the classic "fear of fear" rather than fear of intrusions. Clients may develop avoidances for fear that some catastrophe will befall them (for example, having a panic attack, fainting, looking very foolish, being unable to escape or get help). However, the same therapeutic principles of grading, prolonging and repeating exposure, with homework and self-monitoring apply.

Cognitive Therapy

The rapid growth of cognitive therapy with a range of mental health difficulties has been termed a "cognitive revolution" (Beck, 1991). While the term "cognitive therapy" has been applied to a number of different approaches (e.g. rational emotive therapy—Ellis, 1962), it is the cognitive therapy described by Beck (1976) which is most widely described and practised. Beck (1993, p. 194) defines cognitive therapy as "... the application of the cognitive model of a particular disorder with the use of a variety of techniques designed to modify the dysfunctional beliefs and faulty information processing characteristics of each disorder".

Thus, cognitive therapy aims to educate clients: to identify and monitor negative thoughts, beliefs and assumptions; to identify the logical errors contained in these beliefs; and to find more realistic and helpful alternatives to their current ways of thinking. Cognitive therapy is a time-limited, structured, directive, collaborative and problem-orientated intervention. It draws upon socratic questioning techniques and guided self-discovery, enabling the clients to view their negative thoughts, beliefs and assumptions as hypotheses to be validated in a scientific and systematic way.

Cognitive conceptualisations of post-traumatic stress disorder (Chemtob, Hamada, Roitblat & Muraoka, 1988; Krietler & Krietler, 1988; Janoff-Bulman, 1992; McCann, Sakheim & Abrahamson, 1988) emphasise the importance of the role of cognitive processes which may account for part or all of the psychopathology of abnormal post-trauma reactions. Thus it is posited that interventions are required which are directed towards identifying inappropriate thoughts and beliefs and helping clients reappraise these in order to develop a more helpful view of the traumatic event, themselves and the world.

Although the process of cognitive therapy is well documented in the literature with regard to a range of disorders, e.g. depression (Beck et al., 1979), panic disorder and generalised anxiety (Hawton, Salkovskis, Kirk & Clark, 1989; Freeman, Pretezer, Fleming & Simon, 1990), it is only recently that cognitive techniques have been used with post-traumatic stress disorder (Parrot & Howes, 1991; Resick & Schnicke, 1993; Carroll & Foy, 1992; Thrasher, Lovell, Noshirvani & Livanou, 1996). Although different authors emphasise a variety of specific techniques, they all agree that treatment should be aimed at modifying dysfunctional cognitions via cognitive interventions. We will examine some of these techniques in more detail in the case examples later.

Anxiety Management

Symptom management packages to control anxiety have been used successfully with PTSD, most noticeably with rape survivors (Veronen & Kilpatrick, 1983; Foa et al., 1991). Other groups have had less success with these techniques. Keane et al. (1989), for example, tried to use anxiety management with a Vietnam veteran group as part of their controlled trial. The researchers were unable to report the results of the anxiety management treatment group because the approach was so ineffective and was tolerated so poorly by the veterans that almost all dropped out of treatment.

As stated earlier, anxiety management, often described as Stress Inoculation Training (SIT: Foa et al., 1991), is a package of measures that allow a client to control his or her anxiety. Typically, techniques such as progressive relaxation, thought stopping, breathing retraining and problem solving are taught to clients using education and role play.

Since exposure and cognitive therapy usually evoke affect for therapeutic reasons (i.e. to allow habituation of anxiety or cognitive reappraisal to take place), therapists should not normally wish to interfere with a client's initial affective arousal. Sometimes, however, the degree of affective response is too great for the client to tolerate. When techniques such as grading the stimuli are not able to moderate this affective arousal, it is appropriate to introduce anxiety management techniques such as breathing retraining and panic management.

When using anxiety management within an exposure treatment programme the aim is to provide the clients with sufficient control to remain exposed to the anxiety-provoking stimuli until they experience some habituation. Anxiety management should be used for this purpose only, not because therapists are unable to tolerate high expressed emotion in their clients. There is a danger that some therapists may feel uncomfortable with actually causing affective arousal in clients, albeit for therapeutic reasons. This may lead to a temptation to prevent the expression of high levels of emotion. However, just like clients, therapists must learn to tolerate short-term distress and high arousal levels during exposure sessions in particular, so that habituation is allowed to progress naturally.

EVIDENCE FOR THE EFFICACY OF COGNITIVE BEHAVIOURAL THERAPY

The efficacy of behavioural and cognitive-behavioural interventions in the treatment of PTSD has been demonstrated in the literature. A large range of single case studies have demonstrated the effectiveness of these techniques, particularly exposure and its variants across a wide range of traumas, including war veterans (Keane & Kaloupek, 1982; McCormack, 1985; Weathers & Keane, 1994), assault survivors (Richards, 1989), road traffic accidents (McCaffery & Fairbank, 1985), rape survivors (Wolff, 1977), physical assault (Thrasher et al., 1996), and rape and sexual assault survivors (Lovell, 1992; Kilpatrick & Amick, 1985; Pearson, Poquette & Wasden, 1983).

In the last decade a number of clinical studies using behavioural and cognitive interventions have been reported. These studies have increased in sophistication from uncontrolled studies, through comparisons with waiting list control groups to comparisons with other psychological interventions. Keane et al. (1989) provided one of the first controlled studies of an exposure technique with PTSD. This study was a comparison of implosive therapy (a variant of imaginal exposure) with a waiting list control group in 24 Vietnam veterans meeting DSM-III criteria for PTSD. Using a range of valid and reliable measures, implosive therapy was found to be significantly superior to the control group on some PTSD measures, depression and anxiety, but not on social adjustment. No further change occurred during the six-month follow-up period.

Brom, Kleber and Defares (1989) randomised 112 clients meeting DSM-III criteria for PTSD to either "trauma desensitisation" (a rather weak form of prolonged exposure), hypnotherapy, psychodynamic psychotherapy or a waiting list control group. All three active treatment groups improved significantly when compared with the control group, though few significant differences were noted between the three treatment groups. Richards, Lovell and Marks (1994), compared the relative merits of live and imaginal exposure with 14 subjects who had experienced a range of traumas. Good results were achieved with a 60–80% improvement across a range of symptom-specific and social adjustment measures, and these improvements were maintained at one year follow-up.

Resick and Schnicke (1992) treated sexual assault survivors in small groups and compared them with a waiting list control. They used Cognitive Processing Therapy (CPT)—a combination of a variant of exposure therapy and cognitive restructuring—and found CPT to be superior to the waiting list control.

Foa et al. (1991) conducted one of the most sophisticated controlled studies to date. The authors compared prolonged imaginal exposure, stress inoculation training (SIT), supportive counselling and a waiting list control with 45 rape survivors meeting PTSD criteria. Their results found that prolonged exposure and SIT were significantly superior to supportive counselling and the control group on PTSD symptoms, but not on depression and anxiety. Of particular note is that SIT was significantly superior to exposure at post-treatment, though at 3.5-month follow-up the situation was reversed and there was a trend that those who had prolonged exposure did better than SIT.

In a recent randomised controlled trial (Marks, Lovell, Noshirvani, Livanou & Thrasher, 1996) 87 clients meeting DSM-III-R criteria for PTSD following mixed trauma were randomised to one of four treatment groups: either exposure alone, cognitive restructuring alone, both exposure and cognitive restructuring, or relaxation (placebo control). Patients had 10 weekly sessions of treatment. Independent assessors blind to the clients' treatment condition assessed them at pre- and post-treatment and at one-, three- and six-month follow-up using a range of valid and reliable outcome measures.

Results of the study found that all four treatment groups improved significantly. However, exposure alone, cognitive restructuring alone and the combined exposure and cognitive group were superior to relaxation at post-treatment and follow-up. No significant differences were found between the three active treatment groups at post-treatment or at one-month follow-up. At three- and six-month follow-up, exposure was slightly superior to cognitive restructuring, but those follow-up data were confounded by the patients who did not remain in follow-up in the exposure only and combined exposure and cognitive groups having been significantly more severe than those remaining in follow-up (this was not true for those in cognitive restructuring alone). End scores of those not remaining in follow-up were imputed forward. Analysis of those imputed scores found that the slight superiority of exposure over cognitive restructuring was not significant.

Of further interest was that the combined exposure and cognitive restructuring was not significantly superior to either treatment alone, and exposure alone and cognitive restructuring alone did equally well on re-experiencing symptoms and negative emotions such as guilt and anger. Cognitive restructuring, alone and combined with exposure, was superior to exposure alone on the symptom of detachment.

In summarising the evidence for the efficacy of cognitive-behavioural interventions with PTSD, it is clear that exposure-based therapies are effective for many symptoms of PTSD. There is increasing evidence that cognitive interventions alone are useful for PTSD (Marks et al., 1998; Thrasher et al., 1996). There is some evidence that there is no advantage in using a combination of exposure and cognitive interventions (Marks et al., 1998).

THE PROCESS OF THERAPY

The Rationale and Treatment

The first step in therapy is to assist clients understand that while avoiding dealing with emotional reactions can be initially helpful, long-term difficulties invariably result. A useful way of explaining the rationale for exposure or cognitive therapy is to use the analogy of a factory (Figure 12.2).

Representing the mind as a factory, we can use the diagram to show how raw material (sensory experience) is processed along the conveyor belt to be accommodated and stored. However, when traumatic information is received, this may be so difficult to comprehend that the client avoids thinking about the traumatic event, the conveyor belt stops and processing is halted.

The vicious circle of avoidance and intrusion can be shown by the information being returned to the beginning of the conveyor belt using personal examples of triggers and reminders which can be drawn from the assessment of the client's history.

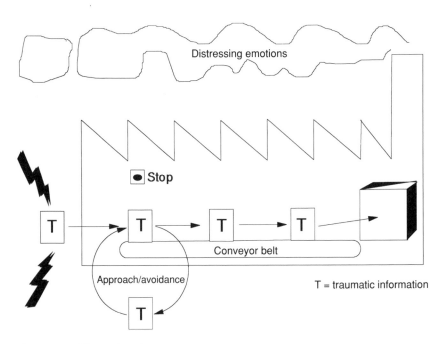

Figure 12.2 The rationale

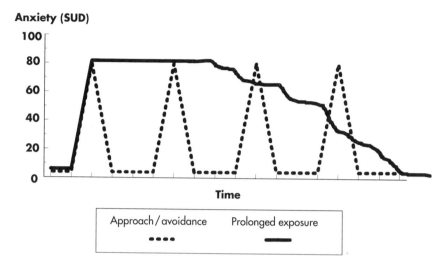

Figure 12.3 Approach/avoidance versus prolonged exposure

The factory can be used to explain the alternatives available. Exposure may create more short-term distress (pollution from the chimney) but lead to improved processing; cognitive therapy represents repairing the machinery of the factory; the status quo is to continue in the intrusion/avoidance cycle.

Finally, if exposure is suggested, it is very useful to draw a graph of the anxiety produced by the approach/avoidance strategy (expressed as subjective units of distress—SUDS) with the alternative habituation curve superimposed to explain the decline in anxiety over time produced by prolonged exposure (Figure 12.3).

Case Example 1: Use of Simple Exposure Techniques

Jane was a 21-year-old bank clerk who had been involved in an armed robbery 18 months previously. Initially distressed by the experience she received two telephone counselling sessions in the first two weeks after the raid. However, within a few weeks she had recovered her spirits with no apparent adverse effects on her health.

One year after the raid she moved to another company doing similar banking work in order to better her prospects. She experienced no problems in her post, serving customers in a branch. However, six months into this job a nearby branch was raided at about the same time as she was watching a series of training videos on robbery procedures. These two events caused her to become anxious and tearful. She experienced intrusive images of her own raid experience, triggered by groups of men, scruffily dressed people, sudden movements and TV violence. She distracted herself from these images by thinking of pleasant things such as ice-cream. She was also beginning to avoid going out alone and walking in areas where she previously felt safe. She was frightened when working at the counter of the branch where she now worked and her concentration was poor.

She was physically anxious when reminded of the raid and had an increased startle response. She met DSM-III-R criteria for PTSD with an Impact of Event Scale (IES) score of 38 and a GHQ-28 score of 6, levels which indicate considerable distress and both lying within the clinically significant range. There was no previous psychiatric or medical history. She referred herself to the company's stress-counselling service because she was disturbed that her old memories had resurfaced in such a dramatic way. She wanted (i) to feel comfortable with her memories; (ii) to get back in charge of her own feelings; and (iii) to feel calm doing her job and walking down the street.

Following the rationale, Jane agreed to an exposure programme starting with writing about her experiences in the raid. She wrote down an account of the raid in the first person present tense as homework and then spent an hour a day reading this account through. Every second day she rewrote the account, each time getting more detail. She recorded her anxiety levels using a 0–8 scale (Figure 12.1). One week later her anxiety had dropped from 8 to 4 after some six hours of exposure homework.

Ten days later, after another six hours of exposure to her written accounts of the raid, she was experiencing anxiety levels of 2. Importantly, her hypervigilance had reduced, she was much less afraid of walking alone and entering her new flat, and less sensitive to groups of men and other intrusive image triggers. When she imagined the raid, she no longer became distressed and did not feel it necessary to distract herself. After this session she agreed to continue the writing exercise until she felt completely comfortable and to return to the training videos which had prompted some of her problems.

At the fourth treatment session she reported watching the videos for a total of two hours during which her anxiety quickly reduced to 0. She also watched a violent TV film without distress, intrusions or avoidance. She did not feel the need to do any more writing, feeling completely comfortable with her memories and her work in the branch. Her IES score was 6 and her GHQ-28 was 0—both scores that were well below clinical significance. There was no need for further treatment, exposure or cognitive therapy. No problems have been reported in follow-up.

Case Example 2: Imaginal Exposure

Ryan was only 14 when he was involved in a disaster at sea as the passenger ship he was travelling on was holed by another vessel and sank. When he presented for help two years later he described feeling lacking in energy with poor concentration and motivation. He could not sleep for fear he would dream about his experiences and found it difficult to look at or think of anything that resembled a boat. His academic performance had deteriorated since the disaster and he avoided contact with other people who had been on the ship. Previously a reasonable swimmer, he had never gone swimming again since the shipwreck.

Treatment was by four sessions of imaginal exposure followed by four sessions of real-life exposure. During the first two sessions he vividly relived the whole of his experiences during the disaster, repeating this for one hour a day at home, using audio-tapes of the sessions. By the third session his anxiety had remained high (7) with no habituation and so a "hot-spot" was identified and a rewind and hold procedure adopted. The hot-spot was a scene in which Ryan had been in the lounge of the ship as it began to list and had seen the water rising above the window as if part of the normal rolling of a ship. However, he had watched in horror as this time the level of water remained above the window. As he concentrated on this scene in his imagination, he recalled believing that he was going to die.

After a week of homework practice using an audiotape of the session he reported anxiety levels falling to 3 while imagining the scene. This was checked in session and a final exposure exercise involving the same scene and the complete account was set for homework. By the fifth session his anxiety had reduced to 1.

At this point his real-life avoidances were tackled. Two sessions were held in the local swimming pool where Ryan gradually entered the water and was helped to dive eventually underwater for rings from the pool floor. Although initial anxiety was very high (8), habituation was rapid. Between each session Ryan also went to the local pool as homework.

Finally, trips were organised on pleasure boat steamers on the local river. Once again, anxiety was moderate to high, initially 6/7, but rapid habituation ensured that the experience was therapeutic. Final assessment revealed that his symptoms were 85% reduced with large improvements in his ability to sleep and concentrate on schooling and subsequent employment. Follow-up to one year revealed complete maintenance of therapeutic gains with no relapse.

MORE COMPLEX APPROACHES

Although exposure appears to confer unambiguous benefits in the treatment of PTSD, a number of researchers have argued that exposure is insufficient to ameliorate the entirety of PTSD symptoms. Keane, Albano and Blake (1992, p. 373) argue that "exposure seems to have the biggest impact on the more anxiety-based and observable, or 'positive' symptoms (e.g. startle response, psychophysiological arousal, nightmares, irritability and anger), whilst negative ones (e.g. numbing, alienation, restricted affect) remain relatively unchanged". Further, PTSD often includes a number of other emotional reactions, not merely fear—for example, shame, anger, guilt, disgust, depression (Pitman, Orr, Forgue, Altman, deJong & Herz, 1990; Resick & Schnicke, 1992). It has been argued that while exposure may reduce fear reactions, other emotional reactions may not diminish in the same way (Pitman et al., 1991; Resick & Schnicke, 1992; Solomon, Gerrity & Muff, 1992).

Other reported problems with exposure are the complications reported by Pitman et al. (1991) which have arisen during or following imaginal exposure with Vietnam veterans. The authors emphasise the importance of post-trauma negative appraisal, and that emotions such as anger, shame and guilt may emerge during or following exposure which may therefore exacerbate such reactions. These arguments have led to the view that a combination of behavioural and cognitive interventions may be the optimal treatment approach (Resick & Schnicke, 1992; Foa et al., 1991; Keane, Albano & Blake, 1992).

At this point it is important to emphasise that such opinions are not supported by the empirical outcome studies. For example, Stress Inoculation Training (SIT), which includes some cognitive reappraisal sessions, did not lead to a better long-term outcome in rape victims (Foa et al., 1991) compared to exposure alone. We, too, have found that the whole spectrum of intrusive, avoidant and hyperarousal PTSD symptoms plus depression have all reduced following a combined imaginal and real-life exposure programme (Richards, Lovell & Marks, 1994). Recently Edna Foa, who has conducted many of the best-designed studies of cognitive and behavioural treatments combined or standing alone, stated that she would choose exposure as her first treatment option with PTSD since it is easier to implement, is as effective as cognitive approaches and is the simplest approach to explain to clients (Foa, 1995). This view was also supported by Marks et al. (1998), despite finding no differences between exposure and cognitive restructuring.

Clinically, however, many therapists have used cognitive techniques effectively to reduce some of the symptoms referred to by Keane, Albano and Blake (1992) and to address the difficulties highlighted by Pitman et al. (1991). From the evidence gathered so far (Marks et al., 1998), cognitive interventions appear to be as effective as exposure, though no more so. They may have great utility, however, in helping so-called "treatment failures", i.e. clients who have not responded to exposure approaches. Much work is currently being done to gain an understanding of the high attrition rate in PTSD treatment studies and to analyse the cognitive processes of clients who drop out or are not responsive to exposure. It may be that cognitive interventions are best utilised to modify the misattributions, negative appraisal and shattered assumptions which lead to the emotional reactions described above if they fail to change with the use of exposure.

Cognitive therapy for PTSD follows a Beckian style of cognitive therapy and comprises (1) the identification and evaluation of negative automatic thoughts that maintain feelings of anxiety, anger, hopelessness, guilt, and low self-esteem; and (2) the identification, critical appraisal and modification of shattered/distorted assumptions and beliefs about the traumatic event, the self, world and future.

Where cognitive restructuring is being considered, the rationale concentrates on explaining that thinking errors and assumptions about the incident have led to a breakdown in the processing mechanisms. Treatment concentrates on the machinery of the conveyor belt itself, challenging these assumptions so that the conveyor belt can be fixed and restarted. The following case study demonstrates the use of cognitive interventions.

Case Example 3

Phillip was a 38-year-old employed, married male. In 1989, he was walking home alone after leaving a party. He noticed a man behind him and, believing he was going to be attacked, began to run. The man ran after him, produced a modelling knife, and demanded his money. Philip handed over his wallet. The assailant then pushed him to the ground and slashed him across the face with the knife three or four times. A passer-by saw the attack and called an ambulance. Phillip was taken to hospital, and required many stitches to his wounds. On referral to our unit some two years later, Philip displayed all the typical features of PTSD.

Following a detailed assessment, Philip commenced treatment. A clear rationale was presented using a combination of Beck et al. (1979), Resick and Schnicke (1992) and Janoff-Bulman's (1992) work to ensure understanding of how distorted thoughts, beliefs and assumptions can arise from a traumatic event, and lead to negative emotional reactions. Treatment was conducted in the Beckian style of cognitive therapy with the initial stages of treatment focusing on the interconnection between thoughts, feelings and behaviour. Philip was taught how to identify and monitor negative thoughts using daily thought records. Common thinking errors were explained and he learnt to recognise these. As the thought records accumulated, themes began to develop and at this stage he was introduced to evaluating and challenging his thoughts, beliefs and assumptions and generating alternatives to them. Two of these themes are detailed below.

1. Shame

Two central thoughts and beliefs were associated with this theme. The first was that Philip believed that he looked like a "villain" due to his facial scarring. This belief led to shame and embarrassment, and resulted in loss of eye contact with others. During therapy he rated his belief that he looked like a villain on a 0–100 scale as 100%.

A number of ways could be used to challenge this thought. The way we challenged it was to ask him to identify the characteristics of "villains', and then compare those with himself. At the end of this session he rated his belief as 50%. He was asked to work further on this belief and to take home an audio-tape of the session. By the beginning of the next session he was rating this belief as 20%, and he once again began to maintain eye contact with others.

Secondly, he believed that he could and should have been able to fight off his attacker. This belief had been reinforced by the subsequent court proceedings, when the assailant pleaded self-defence. The jury believed this, as the assailant was 20 years older than Philip, and a not guilty verdict was returned. Philip rated his belief that he should have been able to fight off his attacker as 80%.

He was asked by the therapist to consider the following: "You believe this thought 80%, thus part of you, i.e. 20%, does not believe this to be true. Can you identify the factors which account for this 20%?" He identified a host of factors, among which were that he "was on the ground when I was knifed", "I have a mate who was mugged the week before me and he is not weak", "if I had tried to fight or struggle then a more serious injury could have occurred". Finally he said, "The more I think about it the more I think it would have been daft to try to defend myself against someone armed with a Stanley knife." He re-rated his belief in the unhelpful thought as 15% and in the alternative thought as 85%.

2. Overestimation of Risk

A second distressing thought which was causing anxiety was that a similar attack would occur in the future, leading him to avoid going out walking at night. As he was not in a position to afford a taxi, this caused considerable handicap to his life. He believed the risk of being reassaulted was 70%. He correctly identified the thinking error in this thought as overestimation.

This belief was challenged by calculating the times that he had been out and the times he was assaulted. He worked out that the actually probability of being reassaulted in terms of his previous life experience of going out at night was 0.01%. He was then asked to explain the difference between perceived and actual risk. He immediately identified the thinking error as overestimation and his strength of belief reduced to 45%. Following this he started to go out more and a few weeks later he was going out at night without difficulty.

At the end of 10 treatment sessions, Philip had improved by approximately 60% across a range of PTSD measures, this improvement being maintained to three-month follow-up.

DIFFICULTIES IN TREATMENT

A number of difficulties can occur during treatment, some of which have been highlighted in the literature and some are from our own clinical experience.

Difficulties Engaging Clients in Therapy

One of the initial difficulties for many clinicians treating PTSD is actually engaging clients in therapy. The literature reports that there is a high rate of poor attendance, and that traumatised individuals are reluctant to use mental health services (Schwarz & Kolowalski, 1992). Further, Solomon,

Gerrity and Muff (1992), in a comprehensive review of treatments for PTSD, note the high attrition rates in these studies.

There are several reasons for poor engagement and compliance. Firstly, therapeutic reluctance actually reflects the symptomatic oscillation from intrusion to avoidance characteristic of PTSD as described by Horowitz (1986). Clients with PTSD are ambivalent about their symptoms, existing for many years in hopeful anticipation that avoidance strategies will keep their traumatic intrusions at bay. One should not forget that for many clients this coping strategy is actually effective, often for considerable periods of time. For some clients it is the eventual breakdown of this strategy, or its limited and intermittent success, which prompts them to seek help. However, despite this breakdown, having successfully coped with the PTSD symptoms for months and years, clients are rarely 100% committed to a new approach.

Secondly, most clients believe that seeking help for a traumatically in-duced mental health problem will require them to at least talk about the initiating trauma. Once again, this is asking them to confront the very experience that they wish to bury and forget. While many clients have a personal sense that this will be a "good thing", they are often very fearful of the effects this may have on them, such as losing control, becoming very emotional, etc.

Thirdly, it is our experience that many clients with PTSD do not have a perception of themselves as "psychiatric cases". Their experience is one of a lifetime history of "normal" mental health. Then one day, following a sudden and unexpected traumatic event, they experience a change in their health leading to a series of bewildering and frightening psychological symptoms. They are reluctant to admit that they have problems and are often concerned not to "waste the therapist's time". This tendency to soldier on makes help-seeking behaviour unlikely. Indeed, at assessment, PTSD clients will often minimise their symptoms and it is only by careful questioning that the full degree of their disturbance will become apparent.

Finally, the high attrition rates in therapy may often be a consequence of the impact of increased affective arousal on clients. Emotional processing requires the presentation of material which evokes arousal. While this normally reduces during therapy, clients have to be assisted through the early stages of confronting their memories or cognitive distortions.

A number of strategies can be utilised to improve attendance rates and to maximise engagement in therapy.

Crucially, a therapist's main aim is to engender trust. In our initial clinical interviews we must communicate to clients a sense of relevant expertise.

Without dominating and leading the interview too directly, therapists can use questions which expose areas of problems which we suspect are likely to be present in a client with PTSD but which the client may not allude to without prompting. A careful mix of client-centred and directive interviewing is most effective in establishing this relevant expertise.

Empathy with the client's distress is, of course, vital. Although too much sympathy tends to be viewed negatively by clients, communicating an empathic understanding of their difficulties is highly effective in building trust. During the assessment or initial interview it is also beneficial to make it explicit to clients that we recognise that:

1. They are being HONEST.
2. They will be RESPONSIVE to a collaborative treatment plan.
3. They have been TRYING TO COPE.

As we have highlighted earlier, a comprehensive, easily understood and well-explained rationale is absolutely essential and allows us to emphasise the collaborative cognitive-behavioural approach. With any therapy, compliance is higher if a client has fully understood the principles of treatment and makes an informed choice following a clear rationale. Once the rationale has been explained the therapist should always check comprehension by asking the client to feedback the main principles underlying the proposed course of therapy.

As one of the symptoms of PTSD is poor concentration, a useful strategy is to give clients a written form of the rationale to take home with them. It is often better to draw diagrams freehand (for example, the "factory" in Figure 12.2) than to provide glossy pre-printed handouts. A rough diagram drawn in session is a first shared session record and has more personal meaning for both therapist and client than a handout, no matter how well printed.

In order to pre-empt difficulties with attendance, the therapist may choose to make it explicit at the initial session that he or she empathises and understands the therapeutic ambivalence inherent in PTSD. One way of doing this is to make clear predictions to the clients that they may find it difficult to attend for subsequent appointments. This is because the therapist, the clinic and our surroundings get incorporated into the triggers and reminders which bring on intrusive traumatic memories. Once we have recognised and made these difficulties explicit, clients can get a sense of relief and understanding if they become anxious before subsequent appointments.

Social support is recognised as a crucial recovery variable post-trauma. Incorporating a family member or other social supporter early on in treatment may also serve to increase compliance and attendance by supporting clients while they undertake homework exercises. However, one must always ensure that social supporters are appropriate and valued in the eyes of the clients. Unfortunately, some family members may be coercing clients rather than co-operating with them in their help-seeking behaviour. Good quality and appropriate social support is the key, not social support *per se*.

It is always a good idea to agree a small homework task with a client after the first assessment interview. Usually this takes the form of a diary-keeping exercise, perhaps monitoring the frequency of intrusions or keeping a sleep record. Engaging a client in collaborative active treatment exercises right at the beginning of the therapy process sets the right positive tone while emphasising the joint nature of cognitive-behavioural therapy.

Finally, as we have discussed earlier, it may be extremely beneficial to introduce some anxiety management skills before stating a programme of exposure or cognitive restructuring. If the client has a history of severe panics and/or is reluctant to consider exposure in particular—for fear of losing control, for example—panic management skills such as breathing retraining are highly appropriate. These should be considered as part of a complete therapy programme and as facilitating future exposure to traumatic memories.

DIFFICULTIES WITH SPECIFIC PROBLEMS

There are numerous difficulties that the clinician may face with particular clients, many of which are no different from those faced in general clinical practice. Some of the main difficulties will be presented here, with special emphasis on problems which are more specific to a PTSD client group. For example, particular difficulties occur with clients who are permanently disabled, bereaved or facially disfigured as a result of their trauma. It is important that treatment focuses on these losses, and incorporates the wider implications of these difficulties into a comprehensive management plan. Individuals with repeated trauma, such as domestic violence or child sex abuse, and clients who remain at continued risk of suicide or self-harm, will require a multi-intervention treatment plan and hence a longer duration of therapy. Within this multifaceted treatment plan, however, cognitive and behavioural interventions will comprise a vital core element.

Many clients are undergoing court cases and or compensation claims, and although our experience is that, for the majority of clients, it does not affect long-term treatment outcome, it clearly has implications for treatment. For example, difficulties include being seen by solicitors for the "other side", fear of seeing the assailant in court, fear of how clients will react in court and fear that they can never put the experience behind them until the case is over. Many clients find it difficult to understand the legal process and a lack of information increases their frustration. Further, the aftermath of the court case can lead to difficulties, particularly disillusionment with the authorities and the legal system. These issues need to be addressed in the process of therapy if successful outcome is to be achieved.

Some emotional reactions may pose specific treatment difficulties. These include guilt, anger, depression, suicidal and homicidal ideation. While guilt does not feature in the DSM-IV (APA, 1994) criteria for PTSD, it is a distressing part of their psychological difficulties for many clients. The best typology of guilt has identified three distinct types: survivor guilt, guilt arising from acts of commission; and guilt arising from acts of omission. Kubany (1994) has written an important article concerning guilt, and describes a number of useful techniques for the practising clinician.

A technique that we have found to be useful has been the use of a guilt cake. Essentially this is done using a pie chart. For example, Joan was walking across a pedestrian crossing with her young daughter when a car failed to stop and ploughed into her daughter. Fortunately, her daughter suffered no serious injury other than severe bruising and many cuts and grazes. Joan believed the accident was her responsibility and felt that her actions had led to her daughter being injured. She rated her belief in this thought as 90%.

In order to help Joan reappraise her beliefs she was asked to identify all the people involved in the car accident, i.e. the driver, her daughter and herself, and was asked to diagrammatically assign the percentage of relative responsibilities and the factors that led to this for each individual (Figure 12.4).

Joan (90%)   "The accident was predominantly my responsibility because I should have seen the car coming and pulled my daughter out of the way."

Daughter (0%)   "It was not my daughter's fault at all."

Driver (10%)   "He was driving to fast, and he failed to stop at a pedestrian crossing."

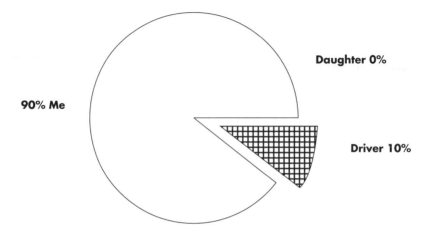

Figure 12.4 Joan's first guilt cake

Joan studied the diagram, and was asked if the levels of responsibility were representative, given the facts she had presented. After a discussion of the accident, including the specific evidence for her beliefs, she felt that she had underestimated the driver's level of responsibility. She was then asked to redraw the "guilt cake". Her second pie chart was drawn as in Figure 12.5.

Driver (100%)   "The driver was driving at least 50 mph in a 30 mph speed limit; he failed to stop at a pedestrian crossing, even though the car coming from the other direction had already stopped; when the car finally saw me and my daughter it was going too fast to stop. When I think about it, the accident was entirely the fault of the driver."

Daughter (0%)   "There is nothing my daughter did that led to the accident."

Joan (0%)   "There is nothing specific that I can think of other than I just wish it had been me and not my daughter."

At the end of the session Joan reported that she no longer felt responsible for the accident. She was asked to take the diagrams home with her and to keep it in her therapy file. Her feelings of guilt had not returned at 12-month follow-up.

We have found this technique to be of great clinical value in decreasing guilt and looking at the incident in a more objective way. Many clients

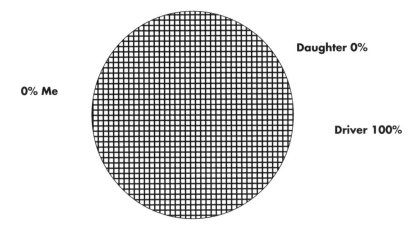

0% Me

Daughter 0%

Driver 100%

Figure 12.5 Joan's second guilt cake

report that it is the visual representation of the "guilt cake" that is particularly effective.

Anger is a common reaction following trauma (Riggs, Dancu, Gershuny, Greenberg & Foa, 1992; Chemtob et al., 1994) and often emerges as a difficulty in treatment. Anger may be directed at the self, an assailant (where one has been involved), those responsible for the incident, or those in authority, i.e. courts, prosecution services, police, etc. Techniques in dealing with anger include Novaco's (1977) SIT package for anger and a similar range of cognitive interventions to those described earlier. Although uncommon, some clients, where they have been assaulted, experience homicidal thoughts and feelings, often centring around vengeance and an "eye-for-an eye". This may lead to a small proportion of clients carrying weapons either through fear of a further assault or with the intention of harming the assailant.

One example of traumatically generated anger is that of John who, while working on a car with his brother, was involved in an accident where another car speeding along the road ploughed into them, killing his brother and injuring him. The prosecution resulted in a non-conviction due to a lack of evidence. Following the court case, John sat outside the driver's house for many hours, watching and waiting for the driver and thinking of how he would harm him. Fortunately, the driver never arrived when John was waiting for him.

One of the techniques we used was to look at the advantages and disadvantages to John and his family of harming the driver. Secondly, he was asked to consider the more global advantages and disadvantages of his anger generally in terms of the impact on himself and his family. During this exercise it became clear to John that his anger was having a negative impact on him and on those closest to him. From this he was able to change the thought "I must seek revenge for the death of my brother" to "My brother would not want me to do this"; "Enough damage has already been done to me and my family"; "I am not sure if I could live with myself if I did seriously harm the driver". Although he remained angry, the homicidal thoughts reduced, as did his behaviour, thus the impact of the anger on his and his family's life reduced considerably.

Depression is not uncommon with those suffering from PTSD (Green, 1994; Keane & Wolfe, 1990) and needs to be assessed and incorporated in the overall treatment plan. A mild to moderate level of depression will usually alleviate with a cognitive-behavioural approach alone. However antidepressant medication may be indicated for those with a moderate to severe level of depression. Although studies have been conducted using antidepressants alone for PTSD (Davidson, 1992; Frank, Kosten, Giller & Dan, 1988) the treatment literature suggests that medication should be used as an adjunctive treatment with other forms of therapy (Solomon, Gerrity & Muff, 1992; Friedman, 1991).

Suicide is quite a common problem in PTSD populations. Studies of PTSD have found associations with major depression and suicidal ideation and attempts (Green, 1994). Suicide plans can arise from depression or from anger. We have seen a number of clients where a plan of suicide involves jumping from a high building outside their place of work, or setting themselves on fire outside the court room.

Cognitive-behaviour therapy, like any other psychological therapy, can only proceed when clients are safe from harming themselves. A suicide management plan which minimises the risk to a client is an essential first step in therapy, and such plans are highly tailored to the individual. They often involve reducing risks by removing tablets, knives, etc., from a client's immediate vicinity; providing social support and family contact at times of greatest risk; and, in some cases, arranging for hospitalisation.

A suicide management plan is based on the development of a trusting relationship with the therapist. It enables the client and therapist to deal with feelings of hopelessness, helplessness and the loss of self-control that is present to an extreme degree in some clients with PTSD. Clearly these needs have to be prioritised in the treatment plan. We would always recommend, however, that the therapist moves on to the exposure or cognitive techniques detailed earlier once active suicidal risk has been minimised.

FUTURE DIRECTIONS FOR TREATMENT

While the recent treatment literature has advanced our knowledge of behavioural and cognitive-behavioural interventions in the treatment of PTSD, much more further research is urgently required. For example, the high attrition rate in therapy noted in many studies and discussed earlier requires further investigation along with better techniques for helping clients both enter and stay in therapy. Although the results of many of the studies show increasingly high levels of clinical improvement, there is often significant pathology remaining. Clear predictors of good and bad therapeutic outcomes need to be identified. Further, many of the studies only report a limited follow-up period. Little is known about relapse rates following treatment and studies need to include much longer-term follow-up.

Some authors have suggested that exposure therapy is likely to be beneficial for anxiety-based symptoms of PTSD, that cognitive therapy is more appropriate for other types of negative emotions, and, hence, that a combination of cognitive and behavioural approaches may provide the optimal treatment approach. However, a recent study (Marks et al., 1998) described earlier found no superiority in the use of a combined approach over either treatment alone.

REFERENCES

Al-Kubaisy, T., Marks, I.M., Logsdale, S., Marks, M.P., Lovell, K., Sungar, M. & Araya, R. (1992). The role of exposure homework in phobic reduction: a controlled study. *Behavior Therapy*, **22**, 599–622.
APA (1994). *Diagnostic and Statistical Manual of Mental Disorders* (4th Edition). Washington, DC: American Psychiatric Association.
Beck, A.T. (1976). *Cognitive Therapy and the Emotional Disorders*. New York: International Universities Press.
Beck, A.T. (1991). Cognitive therapy: A 30 year retrospective. *American Psychologist*, **46**, 368–375.
Beck, A.T. (1993) Cognitive therapy, past, present and future. *Journal of Consulting and Clinical Psychology*, **61** (2), 194–198.
Beck, A.T., Rush, A.J., Shaw, B.F. & Emery, G. (1979). *Cognitive Therapy of Depression*. New York: Wiley.
Beck, A.T., Emery, G. & Greenberg, R. (1985). *Anxiety Disorders and Phobias: A Cognitive Perspective*. New York: Basic Books.

Brom, D., Kleber, R.J. & Defares, P.B. (1989). Brief psychotherapy for post-traumatic stress disorders. *Journal of Consulting and Clinical Psychology*, **57** (5), 607–612.

Carroll, E.M. & Foy, D.W. (1992). Assessment and treatment of combat-related post-traumatic stress disorder in a medical centre setting. In D.W. Foy (Ed.), *Treating PTSD: Cognitive Behavioural Strategies*. New York: Guilford Press.

Chemtob, C., Roitblat, H.L., Hamada, R.S., Carlson, J.G. & Twentyman, C.T. (1988). A cognitive action theory of post-traumatic stress disorder. *Journal of Anxiety Disorders*, **2**, 253–275.

Chemtob, C.M., Hamada, R.S., Roitblat, H.L. & Muraoka, M.Y. (1994). Anger, impulsivity & anger control in combat-related posttraumatic stress disorder. *Journal of Consulting and Clinical Psychology*, **62** (4), 827–832.

Davidson, J. (1992). Drug therapy of post-traumatic stress disorder. *British Journal of Psychiatry*, **160**, 309–314.

Ellis, A. (1962). *Reason and Emotion in Psychotherapy*. New York: Lyle & Stewart.

Foa, E.B. (1995). Presentation to the European Conference on Traumatic Stress, Paris, France.

Foa, E.B., Rothbaum, B.O., Riggs, D.S. & Murdock, T.B. (1991). Treatment of posttraumatic stress disorder in rape victims: A comparison between cognitive and behavioural procedures and counselling. *Journal of Clinical and Consulting Psychology*, **59** (5), 715–723.

Foa, E.B., Steketee, G.S. & Rothbaum, B.O. (1989). Behavioural/cognitive conceptualisations of post-traumatic stress disorder. *Behavior Therapy*, **20**, 155–176.

Frank, J.B., Kosten, T.R., Giller, E.L. & Dan, E. (1988). A randomized clinical trial of phenalzine and imipramine for post-traumatic stress disorder. *American Journal of Psychiatry*, **145**, 1289–1291.

Freeman, A., Pretezer, J., Fleming, B. & Simon, K.M. (1990). *Clinical Applications of Cognitive Therapy*. New York: Plenum Press.

Friedman, M.J. (1991). Biological approaches to the diagnosis and treatment of post-traumatic stress disorder. *Journal of Traumatic Stress*, **4**, 67–91.

Green, B.L. (1994). Psychosocial research in traumatic stress: An update. *Journal of Traumatic Stress*, **7** (3), 341–362.

Hackman, A. (1993) Behavioural and cognitive psychotherapies: Past history, current applications and future registration issues. *Behavioural and Cognitive Psychotherapy*, **21**, Supplement 1.

Hawton, K., Salkovskis, P.M., Kirk, J. & Clark, D.M. (1989). *Cognitive Behaviour Therapy for Psychiatric Problems: A Practical Guide*. Oxford: Oxford University Press.

Horowitz, M.J. (1986). *Stress Response Syndromes*. New York: Jason Aronson.

Janoff-Bulman, R. (1992). *Shattered Assumptions*. New York: Free Press.

Keane, T.M. (1995). Presentation at 1 day Conference "PTSD: trauma and anxiety. Psychological approaches to treatment". Manchester University, England.

Keane, T.M. & Kaloupek, D. (1982). Imaginal flooding in the treatment of a posttraumatic stress disorder. *Journal of Consulting and Clinical Psychology*, **50** (1), 138–140.

Keane, T.M., Fairbank, J.A., Caddell, J.M. & Zimmering, R.T. (1989). Implosive (flooding) therapy reduces symptoms of PTSD in Vietnam combat veterans. *Behavior Therapy*, **20**, 149–153.

Keane, T.M., Albano, A.M. & Blake, D.D. (1992) Current trends in the treatment of post-traumatic stress disorder. In M. Basoglu (Ed.), *Torture and its Consequences: Current Treatment Approaches*. Cambridge: Cambridge University Press.

Keane, T.M. & Wolfe, J. (1990). Comorbidity in post-traumatic stress disorder: An analysis of community and clinical studies. *Journal of Applied Social Psychology*, **20** (21), 1776–1788.

Kilpatrick, D.G. & Amick, A.E. (1985). Rape trauma. In M. Hersen & C.G. Last (Eds.), *Behaviour Therapy Casebook*. New York: Springer.

Krietler, S. & Krietler, H. (1988). Trauma and anxiety: The cognitive approach. *Journal of Traumatic Stress*, **7**, 3–19.

Kubany, E.S. (1994). A cognitive model of guilt typology in combat-related PTSD. *Journal of Traumatic Stress*, **7**, 3–19.

Lang, P. (1979). A bioinformational theory of emotional imagery. *Psychophysiology*, **16**, 495–512.

Lovell, K. (1992). The reality of rape. *Nursing Times*, **88** (25), 52–54.

Marks, I.M. (1987) *Fears Phobias and Rituals*. Oxford: Oxford University Press.

Marks, I., Lovell, K., Noshirvani, H., Livanou, M. & Thrasher, S. (1988). Treatment of post-traumatic stress disorder by exposure and/or cognition restructuring. *Archives of General Psychiatry.*, **55**, 317–325.

McCaffery, R.J. & Fairbank, J.A. (1985). Post-traumatic stress disorder associated with transport accidents: Two case studies. *Behavior Therapy*, **16**, 406–416.

McCann, I.I., Sakheim, D.K. & Abrahamson, D.J. (1988). Trauma and victimisation: A model of psychological adaption. *Counselling Psychologist*, **16**, 531–594.

McCormack, N.A. (1985). Cognitive therapy of posttraumatic stress disorder: A case report. *American Mental Health Counsellors Mental Health Journal*, 151–155.

Mowrer, O.H. (1960). *Learning Theory and Behaviour*. New York: Wiley.

Muse, M. (1986) Stress related post-traumatic chronic pain syndrome: Behavioural treatment approach. *Pain*, **25**, 389–394.

Novaco, R. (1977). A stress inoculation approach to anger management in the training of law enforcement officers. *American Journal of Community Psychology*, **5**, 327–346.

Parrott, C.A. & Howes, J.L. (1991). The application of cognitive therapy to posttraumatic stress disorder. In T.M. Vallis, J.L. Howes & P.C. Miller (Eds.), *The Challenge of Cognitive Therapy: Applications to Nontraditional Populations*. New York: Plenum Press.

Pearson, M.A., Poquette, B.M. & Wasden, R.E. (1983). Stress inoculation and the treatment of post-rape trauma: A case report. *Behavior Therapist*, **6**, 58–59.

Pitman, R.K., Orr, S.P., Forgue, D.F., Altman, B., deJong, J.B. & Herz, L.R. (1990). Psychophysiologic response to combat injury of Vietnam veterans with posttraumatic stress disorder versus other anxiety disorders. *Journal of Abnormal Psychology*, **99**, 49–54.

Pitman, R.K., Altman, B., Greenwald, E., Longpre, R.E, Macklin, M.L., Poire, R.E. & Steketee, G.S. (1991). Psychiatric complications during flooding therapy for posttraumatic stress disorder. *Journal of Abnormal Psychology*, **99**, 49–54.

Resick, P.A. & Schnicke, M.K. (1992) Cognitive processing therapy for sexual assault victims. *Journal of Consulting and Clinical Psychology*, **60** (5), 748–756.

Resick, P.A. & Schnicke, M.K. (1993). *Cognitive Processing Therapy for Rape Victims: A Treatment Manual*. Newbury Park, CA: Sage Publications.

Richards, D.A. (1989). Hidden scars. *Nursing Times*, **85** (22), 66–68.

Richards, D.A., Lovell, K. & Marks, I.M. (1994). Post-traumatic stress disorder: Evaluation of a behavioural treatment program. *Journal of Traumatic Stress*, **7** (4), 669–680.

Riggs, D.S., Dancu, C.V., Gershuny, B.S., Greenberg, D. & Foa, E.B. (1992). Anger & post-traumatic stress disorder in female crime victims. *Journal of Traumatic Stress*, **5** (4), 613–625.

Schwarz, E.T. & Kolowalski, J.M. (1992). Malignant memories: Reluctance to utilize mental health services after a disaster. *Journal of Nervous and Mental Disease*, **180** (12), 767–772.

Solomon, S.D., Gerrity, E.T. & Muff, A.M. (1992). Efficacy of treatments for posttraumatic stress disorder: An empirical review. *Journal of American Medical Association* , **268** (5), 633–638.

Thrasher, S.M., Lovell, K., Noshirvani, H. & Livanou, M. (1996). Cognitive restructuring in the treatment of post-traumatic stress disorder: Two single cases. *Clinical Psychology and Psychotherapy*, **3** (2), 137–148.

Vaughan, K. & Tarrier, N. (1992). The use of image habituation training with post-traumatic stress disorders. *British Journal of Psychiatry*, **161**, 658–664.

Veronen, L. J. & Kilpatrick, D.G. (1983). Stress management for rape victims. In D. Meichenbaum & M.E. Jaremko (Eds.), *Stress Reduction & Prevention*. New York: Plenum Press.

Weathers, F.W. & Keane, T.M. (1994). Posttraumatic stress disorder. In C.G. Last & M. Hersen (Eds.), *Adult Behaviour Therapy Casebook*. New York: Plenum Press.

Wolff, R. (1977). Systematic desensitisation and negative practise to alter the after effects of a rape attempt. *Journal of Behaviour Therapy and Experimental Psychiatry*, **8**, 423–425.

Wolpe, J. (1958). *Psychotherapy by Reciprocal Inhibition*. Stanford, CA: Stanford University Press.

Chapter 13

EYE MOVEMENT DESENSITISATION AND REPROCESSING

Patrick Smith* and William Yule*

INTRODUCTION

Remarkable in many ways, Eye Movement Desensitisation and Re-processing (EMDR) is one of the most recent additions to the armoury of treatments for post-traumatic stress disorders. Following its seren-dipitous discovery (Shapiro, 1989a) and a well-organised interna-tional training programme, extraordinarily rapid treatment effects of EMDR are now claimed for PTSD and a variety of other disorders by a large number of practitioners. However, theoretical explanations of the efficacy of the procedure lag far behind the refinement of clinical practice. At the heart of EMDR is the notion that accelerated processing of disturbing material can be directly facilitated at a neurophysiological level using a variety of dual attention tasks. Accordingly, a by-product of resolution at the neurophysiological level is cognitive and emotional well-being.

This chapter will briefly outline the EMDR procedure, and review the growing number of outcome evaluation studies, before considering some of the recent theoretical explanations that have been offered. EMDR has been used with a variety of populations, and its use with children and adolescents will be considered here.

*Institute of Psychiatry, London

Post-Traumatic Stress Disorders: Concepts and Therapy. Edited by William Yule.
© 1999 John Wiley & Sons Ltd.

PROCEDURE

Origins

It is worth noting that, initially, the approach was not based on the application of scientific principles to clinical problems, but was discovered by chance. Shapiro (1995) describes how, while walking through the woods one day, she noticed that disturbing thoughts began to disappear suddenly: when she recalled them, they were neither as upsetting nor seemed as valid as before. She noticed that, as the disturbing thoughts came to mind, her eyes spontaneously moved rapidly backwards and forwards in an upward diagonal. After recalling disturbing thoughts while deliberately moving her eyes, Shapiro again observed that the thoughts disappeared and seemed to be less upsetting. Following try-outs with colleagues, then a more structured intervention with a traumatised Veterans' counsellor using deliberately invoked eye movements, this led to the first controlled trial with rape survivors (Shapiro, 1989b). Since then, the EMDR methodology has evolved considerably and the currently advocated procedure follows a detailed protocol which is summarised below.

Current Protocol

During the initial full clinical assessment, target memories for reprocessing are identified. In addition, as in treatment approaches which utilise exposure (such as flooding, see Chapter 12), the client's ability and consent to withstand potentially high levels of disturbance is assessed. In EMDR, it is claimed that disturbance may be particularly high (if short lived) because accelerated processing can result in disassociated information and the emotions and physical sensations which were experienced at the time of the traumatic event rapidly becoming consciously accessible. Prior to detailed assessment of particular traumatic memories, the EMDR procedure and effects are explained to the client and eye movements are practised. At this stage, the client is taught relaxation and guided imagery techniques, which will be used in closing the session and by the client between sessions.

A thorough assessment of traumatic memories for reprocessing follows. A target memory for reprocessing is chosen, but the therapist does not need details of the incident. The client may be asked, "When you think of the event, what do you get?": this is used more to gauge the client's current means of encoding the information rather than to get a very detailed account of the incident. A representative image of the target memory is selected by the client, but the clinician does not need a detailed description of the client's visual imagery. A negative cognition that accompanies the memory is identified by the client. These are framed as self-referential beliefs in the present tense (e.g. "I am unworthy") rather than descriptions of the past (e.g. "It was awful" or "I was terrified"). A positive cognition is then identified by asking, "What would you like to believe about the event or yourself?" The positive cognition is rated on the seven-point Validity of Cognition (VOC) scale, where clients are asked for a gut-level rating of how true they feel the positive cognition is. Next, the client is instructed to combine the image and the negative cognition, and to identify and rate the accompanying emotion on a Subjective Units of Discomfort (SUD) scale. The last stage is to identify the location of any physical sensation that accompanies the memory to be targeted. These detailed preparations and assessments having been completed, the client is ready for the treatment stages which incorporate dual attention tasks.

Before beginning the dual attention tasks, the client is told that is important not to purposefully discard any information if it comes up, but just to notice whatever comes up and to report it accurately. The client is asked to bring up the image and the negative cognition, and to notice where it is felt in his or her body. The client is then told to track the therapist's fingers which are moved slowly back and forth across his or her line of vision. When tracking is established, speed is increased until it is as rapid as is comfortable for the client to keep tracking properly. At the end of the first set of 24 bidirectional saccadic eye movements, the client is instructed to "Blank it out" or "Let it go". The clinician asks for brief feedback: "What do you get?" or "What are you noticing now?". This question is as open as possible, and unlike traditional psychological therapies, the client's response is not interpreted, reflected back, paraphrased, summarised or commented on. The client may report changes to the image and will be asked to "Just stay with that" or "Just notice it". A second set of eye movements is carried out. The length of the set can vary and is determined by non-verbal cues from the client. A number of sets will be repeated in a session. While it is not necessary to ask for feedback of SUD ratings after every set, reprocessing is assumed to have reached a plateau once SUDs are rated as 0 or 1.

It is claimed that clients may report a variety of changes during and after sets of eye movements. Any change to the image, sounds, emotions, cognitions, or physical sensations associated with the targeted memory is assumed to indicated that processing is taking place. Clinical reports indicate that images may change in their appearance or content. An image may become more blurred or more broad; additional content may be noticed; the image may become smaller or larger, or move further away or nearer; or at times may disappear altogether. Remembered sounds may change their quality or volume, or remembered dialogue may change its content. Emotions may lessen in intensity, as gauged by SUD ratings, but may also increase, and either event is taken as a sign of processing. Clients may also report a decrease in the intensity of physical sensations, or a shift in the location of bodily sensations.

If no changes take place, the direction of eye movements may be changed, or alternative stimuli used (see below). Should changes be reported, the client is asked just to stay with it, and another set is repeated. This process continues until no further changes are taking place and SUD ratings are at 0 or 1. At this point, the client is asked to bring up the original target image and another set is carried out. Typically, a return to the target memory opens up another association to that memory. Several associations (or "channels") may need to be processed. Once this is done, and a return to the target memory reveals no new associations, images, emotions, cognitions, or sensations, then "installation" of the positive cognition can begin. This may concern the positive cognition that was specified in the original assessment, but can also be a more appropriate cognition that has emerged during the dual attention task. The client is asked how that cognition sounds now, and rates it on the VOC scale. The client is asked to think of the event and hold the positive cognition in mind while a set of eye movements is completed. At the end of the set, the VOC is reported again, and a set repeated until the VOC reaches 7. If the client does not report a 7, this may be due to what Shapiro calls a dysfunctional blocking belief (e.g. "I don't deserve to be healthy"). In this case, the memory that is associated with the blocking belief will become a target for further EMDR work.

Last, the client is asked to hold the memory and the "installed" positive cognition in mind while scanning his or her body for residual tension. The client is asked to notice the tension, and a set of eye movements is carried out while targeting the tension. This stage is complete when the client can notice no residual tension or unusual bodily sensations while holding the memory and positive cognition in mind. The session may be closed using relaxation techniques, hypnosis, or guided imagery as necessary. The client is debriefed about what to expect between sessions (processing may continue spontaneously), and asked to keep a log of disturbing thoughts or memories that arise between sessions.

Additional Procedures

A number of alternatives to left–right saccadic eye movements are now recommended. In the case that left–right movements produce little change, then vertical, diagonal, circular, or figure-of-eight movements have all been used. If the client finds finger tracking difficult, then the therapist may hold one hand at opposite sides of the client's visual field, and alternately raise the index finger of each hand. If the client finds all eye movements uncomfortable, then hand tapping may be tried: the client places both hands palm upwards on the knees while the clinician alternately taps each palm at roughly the same speed as sets of eye movements. Otherwise, auditory stimuli may be used: the client closes his or her eyes while the clinician clicks fingers next to each ear at roughly the same rate as during eye movements.

The basic protocol which is summarised above may work for up to 40% of clients (Shapiro 1995, but see the section below on outcome evaluation). For just over half of clients, then, additional procedures will be necessary, and a number of adjuncts to the standard protocol are advocated. These include techniques to work with abreactions, and techniques to work with blocks, including changing the type of stimulation, focusing on bodily sensations, and deliberately initiating some of the changes to images described above in an effort to "jump start" processing. Shapiro (1995) also describes the "cognitive interweave", a more proactive form of EMDR for working with challenging clients where the clinician takes a more traditional role in offering suggestions and new information, and in using Socratic questioning styles, rather than relying solely on the client's spontaneous processing effects.

Summary

Whatever additional techniques are used, it remains true that what is unique about EMDR is the use of dual attention tasks to facilitate processing at a neurophysiological level. This means that the style of therapy is radically different to most psychological therapies. The therapist gives up a good deal of his or her traditional role. Much of the time, the therapist will have a limited idea of what is happening with the client, but must trust in a poorly understood procedure to resolve blocked processing.

EFFICACY

The current heated debate about whether EMDR works seems to stem from a need to validate the bold claims that are made for a treatment which has apparently poor face validity and a very limited theoretical background. The debate has become somewhat polarised, with negative results being discounted by proponents because researchers had not undergone the requisite training from the EMDR Institute; and positive results being discounted by sceptics due to lack of scientific rigour. What emerges from the brief review below is a large number of single cases and clinical studies which report rapid beneficial results, a small and growing number of comparative outcome studies, but a lack of larger scale studies utilising double blind randomised controls and long-term follow up.

The initial controlled efficacy study (Shapiro, 1989b) showed significant reductions in anxiety for 22 subjects presenting with a number of complaints following a variety of traumatic events. These effects were apparent after a single session and maintained at one- and three-month follow-ups. The placebo control group received a modified flooding treatment, and showed no drop in SUD levels post-session. The control group was then offered EMDR for ethical reasons, preventing a group comparison at follow-up, but forming a "delayed treatment" group. The delayed treatment group responded similarly to the treatment group. Although encouraging, there was a lack of clear criteria for subjects' inclusion in this initial study, and standardised assessment measures were not used, dependent variables being subjective Likert-type ratings of anxiety and changes in validity of cognitions. This first study spurred a number of encouraging clinical case reports.

For example, Wolpe and Abrams (1991) reported a "completely successful" treatment of a 43-year-old woman with PTSD following a rape 10 years earlier: previous behaviour therapy had led to little change. Puk (1991) reported the successful treatment of two cases, one of whom had traumatic memories of childhood sexual abuse. At referral, the 43-year-old woman was having nightmares three to four times a week, and her social functioning, particularly with men, was markedly impaired. Following only three sets of saccadic eye movements targeting different traumatic memories, her SUD levels were reduced to 0, and the frequency of nightmares decreased. At 12-month follow-up, she had had only one nightmare and had had a satisfactory sexual relationship with a male for eight months. Kleinknecht and Morgan (1992) reported successful treatment of a 40-year-old man with an eight year history of PTSD following an incident in which he was shot and left dying. After a single session of EMDR targeting a variety of traumatic memories, significant reductions were noted on the State-Trait Anxiety Inventory (Spielberger, 1974), the Centre for Epidemiological Studies Depression scale (Weissman, Sholomkas, Pottenger, Prusoff & Locke, 1977), and the Brief Symptom Inventory (Derogatis & Spencer, 1982). After treatment, he no longer met the criteria for PTSD, test probes failed to elicit any disturbance, and his personal and professional functioning were improved: these gains were maintained at four- and eight-month follow-up. McCann (1992) reported the successful treatment of a 41-year-old man with severe PTSD following an accident in which he sustained devastating burns which left him with massive scarring, total deafness, bilateral amputations of the arms above the elbow, and severely damaged feet and ankles. Treatment consisted of a single session of EMDR. The man was asymptomatic at one-year follow-up.

While there continues to be an abundance of remarkable clinical case reports in the literature, there are fewer well-controlled outcome trials. Shapiro (e.g. 1995) rightly points out that this is not unique to EMDR, and states that more controlled studies have been done with EMDR than with any other treatment method used in PTSD. Unfortunately, many of these are, at the time of writing, unpublished papers.

There is evidence that EMDR is better than wait list controls and placebos. Rothbaum (1995, unpublished paper) found EMDR to be superior to wait list controls. Wilson, Becker and Tinker (1995) randomly assigned 80 trauma subjects (37 of whom were diagnosed with PTSD) to treatment or delayed treatment groups. Significant differences were found between the two groups, measured by the PTSD Interview (Watson, Juba, Manifold, Kucala & Anderson, 1991) carried out by a blind interviewer, the State-Trait Anxiety Inventory (Spielberger, 1974), the Impact of Event Scale (Horowitz, Wilner & Alvarez, 1979) and the SCL-90-R (Derogatis, Rickels & Rock, 1976). Treatment gains were maintained at 12-month follow-up. Shapiro's initial (1989b) study included an attention placebo group, and found significant differences between treatment and no treatment on SUD and VOC scales.

There is also some evidence that EMDR fares better than traditional VA supportive counselling, group treatment, or relaxation training. Levin, Grainger, Allen-Byrd and Fulcher (1994, unpublished paper) compared EMDR to supportive crisis counselling and no-treatment groups in 45 survivors of Hurricane Andrew in Florida. EMDR was found to be superior to the other groups, as measured by SUD ratings, and Revised Impact of Event Scale (Horowitz, Wilner & Alvarez, 1979) scores at one-month and three-month follow-up. Boudewyns, Hyer, Peralme, Touze and Kiel (1995, unpublished paper) found EMDR to be superior to standard VA counselling in 20 chronic inpatient veterans on standard psychological measures. Carlson, Chemtob, Rusnak and Hedlund (1995, unpublished paper) found EMDR to be superior to a biofeedback relaxation control group and a group receiving routine VA care. It is unfortunate that these studies are as yet unpublished, as this makes it difficult to assess whether subjects were randomly assigned to groups, whether raters were blind to groups, the treatment fidelity of the control groups, the outcome measures used, and the clinical or statistical differences between groups.

At least one published study has compared EMDR to exposure therapy and relaxation groups (Vaughn, Armstrong, Gold, O'Connor, Jenneke & Tarrier, 1994). Subjects were 36 patients with PTSD who were randomly assigned to EMDR, exposure, muscle relaxation, or wait list control groups; and assessed by a blind rater pre- and post-treatment and at three-month follow-up using structured interview and standard self-report measures (State-Trait Anxiety Inventory—Spielberger, 1974; Beck Depression Inventory—Beck, 1978; and the Impact of Event Scale—Horowitz, Wilner & Alvarez, 1979). All groups improved significantly compared with the wait list control, and these benefits were maintained at three-month follow-up. Although there were no significant differences between the different treatment groups, the non-significant trend was for greater reduction in total PTSD symptoms in the EMDR group. In particular, the authors note that EMDR had a striking impact on intrusive symptoms, which further improved at follow-up, and suggest that the marked improvement in flashbacks and nightmares may distinguish EMDR from other treatments.

Silver, Brooks and Obenchain (1995) compared standard milieu treatment alone with milieu treatment plus either EMDR, biofeedback, or group relaxation for inpatient veterans with PTSD. It was found (1) that subjects receiving additional EMDR showed significantly more improvement on three out of eight unstandardised measures of symptomatology than the milieu alone group; (2) that EMDR was superior to relaxation on two out of eight of these scales and superior to biofeedback on five out of eight of the scales. However, this study was hampered by small sample sizes which varied between groups, non-random assignment of subjects to groups, and unstandardised outcome measures.

Two studies have failed to find changes in standardised assessment measures using EMDR. Boudewyns, Stwerka, Hyer, Albrecht and Sperr (1993) found no changes in standardised measures and physiological measures when comparing EMDR to exposure and group therapy in 20 chronic inpatient veterans, although there were positive results for EMDR in self-reported distress and (non-blind) therapist assessment. Jensen (1994) compared EMDR to a standard VA treatment control group in 74 Vietnam combat veterans suffering from PTSD, and found no significant group differences on the structured interviews or VOC ratings; and while SUD ratings were lower in the EMDR group, there were no significant differences on the Mississippi Scale for Combat-related Distress (Keane, Caddell & Taylor, 1986), or on Goal Attainment Scaling (Kiresuk & Sherman, 1968) at post-treatment.

A number of dismantling studies have been carried out in order to delineate the effective components of the EMDR procedure. For example, Renfrey and Spates (1994) randomly assigned 23 trauma victims to either standard EMDR treatment, a modified EMDR procedure in which tracking was induced using a light bar, and a modified EMDR procedure in which subjects fixated a blinking light. Significant reductions were found post-treatment for heart rate, SUD and VOC ratings across all groups. Whereas at pre-treatment, 21 of the 23 met DSM-III-R criteria for PTSD, only five met criteria post-treatment, and these were distributed evenly across treatment groups. There were no between group differences, indicating that something about the general EMDR procedure, rather than eye movements *per se*, was responsible for reductions in heart rate and self-reported distress.

In summary, while there are a good number of encouraging clinical reports in the literature, limited inferences can be drawn from them about the causal nature of the EMDR procedure. Evidence is available that EMDR is better than no treatment (Wilson, Becker & Tinker, 1995), but there is a paucity of well-controlled published comparative outcome studies. A number have noted significant reductions in SUD levels using EMDR, but no significant changes on standardised or physiological measures (Boudewyns et al., 1993; Jensen, 1994). One controlled study found no superiority of EMDR over exposure or relaxation treatments (Vaughn et al., 1994). One component analysis (Renfrey & Spates, 1994) found significant reductions in heart rate, SUD and VOC ratings, but noted that eye movements were not necessary for change.

Nevertheless, while current evidence for the efficacy of EMDR is mixed, the procedure continues to be refined and outcome evaluation studies are ongoing. Lohr, Kleinknecht, Tolin and Barrett (1995), in their comprehensive review of the field, and Shapiro (1995), both provide guidelines for future research, including controlling for non-specific effects, and controlling for client, therapist and situational factors. Therapists should be fully trained in the EMDR procedure; and appropriate, standardised and sensitive outcome measures should be used. Controlled comparative outcome research should examine EMDR's efficacy relative to no treatment, wait list and placebo controls, as well as to other standard treatments such as exposure therapy. Further component analyses may help to elucidate the aspects of the complex EMDR procedure which are critical for therapeutic change.

RATIONALE

While outcome studies suggest that, at the very least, EMDR is a method worth exploring further, it is still far from clear how the method might work. Shapiro (1995) seems to suggest that the changes in mental states evident in EMDR are almost epiphenomenal: "Desensitisation and cognitive restructuring are viewed as byproducts of the adaptive reprocessing taking place on a neurophysiological level." Any underlying theory of EMDR must therefore account for how a rapid non-chemical intervention works directly at a neurophysiological level to produce conscious changes in mental states. A number of theories have been offered, none of which is entirely satisfactory.

EMDR incorporates dosed exposure to traumatic memories and, in behavioural treatments (see Chapter 12 in this volume), the essential components of graded exposure or flooding are assumed to lead to desensitisation. However, the very rapid effects following relatively short bursts of exposure seen in EMDR indicate that exposure and consequent desensitisation alone cannot be the sole explanation here. Indeed, the short bursts of intense exposure alternating with therapist reassurance in EMDR run counter to what learning theory predicts would be effective (Rachman, 1980).

It has been proposed instead that eye movements elicit an orienting reflex which alters neurophysiological function. The orienting response may disrupt a "fused" physiological configuration of the traumatic associative memory network and so allow information processing to resume (Lipke, 1992). Armstrong and Vaughn (1994) have similarly suggested that the physiological orienting response triggered by eye movements may interrupt conditioned escape/avoidance behaviour. Marquis (1991) is more specific, proposing that such a deconditioning effect may be a result of field currents generated by the eye movements "which would interfere with the tracts connecting the frontal lobes to the hypothalamus and hippocampus and in such a way as to weaken the connection between stimulus and emotional response". However, as Shapiro (1995) points out, such theories alone would not account for the increase in positive emotions observed during treatment sessions.

Based on animal studies indicating that repetitive low-voltage currents may change the synaptic potentials that are related to memory processing, and the suggestion that neuronal bursts caused by eye movements may be equivalent to a low-voltage current, Shapiro (1992) has postulated that the changes seen in EMDR treatment may be explained by synaptic changes in mood–memory networks. Under this model, it is assumed that traumatic memories are stored in networks with high bioelectrical valences. Following neuronal bursts, the valence of such networks is shifted downwards so that they are capable of linking up with more adaptive networks. The notion is that any shaking up of the neurophysiological system will automatically lead towards a more adaptive resolution.

A related hypothesis concerns cortical functions. Shapiro (1989a) suggested that EMDR may have a direct influence on cortical functions which leads to a rebalancing of the information-processing system. Some support comes from a case study utilising qualitative electroencephalography (Nicosia, 1994) which showed a normalisation of the synchronisation of slower brain wave activity in homologous areas of the right and left hemispheres. Nicosia (1994) speculates that the rhythmical alternating stimulation during EMDR generates synchronising electrical impulses in the hypothalamus which correct the major phase discrepancy, resulting in increased interhemispheric communication between the two hemispheres and allowing reprocessing of traumatic memories to continue.

One of the most promising explanations of EMDR's underlying mechanism comes from a consideration of dream sleep. Recent work (Winson, 1993) suggests that one function of rapid eye movements (REM) during dream sleep may be concerned with the processing and storage of memory information. A number of other studies (e.g. Ross, Ball, Sullivan & Caroff, 1989) show that the REM state is dysfunctional in traumatised individuals, and Nicosia (1994) has suggested that this suppression of REM is due to the release of norepinephrine during the trauma. The hypothesis is that the alternating attention in EMDR may have the equivalent effects to REM sleep in consolidation of memories. While there is no direct support for this account of the effects of EMDR, it has good face validity and makes clear testable predictions.

Shapiro (1995) also reviews a number of other conjectures concerning the underlying mechanism at work in EMDR. These include distraction, hypnosis, and an induced relaxation response. The suggestion that distraction from the traumatic memory by concentration on eye movements prevents the traumatic memories from being reinforced by anticipatory anxiety seems oversimple, and has nothing to say about how traumatic memories are ultimately processed. Results of EEG studies during EMDR do not reveal the characteristic pronounced alpha, beta and theta waves seen during hypnosis, and therefore make hypnosis unlikely as an explanation of EMDR effects. There is some support for the argument that eye movements may induce a relaxation response (Wilson, Beeker & Tinker, 1995), thus inhibiting an anxiety response, but alternative stimuli such as finger tapping do not produce the same physiologically measured compelled relaxation.

Clearly, explanations of how and why EMDR might work are in their infancy. Common to all the hypotheses offered above is the notion that the processing of traumatic memories becomes blocked or fused at a neurophysiological level. The alternating stimulation in EMDR somehow loosens up frozen memory networks, allowing information processing to take place, the assumption being that any kind of processing will automatically reconfigure or rebalance the neurophysiological state towards an adaptive resolution. None of the models, however, provides a clear and specific account of how a neurophysiological reconfiguring might result in healthy psychological functioning. EMDR then involves a shift in what is regarded as an appropriate level of explanation in clinical psychology and psychotherapy, the emphasis being on physiological mechanisms, with mental states being regarded as byproducts. In the long term, one lasting effect of the EMDR phenomena may be a reconsideration of the kinds of explanation that clinical psychology should seek to provide. Pursuing some of the hypotheses outlined above may result in a broader understanding of the relationship between neurophysiological states and mental states.

EMDR WITH CHILDREN AND ADOLESCENTS

Although developed initially for work with adult trauma survivors, EMDR has been used with a variety of clinical populations, including children and adolescents. Published findings regarding the use of EMDR with children are scarce, but there are currently a number of positive case reports (e.g. Greenwald, 1994) and EMDR has been used with children as young as 4 years old.

The cautions above, about ensuring that adult clients can stop the procedure when they want to, apply equally to children, and the usual care must be taken with children in establishing a safe environment, gaining trust and maintaining rapport, explaining the procedure at an ability-appropriate level, and obtaining informed consent from parents as well as children. In general, EMDR with children tends to be concrete and imagery based, and there will clearly be less emphasis on the articulation of cognitions and emotions with younger children.

When children are referred, their parents will usually be seen first, and an additional focus of history taking will be on the identification of traumatic memories to target. Shapiro (1995) advises against seeing children with their parents, but this will sometimes be necessary with younger children. Parents may sometimes act as a client to demonstrate the safety of the procedure to their child. Before targeting traumatic memories, the therapist will usually complete a number of sets while the child holds a memory or image of a safe and pleasant place or experience in mind. This will be useful at the end of the session, but also helps to encourage trust and creates positive associations with the procedure.

Sets of eye movements or alternative stimulation will usually be shorter with children than with adults, and be interspersed with other activities. The therapist will be more active than with adults in helping the child to identify targets and in keeping the procedure moving through the use of play and other techniques. A variety of stimuli may be used. Most older children will be able to participate in the usual finger tracking and, with younger children, this might be aided with the use of a toy or puppet. For children who have difficulty tracking, the alternating finger method can be used (see page 271 above). Otherwise, finger clicking or hand tapping may be useful, or the child might be asked to focus on alternating spots on the wall.

Older children and adolescents will readily grasp the SUD rating technique, but for younger children, lines or circles of different sizes might be drawn, or the child can simply use his or her hands spread at different distances to indicate distress or discomfort.

Rapid changes in imagery are reported when working with children (Shapiro, 1995), but it is sometimes useful to facilitate change through asking the child to draw the image at intervals during the session, or encouraging him or her to "explode the picture" before the next set of eye movements or hand taps. With younger children, the therapist may help children to install a positive image rather than a positive cognition; and, with slightly older children, the therapist may suggest simple positive cognitions, such as "I'm fine". Greenwald (1994) suggests that installing positive images when working on children's nightmares is particularly effective. If the child dreams about being chased or attacked by monsters, it can help to install images of themselves with a laser gun, for example; if the child dreams about ghosts, it may be effective to install an image of him or her locking the ghost in a box. The VOC is rarely used following installation of positive cognitions or images with children.

At least one published case report (Cocco & Sharpe, 1993) has documented the use of a modified EMDR procedure with a pre-school-age child. A boy of 3 years 9 months had been caught up in a violent robbery at his home. At referral a year later, he met criteria for a diagnosis of PTSD, characterised in his case by separation difficulties, frequent nightmares and enuresis, talking about the event frequently, and seeking reassurance that it would not happen again. Instead of eye movements, auditory stimulation using finger clicks (see page 271) was used; and rather than visualising, the child drew a picture of the event and of his favourite superhero. Two sets of auditory stimulation were used, the first while looking at the picture of the event, and the second while looking at the picture of the superhero and saying what he would do. Following treatment, there was a dramatic reduction in symptoms. The boy ceased having nightmares, talking about the event, and seeking reassurance: these gains were maintained at six months follow-up. Although bedwetting stopped initially, it was back to pre-treatment levels by six months. This report is one of the few published accounts of a successful outcome with a very young child using EMDR, and provides a useful clinical description of adapting the technique. Limited inferences can be drawn from single case reports, and although the authors note that EMDR was the sole therapeutic tool used in treatment, it is unclear which of the components in treatment contributed to the successful outcome.

In summary, very rapid treatment effects are reported with children, and the few reports of a negative outcome are mostly concerned with non-compliance. The EMDR procedure can be imaginatively adapted for use with children. As yet, however, there are no outcome trials available and few published clinical reports: the procedure should therefore be used with care and flexibility by trained professionals until outcome evaluation data and reliable protocols are available.

CONCLUSIONS

Any new and effective treatment for post-traumatic stress is to be welcomed, and it is unfortunate that the debate about the usefulness of EMDR has recently become polarised and politicised. The initial flurry of excitement after its discovery and the publication of encouraging clinical reports has been countered by scepticism among academics and clinicians following mixed results in a limited number of controlled outcome evaluation trials. In a very short space of time, however, EMDR has become popular with clients and a large number of therapists. Dyregrov (1996) suggested recently that the politicisation of the EMDR debate is because, in common with Critical Incident Stress Debriefing, it threatens the power base of traditional psychotherapy: the rapidity of the method means a potential loss of clients to the therapy industry. A number of points should be noted. On the one hand, EMDR grew not out of the application of scientific principles to clinical problems, but was discovered by chance;

controlled outcome trials have not demonstrated its effectiveness over other treatments; and there is no underlying rationale for its effectiveness. Alternatively, a large number of clinicians testify to its efficacy; treatment effects are rapid and lasting with low attrition rates; and it is effective with a variety of disorders. In this polarisation of the debate, EMDR may caused disquiet among clinicians for two reasons, one misplaced and the other justified.

First, in EMDR, the therapist is seen to give up much of his or her traditional role in interacting with the client. No interpretations are made to the client; the therapist does not assist the client in talking through the trauma in detail; and the therapist may not even know enough of the client's experience in order to paraphrase, summarise, or reflect. It seems that few clinical skills are needed to carry out what is essentially a mechanistic procedure. This would be threatening to traditional psychotherapy were it true. It is not, however, and the therapist must call on all his or her clinical skills in assessment and treatment if intervention is to be successful. EMDR will most often be used as part of an overall treatment strategy, and even within the comprehensive EMDR protocol, assisting the client to complete saccadic eye movements is but one part of the procedure. Nevertheless, the misplaced perception of EMDR as an easy-to-administer quick fix for a large number of disorders makes many practitioners uncomfortable.

Second, EMDR seems such an unlikely procedure, and almost smacks of quackery: most importantly, no one understands how it works. Common to all of the initial suggestions about the underlying rationale for EMDR is a working assumption that neurophysiological states are primary: psychological explanations are thereby reduced to neurophysiological ones. This in itself is nothing new, but EMDR entails that neurophysiological states can be accessed directly, rapidly, and non-chemically; and that the brain is a self-righting system which will automatically work towards an adaptive resolution, of which a healthy mental state is a byproduct. While claims of a paradigm shift in clinical psychology seem premature until the effectiveness of the procedure has been demonstrated, further elucidation of the mechanisms underlying EMDR may help in refining information-processing models of PTSD and, more generally, of memory and emotional processing.

EMDR and other rapid treatment techniques, while in their infancy, remain potentially exciting and clinically useful. Further rigorous research is clearly necessary if the claims made for EMDR are to be verified. The search for an underlying rationale has only just begun and, in the long run, may be the most lasting effect of EMDR.

REFERENCES

Armstrong, N. & Vaughn, K. (1994). An orienting response model for EMDR. Paper presented at the meeting of the New South Wales Behaviour Therapy Interest Group, Sydney, Australia, June 1994.

Beck, A.T. (1978). Depression Inventory. Philadelphia: Centre for Cognitive Therapy.

Boudewyns, P.A., Hyer, L.A., Peralme, L., Touze, J. & Kiel, A. (1995). Eye movement desensitisation and reprocessing and exposure therapy in the treatment of combat related PTSD: and early look. Paper presented at the 102nd annual meeting of the American Psychiatric Association, Los Angeles, August 1995.

Boudewyns, P.A., Stwerka, S.A., Hyer, L.A., Albrecht, J.W. & Sperr, E.V. (1993). Eye movement desensitisation for PTSD of combat: A treatment outcome pilot study. *Behaviour Therapist*, **16**, 29–33.

Carlson, J.G., Chemtob, C.M., Rusnak, K. & Hedlund, N.L. (1995). A controlled study of EMDR and biofeedback assisted relaxation for the treatment of PTSD. Paper presented at the 4th European Conference on Traumatic Stress, Paris, France.

Coco, N. & Sharpe, L. (1993). An auditory variant of eye movement desensitization in a case of childhood post-traumatic stress disorder. *Journal of Behaviour Therapy and Experimental Psychiatry*, **24**, 373–377.

Derogatis, L.R. & Spencer, P.M. (1982). The Brief Symptom Inventory: Administration, Scoring, and Procedures Manual—I. Baltimore: Clinical Psychometric Instruments.

Derogatis, L.R., Rickels, K. & Rock, A.F. (1976). The SCL-90 and the MMPI: A step in the validation of a new self report scale. *British Journal of Psychiatry*, **128**, 280–289.

Dyregrov, A. (1996). The process in critical incident stress debriefings. Paper presented at the first European Conference on Traumatic Stress in Emergency Services, Peacekeeping Operations, and Humanitarian Aid Organisations, Sheffield, UK, March 1996.

Greenwald, R. (1994). Applying eye movement desensitisation and reprocessing (EMDR) to the treatment of traumatised children: Five case studies. *Anxiety Disorders Practice Journal*, **1**, 83–97.

Horowitz, M.D., Wilner, N. & Alvarez, W. (1979). Impact of event scale: A measure of subjective stress. *Psychosomatic Medicine*, **41**, 209–218.

Jensen, J.A. (1994). An investigation of eye movement desensitisation and reprocessing (EMD/R) as a treatment for post traumatic stress disorder (PTSD) symptoms of Vietnam combat veterans. *Behavior Therapy*, **25**, 311–326.

Keane, T.M., Caddell, J.M. & Taylor, K.L. (1986). The Mississippi scale for combat related PTSD: Three studies in reliability and validity. *Journal of Consulting and Clinical Psychology*, **56**, 85–90.

Kiresuk, T.J. & Sherman, R.E. (1968). Goal Attainment Scaling: General method for evaluating comprehensive community mental health programmes. *Community Mental Health*, **4**, 443–453.

Kleinknecht, R.A. & Morgan, P. (1992). Treatment of post traumatic stress disorder with eye movement desensitisation. *Journal of Behaviour Therapy and Experimental Psychiatry*, **23**, 43–49.

Levin, G., Grainger, R.K., Allen-Byrd, L. & Fulcher, G. (1994). Efficacy of eye movement desensitisation and reprocessing for survivors of Hurricane

Andrew: a comparative study. Paper presented at the 102nd annual meeting of the American Psychiatric Association, Los Angeles, August 1994.

Lipke, H. (1992). Manual for the teaching of Shapiro's EMDR in the treatment of combat related PTSD. Unpublished manuscript.

Lohr, J.M., Kleinknecht, R.A., Tolin, D.F. & Barrett, R.H. (1995). The empirical status of the clinical application of eye movement desensitisation and reprocessing. *Journal of Behaviour Therapy and Experimental Psychiatry*, **26**, 285–302.

McCann, D. (1992). Post traumatic stress disorder due to devastating burns overcome by a single session of eye movement desensitisation. *Journal of Behaviour Therapy and Experimental Psychiatry*, **23**, 319–323.

Marquis, J.N. (1991). A report on seventy-eight cases treated by eye movement desensitisation. *Journal of Behaviour Therapy and Experimental Psychiatry*, **22**, 187–192.

Nicosia, G. (1994). A mechanism for dissociation suggested by the quantitative analysis of electroencephalography. Paper presented at the International EMDR Annual Conference, Sunnyvale, CA, March 1994.

Puk, G. (1991). Treating traumatic memories: A case report on the eye movement desensitisation procedure. *Journal of Behaviour Therapy and Experimental Psychiatry*, **22**, 149–151.

Rachman, S. (1980). Emotional processing. *Behaviour Research and Therapy*, **18**, 51–60.

Renfrey, G. & Spates, C.R. (1994). Eye movement desensitisation and reprocessing: A partial dismantling procedure. *Journal of Behaviour Therapy and Experimental Psychiatry*, **25**, 231–239.

Ross, R.J., Ball, W.A., Sullivan, K.A. & Caroff, S.N. (1989). Sleep disturbance as the hallmark of post traumatic stress disorder. *American Journal of Psychiatry*, **146**, 697–707.

Rothbaum, B.O. (1995). A controlled study for of EMDR for PTSD. Paper presented at the 29th Annual Convention of the Association for the Advancement of Behaviour Therapy, Washington DC, November 1995.

Shapiro, F. (1989a). Eye movement desensitisation: A new treatment for post traumatic stress disorder. *Journal of Behaviour Therapy and Experimental Psychiatry*, **20**, 211–217.

Shapiro, F. (1989b). Efficacy of the eye movement desensitisation procedure in the treatment of traumatic memories. *Journal of Traumatic Stress Studies*, **2**, 199–223.

Shapiro, F. (1992). Stray thoughts: Frozen in childhood/bio-electrical valence. *EMDR Network Newsletter*, **2**, 1–2.

Shapiro, F. (1995). *Eye Movement Desensitisation and Reprocessing: Basic Principles, Protocols and Procedures*. New York: Guilford Press.

Silver, S.M., Brooks, A. & Obenchain, J. (1995). Eye movement desensitisation and reprocessing treatment of Vietnam war veterans with PTSD: Comparative effects wit biofeedback and relaxation training. *Journal of Traumatic Stress*, **8**, 337–342.

Spielberger, C.D. (1974). *Manual for the State-Trait Anxiety Inventory (Form Y)*. Palo Alto: Consulting Psychologists Press.

Vaughn, K., Armstrong, M.F., Gold, R., O'Connor, N., Jenneke, W. & Tarrier, N. (1994). A trial of eye movement desensitisation compared to image habituation training and applied muscle relaxation in post traumatic stress disorder. *Journal of Behaviour Therapy and Experimental Psychiatry*, **25**, 283–291.

Watson, C.G., Juba, M.P., Manifold, V., Kucala, T. & Anderson, P. (1991). The PTSD interview: Rationale, description, reliability and concurrent validity of a DSM-III based technique. *Journal of Clinical Psychology*, **47**, 179–188.

Weissman, M., Sholomkas, D., Pottenger, M., Prusoff, B. & Locke, B. (1977). Assessing depressive symptoms in five psychiatric populations: A validation study. *American Journal of Epidemiology*, **106**, 203–214.

Wilson, D., Covi, W., Foster, S. & Silver, S.M. (1995). Eye movement desensitisation and reprocessing and ANS correlates in the treatment of PTSD. Paper presented at the 148th annual meeting of the American Psychiatric Association, Miami, FL, May 1995.

Wilson, S.A., Becker, L.A. & Tinker, R.H. (1995). Eye movement desensitisation and reprocessing (EMDR) treatment for psychologically traumatised individuals. *Journal of Consulting and Clinical Psychology*, **63**, 928–937.

Winson, J. (1993). The biology and function of rapid eye movement sleep. *Current Opinion in Neurobiology*, **3**, 243–47.

Wolpe, J. & Abrams, J. (1991). Post-traumatic stress disorder overcome by eye movement desensitisation: A case report. *Journal of Behaviour Therapy and Experimental Psychiatry*, **22**, 39–43.

Chapter 14

PLANNING A PSYCHOSOCIAL RESPONSE TO A DISASTER

Rachel Canterbury* and William Yule*

In recent years there has been increasing interest in the psychosocial consequences of disasters. Although they remain statistically rare events, the last decade saw an increase in the number of major incidents affecting the UK. These included the Bradford City Fire, the King's Cross Fire, the Piper Alpha sinking, the Hungerford shootings, the Lockerbie air crash, terrorist bombings in London and Brighton and the sinking of *The Marchioness* pleasure boat. In addition, UK residents were involved in a number of disasters outside the UK, such as the sinking of the *Herald of Free Enterprise* and the cruise ship *Jupiter*. This list is by no means exhaustive, but illustrates that disasters occur with sufficient frequency and with such cost to those involved as to warrant increased attention. Recognition that disasters carry a risk to mental health has led to calls for post-trauma intervention strategies aimed at reducing psychosocial morbidity. However, it is apparent that the provision of psychosocial care following a major incident raises many complex issues, which as yet are far from being resolved.

BACKGROUND

It is now widely accepted that a significant proportion of people exposed to large-scale disasters go on to develop severe and prolonged psychological reactions. Disorders following severe trauma include post-traumatic stress disorder (PTSD), depression, anxiety, alcohol and substance abuse, dissociative disorders and profound personality change, and rates of co-morbidity are high. There have been no UK epidemiological studies to

*Institute of Psychiatry, London

Post-Traumatic Stress Disorders: Concepts and Therapy. Edited by William Yule.
© 1999 John Wiley & Sons Ltd.

assess rates of PTSD but a recent US survey estimated the lifetime prevalence of the disorder to be 7.8% (Kessler, Sonnega, Bromet, Hughes &
Nelson, 1995). Clearly not all those exposed to disasters will suffer post-
traumatic stress disorders. Raphael (1986) concluded that, in the first week
following a disaster, stress reactions are seen in 20–70% of the affected
population, falling to 30–40% at one year. There is some further reduction
at two years but 15–20% will experience chronic levels of anxiety that will
remain high for more than two years.

DEFINITIONS OF DISASTERS

Within the UK there is no one agreed definition of a disaster, with variations even between government departments (Home Office, 1992). Indeed
there are more than 40 different definitions of disaster in the literature
(Korver, 1987), reflecting the complex, multidimensional nature of the
phenomenon. Factors commonly associated with disasters are that they
are sudden, unpredictable, uncontrollable, involve actual or threatened
loss of life or property, can disrupt or destroy communities, and often give
rise to adverse psychological consequences for survivors. However, what
is considered a disaster by one community may not be perceived as such
by another. Furthermore, the assignation of the label "disaster" may influence both the amount of help offered and the emotional impact of the
event on those involved.

PSYCHOSOCIAL RESPONSES TO DISASTERS

The planning of a psychosocial response to a disaster needs to take account of the enormous variability in psychosocial morbidity following
such events. Levels of distress and the need for intervention will vary
across different disaster situations; across different groups involved in the
same disaster, for example, primary victims, bereaved relatives and
rescue workers; among individuals within these groups; and over time. It
is therefore essential that psychosocial response plans are comprehensive
but flexible. Response plans also need to take account of the characteristics
of the communities they are intended to serve and the resources available
to provide such a response.

Raphael, Wilson, Meldrum and McFarlane (1996) suggest that, in the
immediate aftermath of a disaster, a human and compassionate response
is needed, focusing on safety and survival and the assessment and management of physical injury or threat to life. They point out that, at this

stage, individuals may not be able or willing to talk about their experience. However, some gentle questioning is important to identify those in need of immediate mental health care and those at risk of developing chronic stress reactions. If done supportively, this triage procedure can itself be therapeutic by facilitating the commencement of an integrative working-through process (Raphael, 1986). Ultimately, practical help may be perceived as more useful than specific psychological care (Singh & Raphael, 1981). Providing accurate information and aiding a reunion with family and friends may be invaluable to acute recovery and in preventing psychological problems in the longer term. McFarlane (1987) found that separations of children from parents at this time could lead to adverse effects later.

In the weeks and months following a disaster the differing needs of those involved will become apparent, and psychosocial support should be tailored to meet those needs. The role of psychological debriefing for survivors and workers following disasters was discussed in Chapter 11 of this volume. For those suffering more severe and prolonged traumatic stress reactions, more specific psychological interventions may be required and skilled practitioners should be available to undertake this work. Support for bereaved relatives may be needed over a prolonged period. In addition to bereavement counselling, relatives may need help to cope with tasks such as the identification of bodies, inquests, funerals and memorial services. Systematic but sensitive follow-up is essential to ensure that those affected by disasters receive help appropriate to their needs.

A number of agencies are likely to be involved in the provision of a psychosocial response, including health services, social services and the voluntary sector, and they will bring a range of skills and experience to the disaster situation. Joint planning and training prior to a disaster are essential if best use is to be made of these resources when a disaster occurs.

It is not possible to discuss all the aspects of a psychosocial response in detail, but some of the principles can be summarised as follows (adapted from Adshead, Canterbury & Rose, 1993):

Basic requirements for psychosocial care plans following disasters

1. Services need to be multidisciplinary, multi-agency, and provide services for all those potentially affected by the disaster, but particularly primary victims, bereaved relatives and disaster workers.
2. Services need to be prompt in their response and, where possible, based on an existing traumatic stress service.

3. Special disaster services need to be available for at least three years if there is no existing traumatic stress service, and one year if there is an existing service.
4. Funds need to be made available at the time of the disaster to provide extra manpower and training. Funding needs to be flexible; local managers/fundholders need to be educated about the needs of disaster survivors.
5. Multidisciplinary work and multi-agency work will be required at different times.
6. Ongoing training and exercises are required between disasters, and funds will be required for this.
7. Liaison and communication between agencies is essential and must formally extend over geographical boundaries.
8. Leaflets containing information about traumatic stress responses should be prepared beforehand and staff instructed in their use.
9. There should be provision for data collection and follow-up of those affected by the disaster.

Tasks of a psychosocial response team following a disaster

1. Formation of a core team at the time of the disaster to coordinate the response, identify needs and activate other response networks. The core team should include a psychologist, psychiatrist, suitably trained nurses, social services, and voluntary personnel.
2. Respond to the needs of (i) distressed survivors, including the non-injured, walking wounded and the more severely injured, (ii) distressed relatives.
3. Debrief emergency personnel and other support workers, if there is no existing facility.
4. Identification of special groups such as children or the elderly.
5. Identification of groups at high risk of long-term problems, for example those with a previous psychiatric history.
6. Facilitate research.
7. Review and revision of the psychosocial response after stand down of the core team.

ORGANISATIONAL ISSUES

The various disasters in the UK in the 1980s revealed a tremendous willingness on the part of many individuals and agencies, including social services, health services and the voluntary sector, to offer support and to develop new skills to address the psychosocial needs of those involved in these traumatic events. However, these disasters also exposed many of the difficulties associated with the provision of psychosocial care. Those attempting to provide psychosocial support frequently found that there were no plans in place to guide their efforts. There was a lack of prior training in the nature of post-traumatic stress responses and approaches to psychosocial management and intervention. Services were often already overstretched and additional resources to support an emergency response were often very limited or non-existent. There were problems of poor inter-agency communication with the result that some survivors felt themselves to be plagued by offers of help, while others received no help at all. The problem of coordinating the provision of services was even greater when survivors came from a wide geographical area, often crossing many administrative boundaries.

Two reports have attempted to examine these issues and to make recommendations regarding the future planning of psychosocial responses to disaster. The first is the report of the Disasters Working Party (Allen, 1991), funded by the Department of Health. The Allen Report recommended that local authority social services departments should take the lead role in managing psychosocial needs following disaster, in association with health authorities and other agencies such as voluntary organisations. Guidelines were developed for each agency, identifying tasks to be addressed in planning prior to a disaster, at the time of impact of the disaster, and in the longer term. The areas of responsibility assigned to the director of the lead agency, usually the Director of Social Services of the local authority, included: immediate support; administrative resources; the coordination of voluntary and statutory organisations; the provision of social and psychological services; the provision, training and support of staff; media relations; and formal public relations. The report stressed that such services should be available for a considerable length of time, which has substantial resource implications. It was also suggested that all local authorities should prepare social and psychological support plans as part of emergency planning procedures, and emphasised the need for regular liaison with heads of the emergency services, health and voluntary agencies.

Health authorities were encouraged to ensure that their services, particularly psychological and psychiatric services, were incorporated into local authority plans. It was suggested that health authorities should take responsibility for the care of staff involved in disaster work by providing psychological debriefing. General practitioners were identified as having an important role in diagnosing stress responses and directing sufferers to appropriate services. Voluntary organisations were also seen as having a particular role in the care of disaster workers and, again, it was recommended that their role should be outlined in local authority plans. Joint planning and training exercises involving all agencies were seen as vital. Importantly, the report extended its recommendations to include other agencies such as the police, central government departments, the Press Council, other relevant professional bodies, industry, coroners and chairmen of disaster inquiries, in each case highlighting ways in which these agencies could contribute to an effective psychosocial response. Unfortunately, it is not clear how many of the recommendations of the Allen Report have since been adopted.

The role of health services in providing psychosocial care following disasters was further discussed in a report by Adshead, Canterbury and Rose (1993). This report was also supported by the Department of Health, which asked for advice on the optimal provision of services for victims of major incidents and emergencies. The research team examined the extent to which the English regional health authorities had included provision for psychological care in their emergency plans. It was anticipated that, despite the findings of the Allen Report and the abundance of published studies on the prevalence and severity of post-traumatic stress disorders following disasters, there would be little evidence of planning for psychological care.

Letters were sent to the 14 regional departments of public health enquiring about the psychosocial care element of their major incident plans. Most of the letters were passed on to the regional health emergency planning officers. Specifically, the team sought to discover the provision that was made for the psychological care of victims at regional level; whether regional plans were kept under review; and whether they provided for the full spectrum of potential victims. Information was also sought as to whether a lead agency was identified for the provision of a psychosocial response; whether the plans specified the timing and duration of the response; and whether there had been any estimate of the potential costs of an adequate psychosocial response. In addition, the researchers were invited to attend working groups in two regions that were developing psychosocial response plans. Information was also sought from a number of health districts. Finally, semi-structured interviews were conducted with various professionals in the field including psychiatrists, psychologists, social workers, emergency services personnel and local authority emergency planning officers.

The study found that provision for a psychosocial response was mentioned in most regional plans. However, this provision tended to be general rather than specific and there was an emphasis on hospital-based services with little psychosocial provision except for the injured attending accident and emergency departments. It was frequently assumed that the work would be carried out by chaplains and social workers based in the hospital. There was little mention of provision for relatives or communities, although all regions showed an awareness of the importance of staff care. In contrast, three health regions had adopted a code of practice ensuring a comprehensive psychosocial response, with the suggestion that each district health authority should identify a clinical psychologist who would coordinate the psychosocial response to a disaster by different agencies. Fifty per cent of regions said that they were reviewing psychosocial planning but many were candid in saying that they did not know the level of provision in their districts and were unaware of the clinical services available for sufferers of post-traumatic stress.

Some regions appeared to have accepted the recommendation of the Allen Report that the local authority should be the lead agency in the provision of psychosocial care, and their plans were based around this. Others saw provision of psychosocial care as a health response, entirely separate from local authority responses. Regardless of which agency was designated the lead role, there appeared to be little communication between the various agencies that might be involved, namely health and local authorities and the voluntary sector. In many regions there was no mention of timing and duration of the response and there appeared to be little recognition of the long-term needs of those who develop chronic psychological disorder as a result of a disaster, nor of those who develop problems months or even years after the event. No regional health authority appeared to have made any estimation of possible cost implications of providing a psychosocial response.

In preparing their report, Adshead, Canterbury and Rose stressed the importance of providing services to people suffering post-traumatic stress disorders arising from traumatic events other than large-scale disasters, such as accidents or crime. This is reflected in their recommendations. At an organisational level, it was argued that local and accessible specialist units should be provided to meet the needs of those suffering traumatic stress reactions. These could be related to proposed new health region boundaries. It was suggested that strategies should be in place for the rapid expansion of the service in the event of a local large-scale disaster. Such units could then take responsibility for liaison with other agencies; developing links with similar provider units, to provide effective cross-boundary cover; negotiating funding for both day-to-day and emergency services; and, where possible, make links with academic departments to facilitate research. These units would also be required to undertake a systematic audit and evaluation of their work. The authors agreed that those in need of traumatic stress services should be able to obtain help locally and that local agencies were best placed to initiate such interventions and to liaise with each other. It was therefore recommended that health districts and district hospital major incident plans should include a plan for psychosocial care complementary to those plans held by local authorities.

RESEARCH AND TRAINING

Psychosocial response plans need to be constantly updated to take account of changes in the organisation of statutory services both at a local and a national level. However, both the planning and provision of a psychosocial response are expensive. For example, the cost to the local authority of running the Herald Assistance Unit for 15 months following the sinking of the *Herald of Free Enterprise* in 1987 was £320,000 (Hodgkinson & Stewart, 1991). From a health perspective, one-quarter of the psychotherapy budget was used in treating survivors of the Hungerford shootings, two years after the incident (Jane Knowles, head of West Berkshire Psychotherapy Service, personal communication). It is therefore essential that social and psychological care following disasters is adequately audited and evaluated and that this information is then disseminated. The planning and provision of psychosocial responses to disaster also needs to take account of the ever-growing body of literature on post-traumatic stress responses and evaluation of specific psychological interventions.

As well as training specific to a disaster response, there is a general need to increase the level of knowledge about psychological reactions to trauma. The majority of people suffering from post-traumatic stress disorders have been exposed to individual or small-scale traumas such as accidents or crime rather than disasters. Thus a wide range of professions, including social workers, health care professionals and lawyers, need to be educated about post-traumatic stress, its natural history and prognosis. GPs, psychologists and psychiatrists, in particular, need to develop skills in the assessment and treatment of traumatic stress reactions. Such a broadening of knowledge and skills would increase the resources available at the time of a disaster and would facilitate a more effective response.

THE NEEDS OF CHILDREN FOLLOWING DISASTERS

It is generally recognised that the needs of children following disasters have received relatively little attention by those professionals charged with planning a psychosocial response (Black & Harris-Hendricks, 1997). Neither of the main UK Department of Health sponsored reports (Allen, 1991; Adshead, Canterbury & Rose, 1993) devoted much space to considering the needs of children, although the Allen Report included a very useful appendix by Black (1991), pointing out the many different needs of children.

As discussed earlier (Yule, Chapter 2 in this volume), children may react to a severe trauma or disaster with a wide range of stress, anxiety, depression and bereavement reactions. In particular, and unlike adult reactions, they often show severe separation anxiety and hence it is important that any plans should ensure that children are reunited with their parents or caretakers as soon as possible. It is worth considering whether such a reunion should take place where the accident occurred so that the children can experience the cues associated with the disaster but in the comforting presence of their parent.

The advice of the Allen Report (1991) concentrated on ensuring good cooperation across different helping agencies and suggested that Social Service Departments be given the lead role in dealing with the psychosocial response to disasters. However, children spend a great deal of time in school and, indeed, many of the disasters that affect them directly may occur on the way to or from school, during school hours, or on school journeys. Hence, in planning a psychosocial response to meet the needs of children and adolescents, the school and education authorities must have a much more central role.

This was the thinking behind the booklet written for schools (Yule & Gold, 1993). The argument was that schools provide a framework for stability and continuity in the lives of most children. Whether they are traumatised at school or elsewhere, repercussions will be felt at school and so it is important that schools are aware of this and plan accordingly. Fortunately, most schools will never have to face a major disaster where many children are killed or maimed, but, equally, most schools will have to confront and deal with the effects on pupils and staff of such incidents as a teacher dying, a pupil being killed in an accident on the way to school, or arson destroying property and also threatening lives.

In *Wise Before the Event* (Yule & Gold, 1993) there are strong recommendations that all schools should develop their own contingency plans, identify senior personnel with particular responsibilities and liaise regularly with local child mental health services so that as and when a disaster occurs, there is a greater likelihood of a rational response to the crisis.

INTERNATIONAL PERSPECTIVES

It is well to note that much of what has been discussed has related to a British perspective. Disasters happen all over the world and the precise ways in which psychosocial responses are organised will depend on the way in which local services are developed, the nature and the extent of the disaster, and the resources that remain to deal with it. Other countries have developed their own plans relevant to their situations, and the World Health Organisation (1992) has issued guidelines on the prevention and management of the psychosocial consequences of disasters.

Most such publications recognise that the first need of survivors is to be safe and have their basic needs for food, clothing and shelter met. Based on the adage that early intervention is better than later treatment, most advocate some crisis intervention for survivors even within the first few hours. As we have seen in relation to debriefing (Canterbury and Yule, Chapter 11 in this volume) there is increasing awareness that the timing of such interventions for the primary survivors (as opposed to the emergency personnel) may be crucial with inappropriate interventions causing more harm than good. Somehow, the mental health team needs to make contact with survivors but not necessarily do more than help them settle and get reunited in the first few hours.

It is now clear that large-scale disasters, such as the Armenian earthquake or the Japanese earthquake, will require the mobilisation of considerable resources often internationally. UN agencies such as WHO, UNICEF, UNHCR, International Red Cross and Red Crescent, and UNESCO are among the main international agencies with experience of mounting large-scale emergency responses to disasters in time of peace or war. There are many other humanitarian NGOs (Non-Governmental Organisations) such as Save the Children, Médecins sans Frontières, CARE International, Oxfam, and so on, that now see a major role in providing psychosocial help as well as meeting emergency supply needs and physical rebuilding.

This widespread recognition of the need for the international community to respond to the psychosocial needs of a particular group brings its own challenge. There is little disagreement as to the desirability of helping, but considerable disagreement on how best to do so. Following the Armenian earthquake, Pynoos et al. (1993) organised groups of volunteers, many from the Armenian Diaspora, to go to the affected area and train and support local personnel in providing first aid and specialist therapy in dealing with the post-traumatic stress disorders shown by the children. Careful documentation showed that children in Armenia reacted similarly to children elsewhere in the world and benefited from the structured intervention.

However, others warn against imposing "western" concepts of disorder on populations in diverse cultures. As discussed elsewhere (de Silva, Chapter 6 in this volume) while there are a few conditions that manifest differently in different cultures, as far as stress reactions are concerned there are many more similarities across cultures than there are differences. Obviously, any organisation that intends to help people in another country must respect the ways in which things are done there, unless they contravene the UN Conventions on Human Rights. Some cultures make it easier than others for people to acknowledge emotional problems and each may have different routes to obtaining help. The task of the international organisations and their consultants must be to increase the local capacity to cope with the demands on services and to provide such training and support that new services are sustainable long after the initial emergency is over. Currently, many organisations are finding it difficult to move from the emergency phase to the reconstruction phase in war-torn areas such as Bosnia, Chechneya and Rwanda.

OVERVIEW

With the greater acceptance that, following major disasters, a significant proportion of survivors will have short-or long-term mental health needs, various proposals have been made to ensure a better coordination of services and so a more effective delivery of services at a time when the demand is likely to place any mental health service under strain. Different solutions will be appropriate in different countries according to how their services are already organised. Within the United Kingdom, it is broadly accepted that Social Service Departments should take the lead in coordinating psychosocial responses, although not all authorities have yet developed adequate cross-departmental plans. As far as children are concerned, education authorities and schools have a major role to play.

On the international scene, many UN agencies and NGOs have begun to work in difficult circumstances to try to meet the needs of populations following war and natural disasters. Some of these interventions are beginning to be properly evaluated and it appears that methods worked out to deal with disasters in the UK, USA and Australia have an important role elsewhere, although there will always be local sensitivities that have to be borne in mind. It is to be hoped that where international and national services are set up, the effects of any services offered will be properly evaluated using the types of measures discussed elsewhere in this volume.

REFERENCES

Adshead, G., Canterbury, R. & Rose, S. (1993). *Current Provision and Recommendations for the Management of Psychosocial Morbidity Following Disaster in England.* London: Institute of Psychiatry, University of London.

Allen, A.J. (1991). *The Disasters Working Party. Planning for a Caring Response.* London: HMSO.

Black, D. (1991). Children's needs following a disaster. Appendix IID in A.J. Allen (Ed.), op. cit.

Black, D. & Harris-Hendricks, J. (1997). Organising psychosocial responses to disasters. Chapter 26 in D. Black, M. Newman, J. Harris-Hendricks & G. Mezey (Eds.), *Psychological Trauma: A Developmental Approach.* London: Gaskell.

Hodgkinson, P.E. & Stewart, M. (1991). *Coping with Catastrophe: A Handbook of Disaster Management.* London: Routledge.

Home Office (1992). *Dealing with Disaster* (HC90). London: HMSO.

Kessler, R.C., Sonnega, A., Bromet, E., Hughes, M. & Nelson, C.B. (1995). Posttraumatic stress disorder in the national comorbidity survey. *Archives of General Psychiatry*, **52**, 1048–1060.

Korver, A.J.H. (1987). What is a disaster? *Hospital and Disaster Medicine*, **2**, 152–153.

McFarlane, A.C. (1987). Post-traumatic phenomena in a longitudinal study of children following a natural disaster. *Journal of the American Academy of Child and Adolescent Psychiatry*, **26**, 764–769.

Pynoos, R.S., Goenjian, A., Karakashian, M., Tashjian, M., Manjikian, R., Manoukian, G., Steinberg, A.M. & Fairbanks, L.A. (1993). Posttraumatic stress reactions in children after the 1988 Armenian earthquake. *British Journal of Psychiatry*, **163**, 239–247.

Raphael, B. (1986). *When Disaster Strikes.* New York: Basic Books.

Raphael, B., Wilson, J., Meldrum, L. & McFarlane, A.C. (1996). Acute preventive interventions. In van der Kolk, B. A., McFarlane, A.C. & Weisaeth, L. (Eds.), *Traumatic Stress: The Effects of Overwhelming Experience on Mind, Body and Society.* New York: Guilford Press.

Singh, B. & Raphael, B. (1981). Postdisaster morbidity in the bereaved: A possible role for preventive psychiatry? *Journal of Nervous and Mental Disease*, **169** (4), 203–212.

World Health Organisation (1992). *Psychosocial Consequences of Disasters: Prevention and Management.* Geneva: WHO, Division of Mental Health.

Yule, W. & Gold, A. (1993). *Wise Before the Event: Coping with Crises in Schools.* London: Calouste Gulbenkian Foundation.

Chapter 15

CONCLUSIONS: AN INTEGRATIVE PSYCHOSOCIAL MODEL OF PTSD

Ruth Williams* and Stephen Joseph[†]

In Chapter 1, we began to outline the multifactorial view we have taken in accounting for post-trauma reactions and their variability between individuals. We have referred to the importance of a number of factors in determining the responses of individuals: their personality and individual history; their emotional states at the time of the event and subsequently; the objective nature of the event characteristics; the individual's appraisals of the event and of their emotional states and coping behaviours; their coping behaviours and the responses of others in the post-trauma environment. We have seen these factors as interacting in complex and relatively unexplored ways to account for an individual's state at any particular point in time after the event. We have suggested that these interrelationships may change over time as an individual adjusts to the implications of an event. The symptoms of PTSD emerge as the observable products of this process of adaptation.

In this final chapter we will begin by briefly restating our hypotheses as proposed in the most recent presentation of the model (Joseph, Williams & Yule, 1997) and then consider the implications of the material in this volume contributed by ourselves and our colleagues. We will conclude by raising the most important areas which, in our view, require experimental investigation in taking our understanding further.

*Institute of Psychiatry, London, and [†]University of Essex, Colchester

Post-Traumatic Stress Disorders: Concepts and Therapy. Edited by William Yule.
© 1999 John Wiley & Sons Ltd.

TOWARDS AN INTEGRATIVE
PSYCHOSOCIAL MODEL

Since we are describing a complex process involving an interrelating set of factors, there is some difficulty in expressing this in continuous prose. The main components of the system and their interrelationships are presented in the form of a flow diagram (Figure 15.1). For convenience, the description starts with the traumatic event and continues in a clockwise direction through event cognitions, appraisals, states, coping, appraisals with cognitions being influenced by both personality and/or memory representations and the social environment, culminating in either a repeating circular flow through this cycle or in changes within the representional store that constitute resolution and recovery of state and function. The description is an abbreviated version of that given in Joseph, Williams and Yule (op. cit.)

The occurrence of a traumatic event gives rise to cognitive representations of *event stimuli* being held in memory, due to their personal salience and to the difficulty they present for easy assimilation with other stored representations. These *event cognitions* take two forms: information that is not

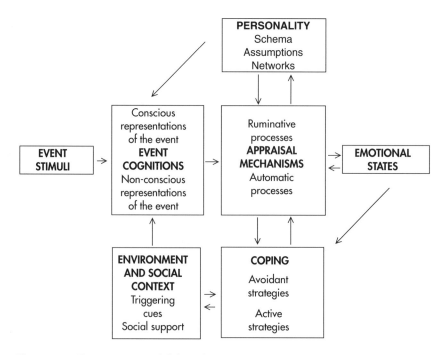

Figure 15.1 Integrative model for adaptation to traumatic stress

available to conscious inspection and information which is intentionally retrievable (after Brewin, Dalgleish & Joseph, 1996). *Event cognitions* provide the basis for the re-experiencing phenomena of PTSD. They are affected by idiosyncratic aspects of the individual's past experience, personality and beliefs and the specific components of the individual's unique experience that presented the greatest subjective threat (i.e they are a product of top-down as well as bottom-up processing).

Event cognitions (often images) form the subject of a further cognitive activity called *appraisal*. Appraisal cognitions are distinguished from event cognitions in being thoughts *about* the information depicted and its further meanings, drawing more extensively and consciously upon representations of past experience in memory and/or aspects of personality. These *appraisal cognitions* might take two forms: automatic thoughts (Beck, 1976) associated with schematic activation and strong emotional states and *reappraisals*, conscious thinking through of alternative meanings, influenced by disclosure to others in the social network (and by memory store, emotional states and coping behaviours). These *appraisal cognitions* might be considered as ruminative behaviour and they constitute a further form of intrusive cognition.

The occurrence of event cognitions and appraisal mechanisms may give rise to the generation of strong *emotional states*, which themselves are capable of becoming the subject of appraisal and reappraisal. As a result of the appraisal processes, emotional states are capable of generating secondary emotional states (e.g. shame about fear, depression about anger, etc.).

The occurrence of these cognitions and emotional states may be distress and attempts at *coping*, including avoidance of thoughts and behaviours. One component of avoidance may be worry, voluntary ruminative activity directed at problem solving and the avoidance of negative imagery (after Wells & Matthews, 1994). It is suggested that some successful avoidance may be an important aspect of adaptive coping but that too much emotional suppression (a type of avoidance) will result in the emotional state of numbness and the dissociation of cognitive and emotional processes. Cognitive suppression (avoidance of cognitions) will result in the recurrence of event cognitions (after Wegner, Shortt, Blake & Page, 1990).

An important aspect of coping will be the seeking of *social support* from the environment. Input from others can interact via appraisal mechanisms to affect the individual's meaning attributions, emotional states, coping and memory stores in a helpful manner or in a way to induce more distress or maintain problematic states.

Ultimately the outcome of many repetitions through the adaption cycle may be the reconciliation of appraisals of event cognitions with memory representations (assimilation) and the adjustment of prior beliefs and/or aspects of personality to take account of new information. The specification of how personality and the experiences of individual development are stored in memory currently encompasses differing concepts such as associative networks, cognitive styles, schema and other theoretical models (Teasdale & Barnard, 1993). This part of the model awaits further work.

Children and Adolescents

To date we have discussed our integrative model with respect to post-traumatic reactions in adults. Chapter 2 of this volume has drawn attention to an increasing recognition in recent years of equivalent patterns of symptoms in children and adolescents where the appropriate questions have been asked. Hence, it may be that the model is applicable to children too, although earlier discussion of risk and protective factors in children has raised a question about the importance of cognitive development to the capacity in younger children for full-scale PTSD. Our model would imply that established expectations are important, as is the ability to read abstract significance into events. It could be, as was suggested in Chapter 2, that the youngest children are protected by their immature cognitive development and that cognitively precocious younger children may be particularly vulnerable.

The importance to the younger child that has been noted of the reactions of parents is consistent with the importance we ascribe, in general, to the response of the social environment. It may be that this is an especially important factor in younger children whose conceptual world is largely mediated by their parents' responses.

Attributional Processes and Coping

Chapter 3's discussion of attributional process and coping has provided some highly relevant content to the abstract cognitive-behavioural features of our model outlined above, as well as the beginnings of empirical exploration. Joseph has proposed that causal attributional processes play an important part in the cognitive processes of appraisal and reappraisal. Specifically, appraisal of an event as uncontrollable and unpredictable will motivate attempts to establish a cause in order to render the world safe once more. In addition, he has suggested that understanding of causation will also be motivated by a need to preserve self-esteem. Thus Joseph adds to the model by providing a cognitive account of the motivation driving the adaptational processes (what Horowitz has termed the "completion tendency"). He also makes a link between such uncontrollability, unpredictability and low self-worth in PTSD and hope-lessness theory, providing another hypothetical explanation in the nature of attributional appraisals for prevalent depressive features inherent in and co-morbid with PTSD.

In discussing allocation of responsibility and blame, Joseph examines the consequences of self and other attributions for emotional states and coping, pointing to the need to preserve control, predictability and self-esteem and to the possible need for complex attributions to resolve difficult emotional conflicts. Negative emotional states consequent to attributional outcomes, such as guilt and shame, may be closely related to specific coping strategies involving reparation on the one hand or social withdrawal on the other.

Finally, Joseph examines attributional style as an enduring personality characteristic that may predict post-traumatic vulnerability. But, consist-ent with the reflexivity of our model, he also suggests that attributional style may be a cognitive factor which can be affected by the processes of appraisal in response to a trauma.

Social Support

Chapter 4 introduces and discusses a range of findings and issues in relation to social support that fills out a component of our integrative model that has lacked concrete content. In doing so Joseph brings into our largely cognitive-behavioural model important considerations of interpersonal needs that such models have largely ignored. He presents important longitudinal evidence from our own research which has dem-onstrated the predictive role of support in reducing distress in disaster survivors.

Joseph makes distinctions within the definition of social support to point to differing interpersonal needs for emotional, cognitive and practical support that may vary with time in the process of adaptation. Cognitive support is related to "account making": the facilitation of the individuals' making a coherent narrative about their experiences to include attribu-tions of causation and responsibility, together with expression of negative emotions.

Contact with others can be perceived as helpful or hurtful. Examining responses viewed as negative, Joseph highlights criticism and absence of expressions of concern and, interestingly examines the role of the survivors' self-presentation in eliciting positive support.

This analysis makes a timely link with communication analysis, which forms an important component of Interpersonal Psychotherapy (Klerman & Weismann, 1984) and has recently received increasing interest in studies of therapy for depression and eating disorders (Elkin et al., 1989). Joseph points to the possible relevance of attachment styles and how they may—mediated by cognitive factors—be related to post-traumatic distress and coping.

In the context of our integrative model, these considerations of inter-personal relationships are comfortably compatible and integrated with a cognitive-behavioural analysis, the model offering a means for analysing the individual case and deciding on priorities for intervention.

Personality

Consistent with our reflexive model, Chapter 5 has attempted to separate out different relationships between personality and PTSD: characterological vulnerability to post-traumatic stress; personality and maintenance of disorder; the effect of PTSD upon personality; and the view of PTSD as representing a personality style. These relationships are represented in our model by the bidirectional influences between appraisal processes and personality, with appraisal forming the mediating mechanism between personality, emotion and coping.

The review of the literature presented in Chapter 5 has made it clear that many personality concepts and theories are in use, with none dominating the field. Particularly troublesome is the absence of research exploring the correspondences between competing frames of reference. In particular, it would be interesting to see the correspondence between measures of self-efficacy or self-esteem and the more traditional personality dimensions. The recently emerging five-factor theory is beginning to be used in PTSD research with some interesting relationships being found, although not always consistent, with factors other than neuroticism, such as openness and agreeableness. These latter factors may prove to be important in considerations of adaptation to change that PTSD crucially involves.

Empirically, the emergence of a strengthening relationship between PTSD and personality factors with increasing time, argues for a major role of personality in maintenance, identified in our model as arising through the effects of personality on coping. Here it would appear that extensive reliance upon avoidant or ambivalent strategies, related to low self-esteem and a view of others as hostile and untrustworthy (?self and others attributed as blameworthy), would link with conceptualisations within the literature of both Traumatic Personality (e.g. Hyer et al., 1991) and Borderline Personality Disorder (BPD) (e.g. Beck et al., 1990). Furthermore, the link between maladaptive coping style and personality leads to a persuasive and intriguing identification of adult BPD with chronic PTSD relating to unassimilated childhood trauma.

Culture

In Chapter 6, de Silva presents more arguments for the importance we have placed in our model to factors in the social environment. He points out that cultural factors will affect, for example, the definition of trauma, the reactions of survivors and the probability and type of post-traumatic symptoms, and the support offered to survivors by their social systems.

He illustrates, in a vivid example from an Asian publication, how reporting the occurrence of rape by one Indian couple had led to ostracism by the family who perceived the family's honour to be at stake. The role of self-blame and avoidant coping can thus clearly be seen to be related to factors in the social environment.

In addition, he points out that the social and cultural system may be affected in significant ways by events such as warfare and major environmental disasters, pointing again to the reciprocally interacting links between post-disaster factors that may occur and to the losses that individuals may suffer to their sense of safety in the world, not only by a disaster itself, but by its consequences in affecting a whole way of life.

In discussing intervention, de Silva adds to our view of support-seeking in recovery by pointing to the importance of social rituals, such as ceremonies to greet soldiers returning from war. One can speculate that such rituals can powerfully support self-esteem for individuals going through a difficult period of transition in moving from a traumatic environment to home and a family group who may be wholly ignorant of the psychological impact of such a change.

Psychobiology

Whereas biological factors go beyond the scope of our psychosocial model, in Chapter 7 Hagh-Shenas et al. raise some interesting psychophysiological observations that might go to improve its descriptive completeness, especially with regard to the effects of neurotransmitter changes on memory. The suggestion that opiate release under high stress produces analgesia at the time and the symptom of emotional blunting post-trauma also may explain the co-morbidity of PTSD with drug and alcohol abuse that has often been observed. The cortical lateralisation studies discussed in Chapter 7 also suggest some experimental verification for the importance of non-verbal cognition in PTSD demonstrated by specifically right hemispherical activity.

Intrusive Thinking

In an interesting and clinically insightful discussion of intrusive cognition in Chapter 8, de Silva and Marks contribute to an important area of neglect in the literature, namely the exact nature of cognitive experience, commonly referred to as intrusions. They draw attention to a distinction between unwanted, negative intrusive verbal (lexical) cognitions and cognitions that take other forms, usually pictorial imagery. This distinction would seem to parallel our distinction between event cognitions (usually images) and appraisals. The authors' examples of specific recollections reported by survivors would seem to bear this out, but de Silva and Marks point out that although images are most common, a blend of verbal and non-verbal recollections are often reported as well as auditory, tactile and gustatory event recollections.

De Silva and Marks go on to provide interesting clinical examples of lexical cognitions which are also reported as occurring intrusively. They suggest that these lexical cognitions can be grouped into three categories: thoughts relating to current and future safety; negative thoughts about the self; and thoughts about the event (citing as examples, questions and statements about event causation). Thus, in addition to appraisals of the event, the authors also draw attention to ongoing appraisals of the self and the world which may relate to event appraisal attributions. Interestingly, de Silva and Marks point to the observation of compulsive cognitions and impulses in a minority of PTSD patients.

Thus, extending the cognitive content of our model, de Silva and Marks provide clinical evidence of varieties of intrusive negative cognition, related to general anxiety disorder and obsessive-compulsive disorder, which would in our view constitute cognitive coping strategies subsequent to traumatisation. Finally, consistent with the purpose of our model, they suggest that the nature of the cognitive experience may be important in informing choice of intervention.

Information-processing Paradigms in Investigating PTSD

The inherent problems in investigating automatic cognitive processes are addressed in Chapter 9, in which Thrasher and Dalgleish review the cognitive information-processing paradigms for assessing cognition and the current evidence with respect to PTSD. Although these methodologies have been as yet little used in PTSD, some predictable results have been obtained with measures of both attentional and memory biases and these are likely to become the subjects of further research activity. As the authors suggest, information-processing measures before or immediately in the aftermath of the experience of trauma may be useful screening instruments to predict those who will develop more severe and long-lasting symptoms, thus aiding the identification of individuals most at risk.

Cognitive Theories

In his important chapter on cognitive theories (Chapter 10), Dalgleish aims to construct a theory which accounts for many of the phenomena of PTSD that have been discussed elsewhere in this volume, and especially the range of individual variation in response observed. He also aims to explain how these features come about in a manner that goes beyond description. Consistent with the cognitive-behavioural focus of our model, he advances a new cognitive theory which focuses on the central components of our broader psychosocial conceptualisation, namely the specification of how information is stored in memory. His theory, therefore, largely encompasses the three cognitive components of our model: event cognitions, appraisal mechanisms and the cognitive aspects of "personality" in the sense of historical information store. His detailed account in this chapter also adds appreciably to a theoretical understanding of the functioning of the system. In doing so, Dalgleish links the cognitive apparatus to a functional understanding of emotions in PTSD and, more generally, as consequences of input information that is processed as having significance for the individual's prepotent goals. The "completion tendency" that drives the attempts to reconcile information is accounted for in a similar cognitive manner as that suggested by Joseph in Chapter 3 as a function of the maintainance of a subjective relative stability of the individual's view of himself or herself and the world.

Looking at the SPAARS model in more detail, the *analogical* system seems similar to what we have less technically termed "event cognitions". The distinction between *propositional* and *schematic* systems is, in our view, not so readily matched onto our model, which has had, thus far, more of an eye to categorising observable products of information processing than to providing a model of the underlying cognitive psychology. It would seem that *both* schematic and propositional systems are involved in what we have termed "appraisal". Following Beck's original cognitive model, we have conceived schematic representation as part of an underlying, relatively inaccessible and stable over time "personality" factor, with appraisal representing the interaction product, relatively accessible, of event information with pre-existing memorial representations. As Dalgleish points out, his own system bears some similarity to another multirepresentational model developed by Teasdale and Barnard (1993), in contrast to Beck's hierarchical model, so it would seem that there is some convergence within cognitive psychology on this point that needs to be considered and tested.

The model of Dalgleish and Power, however, differs from both the original Beck model and that of Teasdale and Barnard in the addition of another, direct *associative* level of representation which, they claim, is not related to schematic high-level meaning structures but simply reflects the unmediated automatic links between stimuli and emotion. This is a very interesting suggestion which goes to explain a difference that has been perceived between those individuals whose emotional problems can be dealt with very largely through reprocessing of current meaning and those whose experience is dominated by intrusive emotional recollections of relatively unprocessed experiences from the past. What is not clear from the summary of the Dalgleish and Power theory, however, is how this associative system differs from the "analogical" level which, in our model, would be represented as the component of intrusive "event cognitions".

In discussing individual differences within post-traumatic responses, Dalgleish makes some interesting suggestions relating to cognitive avoidant coping mechanisms, repression and denial, discussed as if they are information-processing styles as individual difference factors, that may explain both the relative absence of immediate symptoms in some individuals which can be followed by a delayed onset months or years later. This suggestion is similar to the recent views of Horowitz on monitoring versus blunting and repressors/sensitisers discussed in Chapter 5. Dalgleish also proposes, in a discussion that closely mirrors Beck's views about the dysfunctional characteristics of rigidity and absoluteness in some schematic systems, that some individuals hold "overvalued" positive schematic models of self and world that render individuals vulnerable. Another intriguing suggestion made by Dalgleish is that some individuals may have negative schematic models prior to traumatic experience which the traumatic experience goes to confirm rather than to shatter. He draws the inference that these individuals should have less specifically PTSD symptomatology post-trauma and more generalised psychopathological symptoms. Perhaps the latter view ignores the "associative" level of representation as well as the possibility in such individuals of current trauma cognitions providing an entry to recollection of earlier traumatic recollections, a phenomenon which has been reported anecdotally in PTSD (Joseph, Williams & Yule, 1997)

In his discussion of therapy, the implication of the two routes to emotion is discussed, with schematic revision and habituation being viewed as two processes to change in emotional states. It is beyond the scope of this final chapter to begin to examine theories of habituation in relation to cognition. However, Dalgleish's own explanation of failures to habituate do suggest that cognitive factors may be involved. Some animal theorists have pointed to the role of cognition in conditioning (Dickinson, 1987) which might suggest more in the way of top-down processing in the formation and extinction of conditioned associations than has previously been considered. Nevertheless, prolonged exposure is a well-established means to establish a decrement in anxiety, although theoretical explanations may still be divergent.

Crisis Intervention and Critical Incident Stress Debriefing

While discussions on how to develop effective therapies continue to improve individual and group treatments, disasters continue to occur. When a major accident happens, the response of the emergency services for dealing with the immediate aftermath is generally planned and practised. As Canterbury and Yule (Chapters 11 and 14) show, little consideration has been given by the emergency planners for dealing with the psychosocial dimensions; and yet, something has to be done in a crisis. The result has been that various forms of Crisis Intervention have been developed. Critical Incident Stress Debriefing was originally developed to meet the perceived needs of emergency workers themselves, but was adapted and offered to primary victims. While, anecdotally, many people seem to favour such a short-term crisis intervention, there is evidence emerging that it may not be beneficial for all. There remain many issues of how best to make contact with survivors, engage them, but not retraumatise them. Clearly, future developments in crisis intervention will have to learn lessons from controlled studies of the outcome of both individual and group therapies.

Behavioural and Cognitive Behavioural Interventions

In Chapter 12, Richards and Lovell present an account of Cognitive Behavioural Therapy (CBT) in PTSD with useful detail about procedures in
therapy that assist all stages of therapeutic activity from engagement to
successful outcome. They draw attention to avoidant strategies that individuals may employ in exposure to event cognitions that may interfere
with processing and to the usefulness of real-life stimuli both as an aid to
exposure and in dealing with more general issues such as fear of fear.
They argue for the applicability of anxiety management, not so much as
a strongly effective treatment in its own right but with more severely
affected individuals, as an aid to maintaining exposure without escape or
avoidance. Interestingly, they also point to the importance of the attitudes
and responses of others in the social environment in being able to tolerate
high emotional arousal in PTSD patients. Therapists themselves must be
able to do so or else they may abort or avoid full exposure in treatment
sessions.

Although Richards and Lovell are not strong exponents of the importance
of, specifically, cognitive work other than therapeutic exposure, they suggest, like Dalgleish, that cognitive therapies may be more applicable to the
individuals who show most rigidity of thinking and fail or drop out of
exposure treatment, although this hypothesis remains to be tested. This
view is consistent with our multidimensional approach which argues for
a broad assessment of the key features that may be relevant to working
with the individual case.

The authors present an interesting clinical example of reappraising
responsibility for a traumatic event by teasing out all the contributory
factors and assigning weights to their importance in a pie chart. This is
exactly the process of reappraising causal explanation away from a simple
"them" or "me" dichotomy to a more complex interrelationship of factors
which Joseph's discussion in Chapter 3 was suggesting. In addition, their
therapeutic example of dealing with intense anger is a striking example of
the application of Dalgleish's model in drawing upon high-level schematic models and goals in considering the advantages and disadvantages
of acting on feelings.

Eye Movement Desensitisation and Reprocessing

The new and intriguing therapy, EMDR, has been described in detail in
Chapter 13 together with a review of the current outcome literature. The
lack of an unequivocal theory of process makes it difficult to reconcile

within our model at present. Its use of divided attention calls to mind the information-processing paradigms described in Chapter 3 to assess information-processing biases in emotional disorders. The discussion of theory offered by Smith and Yule would suggest that the therapy technique can somehow access the psychophysiological level of functioning and promote change, bypassing the conscious level of experience—all this achieved without pharmacotherapy or electrical stimulation. This is a novel and revolutionary idea which may open the door to even more enquiry into the neurophysiology of emotional states away from descriptive studies and embracing intervention.

DIRECTIONS FOR FUTURE RESEARCH

The discussions presented in this volume provide considerable scope for further research questions to extend our understanding of post-traumatic problems across the age range. In this final section, some of these questions that appear most promising to us will be outlined.

We would identify three broad themes for future research. The first is the need to better understand the architecture of post-traumatic stress reactions. The second is the need for longitudinal research into the aetiology of these reactions based around the recognition that post-traumatic stress is determined by multiple psychosocial factors (as outlined above) which interact in complex and relatively unexplored ways. Such research is needed if we are to understand the factors (apart from exposure to trauma itself) that lead to post-traumatic stress and, consequently, what we, as therapists, might do to promote recovery in our clients. The third is the need for continuing investigation into therapeutic efficacy.

Architecture of Reactions

Here, two questions appear to be most pertinent to us. First, does the diagnostic category of PTSD represent an empirically distinct set of symptoms; and, second, is post-traumatic stress continuous with "normal" behaviour?

First, what the chapters in this volume show is that the range of reactions experienced by survivors is wide, and not simply confined to those symptoms contained within the psychiatric diagnostic category of PTSD. There are also problems of depression, anxiety, substance use, physical health, impairment of social relationships, and so on. The question is therefore whether there is a discrete set of symptoms specific to trauma that are empirically separate from other sets of symptoms (as is implicit in psychiatric classification), or whether the phenomena associated with trauma is an isomorphic set of symptoms that cuts across existing diagnostic classifications. In our opinion, the latter view is the more probable, as the evidence seems to support that view, and we would encourage researchers to adopt a broader view of post-traumatic stress. Here we would also highlight the need to recognize that experience of traumatic events can have positive as well as negative consequences.

Second, there is the question of whether post-traumatic stress reactions are discontinuous from "normal" behaviour or whether they are continuous with "normal" behaviour. It is our opinion, the latter view is more likely, as the evidence seems to support that view, at least with regard to certain symptoms. For example, de Silva and Marks (Chapter 8 in this volume) show that intrusive thinking is not specific to those who experience highly traumatic events but is also found in generalised anxiety disorder, obsessive-compulsive disorder, as well as in non-pathological states.

The importance of understanding the architecture of post-traumatic stress is that we must have a clear idea of what we are trying to find. At present, we would argue that although much progress has been made towards understanding post-traumatic stress, our understanding remains primitive and driven by the needs of psychiatric classification (and legal ramifications) rather those of science with conceptual and empirical work into the architecture of reactions.

Psychosocial Factors

One simple question has driven much of our own research. What is it that leads one person who has experienced a traumatic event to go on to develop severe and chronic problems in living, whereas another person who has experienced the same event is able to get on with life and function effectively, perhaps even find that his or her life has been enhanced in some way? The second key area for future research must be more work into the relationship between psychosocial factors and adjustment (as discussed above). One area of particular interest, and discussed by Williams (Chapter 5 in this volume) is the relationship of prior personality factors to later adjustment. To what extent, exactly, are some people vulnerable to developing post-traumatic stress reactions? How does this vulnerability manifest itself? What are the processes through which this vulnerability expresses itself? If we can find answers to these questions, we will have gone a long way towards understanding how best to help our clients, and to be in the position to develop intervention packages on the basis of this knowledge. Personality, as broadly discussed by Williams, would seem to be crucial in determining how people appraise and cope with what has happened to them. But we need to know more about how the various psychosocial factors, personality, appraisal, coping, emotion, are related to each other and how they interact over time. Our knowledge is building, and social support appears to be an important cornerstone of adaptation. However, we also know relatively little about the processes through which social support works, although we suggest that one aspect of this process is that social support provides a facilitative environment for the expression of emotions, and the construction of new meaning systems.

Intervention and Treatment

The third key area is to continue developing our understanding of ways of facilitating emotional processing in survivors. There are two strands of therapeutic research which seem important to us. First, the development and evaluation of specific intervention packages on the basis of research knowledge. Second, the application of intervention methods from other areas of so-called psychopathology.

First, given the research literature on social support we would recommend the utilisation of techniques through which survivors can be taught ways in which they can foster support from family and friends. For example, this might take the form of training in self-presentational and other communication skills. Other research evidence points towards the benefit of an optimistic attributional style, suggesting that attribution training might also form one component of intervention for survivors who are identified as possessing a relatively pessimistic style. The use of such techniques as these are fairly specific and driven by what the research literature has to say about which survivors adapt best.

Second, most therapeutic research has tended to try out techniques that are already in use with other client groups to see how they fare with post-traumatic stress reactions. As Richards and Lovell (Chapter 12) demonstrate, much work has begun to show the efficacy of cognitive and cognitive-behavioural interventions, and we would encourage this research trend to continue, along with the need for a broader understanding of the relationship between neurophysiological and mental states discussed by Smith and Yule (Chapter 13) in their evaluation of EMDR.

However, we are also beginning to recognise that survivors often find these forms of intervention unpleasant and intrusive and—as Richards and Lovell (Chapter 12) and Canterbury and Yule (Chapter 11) point out—are often reluctant to engage in therapy which is upsetting, will not complete homework assignments, and will drop out of therapeutic trials. Inevitably, therefore, we know more about those who take part in clinical trials, complete homework assignments, and generally take part in clinical research programmes. We know little about the survivors who exist outside the research spotlight. In this respect, we concur with Richards and Lovell when they point to the possibility that a careful mix of client-centred and directive interviewing is most effective in maximising engagement in therapy. We would go further and encourage research into the effectiveness of the person-centred approach and other interpersonal therapies for trauma-related problems. Some would argue that a person-centred approach offers more than simply a means of establishing rapport, it is potentially a powerful therapy in its own right for certain clients. Possibly those clients who are already actively engaged in struggles to find new meaning in their lives, and who feel that they have learnt important lessons from their experiences, may benefit from a person-centred intervention. As with the better established cognitive-behavioural approaches, more systematic evaluation of such counselling approaches is needed before they can be confidently recommended.

CONCLUDING COMMENTS

We would emphasise that research in each of the three areas outlined above must be conducted across age groups and across cultures. As de Silva (Chapter 6 in this volume) points out, much of what we think we know about PTSD as a general psychological process is heavily imbued with the values of western culture. Also, running throughout all these research foci are some fundamental issues about the nature of post-traumatic stress reactions. We would concur with Dalgleish (this volume) that it is the adaptive nature of the emotional system which is the individual's "undoing" following a traumatic event. It would seem, although the evidence remains to be gathered, that people have something akin to a completion tendency as discussed by Horowitz (1986), or network resolution processing as discussed by Creamer, Burgess and Pattison (1992), and the role of therapy is to facilitate this process.

But this remains uncertain and the question of whether or not there is a universal completion tendency would seem to be fundamental to the design of treatment. If someone with all the symptoms of PTSD is in the process of "assimilation" (manifested as phases of intrusion and avoidance) driven by the completion tendency (which varies from person to person in its strength, although not the fact of its presence), then the goal of the therapist must surely be to facilitate the completion tendency. Following Horowitz, the symptoms of PTSD are normal reactions indicative that this process is ongoing, and chronic reactions are indicative of a completion tendency which is "blocked" in some way. It would follow that the role of the therapist is to facilitate the removal of this block and allow the individuals to work through their experiences until they reach the state of completion described by Horowitz. If this is the case, then we must be aware of the possibility that directive interventions, such as exposure, might sometimes work to impede the completion tendency. Should we introduce exposure to clients who are in an avoidant phase (when it would be most painful) or should we facilitate the avoidance (which, after Horowitz, is fulfilling an important protective function) and let it run its course and only consider exposure-based treatments when the client moves into an intrusion phase? Furthermore, are there some people whose "completion" apparently centres around a negative self and world, whose natural healing is so blocked by developmental layers of adverse experiences and for whom, as Dalgleish suggests, no amount of exposure will promote change? These are fundamental questions of continuity and discontinuity between individuals that remain unexplored and need to be addressed in order to start to meet the needs of the full range of traumatised individuals that we see, not just the compliant and motivated who accede to research protocols.

Also, we note that trauma often seems to precipitate a spiritual crisis, in which survivors struggle to establish a greater understanding of transpersonal issues—issues which are often left unexplored within the traditional cognitive and cognitive-behavioural approach which are, by their nature, focused on the alleviation of so-called disorder and the symptoms of disorder. For many, the experience of trauma represents a powerful positive and existential change in outlook, the exploration and facilitation of which are not easily amenable to the techniques of cognitive and cognitive-behavioural therapies.

Finally, we also recognise that therapy for post-traumatic stress has become politicised, with different professional groups claiming expertise and ownership of this area of psychological suffering. Certainly, we would agree that therapy must be subject to research evaluation, and at present the cognitive and cognitive-behavioural approaches have received the greatest amount of evaluation. But we would strongly maintain that professional in-fighting is not to the benefit of our clients, whose problems cut across disciplinary boundaries—those of psychotherapy, psychology and psychiatry.

REFERENCES

Beck, A.T. (1976). *Cognitive Therapy and the Emotional Disorder*. New York: International University Press.

Beck, A.T., Freeman, A., and associates (1990). *Cognitive Therapy of Personality Disorders*. New York: Guilford Press.

Brewin, C.R., Dalgleish, T. & Joseph, S. (1996). A dual representation theory of post-traumatic stress disorder. *Psychological Review*, **103**, 670–686.

Creamer, M., Burgess, P. & Pattison, P. (1992). Reaction to trauma: A cognitive processing model. *Journal of Abnormal Psychology*, **101**, 452–459.

Dickinson, A. (1987). Animal conditioning and learning theory. In H.J. Eysenck & I. Martin (Eds.), *Theoretical foundations of Behaviour Therapy*. New York: Plenum Press.

Elkin, I., Shea, T., Watkins, J.T., Imber, S.D., Sotsky, S.M., Collins, J.F., Glan, D.R., Pilkonis, P.A., Leber, W.R., Docherty, J.P., Fiester, S.J. & Parloff, M.B. (1989). NIMH treatment of depression collaborative research program: general effectiveness of treatments. *Archives of General Psychiatry*, **46**, 971–982.

Horowitz, M. (1986) *Stress Response Syndromes*, Northville, NJ: Jason Aronson.

Hyer, L., Woods, M.G. & Bondewyns, P.A. (1991). A three-tier evaluation of PTSD among Vietnam combat reterans. *Journal of Traumatic Stress*, **4**, 165–194.

Joseph, S., Williams, R. & Yule, W. (1997). *Understanding Post-Traumatic Stress: A Psychosocial Perspective on PTSD and Treatment*. Chichester: Wiley.

Klerman, G.L., Weissman, M.M., Ronnsaville, B.J. & Chevron, E.S. (1984). Interpersonal Psychotherapy of Depression. New York: Basic Books.

Teasdale, J.D. & Barnard, P.J. (1993). *Affect, Cognition and Change: Remodelling Depressive Thoughts*. Hillsdale, NJ: Lawrence Erlbaum.

Wegner, D.M., Shortt, J.W., Blake, A.W. & Page, M.S. (1990). The suppression of exciting thoughts. *Journal of Personality and Social Psychology*, **58**, 495–514.

Wells, A. & Matthews, G. (1994). *Attention and Emotion: A Clinical Perspective*. Hillsdale, NJ: Lawrence Erlbaum.

INDEX

Note: page numbers in *italic* refer to tables. Abbreviations used in sub-headings are: EMDR = eye movement desensitisation and reprocessing; PTSD = post-traumatic stress disorder.

Index compiled by Liz Granger

The Wiley Series in

CLINICAL PSYCHOLOGY